CW01024775

TOLKIEN AND THE MYSTERY OF LITERARY CREATION

Taking his readers into the depths of a majestic and expansive literary world, one to which he brings fresh illumination as if to the darkness of Khazad-dûm, Giuseppe Pezzini combines rigorous scholarship with an engaging style to reveal the full scale of J. R. R. Tolkien's vision of the 'mystery of literary creation'. Through fragments garnered from across a scattered body of writing and acute readings of primary texts (some well-known, others less familiar or recently published), the author divulges the unparalleled complexity of Tolkien's work while demonstrating its rich exploration of literature's very nature and purpose. Eschewing any over-emphasis on context or comparisons, Pezzini offers rather a uniquely sustained, focused engagement with Tolkien and his 'theory' on their own terms. He helps us discover – or rediscover – a fascination for Tolkien's literary accomplishment while correcting long-standing biases against its nature and merits that have persisted fifty years after his death.

GIUSEPPE PEZZINI is Fellow and Tutor at Corpus Christi College, Oxford, and Associate Professor of Latin Language and Literature at the University of Oxford. A classicist by training, he has published extensively on Latin language and literature, Roman comedy, ancient philosophy of language, and fiction theory, ancient and modern. With additional interests in textual criticism and the digital humanities, he is also a prominent Tolkien specialist, was the recipient of a 2021 Philip Leverhulme Prize, and currently serves as Tolkien Editor for the *Journal of Inklings Studies*.

TOLKIEN AND THE MYSTERY OF LITERARY CREATION

GIUSEPPE PEZZINI

Corpus Christi College, University of Oxford

 CAMBRIDGE
UNIVERSITY PRESS

Shaftesbury Road, Cambridge CB2 8EA, United Kingdom

One Liberty Plaza, 20th Floor, New York, NY 10006, USA

477 Williamstown Road, Port Melbourne, VIC 3207, Australia

314–321, 3rd Floor, Plot 3, Splendor Forum, Jasola District Centre,
New Delhi – 110025, India

103 Penang Road, #05–06/07, Visioncrest Commercial, Singapore 238467

Cambridge University Press is part of Cambridge University Press & Assessment,
a department of the University of Cambridge.

We share the University's mission to contribute to society through the pursuit of
education, learning and research at the highest international levels of excellence.

www.cambridge.org
Information on this title: www.cambridge.org/9781009479677

DOI: 10.1017/9781009479714

First published 2025

Printed in the United Kingdom by CPI Group Ltd, Croydon CR0 4YY

A catalogue record for this publication is available from the British Library

Library of Congress Cataloging-in-Publication Data
NAMES: Pezzini, Giuseppe, 1984– author.
TITLE: Tolkien and the mystery of literary creation / Giuseppe Pezzini.
DESCRIPTION: Cambridge ; New York, NY : Cambridge University Press, 2025. |
Includes bibliographical references and index.
IDENTIFIERS: LCCN 2024048270 | ISBN 9781009479677 (hardback) |
ISBN 9781009479714 (ebook)
SUBJECTS: LCSH: Tolkien, J. R. R. (John Ronald Reuel), 1892–1973 – Criticism and
interpretation. | Creation (Literary, artistic, etc.) | LCGFT: Literary criticism.
CLASSIFICATION: LCC PR6039.O32 Z7916 2025 |
DDC 823/.912–dc23/eng/20241112
LC record available at https://lccn.loc.gov/2024048270

ISBN 978-1-009-47967-7 Hardback

G.C.
SINE QUO NON

CONTENTS

Contents

Contents

Contents

Contents

Contents

ACKNOWLEDGEMENTS

The (hi)story and content of this book are analogous: I could not find a better way to describe its origin, methodology, and purpose than to echo Tolkien's self-reflections on his own experience as a writer, as I have tried to reconstruct them. I will not elaborate on this, and I will leave the reader to decide whether this is because I have projected my own experience onto Tolkien or the other way round; or perhaps (as I believe) because literary criticism is itself a form of creative writing, and this is a universal experience (however idiosyncratic), which is enlightened in Tolkien's self-reflective 'theory'.

Certainly, among the many experiences I shared with Tolkien there is the joy of collaboration. This book is (also) dedicated to George Corbett, as it would simply not exist without him, and not just because it was he who, by some strange chance, invited me to give a paper at the Institute for Theology, Imagination and the Arts (ITIA) at the University of St Andrews, back in 2017. All chapters were originally written and delivered as ITIA seminar talks, and have been enormously improved thanks to the encouragement and questions of its audiences.

Stefano Rebeggiani also deserves a special mention: he has accompanied me step by step on the journey, and without his support I would not have recognised that my Tolkien scholarship was not just a 'secret vice', but that rather it cross-fertilises my work as a Classical scholar.

Special thanks also go to Anine Englund, Michaël Devaux, Eden O'Brien, and Edmund Weiner, who read the manuscript before publication and provided invaluable feedback and criticism, as well as to Paolo Prosperi, Guglielmo Spirito, Roger Sylvester, Michael Ward, and Michela Young.

Many friends and colleagues, in St Andrews and Oxford (and beyond), played a role in the history of this book: I will here mention only Mario Brioschi, Rebekah Lamb, Myles Lavan, Emmanuele Riu, Lorenzo Rossi, and Brendan and Judith Wolfe, but there are many others, including especially those of the Oxford Tolkien50 Network (Mark Atherton, David Bernabé, John Garth, John Holmes, Grace Khuri, Simon Horobin, Stuart Lee, and Catherine McIlwaine in particular) and the Tree of Tales Exhibition (especially Oronzo Cilli and Paolo Morandi).

There is a long list of different Tolkien scholars who inspired me in different ways, at different stages: many of these are acknowledged in the book, but here I want to mention at least the names of Federico Guglielmi, Adriano Monti Buzzetti, Verlyn Flieger, Yoko Hemmi, Holly Ordway, Łukasz Neubauer, Ivano Sassanelli, Eduardo Segura, Martin Simonson, and Hamish Williams, as well as the memory of Stratford Caldecott and Simon Stacey.

I am also extremely grateful to my colleagues at Corpus Christi College for their support, and especially to Neil McLynn and Helen Moore for their generosity and encouragement.

I warmly thank Stephen Broadbent and Peter Davidson (together with Anton' De Piro and Rebekah Lamb), for allowing me to use the cover image: this book has grown together with our common Tree, whose realisation I am very much looking forward to.

I am very grateful to the Tolkien Estate and HarperCollins for their generosity in allowing me to quote extensively from Tolkien material. I have a debt of gratitude especially to Cathleen Blackburn and Michael G. Tolkien, for different reasons.

Finally, I would like to thank my wife Elena and J. R. R. Tolkien: they do not know each other directly, but it is their mutual affections that give life to this book.

NOTE ON THE TEXT

A Note on Cross-References

Cross-references in the book generally point to individual sections, numbered as in the table of contents.

A Note on Capitalisation

Following Tolkien's general practice (which, however, is not consistent), I have capitalised the words Elves, Men, Dwarves, Orcs, Hobbits, except when they refer to specific individuals (e.g. "the hobbits Merry and Pippin", as opposed to "a story about Hobbits") or when they are not capitalised in the original quote.

A Note on Quotations

Double inverted commas (" ") are used *always and only* for direct quotes of Tolkien's original text, also including individual words (with references provided in the main body of the text, together with or in proximity to the quote, or in footnotes); single inverted commas (' ') are used for emphasis, qualification, to single out difficult or pregnant terms, and at times also for paraphrasis of Tolkien passages that are not cited verbatim. In Tolkien's quotations, I have used bold to mark emphasis added by myself, primarily to highlight words or phrases I specifically refer to in my analysis. In contrast, italics in quotations is always original.

ABBREVIATIONS

Primary Sources and Abbreviations

Primary texts are cited by page number from the given edition (e.g. LN:111–13 = Leaf by Niggle pp. 111–13), unless otherwise indicated.

All texts by J. R. R. Tolkien are reprinted by permission of HarperCollins Publishers Ltd © (year as per the following list).

ATB	*The Adventures of Tom Bombadil and Other Verses from the Red Book*. With illustrations by P. Baynes. Edited by C. Scull and Wayne G. Hammond. London: HarperCollins, 2014.
BL	*Beren and Lúthien*. Edited by Christopher Tolkien. London: HarperCollins, 2017.
BLT1	*The Book of Lost Tales, Part One*. (*HME* 1, 1983). Cited by chapter and page.
BLT2	*The Book of Lost Tales, Part Two*. (*HME* 2, 1984). Cited by chapter and page.
FG	*The Fall of Gondolin*. Edited by Christopher Tolkien. London: HarperCollins, 2018.
FN	*The Fall of Númenor*. Edited by Brian Sibley. London: HarperCollins, 2022.
HDWM	*J.R.R. Tolkien: The Hobbit: Drawings, Watercolors, and Manuscripts*. Exhibition Catalogue. Marquette University, 1987.
HME	*The History of Middle-earth*. Twelve volumes. Edited by Christopher Tolkien. London: HarperCollins, 1983–96.

Hobbit	*The Hobbit.* 5th edn. London: HarperCollins, 1995 [1st edition 1937, 2nd revised edition 1951]. Cited by chapter and page.

Hobbit — *The Hobbit.* 5th edn. London: HarperCollins, 1995 [1st edition 1937, 2nd revised edition 1951]. Cited by chapter and page.

LB — *The Lays of Beleriand.* (*HME* 3, 1985). Edited by Christopher Tolkien. London: Allen & Unwin 1985. Cited by chapter and page.

Letters — *The Letters of J.R.R. Tolkien: Expanded and Revised Edition.* Edited by Humphrey Carpenter, with the assistance of Christopher Tolkien. London: HarperCollins 2023 [1st edition 1981: Allen & Unwin]. Cited by number of letter and page, with page of the 1981 edition in square brackets (e.g. *Letters* 180:336[231] = *Letters* no. 180, p.336 in 2023 edition = p.231 in 1981 edition). Addressees and date of the letter are normally indicated, except for the following letters that are cited several times in the book:

Letters 25, to the Editor of the 'Observer', February 1938

Letters 43, to Michael Tolkien, 6–8/03/1941

Letters 69, to Christopher Tolkien, 14/05/1944

Letters 89, to Christopher Tolkien, 7–8/11/1944

Letters 96, to Christopher Tolkien, 30/01/1945

Letters 109, to S. Unwin, 31/07/1947

Letters 131, to Milton Waldman, late 1951

Letters 144, to N. Mitchison, 25/04/1954

Letters 153, to Peter Hastings (draft), September 1954

Letters 156, to R. Murray SJ, 4/11/1954

Letters 163, to W. H. Auden, 7/06/1955

Letters 165, to the Houghton Mifflin Co. June 1955

Letters 180, to Mr Thompson, 14/01/1956

Letters 181, to M. Straight, January or February (?) 1956

Letters 183, Notes on W. H. Auden's review of
  The Return of the King, 1956
Letters 186, to Joanna de Bortadano (draft), April
  1956
Letters 187, to H. Cotton Minchin, April 1956,
Letters 192, to A. Ronald, 27/07/1956
Letters 199, to C. Everett, 24/06/1957
Letters 200, to R. Bowen, 25/06/1957
Letters 203, to H. Schiro, 17/11/1957
Letters 205, to Christopher Tolkien, 21/02/1958
Letters 208, to C. Ouboter, 10/04/1958
Letters 211, to R. Beare, 14/10/1958
Letters 212, Draft of a continuation to the above
  letter (not sent)
Letters 241, to J. Neave, 8–9/09/1962
Letters 246, to E. Elgar (draft), September 1963
Letters 247, to Colonel Worskett, 20/09/1963
Letters 297, to Mr. Rang (draft), August 1967
Letters 257, to C. Bretherton, 16/07/1964
Letters 328, to C. Batten-Phelps (draft), Autumn
  1971
Letters 329, to P. Szabó Szentmihályi (draft),
  October 1971
Unpublished letters are referred to according to
  the numbering of the *Tolkien's Collector Guide*
  (*TCG*, see below).

LN   *Leaf by Niggle*, originally published in *Dublin
        Review* (January 1945): pp.46–61. Cited from *TL*
        (pp.93–118).
LotR   *The Lord of the Rings.* 50th anniversary edition.
        London: HarperCollins, 2004. Cited by book,
        chapter and page.
LR   *The Lost Road and Other Writings* (HME 5, 1987).
        Cited by part, chapter and page.

MC	*The Monsters and the Critics and Other Essays.* London: Allen & Unwin, 1983. *Beow.=Beowulf: The Monsters and the Critics*
MR	*Morgoth's Ring* (*HME* 10, 1993). *Ain.=Ainulindalë* (pp.3–44); *Athr.=Athrabeth Finrod Ah Andreth* (pp.303–66).
Myth	*Mythopoeia.* Cited from *TL* (pp.85–90).
NME	*The Nature of Middle-earth.* Edited by Carl F. Hostetter. London: HarperCollins, 2021. Cited by part, chapter and page.
NN	*The Name Nodens.* First published as an Appendix (pp.132–7) in *Report on the Excavation of the Prehistoric, Roman, and Post-Roman Site in Lydney Park, Gloucestershire,* by R.E.M. and T.V. Wheeler (London 1932). Reprinted in *Tolkien Studies* 4 (2007), 177–83.
PME	*The Peoples of Middle-earth.* (*HME* 12, 1996). Cited by chapter and page.
RS	*The Return of the Shadow* (*HME* 6, 1988). Cited by chapter and page.
SD	*Sauron Defeated* (*HME* 9, 1992). *Not.=The Notion Club Papers* (pp.145–327). Cited by part, chapter (except *Not.*) and page.
Sil	*The Silmarillion.* Edited by Christopher Tolkien. London: Allen & Unwin, 1977. *Ain.=Ainulindalë; Val.=Valaquenta; Ak.=Akallabêth; Ring.=Of the Rings of Power and the Third age.* Cited by chapter (except *Ain., Val., Ak., Ring.*) and page.
SME	*The Shaping of Middle-earth.* (*HME* 4, 1986). Cited by chapter and page.
SWM	*Smith of Wootton Major.* Extended edition prepared by Verlyn Flieger. London: HarperCollins, 2005. [1st edition 1967]. *GK=Draft introduction to the Golden Key* (pp.89–96), *Ess.=Smith of Wootton Major Essay* (pp.111–45).

SV	*A Secret Vice: Tolkien on Invented Languages.* Edited by Dimitra Fimi and Andrew Higgins. Revised edition. London: HarperCollins, 2020 [1st edition 2016].
TCG	*Tolkien's Collector Guide* (www.tolkienguide.com/guide/letters/), used as a reference database for unpublished letters.
TCP	*The Collected Poems of J. R. R. Tolkien*, edited by C. Scull and Wayne G. Hammond. London: HarperCollins, 2024.
TI	*The Treason of Isengard* (*HME* 7, 1989). Cited by chapter and page.
TL	*Tree and Leaf.* Second edition. Including *On Fairy-Stories, Mythopoeia, Leaf by Niggle,* and *The Homecoming of Beorhtnoth.* London: Unwin Hyman, 1988.
TOFS	*Tolkien On Fairy-Stories.* Edited by Verlyn Flieger and Douglas A. Anderson. London: HarperCollins, 2008. [1st edition 1947, 2nd edition 1964].
TPR	*Tales from the Perilous Realm.* 2nd edition. London: HarperCollins, 2008.
UT	*Unfinished Tales of Númenor and Middle-earth.* Edited by Christopher Tolkien. London: Allen & Unwin, 1980. Cited by part, chapter, and page.
WJ	*The War of the Jewels* (*HME* 11, 1994). Cited by part and page.
WR	*The War of the Ring* (*HME* 8, 1990). Cited by part, chapter and page.

Introduction

~

This book investigates J. R. R. Tolkien's literary 'theory' and is primarily carried out through the interpretation of his literary works. I purposely put the word 'theory' in inverted commas because I believe that, for Tolkien, "stories come first" in all senses; this is to say that, as he himself suggested, Tolkien's views on the nature and purpose of literature are mainly informed by a self-exegesis, that is, by the "experiment" and "observation" of his own literary work and experience as a writer:

[I] cite myself simply because I am interested in mythological 'invention', and **the mystery of literary creation** (or sub-creation as I have elsewhere called it) and I am the most readily available corpus vile for **experiment** or **observation**. (*Letters* 180:336[231])

This 'experimental' foundation is itself an important element of Tolkien's 'theory' of literature and informs my methodology, which is primarily inductive and exegetical, grounded as it is on a series of close readings of passages from his literary works. These include *The Hobbit* and *The Lord of the Rings*, but also and especially the large corpus of texts belonging to the same mythological framework (the *legendarium*), posthumously published by his son Christopher and other editors after Tolkien's death in 1973. These include *The Silmarillion* (1977), *Unfinished Tales* (1980), the monumental twelve-volume

History of Middle-earth (1983–96), as well as more recent works such as *Beren and Lúthien* (2017), *The Nature of Middle-earth* (2021, edited by C. Hostetter), *The Fall of Númenor* (2022, edited by B. Sibley), and the linguistic material collected in the journal *Parma Eldalamberon* (esp. volumes 11–22, 1995–2015). Other lesser-known stories that do not belong to the *legendarium* are also considered, especially *Leaf by Niggle* and *Smith of Wootton Major*. I will also rely on non-fictional texts to support and expand my exegesis, including the selection of *Letters* collected by H. Carpenter (republished in an extended version in 2023), complemented by occasional references to other letters (published elsewhere or still unpublished), and key essays such as *On Fairy-stories* and *A Secret Vice*, among others (the full list of primary sources is listed in the bibliography).

Despite its scope and specialism, the present book is ideally addressed to a wide and diverse audience, and not just the large cohort of Tolkien readers and scholars (although they are, of course, warmly included). This explains both the general avoidance of critical jargon and the amount of exposition, as well as my perceived need to seek the goodwill of my audience at the beginning of our journey together. My ideal reader is the educated reader of English literature, who might have read *The Hobbit* and/or *The Lord of the Rings* in their youth but has strong doubts and biases about the literary merits and sophistication of Tolkien's enterprise, and may even belittle the genres with which it is often (inappropriately) associated, namely 'fantasy' and 'children's literature'. One of my aspirations is to help correct this bias against the nature of Tolkien's work, still widespread fifty years after his death.

I illustrate its literary depth and complexity by focusing on one of its most distinctive traits: its meta-literary sophistication, that is, its self-reflexive focus on the nature and purpose of literature (cf. *Oxford English Dictionary* s.v. *metaliterature* 'any literary text which takes the nature of literature as its object'). Like many great writers of his generation and beyond, from Virginia Woolf to Jorge Luis Borges, Tolkien was deeply preoccupied by the process of writing and the relationship between literature and reality, or (to introduce key Tolkienian terminology) between 'secondary' or 'sub-created' planes, on the one hand, and 'primary' or 'created' planes, on the other. His texts can also be understood as instantiations and indeed heuristic developments of his understanding of this process, which is deeply embedded in the fabric of his literary work, as Tolkien himself suggested (cf. *Letters* 131, n.*:204[145] "[my work] is, I suppose, fundamentally concerned with the problem of the relation of Art (and Sub-creation) and Primary Reality").

Tolkien's 'theory' of literature is original and idiosyncratic in many respects and yet it cannot be decontextualised from the literary discourses of his age, neither can it be detached from the traditions in which it is anchored. In this book I refer for instance to Walter Pater and Oscar Wilde, whose aestheticist defences of functionless Art are, despite what one might expect, not alien to Tolkien's literary proclivities (as is also suggested by some intriguing similarities between Wilde's *Happy Prince* and Tolkien's *Leaf by Niggle*, both featuring profit-obsessed councillors, disparaging altruistic, 'aesthetic' characters). I also compare Tolkien's work with modernist writers such as James Joyce, whose interest in linguistic experimentalism caught Tolkien's attention, and clearly resonated with his 'secret vice' of language invention, as confirmed by direct evidence. I mention Ferdinand de Saussure, Edward Sapir, and other early twentieth-century linguists, whose work was known to Tolkien and clearly had an impact on his philosophy of language, together with that of Owen Barfield. I also refer to the mythological corpora of Homer and Elias Lönnrot, which provided two important models for Tolkien's *legendarium*, as well as for his authorial persona as a collector and editor of pre-existing oral tales; to Walter Scott, Henry James, and other historical or realistic novelists, who had the same Tolkienian fondness for frame-narratives and the related concern for the "inner consistency of reality" (*TOFS*:77=*TL*:73); and to T. S. Eliot's work on the relationship between tradition and the personal, which was also an important concern for Tolkien. From a different angle, I consider Tolkien's thought in relation to Plato and Aristotle, whose reflections on the relationship between universals and particular embodiments are important paragons for Tolkien's views on the matter; and to medieval mysticism as well as Romanticism, which articulated, in different ways, discourses about the divinely inspired nature of literature and its transcendent vocation, presumably influencing Tolkien, directly or indirectly. Perhaps more surprisingly, I also refer to the theories of Mikhail Bakhtin and Roland Barthes, whose reflections on authorial freedom, the polyphony of (great) literature, and the death of the author, are important counterparts to Tolkien's 'theory'. Other important figures mentioned in my discussion include authors with whom Tolkien was personally related, such as G. B. Smith, C. S. Lewis, and W. H. Auden; texts or collections of texts with which he was particularly familiar, such as *Beowulf* and the Bible; and, also, works apparently remote from Tolkien's reading, such as Manzoni's *The Betrothed*, which yet can be considered, on closer inspection, as intriguing analogues.

In different ways and to different extents, Tolkien's name should be associated with these authors and their works, and his theory and practice of literature could (and should) be fruitfully compared with theirs. In this book I occasionally engage in this work of contextualisation and comparison and provide bibliographical references to relevant studies, but this is not my primary focus. Rather, my aim is to provide a foundation for this kind of comparative work. This is necessary since Tolkien's views (often indefinite and unstable) were never systematically expressed in explicit terms, not even in his most theoretically charged works such as the essay *On Fairy-stories* and the meta-literary short story *Leaf by Niggle*. Rather, Tolkien's views can only be glimpsed in a large corpus of texts, 'absorbed' as they are in the literary fabric of his work and occasionally reflected in fragments from his letters. In this book, I thus approach Tolkien and his 'theory' on their own terms and invite the reader to travel with me into the depths of his sub-created world, in order to collect the scattered tesserae of a complex mosaic, whose reconstruction, I believe, has not yet been attempted systematically.

A Piece of Tolkien Scholarship

This book aims to be original in scope, but all its individual components are founded and built on the ground-breaking research carried out in the past years by several scholars working in the burgeoning field of Tolkien Studies. In writing this book I stand on the shoulders of many giants, especially Verlyn Flieger and Tom Shippey, who courageously dedicated their scholarly expertise to Tolkien and his literature, fostering the development of Tolkien Studies into a proper field of academic research – to which my book aims to contribute. There had been important studies on Tolkien before 2004 (for which see the standard bibliographical reviews by West 1981, 2004; the selected articles in Lee 2017, also collecting later works; also Anderson 2005), the year, that is, when Tolkien's popularity reached one of its peaks, with the triumph of Peter Jackson's *The Return of the King* at the Oscars, and when, more importantly, the first academic journal dedicated to Tolkien was founded (*Tolkien Studies*). However, it is fair to say that scholarly work on Tolkien has dramatically flourished in the past twenty years, and his stature as a literary writer has grown concomitantly, gradually overcoming the academic bias and ghettoisation of the previous decades (still unfortunately fuelled by his 'pop' reception in movies and TV series). More than 400 books on Tolkien have been published in the period 2000–24, many of which were written by established academics (Shippey 2000, 2005; Bloom 2008; Milbank 2009, etc.; also Mosely 1995), and/or published in prestigious academic presses (Gilliver, Marshall, and Weiner 2006; Judd and Judd 2017; Bowers 2019, Bowers and Steffensen 2024 (Oxford University Press); Burns 2017 (Toronto University Press); also Adams 2011b, and Townsend's (2024) *Very Short Introduction to J.R.R.*

Tolkien (both also with OUP)); two publishers in particular have specialised in Tolkien Studies, namely Kent State University Press, with many books related to the subject 'Tolkien, Lewis and the Inklings', and Walking Tree Publishers (based in Switzerland), with its *Cormarë* series specifically dedicated to Tolkien (more than 50 volumes), to which one could also add Luna Press and Cambridge Scholars. To this corpus of Tolkien-related books, one should add thousands of articles, including especially those published by the journals *Tolkien Studies* (West Virginia University Press), *Journal of Tolkien Research* (Valparaiso University), *Journal of Inklings Studies* (Edinburgh University Press), and *Mythlore* (Mythopoeic Society). Several main strands of research can now be identified, from different standpoints and methodologies. In order to contextualise my book and its approach, I illustrate these strands here with a simplified taxonomy, mainly referring, for reasons of space, to a selection of books and edited volumes.

A first strand (1) consists of works focusing on aspects of Tolkien's life, personal and/or professional, especially considered as influencing the birth and development of his literature. Apart from proper biographies (the classic Carpenter 1977, but also Edwards 2014 and Ordway 2023a), I can single out Garth's books (2003, 2020) on Tolkien and the First World War and on the places Tolkien visited as sources of inspiration for his mythology, but there are several other works (Croft 2004, Caldecott and Honegger 2008, Blackham 2008, Ryan 2009, Steimel and Schneidewind 2010 (Part C), Blackham 2011, Phelpstead 2011, Cilli 2014, Cilli, Smith, and Wynne 2017, Ferrández Bru 2018, Croft and Röttinger

2019, Rosegrant 2021, etc.), including a large bibliography on the Inklings (Pavlac Glyer 2007 and Zaleski and Zaleski 2015 in particular, but also Duriez 2015, Hooper 2015, Hilder, Pearson, and Van Dyke 2020, etc.) and the relationship between Tolkien and Lewis in particular (e.g. recently Neaubauer and Spirito 2024). Fimi 2008, Atherton 2012 and Chance 2016 are also interested in Tolkien's real-life experiences, although they also discuss broader cultural influences.

Next (2), there is the group of reference works that have made available a large corpus of material on Tolkien's life and textual corpus. Aside from annotated editions (Anderson 2002, Kane 2009, Rateliff 2011) and encyclopaedic works (Hammond and Scull 2017, Drout 2007a), one can refer to the companions by Ruud 2001 and Lee 2022a and the works by Hammond and Scull 2011, 2015 (on Tolkien's Art), Cilli 2023 ('Tolkien's library'), as well as several extended and annotated editions of Tolkien's minor works and essays (*Smith of Wootton Major* (2005), by Flieger; *On Fairy-stories* (2008), by Flieger and Anderson; *The Adventures of Tom Bombadil* (2014) by Scull and Hammond; *Fragments on Elvish Reincarnation* (2014) by Devaux; *A Secret Vice* (2016, 2020) by Fimi and Higgins; also the recent editions of *The Legend of Sigurd and Gudrún* (2009); *The Fall of Arthur* (2013); *The Story of Kullervo* (2015); *The Lay of Aotrou and Itroun* (2016); *The Battle of Maldon: Together with The Homecoming of Beorhtnoth* (2023); also the recent edition of *The Collected Poems of J. R. R. Tolkien* (Hammond and Scull 2024). To this group, one can also add works with a strong 'sub-creative focus', investigating specific aspects of Tolkien's 'secondary world', such as plants (Hazel 2006, Judd and Judd 2017), place-names (Nagel 2012), maps (Sibley and Howe 2024), poetry (Eilmann and Turner 2013), riddles (Roberts 2013), invented languages (e.g. the issues of the journals *Parma Eldalamberon* and *Vinyar Tengwar*, Hooker 2020), or indeed Tolkien as a whole (e.g. Widdicombe 2020).

A third important strand (3) includes works focusing on source criticism (*Quellenforschung*) and reception: this includes a large group of works focusing on Tolkien's sources of inspiration (cultural, literary and/or linguistic) or literary legacy, and, more generally, on comparative analysis of Tolkien's works and their contextualisation within past (especially medieval), modern, and contemporary literary landscapes. Tolkien's sources or parallels range from biblical narratives (Whittingham 2007) and classical mythology (Williams 2021, 2023, Paprocki and Matz 2022, Williams 2023), to Nordic and medieval literature (Chance 2003, 2004; Chance and Siewers 2005; Burns 2017[2005]; Solopova 2009; Atherton 2012; Ryan 2013; Lee and Solopova 2016; Lee 2022a (Part 4); Gallant 2024, etc.), down to Romanticism and Modern(ist) literature (Simonson 2008a; Fisher 2011; Hiley 2011; MacLachlan 2012; Vink 2012; Eden 2014 (Part III); Wood 2015; Eilmann 2017; Ordway 2021; Sherwood and Eilmann 2024, etc.); no less extensive is the scope of his reception (see, among others, Williamson 2015; Miller 2016; Reid and Elam 2016; Honegger and Fimi 2019; Fimi and Thompson's chapters in Lee 2022a; Bueno-Alonso 2022; Sherwood 2022; Groom 2022; Kascakova and Levente Palatinus 2023; Reinders 2024) and translations (Sherwood 2023b, Hooker 2023).

A fourth strand (4), especially productive in the last few years, is the kind of 'theoretical' research carried out by scholars with interests in philosophy or theology. This has produced a large corpus of works of disparate quality, often aiming to identify a range of (Christian) 'values', 'concepts', or 'theories', both as they are figuratively embodied in the novels and as explicitly addressed by Tolkien in non-fictional texts; among the finest and/or most recent works I can refer to Purtill 2006; Hart and Khovacs 2007; Millbank 2009; Caldecott 2012; Bernthal 2014; Coutras 2016; Mosley 2016; McIntosh 2017; Halsall 2020; Imbert 2022; Estes 2023, 2024; Freeman 2022; Thrasher and Freeman 2023; Dobie 2024; and, less recently, Birzer 2002; Garbowski 2004; Rutledge 2004; also, from a more philosophical or ethical perspective, Smith 2011; Arduini and Testi 2014 (with a useful bibliographical overview at pp. 9–20); Fornet-Ponse; Honegger, and Eilmann 2016; Testi 2018; Siburt 2023. A similarly 'theoretical' approach arguably characterises the recently burgeoning field of 'environmental' Tolkien studies (Campbell 2011; Conrad-O'Brian and Hynes 2013; Fornet-Ponse, Aubron-Bülles, and Eilmann 2014; Jeffers 2014; Simonson 2015, etc.), or, from different perspectives, 'gender' (Chance 2016, Vaccaro and Kisor 2017, Driggers 2023), 'feminist' (Croft and Donovan 2015), or 'racial' (Stuart 2022; also Sherwood 2023a) Tolkien studies.

Finally (5), there are several books that do not neatly fall into one of these categories, and have a more eclectic or idiosyncratic approach; I am thinking for instance of the studies by Flieger (esp. 1997, 2002, 2005, 2012), Shippey (esp. 2000, 2005, 2007), and Fimi (esp. 2008), as well as volumes with a specific monographic focus (Gilliver, Marshall and Weiner 2006; Vaccaro 2013; Honegger and Mann 2016; Helen 2017; Milon 2018; Amendt-Raduege 2018; Bowers 2019; Doyle 2020; Casagrande 2022; Birns 2023; Bowers and Steffenden 2024; etc.) and miscellaneous collections (Bloom 2008; Hunt 2013; Donovan 2015; Ovenden and McIlwaine 2022; Vink 2020c; Bratman 2023; Honegger 2023, among many others; also the bibliographical collection of Lee 2017).

I have taken all these works and related approaches into consideration (excluding those published in 2023–4, after I finished writing), but this book ideally stands apart from (most of) them because of its strong textual focus, rooted in literary criticism, linguistic analysis, and narratological studies, as well as its specific interest in Tolkien's literary 'theory'. In this respect its ideal paragons are the books of Flieger and Shippey, which share a similarly eclectic focus, although they generally feature a less specific interest in meta-literary discourses. There are a few works that do have this kind of focus and approach (including in particular by Bowman (2006), Nagy (esp. 2003, 2005, 2022), Saxton (2013a, 2013b), Drout, Hitotsubashi, and Scavera (2014); see also the chapters in Klinger 2012a, and Kechan 2022), but arguably no comparable monographs; my book aims to be the first comprehensive monograph on Tolkien's literary 'theory', building on previous seminal studies, integrating the approaches and results of the large body of scholarship produced in the past twenty years, and benefiting from the recent publication of new primary sources (including key texts for understanding of Tolkien's philosophical and theological concerns such as *The Nature of Middle-earth*).

Structure and Overview

The book consists of five chapters (I–V), followed by a conclusive, more theoretical chapter (VI) and an epilogue (VII). Each of the main chapters focuses on a formal feature of Tolkien's literary work: the primacy of language-invention and its integration into the narratives (Chapter I); the extensive use of meta-textual frames (Chapter II); the fondness for lacunae, omission, and allusive language, especially as regards "highest matters" (Chapter III); narrative parallelism and cross-referencing inside (intratextual) and between (intertextual) texts (Chapter IV); and unexplained narrative events, (allegedly) transcending the author's intentions (Chapter V). In the second part of each chapter, the theoretical implications of these formal features are discussed, through extensive analysis of internal meta-literary references, the editorial history of Tolkien's texts, comments scattered throughout his letters, and remarks found in his more theoretical texts (*On Fairy-stories* in particular). The analysis is founded on a text-based methodology and is rooted in literary criticism, deliberately diverging from deductive or functional approaches.

Chapter I aims to substantiate and elucidate Tolkien's puzzling claim that *The Lord of the Rings* (*LotR*) should be primarily considered as "an essay in linguistic aesthetic" (*Letters* 165:319[220]). The chapter first analyses a passing reference to the "cats of Queen Berúthiel" (*LotR* 2.4:311), described by Tolkien as the only element in *The Lord of the Rings* "which does not actually exist in legends written before it was begun" (*Letters* 174:331[228]), and about which he had "yet to discover anything" (*Letters* 163:316[217]). This example introduces a discussion of a typical pattern of composition of Tolkien's works, attested from his very early years: this begins as an experience of purely aesthetic fascination for a linguistic entity (e.g. the invented name "Berúthiel"), which is then expanded into a narrative item (e.g. "the cats of queen Berúthiel"), and only later developed into a full, meaningful tale (cf. *UT*: 401–2), through an heuristic process of 'sub-creative discovery'. The second part of the chapter investigates the theoretical implications of such an approach, also benefiting from the recent publication of a complete and annotated edition of Tolkien's seminal linguistic essay *A Secret Vice* (Fimi and Higgins 2020 [2016]). Specifically, the chapter reconstructs Tolkien's perceptions on the value and heuristic potential of a 'gratuitous' aesthetic event, and especially of a linguistic one, given the 'divine' inspiration of language and its original expression of both wonder at and knowledge of created reality. Influences from ancient (e.g. Plato) and modern (e.g. Barfield) philosophies are considered (building on Flieger 2002, 2014d, and Fornet-Ponse, Honegger, Eilmann 2016 and others), but the focus is more on Tolkien's particular view on the dream-like, 'mystical' dimension of language aesthetics, and the way it informs (or rather derives from) his literary practice. For this reason, great attention is given to Tolkien's archetypal fascination for a mysterious verse from an Old English poem ('Hail Éarendel, brightest of angels, above the middle-earth sent unto men!'), which was later integrated (or rather developed) into his literature, with momentous narrative and exegetical implications.

Chapter II reconstructs the complex frame narrative underlying *The Lord of the Rings* (and other works), according to which Tolkien came into possession of a manuscript copy of an old book in an ancient language ("Westron"), consisting of miscellaneous accounts about the first "Three Ages of this World" in five volumes ('the meta-textual frame'). The book allegedly focused on the end of the Third Age and was written by three contemporary authors of Hobbit race (Bilbo, Frodo, Sam), but was soon supplemented by a large bulk of miscellaneous material, of different content, origin, and authorship. Accordingly, this collection was later heavily edited, through a process that included emendation, supplementing, and abridgement, and whose last stage consisted of Tolkien's own compilation and translation. The second part of the chapter investigates the theoretical reasons for, and implications of, this meta-textual frame (which is just one instance within a complex web of frame-narratives underlying his posthumous works). Some of these reasons are related to Tolkien's mythopoetic ambition and urgency for narrative 'realism', probably also informed by literary models that also feature meta-textual frames (e.g. Lönnrot's *Kalevala*); others reflect key aspects of the literary fabric of the novel, including its narrative Hobbito-centrism, as regards both focalisation and themes. More deeply, the meta-textual frame allows Tolkien to express and self-reflect on his own experience as a literary writer: Tolkien considered his stories as something 'other' from him, something given or discovered, free from the control of his rational mind. The meta-textual frame thus reflects Tolkien's own views on his literature as a "puzzle", as the work of "a strange hand", written by "someone else", of which he is only providing an "approximate" report; it also explains why he often declared a fundamental ignorance about many details of the background story, why he indulged in self-exegesis of research on his own books, and why he was convinced that he did not write all that book by himself (cf. *Letters* 328:579[413]).

Chapter III focuses on another key feature of Tolkien's literary technique, namely the lavish use of omissions, narrative lacunae, allusive language, and, more specifically, the deletion of (almost) all the explicit connections between *The Lord of the Rings* and the "highest matters", including the hidden 'divine narrative' underlying the story. According to this narrative, a transcendent divine entity (Eru/Ilúvatar) 'designed' the plot of *The Lord of the Rings*, bringing it to fulfilment through His intermediaries, first the Valar, and then their emissaries in Middle-earth, specifically Gandalf, as revealed in *Unfinished Tales* (*UT*:390). References to this divine narrative are scattered throughout the novel, but always in a 'hidden' or 'glimpsed' form; indeed, as he explicitly claimed, Tolkien "purposely kept all allusions to the highest matters down to mere hints […] or kept them under unexplained symbolic forms" (*Letters* 156:297[201]). The second part of the chapter explores the theoretical implications of this poetics of 'cloaking' or 'glimpsing'. First, this technique provokes the tantalising experience of glimpsing something distant, geographically or temporally, which is vaguely perceivable and yet 'veiled', like "a distant city gleaming in a sunlit mist" (*Letters* 247:469[333]). This experience may evoke in the reader a "heart-racking" longing for something unattainable, which is accordingly at the origin of the attraction of *The Lord of the Rings*. This is a literary strategy with many parallels in ancient and modern literature, but for Tolkien it is more than that. For Tolkien, literature not only comes from the human mind, but also involves some form of participation of and in God's creative power. Human beings are sub-creators, but the light that their works refract comes from a higher Light: incompleteness and cloaking are thus means by which Tolkien acknowledges the mysterious (and arguably mystic) origin of his sub-creations, while at the same time expressing God's high concern for authorial freedom. Tolkien's poetics of cloaking is ultimately related to freedom, "the secret life in creation": (1) the freedom of the writer, who is called to express truth in the cloaked dresses of sub-creation; (2) the freedom of the reader, whose dormant "memory of the high", just like that of the Hobbits, does not need didacticism or catechising, but rather a "rekindling" or "recovery" of desire, brought about by unfamiliar, cloaked forms (such as that of Gandalf); (3) and finally the freedom of God, the "Writer of the Story", Whom the author both respects and evokes by purposefully declining to say all in open, 'primary' terms.

Chapter IV discusses another important feature of Tolkien's literature, that is, the vast amount of narrative parallelisms, both intra- and intertextual, often pinpointed by textual allusions and narrative constants. As a sample case, the chapter focuses on the parallelism between the tales of the hero Beren and the hobbit Frodo, which includes, among other elements, the identity of the enemies fought (spider-like monsters),

the nature and 'methodology' of the quest (characterised by "folly" and "disguise"), and, above all, the form
of denouement (a miraculous, 'eucatastrophic' rescue
by eagles). The analysis is then extended to the comparison between Beren and Aragorn, Frodo and Bilbo,
revealing a complex, interconnected network of narrative parallels, with important meta-literary implications: as discussed in a famous dialogue between Sam
and Frodo (*LotR* 4.8:711–12), Tolkien's characters are
indeed invited to compare the new story that is unfolding through them, with the past 'literary' tales they are
familiar with, and thereby discover unexpected similarities and an ultimate continuity. These narrative parallels are ultimately related to Tolkien's belief in "the
seamless web of story", that is to say, to use an important Tolkienian image, to the view that there is only
one and single Tree of Tales, which sprouts again and
again with new branches and leaves, all different and
yet all similar, since the stock is always the same. This
'organic' image is helpful to understand key aspects of
Tolkien's literary 'theory', which are introduced in the
second part of the chapter: these especially include his
famous aversion to allegory, which is here related to
his belief that literature (just as life) embodies in new
"modes" the same universal "motives", but in a way that
is 'unexpected' and 'unconscious', not as the product of
an intellectual strategy. The chapter concludes with a
discussion of some important ramifications of this theoretical framework: the conviction of an 'organic' narrative continuity between primary and secondary worlds;
the idea of sub-creation as renewal and recovery of primary motives in secondary modes; and the belief of a

'narrative hierarchy' within the Tree of Tales, with all stories correlating with each other in a narrative chain that has its centre in the Gospel Story. Chapter V develops and integrates the analyses of Chapters III and IV through a close reading of one of the most problematic passages of *The Lord of the Rings*, namely the fall of Gandalf in the Mines of Moria and his following return after a journey "out of thought and time" (*LotR* 3.5:502). As noted by Tolkien (*Letters* 156:298–9[202–3]), the language used to describe the event is unclear, and the exact details of what happened to Gandalf after his fall remains ambiguous, to both internal and external audiences (including, apparently, Tolkien himself). With the help of Tolkien's own (elusive) exegesis of the passage, the chapter reveals that Gandalf's 'death' and return should be construed as embodiments of two key meta-literary motives recurrent in Tolkien's mythology: (1) sub-creative submission, which features the sub-creator's humble decision to hand over their sub-creations to the supreme "Writer of the Story" (Eru) and affirm their "naked hope" in Him; this is followed by (2) a direct, miraculous intervention of Eru, which interferes with Gandalf's ontological status and brings him back to life, exceptionally disrupting "the Rules" of the secondary world (Arda); Eru's intrusion transcends the original intentions of Gandalf and his divine authorities – the secondary sub-creators – and results in the enhancement and fulfilment of their plans and wishes, and their eventual integration within a higher creative project. Gandalf's death and return can thus be construed as traces of Eru/God's 'intrusions' in the "mystery of literary creation", in both a primary and secondary sense: the definitive footprint of the divine origin of the event is the prophetic potential of the episode, which is exceptional as regards both Tolkien's 'secondary theology' and his own primary literary 'theory'.

These five main chapters are followed by the concluding Chapter VI, which offers an overview of the main themes addressed in the book and integrates them into a cohesive, overarching framework: the aesthetic and 'gratuitous' dimension of literary inspiration; writing as 'discovery' and 'translation'; the poetics of cloaking and its relation with the freedom of literature (in all senses); the writer as a co-author contributing to a single, polyphonic Story criss-crossing the primary and secondary worlds, and ultimately converging on the Resurrection ("the greatest 'eucatastrophe' possible in the greatest Fairy Story", *Letters* 89:142[100]); the 'death' of the sub-creator as an unavoidable step in any successful sub-creation; the prophetic potential of idiosyncratic literary creations and their eventual enhancement, integration, and redemption. Despite its direct and primary focus on Tolkien's literary 'theory', the chapter remains grounded on the exegesis of a secondary event, namely Gandalf's death and resurrection. In the first part of the chapter, I thus discuss the meta-literary implications of Gandalf's fall and illustrate Tolkien's concern for what can be properly described as a 'death of the author'– to use the concept of the literary critic Roland Barthes, which can be fruitfully compared with Tolkien's 'theory'. This concept is clarified through an extensive discussion of his meta-literary short story *Leaf by Niggle*, in which one can trace all key features of 'sub-creative death' (including especially the surrender of authorial domination and the need for sub-creative co-operation). The second part of the chapter explores other important elements of Tolkien's theoretical framework, focusing on the meta-literary significance of Gandalf's return, and introducing a related concept that I will call 'the resurrection of the author'. This concept is explored through a discussion of five 'gifts' bestowed to Niggle's tree in the eponymous story by the Divine Voices (completion, realisation, ramification, harmony, and prophecy), which conjure up a vision of divine enhancement of human literature, with fascinating eschatological implications.

My book concludes with a brief Epilogue (VII) featuring a very short introduction to the *Ainulindalë* – the cosmogonic myth opening *The Silmarillion*; this myth arguably provides the best illustration of Tolkien's 'theory' of sub-creation and serves as an appropriate 'secondary' summary of the present monograph. This text has often been analysed through the lens of philosophical and theological exegesis (e.g. Collins 2000; Flieger 2002; Eden 2003; Devaux 2007; Houghton 2003; and, more recently, Coutras 2016; McIntosh 2017; Halsall 2020; McBride 2020 (Chapter 1); Bertoglio 2021); here, I will briefly consider the *Ainulindalë* in purely (meta-)literary terms, as Tolkien's archetypal and most elaborate reflection on the problem of the relation of Art and Primary reality. According to this myth, Eru created the world, employing the collaboration of the Ainur (the primeval artists), whom He invited to adorn His music with their "own thoughts and devices". In this meta-literary myth of sub-creation Eru is not merely a passive, detached observer, but constantly participates in the process of sub-creation, by continuing to inspire and correct the Ainur's sub-creating activities, harmonising them with each other and maintaining the freedom to introduce "new and unforetold" entities into the eventual unfolding of their Music. As Eru says to the rebellious Melkor (an image of the self-referential artist), in a passage arguably encapsulating the whole of Tolkien's vision of the "mystery of literary creation": "no theme may be played that hath not its uttermost source in me, nor can any alter the music in my despite. For he that attempteth this shall prove but mine instrument in the devising of things more wonderful, which he himself hath not imagined" (*Sil. Ain.*:17).

I

The Cats of Queen Berúthiel

*Linguistic Aesthetic and
Literature for Its Own Sake*

~

"What is it all about?" This is one of the most common questions that Tolkien's readers – with varying degrees of sympathy – ask about the nature, meaning, and purpose of his peculiar literary enterprise. Tolkien himself addressed the question in a famous letter to his American publisher Houghton Mifflin (written in June 1955), in a piqued response to an early review of *The Lord of the Rings* (*LotR*). His words were notoriously bewildering:

> [*The Lord of the Rings*] is to me, anyway, largely an essay in 'linguistic aesthetic', as I sometimes say to people who ask me 'what is it all about?'. It is not 'about' anything but itself. (*Letters* 165:319[219–20])[1]

Tolkien's ambiguous words were not taken seriously, as he himself noted in a later letter to his son Christopher (written in 1958), in which he lamented that nobody believed him when he said that *The Lord of the Rings* was an attempt to provide a real context to fictional languages

---

[1] I quote Tolkien's letters with number and page from the 2023 revised edition, as well as page number of the old 1981 edition in square brackets (see bibliography). I provide addressee and date for all letters except those listed in the bibliography.

that he found aesthetically agreeable, and which indeed antedated its writing:

> Nobody believes me when I say that my long book is an attempt to create a world in which a form of language agreeable to my personal aesthetic might seem real. But it is true. An enquirer (among many) asked what the L.R. was all about, and whether it was an 'allegory'. And I said it was an effort to create a situation in which a common greeting would be *elen síla lúmenn' omentielvo*, and that the phrase long antedated the book. I never heard any more. (Letters 205:382[264–5])

The aim of this first chapter is to address the question "what is it all about?" by substantiating and elucidating Tolkien's claim about the "linguistic aesthetic" nature of his literary work and its 'gratuitousness', that is to say, its being 'about nothing but itself' or 'for its own sake'.[2] I then explore the implications and ramifications of what could be called a 'philological' approach to artistic creation, in order to introduce Tolkien's vision of the "mystery of literary creation" and, more generally, his complex and peculiar artistic 'theory'.[3]

---

[2] Cf. *Letters* 163:312[213]) and *Letters* 297:542–3[385–6], quoted in I.1.3 and I.1.5 respectively. 'Gratuitous' and 'gratuitousness' will be key words in this chapter, which I normally put in inverted commas to counterbalance the negative connotation that the terms tend to have nowadays in modern English; I will use the words in their etymological sense, connected to both the adverb 'gratis' and the Latin term '*gratia*' (as in *Ars Gratia Artis* 'Art for Art's Sake'), as denoting '(the fact or quality of being) done or made without any external reason or purpose' (cf. *OED* s.v. 2) or '(the fact or quality of) having an end in itself'; in other words, not being about "anything but itself", as Tolkien said about *The Lord of the Rings*.

[3] In this chapter I will build on the work of several scholars who have investigated, especially in the last two decades, the linguistic inspiration of Tolkien's mythology, and its relationship with his views on language

My journey will begin from within Tolkien's secondary plane, that is, the internal, imagined world of Arda – of which Middle-earth (the setting of *The Lord of the Rings*) is a part; here, the secondary plane will be primarily considered in its own right and for its own sake, rather than as a vehicle of literary, philosophical, or theological beliefs, or of any theoretical content in general (belonging or referring to the 'primary' plane, that is, Tolkien's own reality). I believe that this methodological approach is particularly apt to the topic of this chapter, but also necessary for any study on Tolkien in general; this chapter will thus also work as both the blueprint and the justification of the methodology that I will adopt in the rest of the book.

I.1 'Names Come First': From Berúthiel to Eärendil

I.1.1 The 'Undiscovered' Berúthiel and Her Exceptionality

In a crucial stage of the adventure, the Fellowship of the Ring travels through the dark vastness of the Mines of Moria, following the resolve of their leader Gandalf, albeit with doubts, hesitancy, and even some grievance.

invention, and the nature and origin of language in general. I am particularly indebted to Flieger 2002, 2012:242–50, 2014d; Smith 2006, 2011, 2016; Fimi 2008:76–92, 2018; Atherton 2012:179–252; Robbins 2013, Fimi and Higgins 2020: xi–lxv. Cf. also Noel 1980; Medcalf 1999; Lodbell 2004; Shippey 2005:329–78; Gymnich 2005; Segura and Peris 2005; Turner 2007b; Hemmi 2010; Adams 2011a; Weiner and Marshall 2011; Phelpstead 2011; Robinson 2013; the essays in Fornet-Ponse, Honegger, Eilmann 2016; Jarman 2016; Croft 2017; Smith 2017; Imbert 2022: Part One.

In a moment of uncertainty Aragorn addresses his companions with words of comfort:

'Do not be afraid! [...] I have been with him on many a journey, if never on one so dark [...] He will not go astray – if there is any path to find. [...] He is surer of finding the way home in a blind night than **the cats of Queen Berúthiel.**' (*LotR* 2.4:311)

My starting point is an apparently marginal detail of this passage: who is Queen Berúthiel? And what about her cats? These are, apparently, questions with no answer. Indeed, not only is this the first and last time Queen Berúthiel is mentioned in *The Lord of the Rings*, but no other reference to her is found in any other primary Tolkien books, including *The Hobbit* and *The Silmarillion*. This absence is particularly noteworthy for an author such as Tolkien who was obsessed with precision and the comprehensiveness of detail in the building of his secondary world, and who grounded his *The Lord of the Rings* on an all-inclusive, pre-existing corpus of names, characters, and stories. In some few passages from his letters, Tolkien himself noted the exceptionality of Queen Berúthiel and her cats, noting that she was probably the only narrative entity referred to in *The Lord of the Rings* that did not exist in legends already written before its inception.[4] Another important allusion to Berúthiel is found in a famous letter to W. H. Auden,

---

[4] Cf. "I do not think that anything is referred to in *The L. of the R.* which does not actually exist in legends written before it was begun, or at least belonging to an earlier period – except only the 'cats of Queen Berúthiel'" (*Letters* 174:331[228]); "There is hardly any reference in The Lord of the Rings to things that do not actually exist* on its own plane (of secondary or sub-creational reality): sc. have been written. [*The cats of Queen Berúthiel and the names and adventures of the other 2 wizards [...] are all that I recollect]" (*Letters* 180:336[231] with n.*).

which I discuss at length in Chapter II (II.2.2.2) to illustrate Tolkien's self-perception of writing as a discovery:

I knew nothing of the *Palantíri*, though the moment the Orthanc-stone was cast from the window, I recognized it [...], and knew the meaning of the 'rhyme of lore' that had been running in my mind: *seven stars and seven stones and one white tree.* These rhymes and names will crop up; but they do not always explain themselves. I have yet to discover anything about the cats of Queen Berúthiel. (*Letters* 163:316[217])

This crucial passage allusively reveals, in typically Tolkienian fashion, that Tolkien did not hide or omit other narrative information about Queen Berúthiel for some particular reason. Rather, Tolkien paradoxically claims that he himself did not know anything about this enigmatic queen at the time of writing, apart from her name and a vague association with some mysterious cats. Tolkien describes the genesis of Queen Berúthiel and her cats as an instance of a common pattern of his creative practice; according to this, onomastics and their embryonal narrative context ("rhymes and names") "crop up" spontaneously in Tolkien's mind and often "do not explain themselves". Only later does Tolkien "discover" their full "meaning", in a moment of revelation.[5] In the passage quoted, Tolkien talks about names within a context ("rhymes and names"), and in our case-study, the name Berúthiel appears together with some narrative supplements (her identity as a queen and her cats),

---

[5] Cf. also *Letters* 208:385[267] (quoted in Chapter VI, n.32) where Tolkien claims that only when he re-read the book with the eye of the critic he became aware of the dominance of the theme of Death. See also I.2.2.3 and VI.1.3.

however embryonal; but it is clear that for Tolkien, primacy is given to "names". It is "names", that is, "words" and "language", that "come first" for Tolkien, before any narrative contextualisation or development.

This is a point often made in his letters, in which he claimed for instance that to him "a name comes first and the story follows. († I once scribbled 'hobbit' on a blank page of some boring school exam. paper in the early 1930's. It was some time before I discovered what it referred to!)" (*Letters* 165:319[219]).[6] This passage associates this 'linguistic' practice of composition with what for Tolkien was the most unexpected and momentous 'turning point' of his literary career,[7] the genesis of *The Hobbit*. This accordingly originated from a sudden moment of unplanned linguistic inspiration (the name 'Hobbit'),[8] whose narrative implications, and even semantic reference, were "discovered" only after "some time".[9]

I.1.2 The Textual History of Berúthiel: Linguistic Tinkering, Phonoaesthetics, and Narrative Unfolding

One could discount all these claims and discourses as a mere authorial pretence if there was not plenty of evidence

---

[6] Cf. also *Letters* 315, to M. Tolkien, 1/01/1970:566[404] "'Stories' [...] sprout in my mind from names".

[7] Cf. Shippey 2000:1-3.

[8] See Shippey 2011a for a discussion of possible linguistic precedents or influences.

[9] Cf. also Tolkien's words in an unpublished letter (*TCG* 341, 26/10/1958), in which he claimed that the word 'hobbit' generated the Hobbits qua creatures, who "grew to fit to it". On the mysterious genesis of *The Hobbit* and its implications see further II.2.2.1.

to suggest that Tolkien spoke in good faith. In the case of Queen Berúthiel, 'linguistic primacy' is shown by the textual history of the relevant passage quoted earlier, which can be reconstructed in detail thanks to Christopher Tolkien's painstaking work on the early manuscripts of *The Lord of the Rings* (collected in the volumes of the monumental *History of Middle-earth*), and the encyclopaedic effort of Hammond and Scull (2005:283–4). These reveal that the first redaction of the text merely contained a generic comparison of Gandalf's orientation skills to "any cat that ever walked" (cf. *RS* 25:464 n.26). This cat was later given a 'secondary' specificity, through the impromptu addition of an Elvish name of dubious meaning and etymology associated with it ("the cat of Benish Armon"). The name was later changed into "Queen Tamar", "Queen Margoliantë Beruthiel", and finally "Berúthiel". This textual history suggests that a Tolkienian fondness for 'gratuitous' language creation lies at the origin of Queen Berúthiel, which is here used to qualify the otherwise generic (non-sub-creative) reference to "any cat". The fact that Tolkien only tinkered with the form of the name, leaving its narrative context almost unchanged ("the cats") suggests that Tolkien's concern in the creation of our mysterious queen was primarily linguistic.

Although the exact etymology of the name Berúthiel is unclear, its origin certainly had to do with an aesthetic search: that is to say, Tolkien invented the name Berúthiel through a process of 'linguistic aesthetic', aimed to produce a phonetically 'pleasing' word. We are certain about this because all those strange-looking names ("Benish Armon", "Tamar", "Margoliantë") and "Berúthiel" above all display phonological and morphological

features typical of the Elvish languages, which Tolkien
began to invent and develop several decades before the
writing of *The Lord of the Rings*. Languages that, as he
remarked, were supposed to be "specially pleasant", and
through which he tried 'to please himself'.[10] Another
important feature of Tolkien's creative endeavour is
its personal, and even 'egocentric' dimension.[11] This
personal linguist-aesthetic is, however, only the starting point: the next, secondary but necessary, step is to
'unfold' the semantic and narrative content contained in
that linguistic intuition. This could be described as a sort
of 'narrative etymologising' – a difficult but rewarding
task, which many Tolkienian names underwent, including that of Berúthiel.[12]

Although Queen Berúthiel and her cats apparently dis-
appeared from Tolkien's radar after the publication of
The Lord of the Rings, it is clear (as inferred from the passages quoted in the previous section) that he was aware
that there was some unfinished business, which "called
for attention". The matter was unexpectedly forced back
to his attention in 1966, eleven years after the publication of *The Lord of the Rings*, when Tolkien agreed to give
an interview to one of his former students, Daphne R.
Castell, for the journal *New World* (no. 50, "The Realms

---

[10] Cf. *Letters* 144:264[175].
[11] Cf. also *Letters* 328:578[412] "The book was written **to please myself**
(at different levels)", *Letters* 297:536[380], quoted in n.13.
[12] For a collection of cases cf. esp. the lexicographic material collected by
Christopher Tolkien in his Appendix to Part I of the *Book of Lost Tales*
(*BLT* 1:246–97); as Christopher Tolkien points out in his introduction
(246), the perusal of this material "shows in the clearest possible way
how deeply involved were the developments in the mythology and in
the languages".

of Tolkien"). One of Castell's questions concerned Queen
Berúthiel herself. Part of Tolkien's answer is worth quoting in full.

Most of the allusions to older legends scattered about the tale,
or summarized in Appendix A are to things which really have
an existence of some kind in the history of which 'The Lord
of the Rings' is part. There's one exception that **puzzles** me –
Berúthiel. **I don't really know anything** of her. [...] She just
popped up and obviously called for attention, but **I don't really
know anything certain** about her; though **oddly enough I
have a notion** that she was the wife of one of the ship-kings of
Pelargir. She loathed the smell of the sea, and fish, and the gulls.
[...] Berúthiel went back to live in the inland city, and went to
the bad (or returned to it – she was a black Númenórean in origin, **I guess**). She was one of these people who loathe cats, but
cats will jump on them and follow them about [...] I'm afraid
she took to torturing them for amusement, but she kept some
and used them – trained them to go on evil errands by night, to
spy on her enemies or terrify them. ('The Realms of Tolkien',
interview with D. R. Castell, *New World* 50, 147)

The language and imagery used in this passage are
revealing, as well as the logical flow: initially, Tolkien still
professes complete ignorance about Berúthiel ("I don't
really know anything of her"), but this gradually transforms
into 'uncertainty' ("I don't really know anything certain")
and then "a notion" and a "guess", while Tolkien begins
to unfold the narrative seed (perhaps extempore) into a
proper story, still very fragmentary. One can also note
how Tolkien describes the 'discovery' of Berúthiel with a
touch of serendipity and mystery (Berúthiel "popped up",
and "puzzles" Tolkien, who "oddly enough" only knows
about her identity as a queen).

I.1.3 Linguistic Inspiration and the Secret Vice

What I have described so far with Berúthiel is just one
case-study within a large group of Tolkienian narratives
that can be traced back to a linguistic intuition, 'mysterious' and 'gratuitous' at first, and only later 'explained' and
'unfolded' into a story. We have already seen the example
of the word 'hobbit', but there are many other instances.
This pattern of composition could be applied on the
macro-level to the whole of Tolkien's literary work, which
according to Tolkien was "fundamentally linguistic in
inspiration" and whose legends and histories followed the
invention of languages rather than vice versa, and aimed
to 'realise' those languages, providing "the necessary background" for them.[13] This 'fundamentality of language' is a
distinctive trait of Tolkien's methodology, as noted by critics such as Shippey,[14] and is already attested in his earliest

---

[13] Cf. *Letters* 165:319[219] "a primary 'fact' about my work, that is [...]
fundamentally linguistic in inspiration. [...] The invention of languages
is the foundation. The 'stories' were made rather to provide a world
for the languages than the reverse" and *LotR Foreword*:xviiii "[*The
Lord of the Rings*] was primarily linguistic in inspiration and was
begun in order to provide the **necessary background** of 'history' for
Elvish tongues". Also *Letters* 297:536[380] "this process of [language]
invention was/is a private enterprise undertaken to give pleasure to
myself by giving expression to my personal linguistic 'æsthetic' or taste
and its fluctuations. It was largely antecedent to the composing of
legends and 'histories' in which these languages could be 'realized'";
Letters 157, to K. Farrer, 27/11/1954:305[208] "As usually with me
they [the Ents] grew rather out of their name, than the other way
about", *TCG* 1528 (16/04/1956) in which Tolkien stresses that the
Elvish tongues, with their related nomenclature and scripts, are his
"most absorbing interest", and were made before and independently
of his tales; finally, a passage reported by Carpenter (1977:171), cited
in Chapter VI n.11.
[14] Cf. Shippey 2000:56–60, 230–2.

creative experiments. As recalled in a famous passage, after a premature experiment with a story of a dragon, Tolkien was "taken up with languages" for a long time before trying to write a story again, after having been struck by the linguistic impossibility of saying "green great dragon".[15] Tolkien's 'philological priority' is especially confirmed in the textually history of his *legendarium*, which would eventually converge in Christopher Tolkien's 1977 *Silmarillion*. The germs of Tolkien's mythology can be traced back to a series of poems composed in the mid-1910s, still quite undeveloped in both content and taste, and not all clearly integrated in the *legendarium* in the same way; even at that early stage of composition, language invention preceded and compelled storytelling – not vice versa. These early poems include *The Shores of Faery*, a short text composed in the spring/summer of 1915,[16] which Tolkien once described as "the first poem of my mythology".[17] This poem was accompanied (and inspired) by a beautiful watercolour of his own doing,[18] which already included topical Tolkienian images such as "the two Trees", the "lonely hill", and the "haven of the star". It also featured a set of clearly non-English nomenclature, such as Eglamar, Taniquetil, Valinor, and especially Wingelot

---

[15] *Letters* 163:313[214].

[16] Published in *BLT2* 5:271–3 (= *TCP* 181–7).

[17] Cf. Hammond and Scull 2017: *Chronology* 64, 70, *Reader's Guide* 1151. Christopher Tolkien doubted this primacy (attributing it to the Éarendel poem Tolkien wrote in Gedling in 1914, see I.1.5 and cf. *BLT2* 5:271–2) and Tolkien himself later applies this label to other two texts, including *The Fall of Gondolin* composed at the end of 1916 (cf. *Letters* 163:313[213]).

[18] Printed in Hammond and Scull 1995:47–9, with commentary.

and Eärendel.[19] These are of course Elvish names, which were invented by Tolkien before the actual composition of the poem: they all appear in an earlier work, entitled 'Qenyaqetsa' (now published as issue 12 of the journal *Parma Eldalamberon*). This consists of a phonological account and etymological dictionary of Q(u)enya, the first 'Elvish' language that Tolkien devised for his own pleasure.[20] The redaction of this systematic Elvish grammar dates to spring 1915 (cf. Hammond and Scull 2017: *Chronology* 68), but the composition of its lemmata is certainly earlier. The Qenyaqetsa was itself a quite advanced stage in Tolkien's pursuit of language invention, which had begun several years before. This involved both the invention of properly fictional languages and also the fictional reconstruction of unattested words in a primary dead language. Indeed, the very manuscript containing the Qenyaqetsa is preceded by a few pages of notes on (a variety of) the Gothic language, including some original compositions, such as the inscription *Ermanaþiudiska Razda eþþau*

---

[19] On Wingelot/Vingelot see Garth 2003:86–7, noting that the name was derived from the boat of the Germanic hero, Wade (Guingelot), who was also associated with the sea like Éarendel. Cf. also *LB* 2:144, Garth 2014.

[20] For an example of a lemma, cf. "(TAHA) tā (1) adj. † high. (2) av. high above, high up. * Taniqetil (-d)="Lofty snowcap", a great mountain at World's Edge" (*Parma Eldalamberon* 12 (1998), 'Qenyaqetsa: The Qenya Phonology and Lexicon', edited by C. Gilson, C. F. Hostetter, P. H. Wynne, and A. R. Smith:86). On this text and its relationship with the Éarendel poem see Hostetter 1991; Hooker 2020. Cf. also the material now collected in the *Appendix on Names* in BLT1:246–73. For an overview of Tolkien's invented languages see esp. Hostetter 2006, 2007; Weiner and Marshall 2011; Gilson 2020; Smith 2022; also the classic (but now outdated) Noel 1980.

Gautiska tungō ('Language of the Great People, or Gautish [Gothic] tongue').[21] As Tolkien would recall several years later, his experience with Gothic had a momentous consequence, since he discovered in it "not only modern historical philology, which appealed to the historical and scientific side, but for the first time the study of a language out of mere love: I mean for the acute aesthetic pleasure derived from a language for its own sake, not only free from being useful but free even from being the 'vehicle of a literature'" (*Letters* 163:312[213]).[22] I will come back later to this crucial idea of "acute aesthetic pleasure", derived from a "love" for language "for its own sake".

Apart from his experiments in Gothic, by 1915 Tolkien already had long-standing experience in the invention of properly 'new' languages. He retraced the history of this 'hobby' in an important essay originally delivered as a paper to an Oxford literary society, and appropriately titled "A Secret Vice".[23] In this essay, Tolkien gives an account of the different languages he invented (including Nevbosh, influenced by English, French, and Latin, and Naffarin, a mix of Spanish and Italian, and finally 'Quenya'), as well as some illustrative poetic samples in the different languages. These samples include two poems focusing on the tale of Éarendel, the same hero

---

[21] For Tolkien's fondness of original composition in primary dead languages see esp. Rateliff 2014b.

[22] See Robbins 2015 for further influences of Gothic and its literature on Tolkien's mythology.

[23] This has been recently re-edited by D. Fimi and A. Higgins (2020[2016]). The original title of the essay was "A Hobby for the Home", which gave a 'public', shared character to the 'private' dimension of language invention, presented as a 'hobby' that anyone could start in their own 'home'. I owe this point to Roger Sylvester.

mentioned in *The Shores of Faery*, who had been at the centre of Tolkien's poetic attention even before the conscious development of a secondary mythology. Eärendil (with the final spelling of the name, which I will henceforth use) can be considered the most important Tolkienian character, the foundation stone, the igniting spark of all Tolkien's mythology. Moreover, Eärendil's history of composition is archetypal of Tolkien's creative practice, which would be eventually (and lastly) repeated with Queen Berúthiel. Although Eärendil is, from a chronological perspective, at the opposite end of Berúthiel, the two characters are deeply related, as we shall see.

I.1.4 The Thrilling Encounter with Éarendel/ Eärendil

Tolkien strongly opposed the use of the notion of 'invention' to describe his compositional practice.[24] This is particularly true in the example of Eärendil, for which one can certainly talk about 'invention' only in the etymological sense of 'discovery' (from Latin *invenire* 'to find out, discover, encounter'). Eärendil is in fact a pre-existing character, whom Tolkien 'encountered' in 1913–14 during his third year of university while studying Old English in the series *Bibliothek der angelsächsischen Poesie*, edited by Grein and Wülker (1883–1898).[25] The

---

[24] In *On Fairy-stories* Tolkien even posits a contrast between 'uninspired invention' and 'truthful inspiration' (cf. *TOFS*:77 n.1=*TL*:71) and see n.110. I further discuss Tolkien's rejection of 'invention' in II.2.2.2.

[25] On Tolkien's 'encounter' with Éarendel see further Hostetter 1991; Garth 2003:43–7; Shippey 2000:256–61; Morton and Hayes 2008:62–8; Atherton 2012. On the symbolism of Eärendil cf. also Beare 2007.

name appears in an Old English poem known as '*Crist*' or '*Christ I*', preserved in the famous Exeter Book.[26] This poem is a collection of twelve liturgical hymns dedicated to the Advent of Christ, which freely appropriates vestiges of pre-Christian poetic diction into its Christian framework. Specifically, lines 104–5 of this poem deeply struck the young Tolkien, as he would later recall through the persona of Alwin Arundel, one of the main characters in his posthumous work *The Notion Club Papers*:[27]

> *Éala Éarendel engla beorhtost*
> *ofer middangeard monnum sended!*

he chanted. "'Hail Earendel, brightest of angels, above the middle-earth sent unto men!'" When I came across that citation in the dictionary I felt a curious thrill, as if something had stirred in me, **half wakened from sleep**. There was something very remote and **strange and beautiful** behind those words, if I could grasp it, far beyond ancient English. **I know more now**, of course. The quotation comes from the *Crist*; though exactly what the author meant is **not so certain**. (*SD Not.*:236)

In this passage we see some of the key features of Tolkien's creative method: the pure linguistic-aesthetic appeal of a name and the 'uncertainty' of meaning ("strange and beautiful", "not so certain"), which is only better (but never fully) comprehended at a later stage ("I know more now"). Note also the imagery used to describe the experience, equating to that of someone who is "half wakened from sleep".[28] Tolkien referred to that seminal encounter with Éarendel/

---

[26] For a more recent edition see Muir 2000.

[27] For an overview see Shippey 2000:283–9, also noting the similarity of sound in the names Alwin Arundel and Ælfwine Eärendel.

[28] For the imagery of sleeping and dreaming see I.2.2.

Eärendil several times, usually stressing its aesthetic dimension, explaining for instance that he was struck "by the great beauty of this word [...] euphonic to a peculiar degree in that pleasing [...] language".[29] This aesthetic experience comes before anything else, and is to a large extent 'gratuitous' in its pleasurable dimension ("euphonic [...] pleasing"), but at the same time set in motion in Tolkien a 'heuristic' process, a journey of discovery.

I.1.5 *Scientific and Artistic Curiosity: Primary Exegesis and Creative Heuristic*

Tolkien did not stop at linguistic fascination with the beautiful name Éarendel, but rather this compelled him to embark on a heuristic journey to find out its 'meaning' (and thereby, one could say, the significance of his own 'gratuitous' aesthetic experience). For Tolkien, a professional philologist, the first step of this heuristic was a scientific analysis of the etymology and meaning of the term within its primary Old English context. Tolkien provides this analysis in a letter to one of his readers, construing the name as primarily denoting the morning star, presaging the morning, and figuratively John the Baptist, the herald of Christ.[30] This scientific, 'primary' exegesis is just the beginning of the journey, and develops into an artistic or

---

[29] Cf. *Letters* 297:542[385] "The most important name [...] is Eärendil. This name is in fact [...] derived from Anglo-Saxon *éarendel*. When first studying Anglo-Saxon professionally [...] I was struck **by the great beauty of this word** [...] **euphonic to a peculiar degree in that pleasing** but not 'delectable' **language.**"

[30] Cf. *Letters* 297:542[385] with n.6. However, in the same letter (p. 544[387]) Tolkien stresses that this Christian symbolism of *éarendel* is "completely alien" to his use.

(sub-)creative heuristic (a 'learning process'), moved by the desire to discover the true meaning of that aesthetic experience. In Tolkien, this 'secondary' heuristic is primarily conducted, then, in relation to an original creative process. The momentous encounter with that mysterious name led Tolkien to write a first poem about Éarendel (*Éalá Éarendel Engla Beorhtast*, printed in *BLT2* 5:267–9 = *TCP* 86–8), which did not yet consciously belong to his *legendarium*.[31] Tolkien completed this poetic germ in September 1914, between 22 and 25 September, while staying at his aunt Jane Neave's farm in Gedling, near Nottingham.[32] Subsequently, Tolkien gave the poem to

[31] See Garth 2014 for a full discussion of this poem. Cf. also Shippey 2000:256–61.

[32] The exact date of composition is most likely 24 September (cf. *TCP* 86, Hammond and Scull 2017: *Chronology* 61; see also Morton and Hayes 2008, esp. 50–61); this would be appropriate, since in the Anglo-Saxon calendar (cf. Bede *De temporum ratione* 30), as in ancient Christian martyrology (and nowadays in some Orthodox Churches), 24 (or 23) September is the feast of the conception of St John the Baptist (i.e. the *Éarendel* of the *Crist* poem). These dates around the Autumn Equinox are significant also in Tolkien's secondary world, marking the birthdays of Bilbo and Frodo and the start of Frodo's adventure in *The Lord of the Rings* (22 and 23 September), Gandalf's escape from the Tower of Orthanc in an early draft of *The Lord of the Rings* (24 September, cf. *TI* 1:11) and, in the aftermath of the War of the Ring, a series of special days in the year (cf. *LotR Appendix D*:1112 "There were 3 Enderi or Middle-days [...] that corresponded with September 23, 24, 25 old style. But in honour of Frodo Yavannië 30, which corresponded with former September 22, his birthday, was made a festival, and the leap-year was provided for by doubling this feast, called Cormarë or Ringday"). It may also not be completely coincidental that the final meeting ('The Council of Lichfield') of Tolkien's student society at King Edward's School in Birmingham, the Tea Club, Barrovian Society (TCBS), took place on 24–5 September (1915) (see Hammond and Scull 2017: *Chronology* 81), and that *The Hobbit* was published on 21 September (1937).

his school friend G. B. Smith to read,[33] admitting that he did not yet know what it was really about, and promising to "try to find out".[34] It is not an exaggeration to say that all that followed was a fulfilment of that promise.[35]

Again, that early poem about Eärendel was not the end of the journey, but just a stage in Tolkien's 'creative heuristic', which he himself further reconstructs in a letter:

Before 1914 I wrote a 'poem' upon Eärendel who launched his ship like a bright spark from the havens of the Sun. I adopted him in my mythology – in which he became a prime figure as a mariner, and eventually as a herald star, and a sign of hope to men. [...] But the name could not be adopted just like that: it had to be accommodated to the Elvish linguistic situation, at the same time as a place for this person was made in legend. From this, far back in the history of 'Elvish', which was beginning [...] to take definite shape at the time of the name's adoption, arose eventually (a) the C.E. stem *AYAR 'Sea', primarily applied to the Great Sea of the West, lying between Middle-earth and Aman the Blessed Realm of the Valar; and (b) the element, or verbal base (N)DIL, 'to love, be devoted to' – describing the attitude of one to a person, thing, course or

---

[33] G. B. Smith (1894–1916) was one of the fellow members of the TCBS, later a student at Corpus Christi College, Oxford, and a casualty in the Battle of the Somme. After his death, Tolkien edited and prefaced Smith's collection of poems *A Spring Harvest* (excerpted in Atherton 2012). On the relationship between Tolkien and Smith, and the TCBS in general, see Garth 2003, *passim*.

[34] Cf. "he had shown the original Eärendel lines to G. B. Smith, who had said that he liked them but asked what they were really about. Tolkien had replied: 'I don't know. I'll try to find out'" (Carpenter 1977:107). Cf. also Garth 2003:52–3.

[35] Tolkien himself acknowledged this in a letter to C. S. Kilby, in which he wrote that from that line of the *Crist* "ultimately sprang the whole of my mythology" (quoted in Kilby 1976:57). Cf. Garth 2003:44.

occupation to which one is devoted **for its own sake**. (*Letters* 297:542–3[385–6]).³⁶

From that early poem, Tolkien would thus develop a long and complex narrative, fully integrated within, and indeed stimulating, his *legendarium*. This narrative is epitomised in the secondary Elvish etymology that Tolkien (in another stage of his heuristic) eventually 'discovered' for the name Eärendil, meaning 'lover of the sea'. Within Tolkien's *legendarium*, Eärendil is driven by an insatiable love for the sea, which compels him to sail the forbidden route leading from fallen, hopeless Middle-earth back to the land of the gods (the Valar), known as Valinor. There he implores the mercy of the Valar and obtains their intervention against the Satanic Morgoth. After his mission is accomplished, Eärendil becomes the Morning (and Evening) Star, bringer of hope to Middle-earth (just as the Éarendel of the *Crist* poem), and as such will continue to play an important role in *The Lord of the Rings*, as we will see.

It is now time to move to the second part of this chapter, in which I will move away from Tolkien's secondary world and (following Tolkien's own methodology) will try to find out the 'meaning' of what I have been discussing so far.

I.2 'Gratuitous' Creations and the Re-awakening of Sea-Longing

The specific question I will address in this second part of the chapter can be put in the following terms: how did

³⁶ Cf. also *Letters* 131, n.*:210[150] (on the ramified mythological connexions of the Anglo-Saxon name *earendel*, as well as its meaning in Elvish as Great Mariner or Sea-Lover).

Tolkien explain or at least understand his own particular creative method? This, as we have seen, usually begins as an unplanned, mysterious moment of aesthetic-linguistic inspiration (e.g. the encounter with the "strange and beautiful" name Éarendel, the invention of the 'pleasing' word "Berúthiel"), which is then expanded into a narrative item (e.g. from "the tale of Eärendil" to "the cats of Queen Berúthiel"), and gradually developed into a full, meaningful tale, through a process of 'discovery', which is both linguistic/etymological and narrative/literary.

In order to address this question, I will now need to introduce Tolkien's literary 'theory' in more open terms, which, not surprisingly for a sophisticated thinker and committed Christian such as Tolkien, is closely interrelated with his philosophical and theological views. Here I talk of 'theory' and 'views' for the sake of simplification, but, more precisely, I should rather say 'theoretical self-reflections on a creative experience'. That is to say, as already noted in the Introduction, for Tolkien (who was an artist and not a philosopher or theologian), the creative act (linguistic and then narrative) *precedes* the moment of theoretical investigation, which works as a sort of exegesis on a given experience rather than its intellectual source or stimulus. Here I will specifically focus on the very outset of Tolkien's creative experience, the moment and process of inspiration, which I reconstructed in the previous sections in matter-of-fact terms, from Eärendil (arguably the first developed character of the *legendarium*) to Berúthiel (one of the last, least developed ones). There is plenty of evidence, however, that Tolkien did reflect on this experience in theoretical terms, although, as typical of him, never in a systematic manner. I will now attempt to establish some order, drawing from an array of miscellaneous thoughts, explicitly articulated in his essays and letters, or figuratively expressed in his secondary work. Two aspects of his linguistic/aesthetic inspiration particularly caught the attention of Tolkien's self-reflective mind: its 'meaninglessness' and 'unconsciousness'.

I.2.1 From Meaningless Language to Purposeless Art

I.2.1.1 Tolkien on Joyce's Nonsense and the Debate about Language

To illustrate the first aspect ('meaninglessness'), I will start with a short Tolkienian note on James Joyce's *Finnegans Wake*, which was found by Margaret Hiley (2015) among Tolkien's scrap papers (MS Tolkien 24).[37] In a section appropriately titled 'Stream of consciousness', Tolkien notes that in Joyce's novel "the 'meaning' while coherent [...] is so clearly subordinate to sound, that one necessarily pays chief attention to the latter" (MS Tolkien 24 fol. 44=Fimi and Higgins 2020:92). What lies behind these words is Tolkien's tripartite division of language into sound, form, and meaning. These three elements, Tolkien explains, "should cohere and be in a coherent relationship one to another: but this does not of course suggest that any one of them (least of all the 'meaning') is necessarily the most important in a given performance" (ibid. fol. 44–5=Fimi and Higgins 2020:91). In Tolkien's vision, therefore, meaning is not at all the most important

---

[37] Now also printed in Fimi and Higgins 2020:91–2 (whose transcription I follow here). See Fimi and Higgins 2020:lxii–lxv, and Fimi 2018 for a comparison between Joyce and Tolkien regarding their interest in language invention/experimentation and language theory.

element of language; giving priority to meaning, as is inevitable in modern languages, can even be detrimental to the appreciation of the other two elements (sound and form) and their "coherent relationship":

> Normally 'meaning' – and/or [...] visual pictures are so strong that it needs as much training to listen independently or appreciate the independent contribution of the sound part, as to listen to certain subordinate parts of orchestrated music [...] But with a traditional language 'pure sound' is impossible. All the 'sound-groups' have senses (more or less definite) attached to them – their juxtaposition necessarily awakens the 'meaning'-seeking faculty. (ibid. fol. 45=Fimi and Higgins 2020:91–2)

An elaboration of Tolkien's thoughts on the matter, and their broader implications, is found in a passage from his essay *A Secret Vice*:

> In poetry (of our day – when the use of significant language is so habitual that the word-form is seldom consciously marked, and the associated notions have it almost all their own way) it is the interplay and pattern of the notions adhering to each word that is uppermost. The word-music, according to the nature of the tongue and the skill or ear (conscious or artless) of the poet, runs on heard, but seldom coming to awareness. At rare moments we pause to wonder why a line or couplet produces an effect beyond its significance. (*SV*:32–3=*MC*:218)

In this passage, Tolkien develops the idea that meanings ("the associated notions") in modern human languages have an unfortunate primacy above sound, with a resulting loss of delight and contemplation, as well as (paradoxically) of a full appreciation of those very meanings (which conversely may be re-'illuminated' by an aesthetic emphasis on pure sound). Note also the musical imagery, which is key in Tolkien (cf. Chapter VII), as well as the idea that the "sound part" of language has its own independence. The 'independence' of sound, the pleasure in it, and its "symbolic use" are thus very important for Tolkien and should "not be forgotten for a moment", as he points out in another passage in *A Secret Vice*, where he associates this attention to pure sound, independent of meaning, with an experience of aesthetic pleasure.[38] This pleasure-seeking or 'hedonic' approach to language and art in general is key in Tolkien,[39] and is repeatedly asserted in *A Secret Vice*, where the word 'pleasure' (and its derivatives) occurs more than 20 times, especially in contexts emphasising Tolkien's interest in the use of the linguistic faculty "for amusement".[40] Linguistic pleasure is closely related with, and derives from, the contemplation of beauty, and especially with beauty of sound, or

---

[38] Cf. *SV*:18=*MC*:208 "The communication factor has been very powerful in directing the development of language; but the more individual and personal factor – pleasure in articulate sound, and the **symbolic use** of it, **independent of communication** though constantly entangled with it – must **not be forgotten for a moment**."

[39] Cf. also his defence of the "aesthetic aspect of the invented idiom" in a letter written to the secretary of the Education Committee of the British Esperanto Association (published in *The British Esperantist*, vol. 28, 1932:182), and his "strong aesthetic pleasure in contact with Welsh" (*MC*:190; similar ideas are expressed in his unpublished lecture on 'English and Welsh', Tolkien, MS 7 fol. 108).

[40] Cf. *SV*:15–17=*MC*:206 "This idea of using the linguistic faculty **for amusement** is […] deeply interesting to me. […] In these invented languages the **pleasure** is more keen than it can be even in learning a new language […] because more personal and fresh, more open to experiment of trial and error. […] The very word-form itself, of course, even unassociated with notions, is capable of **giving-pleasure** – a perception of beauty which if of a minor sort is not more foolish and irrational than being sensitive to the line of a hill, light and shade, or colour."

"phonoaesthetic" or "phonetic aesthetic" in Tolkien's terms, which he found especially in languages such as Finnish and Greek.[41] Tolkien's appreciation of Joyce's linguistic experimentation is thus related to his own aesthetic and 'hedonic' concern for a language "unassociated with notions", a language that may even appear 'nonsensical' (as the language of *Finnegans Wake*) and produce "a pattern of those clashing woven meanings [...] – even if it be bizarre or dream like", as Tolkien notes in another scrap of those fragmentary notes (MS Tolkien 24, fol. 45=Fimi and Higgins 2020:92).

This reconstructed exchange between Joyce and Tolkien is just one small piece within a much broader mosaic of discourses on language, focusing specifically on the origin of words and the relationship between signifier ('word') and signified ('meaning'). These discourses, which can be traced back to ancient theories of linguistic naturalism,[42] found new vigour in the cultural landscape of the early twentieth century, and involved professional linguists (e.g. de Saussure, Bloomfield, Sapir, Jespersen) and promoters of International Auxiliary Languages (IAR) (particularly Zamenhof and his fellow Esperantists), as well as philosophers and theoreticians (e.g. Paget and Barfield), and (modernist) literary writers (e.g. Gertrude

---

[41] Cf. *Letters* 144:265[176] (on the phonoaesthetic pleasure of Finnish and Greek), *Letters* 257:484[345] (on the "powerfully individual phonetic aesthetic" of Welsh, Finnish, and Gothic). Also *Letters* 180:336[231] on the "marvellous aesthetic" of the language of Greek mythology, *Letters* 297:536[380] quoted in n.13. See Robbins 2013 for an investigation of Tolkien's phonoaesthetics, and its relationship with the features of his invented language, as well as the style of *The Lord of the Rings*.

[42] See Pezzini and Taylor 2019 for an overview.

Stein, Joyce). It would be outside the scope of this chapter to review this debate, or to detail Tolkien's active interest in many of its strands.[43]

This section will, therefore, not systematically compare Tolkien's views on language with that of his possible sources and analogues; rather, I will simply point out that one of the central issues of the linguistic debate of the early twentieth century concerned the arbitrariness of language (qua sounds and word-forms). Are words purely conventional sequences of sounds randomly assigned to meanings and their referents (as per Saussurian theory), which can be either freely manipulated by individuals for the sake of poetic experimentation (as for many modernist writers), or 'rationalised' by enlightened sages to ease communication (as for the proponents of IAR)? Or, conversely, is there any 'objectivity' in word-sounds, any sort of relationship with 'reality' and thus 'truth', even before their assignment to a specific meaning and referent (as according to the theory of phonetic symbolism, discussed by Tolkien in a posthumous essay)?[44] Clearly, Tolkien espoused this second approach in both theory and practice, but at the

---

[43] See Fimi and Higgins 2020:li–lix, Fimi 2018, to which I am particularly indebted in this section. On Tolkien's relationship with modernism cf. esp. Hiley 2011, on his interests in Esperantism, see Cilli, Smith and Wynne 2017. See further Smith 2006, Jarman 2016 for a contrast between Tolkien and de Saussure. There is also evidence (cf. *Letters* 92, to Christopher Tolkien, 18/12/1944:150[105], with n.3) of an aborted collaborative project between Tolkien and Lewis on the "Nature, Origins, Functions" of Language. Only a few notes of Lewis survive (published in *Seven* 27 (2010), 25–9).

[44] Published in Fimi and Higgins 2020:63–80, with notes. See further Flieger 2014d on the influence of Sapir (one of the theorists of phonetic symbolism) on Tolkien.

same time he maintained and integrated all the different aspects and concerns of the former approach, including that typically modernist fondness for individualist linguistic experimentation and its related love for a language "independent of meaning", that is, non-sensical, dream-like, and aesthetically pleasing.

I.2.1.2 Tom Bombadil's 'Nonsense' and Tolkien's Philosophy of Language

A fondness for 'non-sensical' language ("independent of meaning") is thus at the core and at the origin of Tolkien's own creative activity. It may not be completely coincidental that one of the first languages Tolkien invented was called Nevbosh (meaning the 'new nonsense'), and the same term was used to refer to his first experiments in Elvish,[45] as well as the work on the *Silmarillion*, his "private and beloved nonsense".[46] This introduces an important analogy between language (as detached from semantic meaning) and literary creation (as detached from "external meaning or purpose"). In fact, Tolkien uses the word 'nonsense' in his letters to refer to other literary creations of his, including, for example, the collection of verses on Tom Bombadil, allegedly "a little piece of nonsense".[47] Tom Bombadil himself is a character to which the category

---

[45] Cf. *Letters* 4, to Edith Bratt, 2 March 1916:4[8] "my nonsense fairy language".

[46] *Letters* 19, to S. Unwin, 16/12/1937:35[26].

[47] *Letters* 234, to Jane Neave, 22/11/1961:442[311]. Cf. also *Letters* 235, to Pauline Baynes, 6/12/1961:442[312], where he praises her illustrations for *Farmer Giles of Ham* as a series of fantastical or nonsensical pictures.

of 'nonsense' can be properly applied in its literal sense; in *The Lord of the Rings*, he is the author of a series of apparently 'nonsensical' rhymes:

someone was singing a song; a deep glad voice was singing carelessly and happily, but it was **singing nonsense:** *Hey dol! Merry dol! Ring a dong dillo! (LotR* 1.8:118)[48]

Tom's rhymes are only 'apparently' nonsensical, because this is just how they *appear* to the hobbits – the fictional authors of the book and the 'focalisers' of the story, that is, the characters from whose point of view the story is told (the story is 'focalised').[49] Even the text itself suggests, therefore, that there is some deeper, and ancient, meaning behind those apparently meaningless songs:

Suddenly out of a long string of **nonsense-words (or so they seemed)** the voice rose up loud and clear and burst into this song. (*LotR* 1.6:119)

Tom sang most of the time, but it was chiefly nonsense, or else perhaps a strange language unknown to the hobbits, **an ancient language** whose words were mainly those of wonder and delight. (*LotR* 1.8:146)

As illustrated by these two passages, there is a crucial ambiguity in the nature of Tom's language, whether actual "nonsense" or rather "a strange [...] ancient language", filled with "wonder and delight". As noted by Forest-Hill (2015), behind these ambiguous words, there is a complex philosophy of language, partly influenced

---

[48] Cf. also ibid. 120 "singing loudly and **nonsensically**".
[49] On Hobbit focalisation in *The Lord of the Rings* cf. II.2.1.2.

by Owen Barfield.[50] According to this, the language of unfallen creatures (corresponding to the natural language of Adamic humans or the "native" language of children) reflects an original 'virginal' attitude towards reality, which is always approached with wonder as new, with no separation between knowledge and affection, between the scientific and the artistic side. This 'original', 'united', "undivorced" position, which in Tolkien's mythology is only preserved in Valinor,[51] the land of the gods, corresponds to a 'perfect language', made of wholly beautiful words, perfectly featuring a harmony and fitness between sound, form, and meaning.[52]

There are several allusions to this linguistic theory scattered across Tolkien's works, especially in relation to the Elves and their language. One can consider for instance the following passage, whose Barfieldian ring is explicitly highlighted by Tolkien in a letter.[53] This contains an allusion to the 'wonderful' language of the Elves, the primeval name-givers, which has been corrupted with the passing of time and is no longer able to express with

---

50 For an extensive discussion of Barfield's influence on Tolkien's thought and works see esp. Medcalf 1999 and Flieger 2002, 2012:242–50. On Tolkien's philosophy of language cf. in particular Turner 2007b, Fornet-Ponse, Honegger, Eilmann 2016, and the editors' introduction and notes in Fimi and Higgins 2020; also Croft 2017. Cf. also II.2.2.3. For ancient theories of language, comparable in many respects to that of Barfield (and Tolkien), see Pezzini and Taylor 2019, esp. Introduction.

51 Cf. *Letters* 131, n.*:207[148] "The Light of Valinor (derived from light before any fall) is **the light of art undivorced from reason**, that sees things both scientifically (or philosophically) and imaginatively (or sub-creatively) and says that they are good – as beautiful".

52 On Tolkien's views on linguistic fitness see further Smith 2016.

53 *Letters* 15, to A. C. Furth, Allen & Unwin, 31/08/1937:25.

precision real referents (in this case Bilbo's "staggerment"
at the sight of the dragon Smaug):

There are no words left to express his staggerment, since Men
changed the language that they learned of elves in the days
when all the world was wonderful. (*Hobbit* 12:250)[54]

Wonder and newness are thus important features of
the perfect, non-fallen languages of primordial creatures,
such as the Elves, the words-lovers of Tolkien's *legendarium*,[55] but also Tom Bombadil, a semi-divine being who
is both described as "the Eldest" (cf. *LotR* 1.7:131) and
characterised as naïve and childlike.

Other traces of Tolkien's linguistic theory can be found
in the episode and characterisation of Tom Bombadil.
For instance, one could infer that Tom believes in the
primordial unity between signified and signifier, as suggested by the fact that for him to know his own name is
tantamount to knowing who he is.[56] Also significant is the

---

[54] Cf. also *LotR* 2.6:350, where in Lórien Frodo sees colours in a fresh
and poignant way, "as if he had at that moment first perceived them
and made for them **names new and wonderful**".

[55] Cf. *Sil* 3:49 (on the primeval name-giving), 5:60 (on the "great love
of words" of the Elvish people of the Noldor); *LotR* 3.4:465 (on Elves
as the ones who made all the old words and began language), *NME*
1.6:35 (on language as a specifically Elvish gift), 1.8:60–1 (the tale of
the first Elvish name-givers).

[56] Cf. also *LotR* 1.7:124: "'Who is Tom Bombadil?' 'He is,' said
Goldberry" and 131: "'Who are you, Master?' [...]. 'Don't you know
my name yet? That's the only answer',", with Tolkien's commentary
at *Letters* 153:286[191] "Goldberry and Tom are referring to the
mystery of names." For the idea of a natural bond between signified
and signifier cf. also the following response by Gandalf to Bilbo's
question about the name of a stony eyot close to Beorn's house in The
Hobbit: "[Beorn] called it the Carrock, because carrock is his word for
it" (*Hobbit* 7:110).

fact that Tom is described as a name-giver, just like the Elves,[57] and that his very name has evocative powers.[58] Finally, and above all, Tom Bombadil specifically lacks a 'utilitarian', 'possessive', and 'functional' approach to reality, as Tolkien explains in a letter:

He [Tom Bombadil] is [...] the spirit that desires knowledge of other things, their history and nature, because they are 'other' and wholly independent of the enquiring mind, a spirit coeval with the rational mind, and entirely unconcerned with 'doing' anything with the knowledge. (*Letters* 153:287[192])

Tom's 'non-functional' approach to reality echoes Tolkien's anti-functional, or at least non-functional, approach to language.[59] Tolkien's non-functionalist attitude is a manifestation of his 'mere love' for language,[60] of his 'linguistic sensitivity', which, as he suggests in a letter, should itself be related to a more general "passionate love for growing things".[61] Putting all the pieces together, one can relate Tom Bombadil's (apparent) nonsense to an outlook of language detached from its

---

[57] Cf. *LotR* 1.8:144 (the new names given by Tom to Merry's ponies, which they kept for the rest of their lives). Some scholars have described Tom Bombadil as an Adamic figure (cf. esp. Qadri 2014).

[58] Cf. *LotR* 1.8:142, when Frodo calls Tom's name, using the rhyme he taught the hobbits, and he immediately appears in presence.

[59] Cf. *Letters* 180:336[231] "being a philologist by nature and trade (yet one always **primarily interested in the aesthetic rather than the functional aspects of language**) I began with language"; *Letters* 163:312[213] cited in I.1.3. See on this the excellent essay by Fimi (2018).

[60] Cf. *Letters* 163:312[213] "the study of a language out of mere love" (quoted in I.1.3).

[61] *Letters* 163:311[212] "It has been always with me: the sensibility to linguistic pattern which affects me emotionally like colour or music; and the **passionate love of growing things**."

'usefulness' and 'functionality', but rather considered as a 'gratuitous', aesthetic expression of 'love' for 'other things', related to a naïve, primordial relationship with reality, in which everything is perceived as 'new and wonderful' (and thereby truly known).[62]

I.2.1.3 Functionless Art: Beauty versus Power

The dichotomy between 'function' and 'love' is key in Tolkien, and specifically applied to imagination and an artistic discourse in general. For Tolkien, Art itself is an expression of a 'functionless desire', deeply connected with a "passionate love" for reality:

Mortality [...] affects art and the creative (or as I should say, sub-creative) desire which seems to have **no biological function**, and to be apart from the satisfactions of plain ordinary biological life, with which, in our world, it is indeed usually at strife. This desire is at once wedded to a **passionate love of the real primary world** and hence filled with the sense of mortality, and yet unsatisfied by it. (*Letters* 131:204[145])

The love of Faery is the love of love: a relationship toward all things [...] which includes love and respect, and removes or modifies the spirit of possession and domination. Without it even plain 'Utility' will in fact become less useful; or will [...] led only to mere power, ultimately destructive. [...] [Faery] represents love: that is, a love and respect for all things, 'inanimate' and 'animate', an **unpossessive love** of them as 'other'. [...] Faery might be said indeed to represent Imagination [...]: exploratory and receptive; and artistic. (*SWM Ess.*:131,144)

---

[62] For this kind of relationship cf. Oromë's encounter with the Elves (*Sil* 3:49), discussed in VI.1.2. Cf. also *TOFS*:67 (partly quoted and discussed in III.3.2) and *MR*, 1:18 "when all things were new, and green was yet a marvel in the eyes of the makers".

The 'meaninglessness' of Tolkien's language invention is therefore just an aspect of the 'uselessness', 'gratuitousness', or 'powerlessness' of Art. Art derives from one's love for primary reality, which is expressed by the creation of (new) secondary beauty (first exemplified in the name-giving activity of the Elves, artists par excellence), to be aesthetically enjoyed, and contemplated for its own sake (just like the primary reality that stimulated that very creative love). The opposite of Art – to introduce another typical Tolkienian contrast – is Power, which aims instead to 'reform', 'control', 'dominate', and ultimately 'destroy'.[63]

An original aesthetic 'gratuitousness' is thus an important attribute of Tolkien's literary work, from its 'meaningless' linguistic inspiration down to its storytelling. And this is why Tolkien described *The Lord of the Rings* as "a work of narrative art, of which the object aimed at by the author was to be enjoyed as such: to be read with

---

[63] For the contrast between art and power cf. *TOFS*:64=*TL*:53 "the desire for a living, realised sub-creative **art** [...] is inwardly wholly different from the greed for self-centred **power**"; *Letters* 75, to Christopher Tolkien, 7/07/1944:125[87–8] "Unlike **art** which is content to create a new secondary world in the mind, it [i.e. machinery] attempts to actualize desire, and so to create **power** in this World"; *Letters* 131:205[146]; "Their [i.e. the Elves'] 'magic' is Art [...]. And its object is **Art not Power**, sub-creation not domination and tyrannous re-forming of Creation"; *Letters* 181:342[236] "they desired some **'power'** over things as they are (which is) **quite distinct from art**". Cf. also *Letters* 131, n.*:205[146] "The Elves (the representatives of sub-creation par excellence) [...] [fell] into possessiveness and (to a less degree) into **perversion of their art to power**." On Tolkien's emphasis on the powerlessness of Art (versus 'magic' and technology) see in particular Nagy 2019, esp. 167–9. See also Hillman 2023a on the tension between power and pity.

literary pleasure" (*Letters* 329:580[414]).[64] This 'hedonic' rejection of a utilitarian conception of Art, epitomised in the 'meaninglessness of' language invention, is similar to the aesthetic positions of, for example, Oscar Wilde and his former teacher Walter Pater.[65] The aesthetic motto *ars gratia artis* ("Art for Art's Sake") can certainly be applied to Tolkien's creative endeavour, to a large but not complete extent. I have added this latter qualification because, for Tolkien, the purposelessness of Art does have, eventually, an 'unexpected' purpose or function.[66]

---

[64] After the success of *The Lord of the Rings*, Tolkien would stress again and again that his main purpose was to give pleasure (to himself and his readers) and that he was always pleased to learn from his readers that he succeeded in that; this is a point made in many letters including *TCG* 286 (09/04/1957), *TCG* 570 (31/12/1964), *TCG* 738 (16/10/1968), *TCG* 318 (25/01/1973), *TCG* 756 (18/09/1967). In later years the stock reply to his fan readers included a sentence saying that he was always pleased to hear from people who enjoyed his books and that he hoped that it would continue to give them pleasure (e.g. *TCG* 588, 11/05/1965).

[65] For an overview of British (literary) aestheticism, with a focus on Pater and Wilde see Denisoff 2007. Cf. in particular Wilde's Preface to *The Picture of Dorian Gray*, and the following excerpt from a letter written in 1891 (Holland and Hart-Davis 2000:478): "Art is useless because its aim is simply to create a mood. It is not meant to instruct, or to influence action in any way. It is superbly sterile, and the note of its pleasure is sterility. If the contemplation of a work of art is followed by an activity of any kind, the work is either of a very second-rate order, or the spectator has failed to realise the complete artistic impression. A work of art is useless as a flower is useless. A flower blossoms for its own joy. We gain a moment of joy by looking at it." Tolkien would have probably objected to Wilde's neat (however apparent and provocative) dichotomy between Art and (universal) Truth, as well as between Art and Morals. On Wilde's philosophical stance see Bennett 2017, esp. the introduction and essay by Knox.

[66] It would be incorrect, however, to state that Art has no function or purpose at all for aestheticists such as Pater and Wilde. For Wilde specifically, Art does have an ideal function, which is to improve society

Its aesthetic 'meaninglessness' is a starting point (and an essential one), to be recovered again and again, but not the end of the creative journey; as we have seen, even Tom Bombadil's childish 'nonsense' has a deep, ancient meaning. However – and this is a crucial point – this meaning is not immediately and consciously perceived by the Hobbits, but is only eventually discovered at the end of their adventure – which could thus be even described as an adventure of the recovery of meaning.

To explain this final point better, I shall now introduce the second, and related, key feature of Tolkien's creative invention, which is its 'unconsciousness'.

I.2.2 The Unconsciousness of Creation: Dreaming, Art, and Imagination

I.2.2.1 Linguistic Dreams and the Atlantis Complex

Although the word 'invention' might suggest an intentional, intellectual pursuit (however 'meaningless' and 'aesthetic' at its outset), Tolkien always described his creative process as involving a degree of 'unconsciousness'. The most explicit, although figurative elaboration of this conception is found in the posthumous work known as *The Lost Road*. In this aborted time-space novel, originally

by affirming beauty against the ugliness of materialistic reality (a position similar, and yet different from the more 'moral' approach of theorists like Ruskin). Cf. Wilde's words in the *Decay of Lying* (978) "Art takes life as part of her rough material, recreates it, and refashions it in fresh forms [...] and keeps between herself and reality the impenetrable barrier of beautiful style, of decorative or ideal treatment". Even so, Tolkien's position is different, or rather more comprehensive, because its aestheticist moment is fully integrated with its 'ethical' one (see I.2.3.1).

conceived in response to a challenge of C. S. Lewis, two characters from twentieth-century England receive a series of mysterious linguistic dreams made of "fragments of words, sentences, verses", which their recipients write down as soon as they wake up, because they presently disappear.[67] The language of the dreams is sometimes Old English, but more often is an unknown language from an ancient past, that is, one of Tolkien's 'invented' languages including Quenya, Sindarin, and Adûnaic, the language of the ancient Atlantis-like kingdom of Númenor. Númenor in particular will play an important part in the novel, since the 'linguistic dreams' develop into proper images and narratives related to the island of Númenor, back to which the characters would eventually travel. It is clear that this fictional account somewhat reflects Tolkien's own experience; he reveals himself to have had an archetypal dream about Númenor since he was a child – an "Atlantis complex", as he called it, deeply seated in his imagination, featuring a Great Wave coming out of the sea and towering over the inlands. Tolkien had to exorcise this complex by writing, and he reported that the dreams eventually ceased after he had written the story of the Downfall of Númenor, later included in *The Silmarillion*.[68] For Tolkien, it is thus not just language, but also storytelling that originates from dreams, originally unconscious and unexplained. As he explicitly acknowledged (*Letters*

---

[67] Cf. *LR* 1.3:44–5. Christopher Tolkien uses similar words to describe his father's writing practice: "the earliest drafts were put urgently to paper just as the first words came to mind and before the thought dissolved" (*RS Foreword*:4).

[68] Cf. *Letters* 163:311[213] and *Letters* 257:486[347] ("the Atlantis-haunting [...] exorcized by writing about it"; also *Letters* 276:505[361].

163:311[213]), Tolkien "bequeathed" this Atlantis dream to one of his characters, the Gondorian Prince Faramir;[69] indeed, dreams are also present in Tolkien's *legendarium*, often with an important meta-literary significance, carrying implications for Tolkien's views on the nature of literature and art in general.[70]

I.2.2.2 Meta-literary Dreams
in the Secondary World

In one of Tolkien's earliest narrative experiments, now collected in *The First Book of Lost Tales*, we find a character named Eriol, an Old English traveller who becomes the oral recipient of a series of ancient tales about the Elves. His name, appropriately, signifies 'One who dreams alone' (cf. *BLT1* 1:14), and in one of his dream-like visits he is told about an ancestral path called Olórë Mallë, 'the Path of Dreams', leading to 'The Cottage of the Play of Sleep', in the land of the gods (cf. *BLT1* 1:18–19); in later versions of the *legendarium*, this would become the 'Straight Road' from Middle-earth to the West, the very one crossed by Eärendil, and later by Gandalf and his companions at the end of *The Lord of the Rings*. The dreams dreamt by Eriol have a clear 'artistic', musical nature, "as if pipes of silver or flutes of shape most slender-delicate uttered crystal

---

[69] Cf. *LotR* 6.5:962.

[70] For the significance of dreams in Tolkien's works cf. Amendt-Raduege 2006; Hefferan-Hays 2008; Triebel 2008; also Flieger 2007b and Hoffman 2014, who concludes (with an unacceptable but fascinating exaggeration) that "the entire set of adventures of the hobbits may be construed as a pair of 'fully clothed' dream narratives, with the main characters (Bilbo and Frodo) undertaking journeys into their own unconscious, during which each becomes increasingly lucid" (131). See further Pezzini 2021:91–2, and III.1.2.2.

notes and threadlike harmonies beneath the moon upon the lawns" (*BLT1* 2:46), which fills him with longing. This interconnection between dreaming and art/imagination (especially symbolised as 'music') is a leitmotif in Tolkien's works.[71] I here refer in particular to Vala Lórien, who in early drafts of *The Silmarillion* is described as "the lord of dreams and imaginings", or the land of Lothlorien, its full name Laurelindórenan being glossed by Tolkien as the "land of music and dreams" (cf. *Letters* 230, to R. Beare, 8/06/1961:437[308]). Gandalf himself, whose real name is Olórin, evokes a similar association between dreaming and 'functionless' art, as explained in an etymological note found in *Unfinished Tales*, which connects the word *olos* (meaning vision or 'phantasy') to "fair constructions having solely an artistic object", which "had not yet been but might yet be made".[72] All these names (Lórien, Olórin) have thus a common origin in the Elvish root "*lor*', which means 'dream'. The association between dreaming and imaginative creativity is alluded to in more explicit terms by Tolkien in a passage from one of his letters, where he claims that much of the work of composition of his tales goes on at non-conscious levels of his life (other than actual writing), including sleeping.[73]

---

[71] On the connection between dreams and (fantastic) literature cf. also Tolkien's words in *TOFS*:35=*TL*:14 "It is true that Dream is not unconnected with Faërie. [...] A real dream may indeed sometimes be a fairy-story of almost elvish ease and skill – while it is being dreamed."

[72] *UT* 4.2:396–7.

[73] *Letters* 180:336[231]. Cf. also a passage quoted by Carpenter (1977:171) in which Tolkien compares the writing of *The Lord of the Rings* to a seed growing "in the dark out of the leaf-mould of the mind: out of all that has been seen or thought or read, that has long been forgotten descending into the deeps".

I.2.2.3 An All-Pervasive Unconsciousness

For Tolkien, therefore, 'unconsciousness' does not just apply to the first stage of the creative process, the moment of linguistic invention (as in the linguistics dreams in the *Lost Road*),[74] but to all its stages. Tolkien often underlines this 'unconsciousness' in his letters in reference to a wide range of different creative moments, such as the use of motives[75] and sources,[76] the 'thinking out of episodes',[77] the construction of "atmosphere and background", character-invention,[78] up (or down) to "themes", "meaning", "message", and Christian figuration and theology.[79] I will here focus on two passages only:

The Hobbit [...] was unhappily really meant, **as far as I was conscious**, as a 'children's story'. [...] the main idea of the story [...] is really given, and present in germ, from the beginning, though **I had no conscious notion** of what the Necromancer stood for [...] (*Letters* 163:314–15[215])[80]

---

[74] Cf. also *Letters* 324, to G. Tayar, 4–5/06/1971:575[409] on the influence on language invention of submerged memories of names, at times rising "up to the surface".

[75] Cf. *Letters* 337, to Mr Wrigley, 25/05/1972:587[418] (a motive "unconsciously remembered").

[76] Cf. *Letters* 25:41[31], on the unconscious presence of *Beowulf* as one of Tolkien's main sources in the *Hobbit*.

[77] Cf. *Letters* 199:373[258].

[78] Cf. *Letters* 247:470[334], on the mysterious emergence of the Ents, of which Tolkien had no "previous conscious knowledge" (quoted and discussed in Chapter II n.110).

[79] Cf. *Letters* 142, to R. Murray, SJ, 2/12/1953:257[172] on the "fundamentally religious and Catholic" nature of *The Lord of the Rings*, of which Tolkien was unconscious at first since he "consciously planned very little"; also in letter *TCG* 711 (6/12/1965) he confirmed that there was "quite a lot of theology" in *The Lord of the Rings* but that he had discovered how much, with surprise, only after reading an analysis in a theological journal. See further III.1 and IV.2.2.

[80] Quoted at greater length and discussed in II.2.2.2.

As for **'message' I have none really,** if by that is meant the **conscious purpose** in writing *The Lord of the Rings,* of preaching, or of delivering myself of a vision of truth specially revealed to me! I was primarily writing an exciting story in an atmosphere and background such as I find personally attractive. (*Letters* 208:385[267])[81]

Tolkien's emphasis on the absence of a 'message' brings us back to the 'meaninglessness' of language invention, integrating all stages of composition into a single framework.

I.2.3 Tolkien's Contemplative Dynamism: Philology and Etymology

I.2.3.1 The Journey of Creation and Its Aesthetic Drive

All these different creative stages, from language invention to storytelling, are similar and interconnected; they are chained together, in a hierarchical order that ultimately can be traced back to a moment of 'linguistic' inspiration. This, as we have seen, is described as a 'gratuitous', loving act of aesthetic research, which (as seen) should be related to Tolkien's views on the need to recover an original, naïve attitude in the face of reality. This aesthetic 'gratuitousness', with its apparent

---

[81] On Tolkien's repeated attacks against conscious allegory see IV.2.2. For the dichotomy between 'conscious' and 'unconscious' cf. also Tolkien's words on the 'unconscious' understanding of fairy-story by the author of Sir Gawain who "felt instinctively, rather than consciously", the moral potential of fairy-story (conceived as "a real deep-rooted tale, told as a tale, and not a thinly disguised moral allegory") (*MC*:73).

'meaningless' and 'unconsciousness', applies to all stages of the composition, and it is the spark that leads Tolkien, the artist, to move from one stage to the other, from the language invention to storytelling and world-building, in a restless, endless artistic adventure.

Tolkien often alludes to this never-ceasing aesthetic journey of sub-creation, which moves from one stage of aesthetic research to the other. Consider in particular the following passages, in which Tolkien uses the same imagery of organic development to refer to different stages of the creative process:

The instinct for 'linguistic invention' – the fitting of notion to oral symbol, and pleasure in **contemplating** the new relation established [...] is capable of **developing** into an art, with refinement of the construction of the symbol, and with greater nicety in the choice of notional-range. [...] it is the **contemplation** of the relation between sound and notion which is a main source of pleasure. [...] The very word-form itself, of course, even unassociated with notions, is capable of giving pleasure [...] It is then in the refinement of the word-form that the next progress above the Nevbosh stage must consist. (*SV*:15–17=*MC*:206)

The imaginary histories grew out of Tolkien's predilection for inventing languages. He **discovered** [...] that a language requires a suitable habitation, and a history in which **it can develop**. (*Letters* 294, to C. and D. Plimmer, 8/02/1967:527[374–5])

[...] perfect construction of an art-language it is found necessary to construct at least in outline a mythology concomitant. [...] to give your language an individual flavour, it must have woven into it the threads of an individual mythology [...] your **language construction will *breed* a mythology**. (*SV*:23–4=*MC*:210)

From passages such as these and others,[82] one can thus reconstruct a journey of composition, from language invention down to world-building. After the initial 'linguistic inspiration', the true artist is not content with the 'discovery' of a perfectly pleasing sound; the next necessary step will be to discover the semantic referent of the word (the 'fitting of notion to oral symbol'). This then develops into an art "with refinement of construction" and "greater nicety in the choice of notional-range".[83] After a 'linguistic' and 'etymological' stage, the artist will then strive (for the sake of the same 'perfect construction') to devise a narrative context to that 'notion'; that is, to write a story about it (and that is why, for Tolkien, "stories spring from names").[84] But even this is not yet enough:

[82] Cf. also *Letters* 165:319[219] on the making of stories aimed to "provide a world for the languages"; *Letters* 131:202[143] on the development of Elvish languages, "deduced scientifically from a common origin".

[83] Cf. in this respect the description of the linguistic artistry of the Ñoldor/Noldor (the most artistic of the Elves), as the ones most ready to change speech to make it fit better all things that they knew or imagines (cf. *Sil* 5:60). This suggests, among other things, that it would be a mistake to associate Tolkien too closely with any form of linguistic primitivism: Art involves (and indeed needs) change in its effort to achieve (rather than go back to) greater linguistic fitness.

[84] Tolkien follows the same journey of composition, in its different stages, also when starting from 'primary' linguistic or narrative material (e.g. a fragment, or even a reconstructed word of Gothic), as for instance in his academic essay 'The Name Nodens' (*NN*), originally published in 1932 and reprinted in *Tolkien Studies* 4 (2007). Tom Shippey famously describes this practice as the reconstruction of an 'asterisk-reality' (on which cf. Shippey 2005, esp. 22–6, Drout 2007b; see also Rateliff 2014b, Robbins 2015). On the connection between language and mythology cf. also *Letters* 180:336[231] in which Tolkien talks about the interdependence between legends and (living) languages.

both a name and a story need a background, a larger chronological setting, a network of narrative connections, and so on, and eventually the full creation of a secondary world and a comprehensive mythology.[85] Each stage produces, arguably, a 'pleasure of contemplation' in the artist. But – and this is a crucial point – the artist's contemplation is dynamic, not static: it is a restless contemplation that urges the artist to develop in the creative journey. That is to say, the contemplative gaze of the artist never stops on a particular frame, but, driven by its (inspired) aesthetic urge, widens into discovering more and more about the context and origin of the original detail.

We find a beautiful, analogical description of this artistic process of 'aesthetic widening' in Tolkien's meta-literary short story *Leaf by Niggle*:

He used to spend a long time on a single leaf, trying to catch its shape, and its sheen, and the glistening of dewdrops on its edges. […] There was one picture in particular which bothered him. It had begun with a leaf caught in the wind, and it became a tree; and the tree grew, sending out innumerable branches, and thrusting out the most fantastic roots. Strange birds came and settled on the twigs and had to be attended to. Then all round the Tree, and behind it, through the gaps in the leaves and boughs, a country began to open out; and there were glimpses of a forest marching over the land, and of mountains tipped with snow. (*LN*:94)

For Tolkien, literature (and art in general) is thus a philological and etymological process, in the literal sense of the words: an aesthetic journey of research into language and thereby reality, driven by love ('philos'), but

---

[85] Cf. also *Letters* 205:382[264–5], quoted at the opening of this chapter.

also tending to 'truth' ('etymon'). In contrast to the approach of many modernists and aestheticists, 'truth' is a category that Tolkien fully applies to the literary process, and is indeed applicable from the very early stage of language inspiration. This explains the scientific rigour that he always showed in his language invention, however idiosyncratic and pleasure-seeking that might be.[86] This approach reflects his own professional expertise as well as, for instance, his interest in Esperantism.[87] The same concern for linguistic truth also accounts for Tolkien's attention to the 'objectivity' of word-forms even before their semantic referentiality – an approach typical of theories of phonetic symbolism, as we have seen (I.2.1.1). For Tolkien, a tension for 'objective' truth is not in contradiction with the 'gratuitous' affirmation of a personal aesthetic drive – quite the opposite.[88] Each step of the artistic journey is 'gratuitous', 'meaningless', singular ('the single leaf'), and needs to be so in order to produce that 'gratuitous' beauty that urges the artist to proceed to the following stage: the deeper meaning (and eventually the 'truth') is discovered and is consciously recognised only after each aesthetic event, that is, 'eventually', in the etymological sense of the term. Since, for Tolkien, beauty and truth are interconnected, there is no beauty

---

[86] The decision to abide by objective rules (i.e. the opposite of a 'relativist' position), even in one's own invented languages, is for Tolkien an important requisite of Art, and a necessary act of humility which distinguishes it from the "despotic" approach of Power (cf. *SV*:33, quoted in Chapter VI, n.3).

[87] See n.43.

[88] Cf. I.2.4, III.3.4, and IV.2.2.2. For the Christian and/or Neoplatonic ancestry of the idea of a close connection between Beauty and Truth see Coutras 2016; also Halsall 2020.

that does not ultimately lead to truth; but in order to do so, beauty needs to be *true* beauty, which is freely and one could say 'mercifully' created, and first affirmed for its own sake only, to be loved and contemplated, without any conscious concern for its meaning and function.[89]

I.2.3.2 Not (Just) Psychology: Rationality, Awakening, and Inspiration

Tolkien's dynamic journey of creation involves, at all of its stages, a degree of 'unconsciousness', which is evoked by the common association between dreaming and artistic creation. Although all this certainly has fascinating psychoanalytic implications,[90] it would be a mistake to interpret Tolkien's emphasis on the 'unconsciousness' only in personal psychological terms, as if artistic creation were for him a purely individual, irrational emergence of the subconscious (however embedded in a relational context).[91] First of all, this kind of dream-like, instinctive

---

[89] Cf. Tolkien's definition of love ('(N)DIL' in Elvish, as in Eärendil), as being devoted to "a person, thing, course or occupation [...] for its own sake" *Letters* 297:542–3, quoted in I.1.5).

[90] Tolkien himself refers to Jung in an unpublished letter, comparing the Atlantis Complex that disturbed his own dreams to other images that "disturbed Jung's dreams" *TCG* 812 (to Maria Mroczkowska, 1969). For examples of psychanalytical readings of Tolkien cf. O'Neill 1979 (reading *The Lord of the Rings* in Jungian terms) and more recently Robertson 2016 (arguing that *The Lord of the Rings* is a report of a dream) and (more scholarly) Rosegrant 2021.

[91] I am here alluding in particular to theories of the mind of either Freudian or Lacanian ancestry. Freud (or rather the standard Freudian view) posits a neat distinction between individual (ego) and external reality, and a relationship between the two negotiated at different levels of the psyche. In contrast, Lacan describes the 'I' in more relational terms, as embedded within an intersubjective relationship with the Other. This is not the place to discuss the similarities and

mental process is for Tolkien completely 'rational', as he often says in his essays and letters.[92] Moreover, this dream-like artistic experience is a reawakening of a true gaze on reality, as we have seen in the description of the encounter with Eärendil ("as if something had stirred in me, half wakened from sleep", *SD Not.*:236, quoted in I.1.4), and as Frodo suggests at the end of his (dream-like) adventures, saying that the return to the Shire felt more to him "like falling asleep again".[93] Above all, the artistic 'dreaming', however personal, is not just the mechanical product of the psychological experiences of single individuals, however intertwined with and informed by their relationship with their social context. For Tolkien, the artistic event is an 'inspiration' in the etymological sense; it is an echo of some other voice, a dream that "some other mind is weaving", as Tolkien explains in *On Fairy-stories*, distinguishing normal from Faërian dreaming.[94]

differences between Tolkien, Freud, and Lacan at length, especially with regard to the different outlooks on dreaming and its relationship with imagination. Here, I can only point out that dreaming (as well as imagination) in Tolkien does not just have an intersubjective dimension (as in Lacan, but not in Freud) but also a specific transcendental character (as being inspired by, and giving access to an Entity belonging to a higher, metaphysical plane), which makes his views different to (although not incompatible with) Lacanian theories of the mind.

[92] Cf. *TOFS* n.1:60=*TL*:48 "**Fantasy is a rational** not an irrational activity"; also *Letters* 89:143[101] where Tolkien recalls having "one of those sudden clarities which sometimes come in dream", which did not come as the result of an argument, and yet gave him the same sensation "as having been convinced by reason (if without reasoning)".

[93] *LotR* 6.7:997.

[94] *TOFS*:63=*TL*:52 "The experience [of a 'Faërian drama'] may be very similar to Dreaming and has [...] been confounded with it. But in Faërian drama you are in **a dream that some other mind is weaving**, and the knowledge of that alarming fact may slip from your grasp."

I.2.4 The 'Otherness' of Artistic Dreams and the Indwelling of the Imperishable Flame

This idea of the 'otherness' of artistic dreams is very common in Tolkien's *legendarium*. Specifically, in *The Silmarillion*, and even more explicitly in its earlier drafts, dreams are often attributed to the Valar, the 'gods' of Middle-earth and its primeval sub-creators, and especially to the Vala Ulmo, who often sends "messages and dreams" to inspire the characters' actions and dispositions, including for instance those of the elf Turgon.[95] Dreams also play an important role in *The Lord of the Rings*, as well as, more generally, sudden moments of unconscious inspiration, often with meta-literary implications. Although there are many examples, let me focus on one important passage, which follows the initial, unsuccessful confrontation between the hobbit Sam and the monster-spider Shelob:

'Galadriel!' he [sc. Sam] said faintly, and then he heard voices far off but clear: the crying of the Elves as they walked under the stars in the beloved shadows of the Shire, and the music of

---

For the connection between Faery and dreaming see also *SWM Ess.*:114–15.

[95] For instance: *BL*:54 (a dream of the Valar about Beren that came to Lúthien); *Sil* 18:158 (dreams sent by Ulmo to Turgon warning him of woe to come). Cf. also *Sil* 13:114 (the dreams sent to the elves Turgon and Finrod, which each believed to be messages sent to each of them alone); 17:143–4 (the troubling dreams sent to Thingol about the coming of Men); 18:158 (the dreams sent to Turgon from Ulmo); 24:246 (the dreams sent to Eärendil, which drove him back from his journeys), on which see I.2.5.1. Also at this stage, however, one can trace Tolkien's tendency to conceal the divine origin of dreams (cf. for instance *BLT*2 2:116 n.10 where the expression "dreams the Valar sent to them" was changed in the same manuscript into "dreams came to them").

the Elves as it came through his sleep in the Hall of Fire in the house of Elrond. Gilthoniel A Elbereth! And then his tongue was loosed and his voice cried in a language which he did not know. (*LotR* 4.10:730)[96]

Here we see all the key elements I have discussed: the sudden origin of a linguistic inspiration, 'meaningless' to its recipient ("a language which he did not know"); the dream-like imagery ("through his sleep"), recalling a dreamlike performance that Frodo listened to in Rivendell;[97] the 'otherness' ("he heard voices far of"), as well as its meta-literary implications ("the music of the Elves", the hymnic nature of Sam's invocation). In fact, in *The Lord of the Rings*, art and dreaming often go together, and especially in relation to the Elves, the 'Artists' par excellence in Tolkien's *legendarium*.[98]

What lies behind all this is the idea (or perhaps better this 'self-reflected experience') of Art (and imaginative literature in particular) as divinely inspired, which is often expressed in Tolkien's works through the imagery of a 'divine vision'. This imagery is central in particular in the cosmogonic myth opening *The Silmarillion*, the "Music of the Ainur" or *Ainulindalë*. This myth has key meta-artistic implications, as Tolkien himself

[96] Cf. Tolkien's comment on this passage at *Letters* 211:398[278], noting that Sam was inspired to make this invocation, and that its words were "composed or inspired for his particular situation".

[97] *LotR* 2.1:233.

[98] Cf. *LotR* 1.3:81–2 (Sam and Pippin meeting the Elves for the first time, enjoying the sound of their voices, and feeling "as if in a dream" and "in a waking dream"); *LotR* 2.1:233 (Frodo in the hall of Rivendell, wandering "long in a dream of music", which turned into Bilbo singing a song about Eärendil).

suggested,[99] and for this reason I will often refer to it in the following chapters, before concluding with a full discussion of (or rather introduction to) it in Chapter VII. In this myth, the Valar (or Ainur as they are first called) are invited by Eru/Ilúvatar (a God-like entity) to participate in an artistic event, which will result in the creation of Tolkien's secondary world (Arda). Each Vala (or Ainu) is called to contribute to this primordial concert with their "own thoughts and devices" (*Sil Ain.*:15), and thereby add their own (sub-)creations to the general artwork of Eru. Appropriately, in early versions of the story, the creations of the Valar/Ainur, which correspond to physical elements in the created world, are explicitly described as their own personal dreams. For instance,

water was for the most part the dream and invention of Ulmo, an Ainu whom Ilúvatar had instructed deeper than all others in the depths of music. (*BLT1* 2:56)[100]

And yet, as already suggested by this passage, the 'authorship' of the Ainur's sub-creations is only secondary: Eru instructed them in their art, and inspired them in the first place, and it is Eru who remains the ultimate source of their artistic endeavour at all of its various

---

[99] Cf. *Letters* 212:405[284] "**The Ainur** took part in the making of the world **as 'sub-creators'** [...] They interpreted according to their powers, and completed in detail, the Design propounded to them by the One". Cf. also *Letters* 153:288–9[193–4], *Letters* 257:485[345] ("the angelic first-created [...] carrying out the Primeval Design"), *BLT1*:53 (Eru explaining to the Ainur that the story he laid before them was "related only as it were in outline"); see further Chapter VII.

[100] Cf. also *BLT1* 2:57 "our dreams".

stages. Eru Himself points that out, at the time when He shows to the rebellious Melkor (and all the other Ainur) a vision of their Music – the artistic event, now 'realised', to which they all contributed, and which yet remained 'other' than them:

'thou, Melkor, shalt see that no theme may be played that hath not its uttermost source in me, [...] Behold your Music!' And he showed to them a vision. [...] and they saw a new World made visible before them [...] and it seemed to them that it lived and grew. [...] 'This is your minstrelsy; and each of you shall find contained herein, amid the design that I set before you, all those things which it may seem that he himself devised or added.' (*Sil Ain.*:17)

This idea of Art's divine vision (closely related to that of divine inspiration) is figuratively expressed in several other places, including in the short stories *Leaf by Niggle* and *Smith of Wootton Major*, which both feature artistic characters (the painter Niggle, the artisan Smith) having meta-artistic visions ("visions of mountains" for Niggle,[101] visions of the great Tree of the King in the land of Faërie for Smith);[102] it is also occasionally expressed by Tolkien in theoretical terms.[103] This idea

---

[101] *LN*:100. See further I.2.5.1 and VI.1.5.

[102] Cf. in particular *SWM*:24 quoted in IV.3.3. On the meta-literary implications of the tale see Tolkien's own notes and essay on it (*SWM*:105–45, esp.106 "a time comes for writers and artists, when invention and 'vision' cease and they can only reflect on what they have seen and learned") and Flieger 2007c; also Shippey's 2008 introduction.

[103] Cf. *TOFS*:32 n.1=*TL*:10 "even if they [the Elves] are only creations of Man's mind, 'true' only as reflecting in a particular way one of Man's **visions of Truth**"; also *Letters* 95c, to Christopher Tolkien, 15/01/1945:156 (on reflections of strange, beautiful,

has a Romantic heritage,[104] but is elaborated by Tolkien into a very original Christian aesthetic discourse, which is arguably closely related to (and develops) the notion of the inspiration of the Holy Spirit – a notion that Tolkien explicitly introduced in a letter,[105] and figuratively expressed in his mythology.[106] Indeed, in the *Ainulindalë*, the personal, artistic talent of the Valar derives from the gift of the "Flame Imperishable", with which they have been kindled, so that they can show forth their powers "each with their own thoughts and devices".[107] Even the full comprehension of each Valar's creative contribution will only be possible through the bestowal of a 'Secret Fire', which will be fully given at the end of time.[108] The indwelling of the Flame Imperishable is thus at the core of the mystery of literary creation, as it bestows reality to both sub-creations and their sub-creators and provides

and true things having power "quite beyond the cracked and murky mirrors"). The imagery of 'reflection', which is common in Tolkien (and central e.g. in *Mythopoeia*), is arguably closely related to that of 'vision'.

[104] On the Romantic ancestry of the idea of art and imagination as a 'divine vision' see in particular Thayer 2016a; also Seeman 1995, Sherwood and Eilmann 2024 (esp. the chapters in the section 'Imagination, Desire, and Sensation'). Cf. also Tindall and Bustos 2012 for a (fanciful but intriguing) comparison with Homeric and shamanist discourses on art and poetry as visionary experiences.

[105] *Letters* 63, to Christopher Tolkien, 24/04/1944:109[75] "the Holy Spirit seems sometimes to speak through a human mouth providing art, virtue and insight he does not himself possess".

[106] According to Kilby (1976:59) Tolkien explicitly acknowledged in a conversation with him that the Secret Fire was the Holy Spirit.

[107] *Sil Ain.*:15 "since I have kindled you with the Flame Imperishable, ye shall show forth your powers in adorning this theme, **each with his own thoughts and devices**, if he will".

[108] *Sil Ain.*:15–16 (quoted and discussed in VI.2.5).

a channel for Eru's collaborative authorship.[109] As succinctly put by Tolkien in a note to the posthumous text *Athrabeth* (*MR Athr.*:345), the Flame Imperishable "refers [...] to the mystery of 'authorship', by which the author, while remaining 'outside' and independent of his work, also 'indwells' in it".

Inspiration (in its etymological sense) is thus a key event for Tolkien, which distinguishes "real" Art from "uninspired invention" and provides a mysterious channel between primary and secondary reality;[110] it also ultimately explains the paradoxical 'otherness' of private artistic inventions. I will not elaborate further upon this here, not least because I am convinced that Tolkien would have preferred to leave all this at the level of an artistic intuition.[111]

There remains, however, an important question that one should not fail to address: "What is it all about"? After all this 'gratuitous' digression about meaningless

---

[109] The ontological role of the Imperishable Flame is even more explicit in some versions of the *Ainulindalë* (cf. *BLT1*:53, "the Secret Fire that giveth Life and Reality", 55 "One thing only have I added, the fire that giveth Life and Reality".

[110] Cf. *TOFS*:77=*TL*:73 (discussed at VI.2.2) "the peculiar quality of this secondary world (if not all the details)* are derived from Reality [*For all the details may not be 'true': it is seldom that the 'inspiration' is so strong and lasting that it leavens all the lump, and does not leave much that is mere **uninspired 'invention'**]."

[111] One could add here that Tolkien probably believed that divine inspiration of the Holy Spirit was not restricted to Christians only, and that the re-integration of a non-Christian 'channel of inspiration' into a Christian framework was only necessary at an institutional level, as can be inferred from a note to *Letters* 250, to M. Tolkien, 1/11/1963, n.*:476[339]) "it is our duty to tend the accredited and established altar, though **the Holy Spirit may send the fire down somewhere else.** God cannot be limited [...] and may use any channel for His grace".

language, I surely must return to my opening question about the 'meaning', 'function', or 'message' of Tolkien's creative project. I will now openly address the question, in what will be the final leg of my journey in this chapter. This will begin from the small university town of St Andrews, in Scotland – a place that has an important connection with Tolkien.

I.2.5 Sea-Longing and Creative Nostalgia

I.2.5.1 St Andrews and the Horns of Ylmir

On at least one occasion, in the summer of 1910 or 1911, Tolkien visited St Andrews to visit his aunt Jane Neave, who was at that time Lady Warden of University Hall. The landscape of St Andrews clearly made an impression on Tolkien's imagination, and a drawing of his from this time survives, depicting St Andrews from Kinkell Brae.[112] It was probably in St Andrews that Tolkien encountered for the first time the Great Sea on the steep cliffs of the town; this moving experience apparently compelled him to write a twelve-line poem ('The Grimness of the Sea'), which is one of his earliest poetic attempts (now published in *TCP*:61).[113] This poem was the "original nucleus" of a

---

[112] See *TCP*:61–2, with Hammond and Scull's discussion of the probable St Andrews origin of the poem. I am very grateful to Wayne Hammond and Christian Scull for sharing with me this material in advance. On Tolkien's trip(s) to St Andrews in the 1910s, and its influence on the development of his imagination, cf. Hammond and Scull 2017: *Chronology* 24, 37. Cf. also Hammond and Scull 1995:45–7 with their relevant addenda and corrigenda (available at www.hammondandscull.com/addenda/artist.html; consulted on 6 February 2024).

[113] Cf. Hammond and Scull 2017: *Reader's Guide* 556–7.

series of later compositions, preserved in different versions, which have been collected by Hammond and Scull as no. 13 in the recently published Tolkien's *Collected Poems* (*TCP* 61–78). Here a few lines from a late draft, titled 'The Horns of Ylmir':

> I sat on the ruined margin of the deep-voiced
>   echoing sea
> Whose roaring foaming music crashed in endless
>   cadency; [...]
> 'Twas in the Land of Willows that I heard
>   th'unfathomed breath
> Of the Horns of Ylmir calling – and shall hear them
>   till my death.
>
> (*The Horns of Ylmir*, 1914; *SME* 3:216–17)

This poem was eventually integrated into Tolkien's *legendarium* and associated with an important iconic episode, namely the epiphany of the sea-god and great dreamweaver Ulmo (or Ylmir is early texts) to the man Tuor on the shores of the Western Sea, and the revelation to him of an important vocation.[114] More specifically, according to an early version of the episode, it is said that the 'vision' compelled Tuor (as happened to Tolkien) to compose a song (the *Horns of Ylmir* itself!), which expressed his longing for the Sea and its music (cf. *SME* 3:142,213–17). As often in Tolkien's *legendarium*, the encounter with the beauty of creation results in the creation of new, secondary beauty.

In the published 1977 *Silmarillion*, the 'Music of the Sea' is no longer restricted to a single episode, but is rather

---

[114] *Sil* 23: 238–9 (Ulmo sets in Turgon's heart the desire to depart, and he travels to the shores of the Great Sea, where Ulmo appears to him, out of a great storm **from the west**).

described as an ongoing, multiple event, specifically associated with the original 'immortal Music' of Creation – the primeval artistic entity inspired by the 'Flame Imperishable' and mediated through the Valar/Ainur, the *ur*-artists (see Chapter VII).[115] The exposure to such Music, in its different forms, instils an insatiable sea-longing 'for they know not what' in the creatures, and an invitation to sail West and cross the Sea, beyond the borders of mortal lands. Many other Tolkienian characters share Tuor's same experience, including, for instance, the elf Legolas in *The Lord of the Rings*, who will have no peace again after sea-longing has been stirring in his heart (cf. *LotR* 5.9:873).[116]

In Tolkien's work, this experience of the 'reawakening' of longing is often associated with a dream-like event – imagery that, as we have seen, has important meta-literary significance.[117] We also find this association in *The Lord of the Rings*, especially in relation to a momentous dream of Frodo, in which he hears the sound of the Sea for the first time, and is filled with desire:

[115] *Sil Ain.*:19 "in water there lives yet the echo of the Music of the Ainur more than in any substance else that is in this Earth; and many of the Children of Ilúvatar hearken still unsated to the voices of the Sea, and yet know not for what they listen". Cf. also *Sil Val.*:27 (Ulmo's unseen visits to the shores of Middle-earth, making music will remain always in the hearts of those who listen to it). On music in Tolkien's work see the essays collected in Steimel and Schneidewind 2010 and Eilmann and Schneidewind 2019.

[116] Scholars have noted how sea-longing (with its spiritual implications) is also prominent in the Old English poem *Seafarer*, which might well have been an important source for Legolas' song in *The Lord of the Rings* (see Wilcox 2003). On the connections between this nostalgia and the Romantic concept of *Sehnsucht* see Vaninskaya 2020.

[117] Cf. already the early characterisation of the sea-traveller Ælfwine (*BLT2* 6:314), who held "converse with the hidden Elves", dreaming "dreams filled with longing".

he fell into a vague dream, in which he seemed to be looking out of a high window over a dark sea of tangled trees. [...] he heard a noise in the distance. [...] he knew that it was not leaves, but the sound of the Sea far-off; a sound he had never heard in waking life, though it had often troubled his dreams. [...] A great **desire** came over him to climb the tower and **see the Sea**. (*LotR* 1.5:108)

This dream would necessitate full interpretation, which cannot be explored here. I will only say that Frodo's "desire [...] to see the Sea" is related to his characteristic 'restlessness' and desire to leave the Shire and travel to the Wide World, itself inspired by "strange visions of mountains", which came to him in his dreams.[118] And among the restless characters struck by the longing for the Sea, we of course find the archetypal hero Eärendil himself, compelled by dreams to sail the Secret Way to the land of the gods.[119]

I.2.5.2 Eärendil's Hope: The Inspiration of Creative Desire

Eärendil's sea-longing concerns the desire of creatures to reconnect with some lost divinity, a desire that, crucially,

---

[118] *LotR* 1.2:43 "[Frodo] found himself wondering at times [...] and **strange visions of mountains** that he had never seen came **into his dreams**. He began to say to himself: 'Perhaps I shall cross the River myself one day'". Cf. also *TI* 1:6.

[119] Cf. *Sil* 24:246 (Eärendil's 'swift desire' to sail West). On Eärendil's Sea-longing and its meta-artistic and religious significance see Garth 2003:43–7, esp. 46: "on a human scale [Eärendel's myth] is also a paean to imagination 'His heart afire with bright desire' [...] Eärendel overleaps all conventional barriers in a search for self-realisation in the face of the natural sublime. In an unspoken religious sense, he seeks to see the face of God". Cf. also Shippey 2000:287–9 for an overview of Eärendil's medieval precedents.

is itself inspired by that very divinity. The inspired origin of sea-longing also explains its close association with 'hope'.[120] Eärendil is the 'sea-lover' but also the 'carrier of hope' (Gil-Estel, "the star of high hope", the one that comes "beyond hope"),[121] and he reappears in this role in *The Lord of the Rings* in several momentous episodes,[122] and especially in one of the story's most desperate moments, namely Frodo's encounter with the monster Shelob:

For a moment it glimmered, faint as a rising star struggling in heavy earthward mists, and then as its power waxed, and hope grew in Frodo's mind, it began to burn, and kindled to a silver flame, a minute heart of dazzling light, as though Eärendil had himself come down from the high sunset paths with the last Silmaril upon his brow. [...] Aiya Eärendil Elenion Ancalima! He cried, and **knew not what he had spoken**; for it seemed that **another voice** spoke through his, clear, untroubled by the foul air of the pit. (*LotR* 4.9:720)

Frodo's cry, which is 'inspired' ("another voice") and (apparently) 'meaningless' to him ("knew not what he had spoken"), is indeed a direct quote from that very passage from the Old English poem (*Crist*) that struck

---

[120] As the wise elf Finrod explains (*MR Athr.*:320), "desire may be the last flicker of Estel [i.e. naked hope in God]" (see V.1.6). Cf. also Frodo's dream in an early draft of *The Lord of the Rings*, where hope and the sound of the Sea are explicitly connected (*TI* 2:34 "[the] mingled fear and hope [of Frodo's Sea-dream] remained with him all the day; and for long the far sound of the Sea came back to him whenever great danger was at hand").

[121] *Sil.* 24:298 (on which cf. V.1.6 with n.18).

[122] It is under the "white fire" of Eärendil's star, "most beloved by the Elves", that Galadriel rejects the temptation of the Ring and the shadow of Sauron, embracing the hope of Frodo's mission (cf. *LotR* 2.7:365).

Tolkien so much at the beginning of his creative adventure, which here finds its ultimate 'function', as a cry of desire and, therefore, hope in the middle of darkness. The hope-bringing, prophetic nature of the character Éarendel in the *Crist* (see I.1.4) is thus maintained in Tolkien's secondary world and associated with an inspired sea-longing. This association is essential, and, I believe, has momentous implications for Tolkien's decisions, as a committed Christian, to write a pre-Christian tale that addressed a post-Christian world, a topic I will address in Chapter III.

I.3 The Paradox of Creation and the Purpose of Purposeless Beauty

Eärendil can thus be considered as the archetype of many Tolkienian characters, including Frodo, Legolas, Bilbo, and many others, who carry within themselves a divinely inspired sea-longing, and a confused hope hidden within it. But what has all this sea-longing got to do with art, language, and storytelling, and with the meaning and purpose of *The Lord of the Rings*? It would suffice to highlight, as we have seen, that the water of the sea is described as the musical dream of Ulmo, one of Tolkien's *ur*-artists, and as an echo of the original Music, inspired by the Secret Fire or Flame Imperishable, and itself inspiring new songs, as in the case of Tuor. But to be more explicit, the reawakening of sea-longing is possible only through the encounter with the 'gratuitous' beauty of an artistic creation of any kind, primary (created) or secondary (sub-created, inspired). For example, the sea at St Andrews for the young Tolkien; the water of

Ulmo and its ancestral music, which compels the restless Eärendil; but also poetic creations, including that beautiful, mysterious couplet from an Old English poem, from which everything originated; and similarly, the poem about Eärendil, composed by Bilbo and heard by Frodo in Rivendell in a dream-like situation (*LotR* 2.1:233–7), together with the Elvish hymn to Elbereth, later recalled in moments of distress;[123] and finally, with a meta-literary twist, *The Lord of the Rings* itself, which recounts all these stories and is nothing but the final creative fruit of that original linguistic fascination.

All these different creations are connected, first of all because (as we have seen) the encounter with an artistic entity on any given plane compels its recipient to create, gradually and 'eventually', new art on a lower plane. This can be a song, a poem, or indeed a whole *legendarium*, in an interrupted chain of aesthetic events, which all together make up a variegated and yet organically integrated Creation ("The Tree of Tales"[124]). Because they are all inspired, all these creations ultimately find their origin in God (Eru). For Tolkien, God never interrupts His creative activity, directly in the primary creation and even perhaps more importantly 'mediately', through the inspired collaboration of the inspired sub-creator, struck by beauty.[125] Secondly, all these artistic, desire-awakening events are characterised by the same 'gratuitous', 'meaningless', 'purposeless' beauty. This 'gratuitousness' is the trademark of inspired beauty, and it is indeed, for Tolkien, the trademark of God, who creates primary

---

[123] Cf. III.1.1.   [124] For this concept and its ramifications cf. IV.3.3.
[125] Cf. *Letters* 153:283[188], quoted and discussed in VI.2.3.

Beauty for its own sake only, with no apparent 'purpose'. As Tolkien explains in a letter to one of the daughters of his publisher:

I think that questions about 'purpose' are only really useful when they refer to the conscious purposes or objects of human beings, or to the uses of things they design and make. As for 'other things' their value resides in themselves: they ARE, they would exist even if we did not. But since we do exist one of their functions is to be contemplated by us. [...] because these things are 'other' and we did not make them, and they seem to proceed from a fountain of invention incalculably richer than our own. Human curiosity soon asks the question HOW: in what way did this come to be? And since recognizable 'pattern' suggests design, may proceed to WHY? (*Letters* 310, to C. Unwin, 20/05/1969:560–1[399])

And yet (as Tolkien explains in this beautiful passage, with a key paradox), because this 'gratuitous' Beauty *exists*, it assumes the 'function' to be contemplated and enjoyed by His creatures, and may thereby (re)awaken their wonder and curiosity, and eventually lead them through the path that leads to the recognition of a Creator. As in the archetypal case of Tuor, those who let themselves be wounded by the beauty of 'purposeless' things cannot but develop within themselves an insatiable longing for their divine origin. Becoming, in turn, sub-creators of new beauty, they continue to reawaken sea-longing in other people, including, eventually, the readers of *The Lord of the Rings*.

In summary, for Tolkien, artistic creations on any planes, including *The Lord of the Rings*, have the primary meaning and purpose of creating new 'gratuitous' beauty, in order to "to re-establish sanity, cleanliness, and the love of real and true beauty in everyone's breast" (to quote from a passionate letter of G. B. Smith's, written to Tolkien on 24 October 1915, in which he reaffirmed the vocation of the TCBS).[126] In his immediate context, this stood as a challenge to a world darkened by war, and in which ever-greater priority was afforded to the useful and functional, and thus violent and dehumanising. By contrast, the primary and secondary creations described by Tolkien are all 'about themselves', and need to be so, because only through their divinely inspired 'gratuitousness' can they hope to attract fallen creatures to 'escape' from the prison of appearances,[127] and travel on the path that leads, eventually, to the discovery of the 'meaning' and the related recognition of a loving Creator – this is, if any, their eventual 'purpose'.

Although this may all seem paradoxical, it is, as we have seen, the mysterious paradox of Beauty, which is another facet of the paradox of Mercy, which Tolkien describes in an important letter (*Letters* 192), in reference to the momentous decision of Frodo to spare Gollum in *The Lord of the Rings* (cf. esp. 4.1:615), echoing that of Bilbo in *The Hobbit* (5:102, recalled at *LotR* 1.2:59). This is described as a 'gratuitous' exercise of unplanned mercy and "extravagant generosity", which is rewarded, because of that very 'gratuitousness', with the "extravagant generosity" of God.[128] Therefore, just as human

---

[126] Cited by Hammond and Scull 2017: *Chronology* 81. I owe this reference to Michaël Devaux.

[127] On the concept of escape cf. *TOFS*:69–70=*TL*:60–2 and see III.3.2.

[128] *Letters* 192:363[253] (on Frodo's miraculous triumph as a consequence of his exercise of pity and mercy – correlated instances

mercy, purposeless and yet meaningful, is analogous to the creative mercy of God,[129] the aesthetic 'generosity' of an inspired human creation is a reflection of the original 'gratuitous' generosity of the primary Creation of God.

One could justly claim, then, that to reawaken the sea-longing, or the "memory of the high" as Gandalf would say,[130] is perhaps the 'purpose' of *The Lord of the Rings*. But this 'purpose' is accomplished only because the book was not originally written with that in mind and did not involve any 'conscious', 'intellectual' purpose or meaning of any kind: it was, that is to say, an "essay in linguistic aesthetic", it was "about itself"; and because of this aesthetic 'gratu-itousness', inspired by and analogous to that of God, it has been able to reawaken, however confusedly, the longing for the Sea, the desire to walk again on the path that leads to meaning, and the prophetic hope that all this contains.

I.4 Epilogue: Berúthiel's Fate

To conclude this chapter, let me quote a short literary creation, one of the very last composed by Tolkien during

of extravagant generosity). Tolkien repeatedly acknowledged the literary significance of this theme in *The Lord of the Rings* as for instance in *TCG* 214 (24/10/1955) in which he described his book as an exemplary legend of "the triumph and the defeat of Pity". For a study of pity in *The Lord of the Rings* see Hillman 2023a.

[129] On mercy as a key quality of God cf. *Letters* 246:460[326] "that strange element in the World that we call Pity or **Mercy**, which is also an absolute requirement in moral judgement (since it is present in the Divine nature). In its highest exercise it belongs to God." God's mercy has also to do with the acceptance and integration of human sub-creative desire: cf. on this V.1.7 (Aulë's sub-creation of the Dwarves).

[130] Cf. III.2.1 with n.95.

his life. This is again from a scrap paper, difficult to read and now printed in *Unfinished Tales*, in which Tolkien reveals his eventual discovery of Berúthiel's fate – an information-obsessed, art-loather, barren queen, who yet will eventually sail, just like Eärendil, and all other Tolkienian characters, on the Great Sea. It stands as an epitome of Tolkien's artistic journey, from a 'gratuitous' linguistic invention to the discovery of an omnipresent, irresistible Sea-Call lying beneath that.

Berúthiel lived in the King's House in Osgiliath, hating the sounds and smells of the sea […] she hated all making, all colours and elaborate adornment, wearing only black and silver and living in bare chambers […]. She had nine black cats and one white, her slaves, with whom she conversed, or read their memories, setting them to discover all the dark secrets of Gondor, so that she knew those things 'that men wish most to keep hidden', setting the white cat to spy upon the black, and tormenting them. […] her name was erased from the Book of the Kings […] and King Tarannon had her set on a ship alone with her cats and set adrift on the sea before a north wind. The ship was last seen flying past Umbar under a sickle moon, with a cat at the masthead and another as a figure-head on the prow. (*UT* 4.2:402)

II

The Authors of the Red Book

Meta-textual Frames and Writing as
Discovery and Translation

∼

In Chapter I, I showed how Tolkien frames his literary creation as a process of 'discovery'; this normally begins with a purely aesthetic and 'gratuitous' fascination for a particular linguistic entity and develops through the gradual invention (or rather 'revelation') of the narrative contexts, implications, and meanings of that original intuition. In this chapter, I will continue to investigate the notion of writing as 'discovery', as it is expressed within Tolkien's narratives, and thereby introduce some further ramifications of his literary 'theory'. I will thus focus on another important feature of Tolkien's *legendarium*, that is, the pervasive presence of a complex 'meta-textual frame', expressing in secondary terms Tolkien's perception of his own experience as a literary writer. This meta-textual frame includes an overarching narrative of the composition, transmission, and publication of his literary works as well as the related concept that Tolkien is only presenting an approximate rendition of texts originally written by a variety of other authors. To claim that Tolkien is the (only) author of *The Hobbit*, *The Lord of the Rings*, and other works would thus mean to miss a crucial feature of the literary fabric of his books; more importantly, such a claim would overlook other key dimensions of Tolkien's vision on the "mystery of literary creation", which I will explore in the second part of this chapter (II.2).

II.1 The Meta-textual Frame of Middle-earth

By 'meta-textual frame' I refer to a particular subtype of frame narrative, that is, of "a story in which another story is enclosed or embedded as a 'tale within the tale'" (Baldick 2008 s.v.). Frame narratives are found in many works from a variety of literary traditions, from *The Thousand and One Nights* to Boccaccio's *Decameron*; from the Buddhist collection *Jātakaṭṭhavaṇṇanā* to Chaucer's *Canterbury Tales*; from the ancient Egyptian tale *The Eloquent Peasant* to Mary Shelley's *Frankenstein* and Emily Brontë's *Wuthering Heights*. In one particular type of frame narrative (which I will call 'meta-textual frame'), the author or narrator presents the main, embedded story as being based on, reproducing, and/or translating the text of an earlier work, usually preserved in a (re)discovered book or manuscript. Meta-textual frames are found, for example, in Cervantes' *Don Quixote* (allegedly derived from an original Arabic text); *Platone in Italia* by Vincenzo Cuoco (allegedly translated into Italian from a lost work of Plato); many nineteenth-century novels, both historical and not, including Potocki's *The Manuscript Found in Saragossa*, Scott's *Waverley Novels*, Manzoni's *The Betrothed*, and James' *The Turn of the Screw*; more closely to Tolkien, C. S. Lewis' *The Screwtape Letters*.[1] A recurring

---

[1] Cf. C. S. Lewis, *The Screwtape Letters*, Preface: "I have no intention of explaining how the correspondence which I now offer to the public fell

feature of meta-textual frames is the paradoxical concern for both historicity and literariness. To illustrate this, I will briefly focus on Alessandro Manzoni's historical novel *The Betrothed* (published in 1840) – an apparently exotic novel, and yet one that it is not entirely impossible Tolkien might have heard of.[2] This Italian novel is prefaced by an authorial note beginning with a fictional quote from an allegedly rediscovered seventeenth-century manuscript, written in a baroque, almost illegible Italian; the author/editor soon stops quoting from the manuscript, and states that he has decided to rewrite and rearrange the original text, for the sake of his modern readers. In this way, Manzoni asserts both the (fictional) historicity of the story he is going to tell and, at the same time, acknowledges that this has been mediated by his own literary voice, on both a narrative and linguistic level.

There is plenty of explicit evidence showing Tolkien's fondness for meta-textual frames and narrative frames in general; most of this evidence is found in posthumous works, specifically in the texts collected by Christopher Tolkien in the monumental *History of Middle-earth*. The

---

into my hands." For an overview of this motive in Tolkien's literary precedents cf. Neuhaus 1990, Tarr 2017. For a discussion from the specific perspective of Tolkien scholarship see in particular Flieger 2005:55–84; Henige 2009; Brljak 2010 (referring to Rider Haggard's *She* and *King Solomon's Mines*, Poe's *Manuscript Found in a Bottle*, and comparing Tolkien's metafictional interest with those of Borges); Sherwood 2020.

[2] On similarities between Tolkien and Manzoni see Monda 2019. Manzoni's *The Betrothed* was one of Cardinal Newman's favourite books, and three copies of it are preserved in the Birmingham Oratory (together with several other of Manzoni's books). It is possible, although unprovable, that Tolkien had indirect access to the collection of the Oratory Library through Father Francis Morgan.

germ of an overarching meta-textual narrative already appears in his early work *The Book of Tales*, and is indeed related to that very line from an Old English poem that was at the centre of the analysis of Chapter I (I.1.4). In this early version of the *legendarium*, a mariner named Eriol, a "son of Eärendil" and "a man of great curiosity", arrives on the island of Tol Eressëa, where he encounters members of an ancient people ("the Gnomes", who would become the Elvish people of the Noldor or Ñoldor in later versions of the *legendarium*). In a series of oral performances, these proto-Elves relate to Eriol tales about the creation and the ancient ages of the world; these stories would be integrated, many years later, into *The Silmarillion*.[3]

Over several years, Tolkien repeatedly rewrote and changed this meta-textual frame; and it is now extant in a variety of different versions, which often include explicit links with the primary world and complex textual histories. In one among the several variants, the human traveller Ælfwine (or Widlást) is presented as an Anglo-Saxon man, born in Britain in around 869 AD; after visiting Tol Eressëa and learning about the stories of the Elder Days (i.e. the *Simarillion*) from the Elvish loremaster and recorder Pengoloð, Ælfwine returns to England to translate into Old English the tales he heard (and read) during his journeys.[4] His works lay forgotten for many

---

[3] References to a framework of orality are common in *BLT1* and *BLT2*, and later works of the *legendarium*, and traces of it can also be occasionally identified in *The Lord of the Rings* (see on this Prozesky 2006 and later in this chapter, esp. II.1.5, and nn. 46 and 52).

[4] References to this meta-textual frame abound in the volumes of the *History of Middle-earth*, and include explicit first- or third-person narrator references, "translator's notes", marginal or interlinear glosses, fictional paratextual material, ancient scripts, and so on.

centuries, but were eventually rediscovered, translated, and redacted by a series of following editors. Despite their differences, these versions generally maintained the original narrative core, featuring an ancient traveller compiling oral stories, recorded directly from Elves living in a distant island, as well as the general conceit that Tolkien's works were originally authored by someone other than him.[5] In the 1977 published version of *The Silmarillion*, Christopher Tolkien decided not to include any open references to these meta-textual narratives,[6] but, as he confessed, he later regretted the

There are also some fragments of *Silmarillion* material directly written by Tolkien in Old English and allegedly authored by Ælfwine or Eriol (collected in *SME*:281–3).

[5] The early drafts of *The Lord of the Rings* implicitly maintained this English link, connecting primary and secondary worlds (cf. *PME* 1:3 where the narrator says that the hobbits spoke a language very similar to that of his own human ancestors; cf. also *TI* 23:424 connecting the Language of the Shire with Modern English). This link was transformed and concealed (cf. II.1.8 and see Brljak 2010:14–19), but not wholly eliminated (cf. IV.2.1). On meta-textual frames in the *Book of Lost Tales* and the *Silmarillion* material in general see in particular Noad 2000, Garnier 2003, Flieger 2007a, Atherton 2012, esp. 97–118, 189; cf. also Lewis and Currie 2009 for the speculation that Tolkien's meta-textual frame originally featured a connection with the Arthurian cycle. References to the meta-textual frame are also common, and at times blatant also in other posthumous works of the *legendarium*; one can refer for instance, among many, to the "Comments of the Eldar" (recently published in Devaux 2014:102–29), a fragmentary text allegedly authored by "Elvish loremasters", discussing from the Elves' perspective key philosophical questions related to their nature and destiny. Cf. also *NME* 1.9:67 (scribal errors), 2.3:183 (a document preserved in the archives of Gondor, probably made at the orders of Elendil), 2.8:203 (one of many cases of the marginal note "Quoth Aelfwine"), 3.16:352 (a Gondorian commentator), for example.

[6] To give just one example of many: all the original Tolkien versions of the *Ainulindalë* myth, which opens the *Silmarillion* (cf. Chapter VII), contain extensive meta-textual material, both in the paratext

decision.[7] Complex meta-textual frames are also found in Tolkien's unfinished and unpublished time-fictions, *The Lost Road* and *The Notion Club Papers* (see Flieger 2022), which, similarly, are partly integrated in the *legendarium*. Finally, meta-textual references are common and explicit in the earlier versions of *The Lord of the Rings*, which, for instance, originally ended with an epilogue featuring Sam Gamgee writing on "sheets of loose paper" and reading excerpts from a "large red book" recording his own story, to the eager ears of his numerous children.[8]

In this chapter, my main focus will be on the 'published' meta-textual frame, that is, on the meta-textual frame that can be reconstructed from Tolkien's published works; this especially includes *The Lord of the Rings* and *The Hobbit*, but also *The Adventures of Tom Bombadil*. *The Silmarillion* will also be considered occasionally, but with due caution and only tangentially. This is because Tolkien did not see this book into publication, and this affected the coherence and clarity of its underlying meta-textual frame, as Christopher Tolkien intimated.[9] In contrast, there are

and the narrative itself (e.g. *MR Ain*. 8 "This was written by Rúmil of Túna and was told to Ælfwine in Eressëa (as he records) by Pengoloð the Sage [...] The Music of the Ainur and the Coming of the Valar. These are the words that Pengoloð spoke to Ælfwine concerning the beginning of the World." All this material was removed in the 1977 *The Silmarillion*).

7 Cf. *BLT1 Foreword*:5 "it is certainly debatable whether it was wise to publish in 1977 a version of the primary 'legendarium', standing on its own and claiming, as it were, to be self-explanatory. [...] this I now think to have been an error".

8 See *SD* 1.9, esp.:121–4. See further Flieger 2005:77–80; duPlessis 2018.

9 This does not mean that in *The Silmarillion* there are no elements underpinning a meta-textual frame: for instance, as noted by

several hints, of varying degrees, showing that Tolkien developed and integrated into all his published tales a version of the meta-textual frame, which has important influences and implications on their narrative fabric. At the same time, it is to be the case that in the writing and editing process, Tolkien decided to make the meta-textual frame less perceptible to the reader; that is, that he took care to conceal the identity of the 'real authors' of his tales.

In the past two decades, several scholars have highlighted the underlying meta-textual narrative of Middle-earth and its literary significance.[10] In this chapter, I will build upon these recent works, aiming to expand on the complexity of Tolkien's meta-textual frame, as well as

Christopher Tolkien himself (*Sil* Foreword viii), the contrast in narrative speed and detail between different parts of the work can be related to the different temporal distance of the narrated events from the time of the fictional author(s). More generally, the heterogeneity of styles, focalisation, and degree of narrator's knowledge, can be explained as reflecting its fictional compilatory nature, as if *The Silmarillion* were a collection of different tales, deriving from a variety of sources composed in different formats by multiple authors over a long span of time; this implicit meta-textual heterogeneity gives an important contribution to the 'literary depth' of the published *The Silmarillion*, although probably to a lesser level than in its unpublished drafts, where the meta-textual frame is often very explicit. On this see in particular Joosten 2013 (esp. on the relation between poetic and prose texts); Nagy 2004; Drout, Hitotsubashi, and Scavera 2014, with bibliography. For an attempt at identifying a single fictional authorship in *The Silmarillion*, see instead Wise 2016. See further n.80; also II.1.7, IV.1.1.

[10] See in particular Nagy 2003, 2005, 2007, 2012; Flieger 2000, 2005:55–84, 2006, 2007a; Bowman 2006; Brljak 2010; Drout, Hitotsubashi, and Scavera 2014; Vink 2020b; cf. also Agøy 2007; Oberhelman 2008; Klinger 2012b; Brückner 2012; Cristofari 2012; Atherton 2012, esp. 61–72, 77–80, 93–5, 107–18; Vanderbeke and Turner 2012; Kokot 2013; Thiessen 2014; Wise 2016; Stefani 2020; Glover 2020:6–10; Sherwood 2020; González de la Llana 2020; Nagy 2022:97–9; Lee 2022b.

to delve into its meta-literary significance. This study is particularly indebted to Flieger's (esp. 2000, 2005, 2006) and Brljak's (2010) works, with which it has some points of affinity, especially in its first part; however, I disagree with their shared conception of the meta-textual frame as a mere authorial conceit, ultimately destined to "collapse", rather than as a coherent "structural factor" (albeit ultimately unrevised). Thus, for example, I will construe narrative elements, such as multiple focalisations and interlaced narratives (cited by Flieger as counter-evidence to the meta-textual frame), as actually depending on that very frame, together with the number of explicit hints scattered throughout Tolkien's published works.

II.1.1 The Paratext of The Lord of the Rings

The most explicit and comprehensive evidence about the fictional textual history of Tolkien's works (the meta-textual frame) is not found in external or unpublished sources, but in *The Lord of the Rings* itself, both in the paratextual sections (*Prologue* and *Appendices*) and in the main text.[11] Just before his final journey to the Grey Havens and beyond, the hobbit Frodo hands over all his possessions to his friend Sam. These include:

a big book with plain red covers; its tall pages were now almost filled. At the beginning there were many leaves covered with Bilbo's thin wandering hand; but most of it was written in Frodo's

---

[11] In this chapter I will not consider all types of meta-textual references (such as the famous meta-textual dialogue between Sam and Frodo on the Stairs of Cirith Ungol (*LotR* 4.8:711–12), which will be analysed in Chapter IV), but only those that depend on and evoke the underlying frame narrative.

firm flowing script. It was divided into chapters but Chapter 80 was unfinished, and after that were some blank leaves. The title page had many titles on it, crossed out one after another, so:

My Diary. My Unexpected Journey. There and Back Again. And What Happened After. Adventures of Five Hobbits. The Tale of the Great Ring, compiled by Bilbo Baggins from his own observations and the accounts of his friends. What we did in the War of the Ring.

Here Bilbo's hand ended and Frodo had written:

THE DOWNFALL OF
THE LORD OF THE RINGS
AND THE
RETURN OF THE KING

(as seen by the Little People; being the memoirs of Bilbo and Frodo of the Shire, supplemented by the accounts of their friends and the learning of the Wise)

Together with extracts from Books of Lore translated by Bilbo in Rivendell. (*LotR* 6.9:1026–7)

This cryptic passage is a mine of information – a 'fortunate crack' that gives a glimpse of an elaborate meta-textual frame, underlying the novel and indeed the whole *legendarium* of Middle-earth. This pivots on the ancestral "big book with plain red covers", or more simply the "Red Book".[12]

---

[12] On the Red Book cf. in particular Flieger 2006 (connecting the conceit with the 1934 discovery of the Winchester Manuscript of Malory's *Morte d'Arthur*) and Bowman 2006 (perceptively contextualising it within Tolkien's broader meta-narrative concerns); see also Fimi 2008:128 and Klinger 2012b (both discussing some alleged inconsistencies, including e.g. the description of Frodo's final vision of Eldamar); Alfaiz 2015, esp. 89–90 (describing the Red Book as a *lieu de mémoire*); Birns 2015 (questioning the widespread assumption that the Red Book of Westmarch neatly coincides with *The Lord of the Rings*). Cf. also Vanderbeke and Turner 2012 for an extensive deconstruction of the conceit (a bit too defeatist); Phelpstead 2011:62–3 for the identification of a possible primary model, namely the famous Welsh manuscript *Red Book of Hergest*. Another possible

II.1.2 The First Author of the Red Book: Bilbo Baggins

The fictional paratext also reveals the identity of the first writer of the Red Book, who authors its opening text, namely the hobbit Bilbo Baggins. Although the heading *The Hobbit* does not appear in the list of provisional titles "crossed out one after another" by Bilbo, there are few doubts that the "many leaves covered with Bilbo's thin wandering hand" form the textual archetype of what is now known as *The Hobbit*. Tolkien explicitly confirms this at the very beginning of the Prologue to *The Lord of the Rings*: "Further information [sc. 'Concerning Hobbits'] will also be found in the selection from the Red Book of Westmarch that has already been published, under the title of *The Hobbit*. That story was derived from earlier chapters of the Red Book, composed by Bilbo himself, [...] and called by him *There and Back Again*" (*LotR Prologue*:1).

An indirect hint to Bilbo's authorship of *The Hobbit* is already found in the book itself at the very end of the story, when Bilbo sits in his study to write his memoirs, which he thought of calling "There and Back Again, a Hobbit's Holiday" (*Hobbit* 19:349).[13] Similar meta-textual allusions are also scattered across *The Lord of the Rings*,

inspiration for the conceit is the *Red Fairy Book* by Andrew Lang, which Tolkien read with great interest in his early years.

[13] In a lecture 'on Dragons and Dinosaurs' delivered at the University of Oxford on 1 January 1938, Tolkien quoted some bits of The Hobbit attributing them to his "friend Baggins", and even ascribed to him the authorship of the illustration of Smaug. See further Atherton 2012:213–16 on Bilbo's eventual transformation into an author and scholar, noting his similarity with Rúmil, the author-philologist of the meta-textual frame of *The Book of Lost Tales*.

typically in the form of references to Bilbo's secret book. Frodo thought he was the only person who had read this work, but it was, in fact, also known to Merry, who managed once to have a "rapid glance" at it before Bilbo took it away after his departure (cf. *LotR* 1.5:105).

In *The Lord of the Rings*, there is even a direct quote from *The Hobbit* explicitly ascribed to Bilbo:

That house was, as Bilbo had long ago reported, 'a perfect house, whether you like food or sleep or story-telling or singing, or just sitting and thinking best, or a pleasant mixture of them all'. (*LotR* 2.1:225 [= *Hobbit* 3:61])

There is an event from *The Hobbit* (or rather from Bilbo's diary) that receives particular meta-textual attention in *The Lord of the Rings*: Bilbo's narrative of the finding of the Ring and his escape from Gollum's cave. In several points, it is said that two variants of this narrative existed: a 'fake' story told by Bilbo to the dwarves at the time of the event and eventually written down in his book in the version read by Frodo, according to which the Ring was given by Gollum to Bilbo as a present;[14] and a second, accurate story, revealed only to his closest friends and eventually to all members of the Council of Elrond;[15] this is essentially the version one can now read in Chapter 5 of *The Hobbit* ("Riddles in the Dark"). According to Tolkien's meta-textual frame, this second version remained at an oral stage for a long time and was not included in the Red

[14] Cf. *LotR* 1.1:40 (Frodo confirming to Gandalf that Bilbo revealed to him the true story and not the one he told the dwarves and put in his book).
[15] Cf. *LotR* 2.2:249 (Bilbo apologising to the dwarf Glóin and saying that he will now tell the true story in full).

Book and its first copies. And yet it was eventually written down and incorporated in later versions, as explained in the Prologue to *The Lord of the Rings*.[16]

What is the point of this double version, which resulted in a textual variance? First, from a narrative point of view, the existence of a 'fake' version of the story helps to shroud the Ring with a shadow of deception and evil, and characterise its finder, Bilbo, as haunted by a morbid obsession to justify his ownership.[17] This is, however, only a post-event explanation of something that is primarily a 'real' fact. The two aforementioned narratives do exist, first, in the real or 'primary' world (to use Tolkien's terminology): the former narrative is the one found in the first edition of *The Hobbit* (1937) whereas the second is the one printed from its second edition onwards, which resulted from the revisions Tolkien made in 1951 in order to harmonise *The Hobbit* with the forthcoming *The Lord of the Rings*.[18] We can thus begin to introduce a key feature of Tolkien's meta-textual frame: that real, primary literary events or features (such as the revision of a chapter of the *Hobbit*'s first edition) are expressed and integrated in the secondary world as narrative elements (a lie engendered by the Ring's corrupting power originated as a variance in the fictional transmission of the texts). I will come back to this point later on, since the whole meta-textual frame can be described in similar terms.

---

[16] *LotR Prologue*:13 (revealing that neither Bilbo nor Frodo altered the fake account, which explains why this appeared in several copies of the Red Book; the true account, derived from notes by Frodo or Sam, was preserved as an alternative version in other copies).

[17] Cf. for instance *LotR* 1.1:34 "It is mine isn't it? I found it, and Gollum would have killed me, if I hadn't kept it. I'm not a thief, whatever he said."

[18] For a comparison between the two versions see Rateliff 2011. Cf. also 1981; Christensen 2003; Garnier 2003; Honegger 2013.

II.1.3 The Second Author of the Red Book:
Frodo Baggins

With its reference to "Frodo's firm flowing script", the passage quoted in II.1.1 also reveals the second important author of the Red Book, the hobbit Frodo, who wrote the main text contained in the Red Book, that is, the account of the War of the Ring.[19] Moreover, according to Frodo's intention, this secondary text would form a unity ("the memoirs of Bilbo and Frodo") with the other, preceding text written by Bilbo. In contrast to Bilbo's authorship, there are not many explicit references to Frodo's authorial role in *The Lord of the Rings*, which is nevertheless often foreshadowed or alluded to. In his first visit to Bree, for instance, Frodo introduces himself as a prospective writer of a book about the life of the Hobbits outside the shire (cf. *LotR* 1.9:155). Frodo's authorial self-presentation is realised on his way back when he explains to the inquiring people of Bree that he has not written the book yet but promises that he will put his notes in order as soon as he is back home (*LotR* 6.7:995). Since this book is supposed to deal with the affairs "away south", Frodo's answer becomes an allusive reference to the actual writing of his account of the war during his final years in the Shire.[20]

One might be tempted to conclude that the author of *The Hobbit* is Bilbo and that the author of *The Lord of the*

---

[19] Given its heading and content, this text seems to correspond to what is now known as *The Lord of the Rings*, although the two titles are not identical.

[20] As later confirmed, Frodo began and concluded this writing activity, both editorial and authorial, during his final couple of years in the Shire (1420–1): "he took to a quiet life, writing a great deal and going through all his notes" (*LotR* 6.9:1027).

Rings is Frodo: Tolkien's meta-textual frame, however, is much more complex. Indeed, it is not at all obvious that the two archetypal texts of the Red Book ('Bilbo and Frodo's memoirs') neatly coincide with their 'real' counterparts, *The Hobbit* and *The Lord of the Rings*, or that Bilbo and Frodo are their only two respective authors.

II.1.4 Bilbo's Extended and Incomplete Authorial Role

First, there are plenty of references in *The Lord of the Rings* to the incomplete status of the first text, Bilbo's diary, the supposed source of *The Hobbit*. At the beginning of *The Lord of the Rings*, for instance, before his departure from Rivendell, Bilbo reveals that he has to finish his book, and that he is still pondering about giving it a traditional ending ("he lived happily ever after").[21] And yet, despite Bilbo's ambitions, his diary is still incomplete at the time of the Council of Elrond, although he spent several years in the peace of Rivendell.[22] An important reason for the book's 'incompleteness' is Bilbo's realisation that the tale went on, someone else (Frodo) was called to "carry on the story",[23] and that what initially looked like Bilbo's

---

[21] *LotR* 1.1:32 "I can finish my book. I have thought of a nice ending for it: and **he lived happily ever after** to the end of his days"; also *LotR* 2.2:269 (another proposed "good ending" to Bilbo's book).

[22] Cf. *LotR* 2.2:277 "his book [...] still seemed very incomplete"; also *LotR* 2.1:232, quoted II.2.1.1.

[23] *LotR* 2.1:232. Cf. *LotR* 2.2:269 "there will evidently have to be several more chapters, if I live to write them. It is a frightful nuisance. When ought I to start?". On the implications of Bilbo's realisation of the 'endlessness' of story see II.2.1.1, IV.3.2, and cf. Bowman 2006, esp. 273–8.

individual story was in fact a collective Hobbits tale.[24] New chapters should have been added to his first tale, and initially Bilbo considers himself to be the one charged with that task. The old hobbit also started (or intended) to draft the initial chapters of *The Lord of the Rings*, and this is confirmed by the same paratext of *The Lord of the Rings*, where Bilbo mentions in his own hand the tale of "What Happened after" the events of his "unexpected journey", compiled "from his own observations and the accounts of his friends". There are many references in *The Lord of the Rings* to Bilbo's wish to add Frodo's 'new chapters' to the previous story, which yet remains "our story".[25] Frodo's chapters, as Bilbo calls them, are thus part of the same 'Hobbit story' begun by Bilbo and written down by him; at the same time, they belong to a new, second book, which includes, per Bilbo's initial intention, the events now recounted in Book 1 of the *Fellowship of the Ring*, up to Frodo's arrival in Rivendell.[26]

Thanks to Gandalf's explicit warning, Bilbo realises that it is too soon to think of an ending for this second book because the new story is only at its beginning. This is not just a second book, but a real sequel; Frodo's journey to Rivendell is only the first step of a long adventure, as Gandalf points out to him: "I should say that your part is

---

[24] This transition from an individual to a collective narrative self-awareness is also reflected in the evolution of the titles of Bilbo's book, from the singular "**My** Diary My Unexpected Journey" to the plural "Adventures of Five Hobbits. [...] What **we** did in the War of the Ring". I owe this point to Michaël Devaux.

[25] Cf. *LotR* 2.1:238.

[26] Cf. *LotR* 2.2:249, "I tried to make a few notes [...] There are whole chapters of stuff before you ever got here!"; also 2.3:273; 278 "I should like to write the second book, if I am spared."

ended, unless as a recorder. Finish your book, and leave the ending unaltered! There is still hope for it. But get ready to write a sequel, when they come back" (*LotR* 2.2:270).

Despite Gandalf's words, Bilbo's authorial role is often highlighted in the rest of *The Lord of the Rings*, in connection with his role as a poet and adaptor of Elvish poems.[27] Moreover, Bilbo continues to be described as the intended 'recorder' of the hobbits' new adventure.[28] At the end of the novel, when the victorious hobbits come back to Rivendell, having destroyed the Ring, it is still Bilbo who is supposed to write down the full story of the War of the Ring, compiling it from the reports his friends try to give to him before he inevitably falls asleep.[29] In the end Bilbo did not fulfil his role as recorder: he did not edit his notes or, apparently, even manage to finalise his first book. Bilbo thus entrusts both tasks to Frodo in Rivendell, after he realises that he will not be able to write up their story himself, asking him to collect all his notes and papers, and, with the help of Sam, 'knock things into shape' (cf. *LotR* 6.6:988).

II.1.5 *Frodo and the 'Collective' Narratives of* The Lord of the Rings

Frodo accepts Bilbo's investiture and will dedicate his last few years in the Shire to writing the account of the war and to 'tidying up' Bilbo's first book. We can, thus,

---

[27] Cf. *LotR* 2.3:277.
[28] Cf. *LotR* 3.3:458 "You will get almost a chapter in old Bilbo's book, if ever I get a chance to report to him"; 6.4:956 "Frodo will have to […] write it all down. Otherwise he will forget half of it, and poor old Bilbo will be dreadfully disappointed."
[29] Cf. *LotR* 6.6:986 (the four hobbits telling Bilbo in turn all that they could remember of their journeys and adventures, with Bilbo pretending to take notes but often falling asleep).

note that Bilbo's authorial voice is not the only one in *The Hobbit*, which was polished up by Frodo; neither should it be completely discounted from *The Lord of the Rings*, since this was partly compiled from Bilbo's notes, particularly those taken at the time of the Council of Elrond and covering the events up to that point.[30] Frodo's role in the writing of the Account of the War is first intended by Bilbo to be editorial, aiming to 'knock things into shape', that is, to compile different notes into a coherent narrative. These include more than Bilbo's notes: as the paratext declares, Bilbo and Frodo's memoirs are "supplemented by the accounts of their friends and the learning of the Wise" (see II.1.1). Just like Bilbo, Frodo is thus primarily a 'compiler', who puts together the reports and accounts of the characters involved in the story, and especially those of the other three hobbits (Sam, Merry, and Pippin).

The 'collective' and 'compiled' nature of *The Lord of the Rings* is another important feature of the meta-textual frame, evoked in the text by many narrative devices. A most common one is the 'remembering formula', which presents parts of the narrative as memories. One can consider for instance:

Pippin afterwards recalled little of either food or drink [...]. Sam could never describe in words, nor picture clearly to himself, what he felt or thought that night, though it remained in his memory as one of the chief events of his life. (*LotR* 1.3:82)[31]

---

[30] That is, the events now included in the First Book of *The Fellowship of the Ring*.

[31] Cf. also *LotR* 1.7:128 "**As far as he could remember**, Sam slept through the night"; *LotR* 3.3:450 "**Neither Pippin nor Merry remembered** much of the later part of the journey"; *LotR* 3.4:463 "Often afterwards Pippin tried to describe his first impression of them"; *LotR* 5.2:787 "**Gimli remembered** little".

Most of these remembering formulas belong to passages in which Frodo is not present; they especially abound in books three and five of *The Lord of the Rings*, which are narrated from the perspective of other characters, such as Merry and Pippin.[32] All of these 'memories' should thus be construed as being recalled at a later stage by one of the characters who is reporting to Frodo and Sam. Some of these reporting moments are explicitly referred to in *The Lord of the Rings*; this includes the example mentioned in the previous section in Rivendell with Bilbo, and also the scene in the field of Cormallen after the destruction of the Ring, when Frodo and Sam's friends tell them everything that happened after the breaking of their Fellowship at Parth Galen.[33] There are a few other explicit allusions to reporting moments in the published text,[34] and we know that in Tolkien's vision

---

[32] There are a few cases in other books in which the 'remembering formula' is applied to Frodo himself. Cf. *LotR* 2.3:282 "**Frodo remembered** little of it, save the wind"; *LotR* 2.8:377 (Frodo interpreting, "long afterwards [...] as well as he could", the Elvish words that remained graven in his memory). These references, however, can point to the same meta-textual frame: in coherence with it, the non-omniscient narrator of *The Lord of the Rings* has not only to rely on the accounts of the other characters to fill gaps in the story in which he was not directly involved, but he must also recall at a later stage the events that happened to him.

[33] *LotR* 6.4:955. Cf. also *LotR* 1.3:102 (Pippin giving an account to Merry of his journey with Frodo and Sam from Hobbiton to Crickhollow), *LotR* 3.5:496 (Aragorn recounting to Gandalf the events after his fall in Moria and his return as the White Rider), *LotR* 6.2:926 (Sam telling Frodo about his fight with Shelob and his adventure with the Orcs).

[34] Cf. *LotR* 3.9:563–4, when Pippin relates his adventure with the Uruk-hai to Aragorn, Legolas, and Gimli. He explicitly signals that his tale begins at the moment when he wakes up "in the dark" and finds himself "all strung-up in an orc-camp". This tale neatly corresponds to the content of chapter 3.3 ('The Uruk-hai'), which begins with

the most important example took place in Minas Tirith, after Aragorn's crowning; this was not included in *The Lord of the Rings* and is only mentioned in the *Appendices* (p. 1079), but can be found in *Unfinished Tales*, in a section recording some of the conversations the hobbits had with Gandalf, asking him 'questions about all that came into their minds' (cf. *UT* 3.3:329).

An interesting feature of this section is the first-person narrative. As Christopher Tolkien notes in his introduction (*UT* 3.3:321): "The 'He' of the opening sentence is Gandalf, 'we' are Frodo, Peregrin, Meriadoc, and Gimli, and 'I' is Frodo, the recorder of the conversation; the scene is a house in Minas Tirith, after the coronation of King Elessar." The first-person narrative is never used in *The Lord of the Rings*, which always uses the third narrative person; this fact itself might be related to its intended 'plural' authorship, meta-textually justified by presenting Frodo as a recorder of accounts. Together with the remembering formulas, these reporting moments should be construed as depending on and underpinning the underlying meta-textual frame, as well as justifying another important feature of the narrative fabric of the novel, that is, the extensive use of multiple focalisations and interlaced narratives.[35]

Pippin waking up from a bad dream. Notably, this part is omitted by the narrator, who starts reporting Pippin's tale only after highlighting its complete novelty ("now we come to a part of the story you know nothing about"). Cf. also *LotR* 3.3:458 when Pippin and Merry "compare notes" after their escape from the Orcs, with the latter saying to the former that his deeds will deserve "almost a chapter in old Bilbo's book".

[35] On focalisation as an important element of Tolkien's world-building see esp. Turner 2019. On interlaced narratives, their nature, ancestry,

II.1.6 Sam's Authorial Voice: Narrative, Style, and the Meta-textual Frame

Bilbo and Frodo cannot be considered the only independent authors of the two texts of the Red Book, because of yet another important tessera of the meta-textual mosaic; in addition, the hobbit Sam plays an important authorial role, an editor and reviser (as declared by Bilbo), and also one of the writers of the final chapters of the book. The paratext of *The Lord of the Rings* reveals that the manuscript handed over by Frodo to Sam is unfinished, with the writing of the few remaining leaves entrusted to Sam.[36]

There is also a clue to the exact starting point of Sam's authorial hand, which is the number of his supposedly unfinished chapter (80). Since *The Hobbit* includes nineteen chapters and *The Lord of the Rings* sixty-three chapters, one can infer that the final chapter of the novel, that is, the one including the paratext, is the eighty-first of the Red Book and thus that the unfinished eightieth chapter is the previous one, "The Scouring of the Shire". More than this cannot be said with certainty, although I am inclined to think that Frodo's hand is supposed to conclude with the Horn-cry of Buckland ("Awake! Awake! Fear, Fire, Foes! Awake! Fire, Foes! Awake!", *LotR*

and parallels see in particular West 1975; Shippey 2000:102–11 (with graph at p. 104), 2003; Bowman 2006:281–4; Chapter IV; also Rosebury 2003:27–8; Shippey 2016; Kokot 2013, rightly emphasising their connection with the meta-textual frame.

[36] Cf. *LotR* 6.9:1026–7, quoted earlier ("'I have quite finished, Sam [...] The last pages are for you'"). Also *Letters* 131:229 on Sam struggling to finish the Red Book ("nearly completed by Frodo") in the years after Frodo's departure.

6.8:1007), right after Sam's departure to Cotton's farm and before the battle properly begins. What follows is mostly told from Sam's perspective.[37] Moreover, in contrast to Frodo's leading part in the first part of the chapter,[38] Frodo's role in the action clearly decreases after this point (ibid. 1016 "Frodo had been in the battle, but he had not drawn sword"). Frodo is not at all interested in the battle of Hobbiton (and thus, one should assume, in its narrative). A formal feature of the text, the apparent change of focalisation, is therefore meta-textually justified by a supposed authorial change in the writing of the text; and this is not the only one. Another formal feature related to the meta-textual change of narrator concerns style: in the second part of the chapter, after Merry's battle cry, one can notice a lowering of register, featuring plenty of contractions and analogous colloquial forms and words,[39] which are characteristically attributed to Sam throughout the book. To focus on one example: the low-register hypocoristic term 'lad' is never used in *The Lord of the Rings* except in direct speeches by Hobbits or Orcs.[40] The only three real exceptions are found in this

---

[37] Cf. *LotR* 6.8:1007 "Behind him Sam heard a hubbub of voices"; 1008 "Sam hurried to the house"; 1014 "into the middle of this talk came Sam"; 1016 "Even Sam's vision in the Mirror had not prepared him for what they saw"; 1020 "'I shan't call it the end, till we've cleared up the mess,' said Sam gloomily."

[38] Cf. *LotR* 6.8:1001 "I [i.e. Frodo] am going where I please"; 1003 "He won't be so eager when Mr. Frodo has finished with him"; 1005 "I am on my way to call on Mr. Lotho".

[39] Cf. *LotR* 6.8:1009 "the ruffians can't come at 'em".

[40] Cf. *LotR* 3.3:458 "Evidently Mauhúr and his **'lads'** had been killed." An irrelevant exception: Bergil of Minas Tirith is often referred to as 'lad' (*LotR* 5.1 "said the lad", x3), but in this case the term is not hypocoristic.

chapter, and only in its second half.[41] This sort of stylistic change matches the supposed identity of the author of the passage, the hobbit Sam, whose language is characterised throughout the novel at a low register.[42]

Thus, there is a concealed correlation between narrative and stylistic features and the underlying meta-textual frame. This correlation is not only found in these final chapters, but is also a widespread feature of the literary fabric of *The Lord of the Rings*, discernible above all in its stylistic diversity.[43] For instance, the first book of *The Fellowship of the Rings* displays a considerably lower register than the later books, more similar to that of *The Hobbit*.[44] Applying Tolkien's meta-textual frame, we can

[41] *LotR* 6.8:1010 "a dozen **lads** on ponies"; 1007 "Farmer Cotton with three of his **lads**"; 1008 "many younger **lads**".

[42] In a letter to the BBC producer Terence Tiller (10/09/1955), responding to a request about accents of *The Lord of the Rings* characters for a famous radio dramatisation, Tolkien noted that the difference between "gentlehobbits" and "the Great" was more "one of period [...] than dialect" and that Hobbits used "our own rather slack colloquial", speaking as we do "at our most unstudied". Sam, however, could be given a "country accent" of some kind, with "a rustic tone and vowel-colouring" (quoted in Lee 2022c:147, 150).

[43] On intertextual and intratextual stylistic variation of Tolkien's works see further II.2.1.2.

[44] This was, of course, originally a mere consequence of the fact that *The Lord of the Rings* was initially conceived as a sequel to *The Hobbit*; yet this 'editorial fact' was arguably eventually given secondary significance by Tolkien. Tolkien himself noted that there is a great stylistic variety in *The Lord of the Rings*, with a general ascending trend of 'heightening' of the linguistic register while the story proceeds (cf. *Letters* 131:221[160] on the style of *The Lord of the Rings* including "the colloquialism and vulgarity of Hobbits, poetry and the highest style of prose" and ibid. 223 on the rising of style accompanying the changes of the characters; *Letters* 193, to T. Tiller, 2/11/1956:364[254] "I paid great attention to such linguistic differentiation as was possible", *LotR Appendix* F:1133–4). Cf. also *Letters* 131:221[159] on the stylistic

link this stylistic feature with the intense presence of Bilbo's authorial voice in this very book through the notes taken by him in Rivendell. There would also be much to say on the abundance of 'light talk' in the chapters of the story concerning (and allegedly reported by) the hobbits Pippin and Merry, or on the use of authorial empathy and focalisation, but this would be a topic for another work.

We can sum up the meta-textual narrative reconstructed here in the following way: what are now known as *The Hobbit* and *The Lord of the Rings* originally formed a single volume of eighty-one chapters, written by three intermingling Hobbit hands ("as seen by the little people"). Bilbo Baggins drafted (but did not finalise) the first nineteen chapters (the archetype of *The Hobbit*) and sketched notes for the following twelve chapters (book 1 of *LotR*). Frodo Baggins (presumably) polished up Bilbo's early chapters and wrote the main bulk of the text, compiling Bilbo's and his own notes and incorporating the (oral) accounts of his friends, especially his fellow hobbits. Finally, Sam Gamgee completed chapter 80 of the book, left unfinished by Frodo, wrote the final chapter, and, as envisaged especially in the unpublished epilogue, incorporated some editorial changes to the entire volume, also availing himself of the help of his friends.[45]

---

differentiation in *The Hobbit*: "the tone and style change with the Hobbit's development, passing from fairy-tale to the noble and high and relapsing with the return"; on this see further Atherton 2012:67–73. For an investigation of linguistic characterisation in Tolkien's works see the recent study by Kullman and Siepmann 2021 (esp. 192–226, and 259–96).

[45] Cf. *SD* 1.11:123–4, where it is also revealed that Sam had also to rewrite "in proper style" what Frodo had only sketched in outline form, and for that purpose he asked for the help of Merry, who was "clever at writing".

II.1.7 The Other Volumes of the Red Book and Its Textual History

This already elaborate account is still only a small part of the meta-textual frame of Tolkien's works. In the first place, the Red Book did not only consist of the text of the eighty-one chapters, but also included "extracts from Books of Lore translated by Bilbo in Rivendell".[46] More information about these "Books of Lore", abridged by Frodo in the 'appendix' to his memoirs, are scattered throughout *The Lord of the Rings*. From these one learns that Bilbo's books were three in number, "made at various times", and that they were given by Bilbo to Frodo during their last conversation in Rivendell.[47] There are also a couple of references to some of the original Elvish sources of these translated Books of Lore,[48] and one of these reveals the name of their original Elvish author, namely Elrond himself.[49] These three Books of Lore dealt with the tales from the forging of the Ring to the

---

[46] Bilbo's role as a 'translator' of Elvish poetry is also often alluded to in the work, and some of his translated poems are even recited by characters in parts of the story: cf. *LotR* 1.11:186 "the lay that is called The Fall of Gil-galad [...]. Bilbo must have translated it". It is plausible that these supposedly oral traditions were imagined to be eventually included in Bilbo's "Translations from the Elvish".

[47] *LotR* 6.6:987 (three Books of Lore labelled on their red back "Translations from the Elvish, by B(ilbo) B(aggins)").

[48] *LotR* 2.3:277 (Aragorn and Gandalf pondering books of lore preserved in the house of Elrond).

[49] See Thiessen 2014 for the contention that it is an Elvish authorial voice that prevails in the tales of Middle-earth, and *The Silmarillion* specifically; cf. also Freeh 2015 on possible ways the elvish focalisation is reflected in the treatment of the subject-matter. In contrast, Agøy 2007 (159) and Wise 2016 (118) suggest that the narrator of *The Silmarillion* is a Man speaking to an audience of Men (who presumably lived in the Fourth Age or later).

last alliance;[50] they also dealt with the events of the 'First Age of the World', that is, with what is now the content of *The Silmarillion*.[51] Therefore, the Red Book also included *Silmarillion* material, originally authored by Elrond, at least in part,[52] but abridged, translated, and edited by Bilbo.[53] Given its 'translated' and 'abridged' nature, one must infer that this material was only an approximate rendering of the original version and contained simplifications and misunderstandings, as Tolkien himself points out.[54] I will come back to this point in the second part of this chapter (II.2).

[50] That is, the content of the very last chapter of *The Silmarillion* ("Of the Rings of Power and the Third Age"). Cf. *LotR* 2.2:242 "that history [i.e. of the Ring during the Second Age] is elsewhere recounted, even as Elrond himself set it down in his books of lore".

[51] Cf. *LotR Prologue*:15 "These three volumes were found to be a work of great skill and learning [...] they were little used by Frodo, being almost entirely **concerned with the Elder Days**." Following Christopher Tolkien (*BLT1*:6), quoting Foster 2022 [1971], one can thus reasonably link Bilbo's Books of Lore with the collection of tales eventually published in *The Silmarillion*, even if it would be of course incorrect to make them coincide.

[52] The *Note on the Shire Records* specifies that Bilbo used "all the sources available to him in Rivendell, both living and written", with a plural reference that suggests that Elrond was not the only author of Bilbo's Elvish sources, even just because these also included oral material. In *Unfinished Tales* (3.3:224) it is revealed that the original author of the section *The Downfall of Númenor* was Elendil, Aragorn's ancestor. Cf. also *LotR Prologue*:2, mentioning records preserved by the Elves, dealing with their ancient history.

[53] As noted by Nagy (2014:112), in his published works Tolkien therefore modified the original frame-narratives of the *Silmarillion* (cf. n.1) and made this "the work of Bilbo Baggins, collecting and translating Elvish Texts in Elrond's house in Rivendell". Consequently, as put by Noad (2000:65) "the whole mythology finally devolved into the single 'vehicle' of the Red Book".

[54] On this cf. Agøy 2007, 144–5, Nagy 2022:98–9.

We have thus added another important author of the
Red Book (the Half-Elven Elrond) and another important facet of Bilbo's role (that of translator). But the
meta-textual frame is still not complete, since, in Tolkien's
vision, this frame did not only encompass the redaction
of the Red Book, but also its subsequent textual history.
In this case there is no need for reconstructions, as this
textual history is sketched out by Tolkien in a detailed
note he added to the 1965 edition of *The Lord of the Rings*
and appended to the Prologue (the "Note on the Shire
Records").[55] Tolkien's account is intricate but clear and
can here be paraphrased as such: Frodo's original book
was later appended by four supplemental volumes: the
full three books of Bilbo's translations from Elves, and
a final volume featuring miscellaneous material, written
or compiled at different times by a number of authors,
including Merry Brandibuck and Gimli the Dwarf. The
original Red Book was lost, but many complete or partial
copies were made of it, including a full five-volume edition ("The Thain's Book"), which was emended, annotated, and supplemented in Minas Tirith. *The Lord of the
Rings* is an abridgement derived from a copy of this edition, incorporating Frodo and Sam's chapters from the
first volume and 'selections' from the fifth volume,[56] and
including the Tale of Aragorn and Arwen, redacted in
Gondor by Faramir's grandson.

Just as the early part of the meta-textual frame (concerning the writing of the ancestral Red Book) is evoked

---

[55] Cf. *LotR Prologue*:14–15. See Brljak 2010, esp. 6–14 for a discussion of
the fictional history of transmission of the Red Book.

[56] Cf. *LotR Appendix A*:1033 "only selections from them [i.e. Tolkien's
alleged sources], in most places much abridged, are here presented".

by narrative and stylistic changes, so too is the latter part (concerning the Red Book's editorial history) harmonised in the text through the use of formal features; the Appendices are full of scribal glosses, later notes, and editorial references that are meant to match the elaborate textual history detailed in the Note on the Shire Records.[57]

II.1.8 The Hidden Presence: Tolkien's Authorial/Editorial Voice

The most important feature of the Note on the Shire Records, however, is precisely the presence of Tolkien's authorial voice, which connects the meta-textual frame outlined earlier with his actual writing of *The Lord of the Rings* (or rather, according to the narrative, his compiling and translating of it). In the passage just quoted, as in the prologue in general, Tolkien is speaking in his own authorial persona; this is shown by the statement that "This

[57] Narrative formulas, for instance, imply that parts of the Appendices are authored by Hobbits, presumably living in Brandibuck Hall or the Great Smials (cf. *LotR Appendix A*:1039 "before we came to the Shire"). Other references instead point to Gondor and to Findegil, the scribe of the King (cf. ibid. 1043 n.1 "the King tells us"; 1050 n.1 "as we have learned from the King"). In general, a complex system of diacritics, explained by Tolkien in the opening section, is used to evoke the variety of 'sources' available to the 'compiler' of *LotR*. Cf. *LotR Appendix A*:1033 "Actual extracts from longer annals and tales are placed within quotation marks. Insertions of later date are enclosed in brackets. Notes within quotation marks are found in the sources. Others are editorial." On the literary importance of the appendices, and the paratext material in general, and their contribution to the narrative sophistication of *The Lord of the Rings*, especially in relation to its meta-textual frame, see in particular Turner 2008; also Chandler and Fry 2017.

account of the end of the Third Age is drawn mainly from the Red Book of Westmarch" (*LotR Prol.*:14) and also by the reference to the publication of *The Hobbit*, which is said to have been "derived from the earlier chapter of the Book" and above all to have been "already published".

There is a further notion, which the Note does not state explicitly, but clearly implies, and which indeed underlies the whole meta-textual frame; this is that Tolkien is in possession of a manuscript descending from the Red Book, specifically one of the descendants of the "Thain's book", allegedly revised in Gondor. This is the point where the meta-textual frame of *The Lord of the Rings* is developed, through Tolkien's authorial persona, into a full frame narrative, featuring Tolkien himself in his 'professional role' of editor and critic of ancient texts.[58] This narrative, which criss-crosses and connects primary and secondary planes, is never explicitly articulated in Tolkien's works, but is hinted at in several places. For instance, in *Appendix F* of *The Lord of the Rings* Tolkien claims to have transcribed the "ancient scripts" and translated their content into English.[59] Moreover, there are a few remarks in *The Lord of the Rings* itself where the narrator can neither be Frodo nor Sam, but must be the very compiler of *The Lord of the Rings*, that is (probably) Tolkien himself. These include a passage in which there

---

[58] For Tolkien's academic work as editor of ancient (medieval) texts see especially the overview by Shippey 2022.

[59] Cf. *LotR Appendix E*:1113 ("The Westron [...] has been entirely translated into English equivalents. [...] **In transcribing the ancient scripts** I have tried to represent the original sounds)." See Turner 2003b for an insightful discussion of some of the features and implications of Tolkien's fashioning of his works as pseudo-translations.

is a meta-textual reference to the very chapter of the Red Book dedicated to the Battle of Bywater, and to the fact that the names of the participants in the battle would have been learnt by heart by future Shire historians.[60]

However, the most explicit reference to Tolkien's authorial presence is hidden in the dust jacket of the first edition of *The Hobbit* and the title pages of *The Lord of the Rings* in the friezes of runic letters, which respectively transliterate as:

The Hobbit or There and Back Again being the record of a year's journey made by Bilbo Baggins of Hobbiton, **compiled** from his memoirs by J.R.R. Tolkien and published by George Allen and Unwin Ltd. (*Hobbit* 1937 edition, Dust Jacket)

The Lord of the Rings **translated** from the Red Book of Westmarch by John Ronald Reuel Tolkien. Herein is set forth the history of the War of the Ring and the Return of the King as seen by the Hobbits (*LotR* 1954–5 edition, title pages)[61]

Besides confirming the 'Hobbito-centrism' of his books (see II.2.1.3), this hidden paratextual material

---

[60] *LotR* 6.8:1016. Cf. also *LotR* 2.6:342 ("in those days"); 3.1:342 ("in Gondor in after-days it was long said"); 4.4:661 (the Mûmakil "does not walk now in Middle-earth" and its descendants [i.e. common elephants] that "live still in latter days" are only memories of his majesty); 5.3:803 "for many long lives of men thereafter"; 5.6:849 "long afterward [...] in Rohan". There are also special cases in the *Prologue* in which clearly Tolkien is speaking with his own human authorial persona, describing the hobbits as being more "numerous formerly than they are today" (*LotR Prologue*:1), and calling "us" (i.e. Men) "the Big Folk" (ibid.).

[61] The paratext also introduces the important epithet "of Westmarch", which refers to the place where the book was preserved by Sam's descendants (the Fairbairns family), as stated in the *Appendices* and *Prologue* (cf. *LotR Prologue*:14 and *Appendix B*:1097).

paradoxically reveals that, despite what the presence of his name under the title might suggest ("by J. R. R. Tolkien"), Tolkien fashioned himself a 'compiler', a 'scribe', a 'translator', not an author,[62] – a conceit noticed by some of his most perceptive readers, including the writer Arthur Ransome.[63] This is another important element of the frame narrative of Tolkien's works, which introduces a further layer of complexity to the (fictional) transmission of the text and associates Tolkien, the author in the primary world, with the authors of his secondary world, who are also described as 'compilers' or 'recorders'. This is not the only quality that Tolkien shares with his fictional authors: the second frieze reveals that, just like Bilbo, Tolkien is also (and primarily) a 'translator'.[64] Tolkien's

---

[62] Tolkien's self-fashioning as a recorder and translator is also present in his letters (cf. especially *Letters* 131:204[145] "I always I had the sense of recording what was already 'there', somewhere: not of 'inventing'", *Letters* 214, to A. C. Nunn, late 1958/early 1959:412[289] "in the matter of the Third Age I regard myself as a 'recorder' only. The faults that may appear in my record are [...] omissions and incompleteness of information" and see nn.67, 68). It is predominant in the *Foreword* of the first edition of *The Lord of the Rings*; this was changed in the 1966 version (see on this Bratman 2006), but the conceit remained in the *Appendices*. Cf. also Butler 2013 for the claim that the conceit of multiple translators also helped Tolkien to account for some narrative inconsistencies. For a collection and analysis of Tolkien's paratextual material, see Croft 2018, noting that Tolkien's revisions for the 1951 edition introduced the "first true appearance in print of the metafiction of Tolkien as the translator and editor of the Red Book of Westmarch" (186). Cf. Rateliff 2011:751–6. A more indistinct meta-textual frame was, however, already present in the first edition of *The Hobbit* (noted later).

[63] See n.67.

[64] On the similarities between Bilbo and Tolkien as writers and recorders of stories, and as authors in general, see further Klarner 2014, Birns 2015, González de la Llana 2020 (the latter usefully comparing and contrasting Tolkien and Borges). On Tolkien's role as a translator and his (fictional) theory and practice see Vink 2020b.

translating role is, in fact, often emphasised in both *The Hobbit* and *The Lord of the Rings*,[65] as well as in his other writings.[66] This is another key feature of the meta-textual frame of *The Lord of the Rings*; not only does it add a further stage to its already complex meta-textual history, but it also presents Tolkien's works (already described as 'abridgements') as 'mediated', 'approximate' texts; in a word, as 'translations' – a notion also maintained in several letters to his readers.[67]

II.1.9 Summing Up

We can now try to summarise the complex meta-textual frame narrative underlying Tolkien's works: Tolkien has come into possession of a manuscript copy of an old book in an ancient language ('the Westron'),[68] consisting of

[65] Cf. *LotR Appendix E*:1113; *LotR Appendix F*:1133 (Common Speech turned into modern English); 1134 (all Westron names translated according to their senses); also *Letters* 144:263[175] (Tolkien translating all Westron words into English terms, "with some differentiation of style to represent dialectal differences").

[66] Tolkien duly maintains his role as a transcriber also in his posthumous secondary linguistic works, in which he scientifically describes the phonology and grammar of Elvish languages (cf. Gilson 2010, e.g. 68 "The transcription used in this grammatical account is not that usually employed in the legends and histories for the representation of Elvish words and names").

[67] Cf. esp. his correspondence with Arthur Ransome (published in Hall and Kaislaniemi 2013), who had written to him pointing out some linguistic infelicities in the *Hobbit*, humorously addressing him as a mere 'human scribe', yet "to whom must all be grateful for the chronicle". Tolkien replied maintaining the conceit, and accepted some of the proposed changes, explaining some of the original errors as 'loose renderings' in English of the Dwarves' (imperfect) speech. See also the following note.

[68] In an unpublished letter to two early readers of *The Hobbit* (Leila Keane and Pat Kirke, 3/08/1943, *TCG* 119), Tolkien invited them

miscellaneous accounts about the first 'Three Ages of this World' in five volumes. The book originally focused on the end of the Third Age and was written by three contemporary authors of Hobbit race (Bilbo, Frodo, Sam), but was soon supplemented by a large bulk of miscellaneous material of different origin, authorship, and content. Tolkien is now translating extracts of this book into English and compiling them into separate volumes (*The Hobbit* and *The Lord of the Rings*, as well as, at least according to this version of the frame, the incomplete *Silmarillion*). Returning to my opening questions: *The Hobbit* was originally authored by Bilbo, but was partly emended by Frodo; *The Lord of the Rings* was authored by Frodo and Sam, but incorporated accounts of Bilbo and several other characters; *The Silmarillion* (or more precisely its archetype) was (at least partly) written by Elrond and later translated by Bilbo. All three original works were later heavily edited in a process that included emendation, supplementing, and abridgement, and whose last stage consists of Tolkien's own compilation and translation.

Now that the first part of this chapter's journey is complete, we still have to address the ever-important question: why? Why did Tolkien develop such an elaborate meta-textual frame? What is its purpose and meaning?

to decipher the runic inscription around the edges of the book. He noted that they would find out that the book had been compiled from the memoirs of Bilbo Baggins, adding a vague reference to the way they survived and came down to him ("how they survived is another matter"). He also explained that he had translated the original lingua franca spoken at the time of Bilbo into English to make his accounts readable.

II.2 The (Double) Meaning of the Meta-textual Frame

In order to address the question about the meaning of the meta-textual frame, we first need to distinguish between two different perspectives, one internal and the other external to the stories. The meta-textual frame, in other words, is meaningful on two different planes at the same time: the fictional world of the story (the 'secondary world', according to Tolkien's terminology) and Tolkien's real world ('the primary world'). In Tolkien's vision, elements within the 'secondary' world have a value within its ontological and narrative framework, but, at the same time, they have a mysterious relationship with 'primary' elements. A few short quotations from Tolkien's letters will help to introduce his apparently paradoxical conviction:

I sense amongst all your pains [...] the **desire to express your feeling** about good, evil, fair, foul in some way: to rationalize it, and prevent it just festering. In my case it generated Morgoth and the History of the Gnomes. (*Letters* 66, to Christopher Tolkien, 6/05/1944:113[78])

I took to 'escapism': or really **transforming experience into another form and symbol**, with Morgoth and Orcs and the Eldalie (representing beauty and grace of life and artefact) and so on (*Letters* 73, to Christopher Tolkien, 10/06/1944:122[85])

There is a great deal of linguistic matter [...] included or **mythologically expressed** in the book. (*Letters* 165:319[220])

As shown by these passages, according to Tolkien primary 'experiences', 'feelings', or 'matters' are expressed through elements of the secondary world with which they maintain a sort of 'symbolic' relationship. Crucially, however, this expression is 'artistic' and 'transformative', in the sense that it involves the (unintentional) transformation of primary experiences into another, aesthetically defined secondary code; in Tolkien's case, this would be the literary code of his mythology. That is to say, Tolkien does not conceive his work as an intellectual act consisting of the assertion of pre-existing convictions under the veil of literary fiction; rather he views it as the artistic (or 'sub-creative', 'mythological', 'literary') expression of non-rationalised experiences. This explains why secondary elements have a paradoxical primacy and a value in their own right, while at the same time not being completely detached from 'primary elements'; it also justifies and illuminates Tolkien's notorious aversion to allegory (as will be demonstrated in detail in Chapter IV); above all, it accounts for his passionate apology for his secondary world in its own right and his persistent prioritising of the coherence and beauty of the Story over its possible allegorical meanings, as well as his belief in the heuristic potential of literature. In the following chapters, I will develop a full discussion of these ideas and Tolkien's underlying vision of "the mystery of literary creation" in general. Here I will start by pointing out that, in Tolkien's theory, narrative elements are perfectly coherent (and indeed necessary) within the framework of the secondary world, but they also have a mysterious relationship with elements in the primary world, from which they ultimately derive and which they artistically express.

To both give an example and return to the focus of this chapter, I shall refer to the already-mentioned case of the two versions of the finding of the Ring in *The Hobbit*. Within Tolkien's 'secondary' world it is perfectly credible (and it is necessary from a narrative and thereby aesthetic point of view) that Bilbo should have given a false version of the story to the dwarves, under the corruptive effects of the Ring, and that this should have been the version that first entered the textual tradition of his diary.[69] But at the same time, the alternative version of the story actually exists in the real world, being the one printed in the first edition of *The Hobbit*.[70] This element of the meta-textual frame is thus true and meaningful in both the secondary and the primary reality.

II.2.1 The 'Secondary' Function of the Meta-textual Frame

II.2.1.1 Realism, Historia, and the Mythopoetic Ambition

The double-narrative of the finding of the Ring must be explained first of all, therefore, as an instance of a necessary, 'realistic' element within Tolkien's imaginary universe, and the same can be said, analogically, for all the other features of Tolkien's meta-textual frame, and indeed for its very existence. The first explanation for the meta-textual frame is thus its narrative necessity within the secondary plane. A coherent story, in order to be accorded belief and given the status of *vera historia*,[71] also

---

[69] Cf. Gavaler and Goldberg 2020.

[70] Later revised by Tolkien before the publication of *The Lord of the Rings*, and incorporated into it almost by chance (cf. *Letters* 128, to Allen & Unwin, 1/08/1950, and see Rateliff 2011).

[71] On Tolkien's fashioning of his work as *vera historia* cf. *Letters* 281, to R. Unwin, 15/12/1965:510[365] (the Hobbit saga as a *vera historia*). Cf. also Tolkien's letter of recommendation for C.S. Lewis' novel *Out of the Silent Planet* (*Letters* 26, to S. Unwin, 4/03/1938:43[33]) (described as a *vera historia* of a journey to a strange land blended with mythos, which Tolkien allegedly found irresistible).

needs a textual history, and especially so in the case of a story that claims to be set in the same world as ours, in a distant imagined past.[72] In this respect, the meta-textual frame thus plays a similar role to that of the (aesthetically) invented languages of Middle-earth (among many other 'sub-created' features), which, as Tolkien remarked, aimed to give "an air of reality", as if his stories were a sort of real feigned history.[73] Tolkien's meta-textual frame thus provides internal realism, as well as what scholars call 'impression of depth', thereby performing the same function assigned to meta-textual frames in most nineteenth-century (realistic) novels.[74] But there is more.

The meta-textual frame, and specifically Bilbo's fictional authorship of *The Hobbit*, also allowed Tolkien to overcome what he considered "an insuperable obstacle", namely the fact that the original published version of *The Hobbit* ended with the traditional narrative closure "Bilbo 'remained very happy to the end of his days and those were extraordinarily long'".[75] As neatly put by Bowman

---

[72] On the imagined temporal setting of *The Lord of the Rings*, and its implications, cf. IV.2.1 with n.59.

[73] Cf. *Letters* 15, to A. C. Furth, Allen & Unwin, 31/08/1937:25[21] "The magic and mythology and assumed 'history' and most of the names [...] give the narrative **an air of 'reality'**"; *Letters* 19, to S. Unwin, 16/12/1937:35[26] "[the names] are good, and a large part of the effect. They are coherent and consistent and made upon two related linguistic formulae, so that **they achieve a reality**." On Tolkien's famous preference for "history, true or feigned", and his construction of his fiction as 'real history', cf. Joosten 2013 (esp. 153–4); Nagy 2005; Morrison 2005; Kerry 2005.

[74] On the "impression of depth" cf. IV.1.1 with n.8. On the use of meta-textual frames as a 'veracity mechanism' cf. also Davidsen 2016, esp. 535–4 (= Davidsen 2018, chapter 2).

[75] *Letters* 31, to C. A. Furth, 24/07/1938:49[38] quoting *Hobbit* 19:349. Cf. Anderson 2002:361 with n.13.

in her insightful analysis (2006:274): "The most immediate consequence of this construction [i.e. the meta-textual frame] is to disown the troublesome sentence at the end of *The Hobbit* and attribute it to Bilbo; the frame device effectively places the entire book inside quotation marks." But why did Tolkien consider that original ending so "insuperable" in the first place? Clearly because of that same concern for internal 'realism', and the same effort to present the work as *vera historia*, which would have been jeopardised by the contradiction of adding a continuation to a supposedly ended narrative. The meta-textual frame solved the problem, casting *The Hobbit* ending as the mere wishful closure of the narrator, which is indeed the manner Bilbo repeatedly refers to it in *The Lord of the Rings*.[76] In fact, as already mentioned earlier (II.1.4), and noted by Bowman (2006:274), Bilbo's obsessive desire to finish the book will not be fulfilled, and he will have to realise that the stories can never have an end:

Don't adventures ever have an end? I suppose not. Someone else always has to carry on the story. Well, it can't be helped. I wonder if it's any good trying to finish my book? (*LotR* 2.1:232)

Therefore, Bilbo's authorship of the *Hobbit*, and by analogy all the multiple authorships of Tolkien's work in general, contribute to affirm the idea that every individual tale is only a part of a larger, never-ending Story, and for that reason individual openings and closures are only apparent and ultimately impossible. The endlessness of

---

[76] Cf. *LotR* 1.1:32 and *LotR* 2.2:269, cit. in n.23; also *LotR* 2.3:273 and *TI* 1:4 (a note on Bilbo's "motive writing book" and related restlessness). See II.1.4.

Story, and the related idea of the 'partiality' of individual narratives, are key ideas in both Tolkien's literary theory and primary *Weltanschauung*, to which he will dedicate an important section of *On Fairy-Stories*, explicitly alluding to Bilbo's wishful ending. I will discuss these ideas and their implications at greater length in Chapter IV (IV.3.1): here I only stress that the meta-textual frame, which to a certain extent also originated from the challenge posed by that problematic closure of *The Hobbit*, provided Tolkien an opportunity to reintegrate into a single realistic framework what would have otherwise been 'unreal', at both a superficial level (Bilbo's story did not end with the *Hobbit*) but also a deeper one – because real stories never end, and are always parts of a larger 'mythological' corpus.

In fact, the realistic function of the meta-textual frame should also be related, more generally, to Tolkien's mythopoetic ambition, that is, to his desire to create a national mythological corpus, on the model of Homer's poems,[77] and more recently for him, of Elias Lönnrot's *Kalevala*, the Finnish national poem.[78] The comparison with the *Kalevala* is illuminating: despite most of *Kalevala* being his own work, Lönnrot always posed as a mere compiler of collective, real tales, handed over from the distant past and embodying the spirit of Finnish tradition. As we have seen already, Tolkien also (along with Bilbo) described himself as a compiler of collective tales, and 'collectiveness' is a central feature of the meta-textual

---

[77] On Homeric influences in Tolkien cf. Pepe de Suárez 2013; also Pezzini 2021.

[78] On the link between the meta-textual frame and Tolkien's mythopoetic ambition see cf. Flieger 2005:63; Thiessen 2014:199–200.

frame of *The Lord of the Rings*.[79] Moreover, as Flieger well explained, the meta-textual frame, featuring a single archetypal book translated by Tolkien at different stages, allows Tolkien to integrate its works into a unified mythological corpus.[80] Although most of the meta-textual references are found in *The Lord of the Rings*, they often allude to other works, integrating them into the same frame narrative. Meta-textual references are also found in all its other Middle-earth-related works: apart from the already-discussed cryptic paratext of *The Hobbit*, there are several meta-textual hints also in *The Silmarillion*,[81]

---

[79] On the literary (and linguistic) influence of *Kalevala* on Tolkien's work see Flieger 2004; Shippey 2018; Kahlas-Tarkka 2022. Another important precedent for Tolkien, particularly in relation to the oral nature of the meta-textual frame, is the poet James Macpherson, who presented himself as the recorder of a lost oral poetic tradition, the (fictional) Scottish bard Ossian (see Sherwood's perceptive 2020 study, which also discusses the case of the poet-forger Thomas Chatterton).

[80] Cf. Flieger 2005:83–4, in particular (84) "If we are to take Tolkien's work as he wrote it and as he clearly wanted his audience to read it – as a true mythology, with all the layering and multiple narrators and overlapping texts and variant versions that characterise mythologies in the real world – then we must allow that, like those real-world mythologies, all the parts, even the apparently inconsequential ones, are in in the greater service of the whole."

[81] Cf. for instance *Sil Ring.*:312 "those who saw the things that were done in that time [...] have elsewhere told the tale of the War of the Ring". Cf. also *UT* 3.1:276, which reveals that the full story of Isildur's fate (i.e. the content of that very chapter 3.1) was written down during the time of the kingdom of Aragorn/Elessar in the Fourth Age. Similarly, in *UT* 4.3:412, Christopher Tolkien notes that the Tale of the Years (i.e. *Appendix B* of *LotR*) was supposed to have been composed in the Fourth Age. Thus, some of the information presented there, however assertive, should be considered as mere deductions. Additionally, in *UT* 4.1:386, a legend about the fate of the Númenóreans in the Second Age (*The Mariner's wife*) is mentioned, a copy of which was preserved in Gondor. See further n.9.

as well as *The Adventures of Tom Bombadil* (appropriately subtitled "and Other Verses from the Red Book"),[82] all referring to the same unifying frame. All these contribute to the 'internal' realism of the works, since, on the model of real mythologies,[83] they convey a sense of 'wholeness' and unity of their underlying secondary reality.

II.2.1.2 *Stylistic Realism, Narrative Focalisation, and 'Philosophical' Bias*

The realistic function of the meta-textual frame is not only valid at a large scale, but it also affects the literary fabric of the text, down to the level of its stylistic and narrative features. First of all, the meta-textual frame reflects and justifies the stylistic variety of Tolkien's works, both intratextually (as already shown) and intertextually: for instance, there is an evident contrast between the high-flown and archaising tone of the material eventually collected in *The Silmarillion* and the simple, fairy-story-like style of *The Hobbit* and its intrusive, paternal narrator,[84] or the stylistic medley that is used in *The Lord of the Rings*.[85] These stylistic variations find a 'realistic' justification in

---

[82] Cf. *ATB*:29 (presenting the Tom Bombadil poems as deriving from loose leaves or marginal notes in the Red Book).

[83] Lee (2022b: 61) points out the similarity between the meta-textual frame, especially as regards the fictional history of transmission, and medieval antiquarianism, with which Tolkien was well acquainted thanks to his academic work.

[84] On the paternal narrator of the *Hobbit*, and Tolkien's ambiguous criticism of it, see Shippey 2000:18–21, Rearick 2012.

[85] On stylistic variety in Tolkien's works, inter- and intratextual, see further Shippey 2000:39–45, 68–77, 221–5, and Shippey 2005:63–106, 237–52; cf. also the seminal Kirk 1977, and more recently Turner 2003a; Drout 2004; Walker 2009, esp. chapter 2; Kullman 2009; Reid 2009; Joy 2013; Kullman and Siepmann 2021.

the meta-textual frame, and specifically in the identities of the authors of the different works: an Elf for the *Silmarillion* material, the down-to-earth and paternal Hobbit Bilbo for *The Hobbit*,[86] and the ennobled, gradually 'elvenised' Hobbit Frodo for *The Lord of the Rings*.[87] Similarly, on the narrative level, the multiple focalisations that can be identified in different parts of *The Lord of the Rings* match the 'collectiveness' of the meta-textual frame, with Frodo compiling from Bilbo's notes and the memories of his friends, as already pointed out (II.1.5).

The stylistic variety and narrative focalisation underpinned by the meta-textual frame is not just a formal ornament, but has important implications related to the multiplicity of views and understandings of reality that are integrated within Tolkien's *legendarium*, as well as Tolkien's own holistic literary vision. As noted by Tom Shippey, apropos of stylistic variety in *The Hobbit* (2000:41) a "[s]uperficial clash of styles leading to a deeper understanding of unity is in the end the major theme (even the major lesson) of *The Hobbit*".

I will further illustrate what is a distinctive feature of Tolkien's literature in toto by presenting a case study of a linguistic variation of momentous significance related to the use of the word 'luck'. As pointed out by Shippey (2005:esp. 152–4), this word has in fact greater philological weight than its current use would suggest: 'luck' originally referred not to random chance, but, rather, to "a continuous interplay of providence and free will [...] encapsulating

---

[86] For Bilbo's characteristic paternal attitude see for instance *LotR* 6.6:987 (Bilbo giving good advice to Merry and Pippin).
[87] Cf. *LotR* 4.5:668 (Faramir noting Frodo's "strange [...] Elvish air") and 4.10:733 (Frodo's "Elvish beauty").

ancient philosophical problems" (ibid. 153).[88] The semantic pregnancy of the word, however, is not immediately
perceived by the hobbits, its standard users. In fact,
this term is distinctively frequent in *The Hobbit*, with
twenty-eight occurrences evenly distributed, including
twelve directly used in non-direct speech by the narrator
(i.e. Bilbo, according to the meta-textual frame). In contrast, the word is never found in *The Silmarillion* (allegedly
authored by Elves), and in *The Lord of the Rings* it is more
than four times less frequent than in *The Hobbit*, and above
all it is stylised as low-register and restricted for linguistic characterisation: in *The Lord of the Rings* the word
'luck' is never used by the narrator; rather, twenty-eight
out of the thirty-seven occurrences of the word are found
in direct speeches of low characters, including the orc
Shagrat and the innkeeper Butterbur,[89] but especially hobbits (twenty-four occurrences, including four by Bilbo).[90]
That the word has a 'Hobbit association' is also suggested
by the fact that in the other six occurrences in which it
is used by high characters, these are always in conversation with Hobbits.[91] The remaining three occurrences are
found in the Prologue, all referring to Bilbo's finding of
the Ring and escape from Gollum's cave: "he put his hand
on a ring [...] **It seemed** then like **mere luck**. [...] In the
end Bilbo won the game, more by **luck** (as it seemed) than
by wits. [...] once more he was saved by his **luck**" (*LotR
Prologue*:11–12).

---

[88] Cf. also Shippey 2000:27–8, 143–7.   [89] *LotR* 737:995 (x3).
[90] *LotR* 43:107 (x3), 109 (x2), 270, 273, 278, 281 (last four by Bilbo), 590,
   596, 609 (x2), 914, 921, 928 (x3), 929, 930, 935 (x2), 1003.
[91] *LotR*:147 (Tom Bombadil), 183, 336, 597 (Aragorn), 310 (Gandalf),
   564 (Gimli).

The most frequent and important use of the word 'luck' in *The Hobbit* itself is in the context of a (self-)exegesis of that particular Gollum episode, and of the apparent fortune of Bilbo ("the Luckwearer") in general.[92] However, as already suggested by the qualifying remarks of the *LotR Prologue* ("it seemed"), the word 'luck' is imprecise, because, at least in the hobbit's default linguistic perception, it underpins a world view that construes the success of an individual story as a random and self-sufficient event, rather than a purposeful episode within a larger providential horizon. As declared by Gandalf in his final dialogue with Bilbo:

Surely you don't disbelieve the prophecies, because you had a hand in bringing them about yourself? You don't really suppose, do you, that all your adventures and escapes were managed by mere luck, just for your sole benefit? [...] you are only quite a little fellow in a wide world after all! (*Hobbit* 19:351)

With his implicit counter-exegesis, which derives from his actual knowledge of a 'providential design', Gandalf is not just correcting the linguistic imprecisions and narrative partiality of Bilbo the character, but also those of Bilbo the narrator, both of whom have extensively used the word 'luck' in the course of the story, without understanding its relationship with the concepts of providence and free will (cf. Shippey 2005:153): one could say that, in

---

[92] *Hobbit* 5:92 "Bilbo was saved by pure luck"; *Hobbit* 9:206–7 "Bilbo [...] saw that luck was with him [...] Luck of an unusual kind was with Bilbo then"; *Hobbit* 12:246 "Mr. Baggins [...] so possessed of good luck far exceeding the usual allowance"; 246–7 "Perhaps I have begun to trust my luck more than I used to"; 258 "I am Ringwinner and Luckwearer".

typical Tolkienian fashion, Gandalf's education consists in recovering the semantic depth and complexity hidden in a banal, trite word such as 'luck'.

Gandalf will return to the issue in his crucial dialogue with Frodo at the beginning of *The Lord of the Rings*, where he gives Frodo a better interpretation of the crucial Gollum episode, in more precise (but not yet totally explicit) language (*LotR* 1.2:56). I will discuss this important passage in Chapter III (III.1.2.5), widening the analysis to consider other related key words ('chance', 'fate', and 'fortune'), and discussing its relationship with the 'divine narrative' underlying *The Lord of the Rings* and Tolkien's 'poetics of cloaking' in general. Here, I only highlight that all this linguistic, stylistic, and 'philosophical' variety is in harmony with the meta-textual frame, and its multiplicity of narrators and focalisations. More specifically, the meta-textual frame adds further 'realism' to that very variety, justifying a plurality of different, and even contrasting, views, and allowing the presence of imperfect, or even mistaken, understandings of reality, which are ultimately integrated into a single, multiple but hierarchical framework (Bilbo's imprecise language and understanding are accepted, but not equated with those of Gandalf, and for that reason they need to be eventually corrected by him).[93]

The meta-textual justification of imprecise language and related world view is a widespread feature of Tolkien's literary works. For instance, Lewis (1996)

---

[93] In *Unfinished Tales* (3.3:323 and 335), Gandalf himself stresses that the story of *The Hobbit* was written from Bilbo's imperfect point of view and that it would have sounded very different if he had written the account himself.

identified a number of internal contradictions within the narrative framework of *The Silmarillion*, which he construed as deriving from the "political biases" of their different sources and narrators. Building on Lewis' work, and moving to the primary plane, Gallant (2020a) convincingly explained the conflict between Tolkien's primary reservations on ideals of Northern courage and their apparent embodiment in *The Silmarillion* in relation to the Elvish identity of its "intradiegetic narrators" and its presentation as "fictional historiography".[94] Another important meaning of the meta-textual frame is thus to make 'realistic', and 'realistically' integrate, the multiplicity of views and voices (at times contradictory) – a typical feature of Tolkien's literary corpus, often puzzling his critics.[95]

II.2.1.3 Hobbito-Centrism: Narrative and Themes

Despite all this multiplicity, however, in one important sense the narrative perspective of *The Lord of the Rings* is 'singular', and this is that it is a Hobbit perspective, a fact that is aptly justified by the Hobbit identity of the book's specific author(s). This is another important 'internal' function of the meta-textual frame: that is, to emphasise and justify the Hobbito-centrism of

---

[94] Cf. in particular Gallant 2020a:42 "Such reservations and criticisms [of Tolkien on the northern theory of courage] may be seen in the illustrative narration technique used to narrate the fictional history of the Eldar. [...] The historical bias and moral authority of the Elvish *wyrdwrīteras* gives their entire history, in Alex Lewis's words, 'a realism far removed from mere contrivance'" (= Lewis 1996:164).

[95] Cf. Chapter IV, n.74, and VI.2.4.

the book. This Hobbito-centrism is not just a narrative accident, but a fundamental element, related to one of its main underlying themes, namely to quote Tolkien himself, "the ennoblement (or sanctification) of the humble" and "the place in 'world politics' of the unforeseen and unforeseeable acts of will, and deeds of virtue of the apparently small, ungreat, forgotten in the places of the Wise and Great".[96] *The Lord of the Rings* is written by Hobbits because the whole story is about Hobbits, and more precisely about their "ennoblement" and their contribution to the history of the world.[97] All these themes were most dear to Tolkien, as he often acknowledged.[98]

---

[96] Cf. *Letters* 131:221[160] "as the earliest Tales are seen through Elvish eyes [...] this last great Tale [...], coming down from myth and legend to the earth, is seen mainly through the eyes of Hobbits, through Hobbits, not Men so-called, because the last Tale is to exemplify most clearly a recurrent theme: **the place in 'world politics' (etc.)**"; *Letters* 181:343[237] "[The structure of the narrative] is planned to be 'hobbito-centric', that is primarily a study of **the ennoblement (or sanctification) of the humble**". Cf. also *Letters* 186:353–4[246] (the hobbit focalisation as related to "another main point in the story", summed up by Elrond's words at *LotR* 2.2:268 "such is oft the course of deeds that move the wheels of the world: small hands do them because they must, while the eyes of the great are elsewhere").

[97] Some important moments in which the hobbits' ennoblement is openly thematised in *The Lord of the Rings* are the dialogues between Merry and Pippin at the House of Healing (*LotR* 5.8:870 "there are things deeper and higher"), Gandalf and the hobbits on the journey back (6.7:996 "you are grown up now"), Saruman and Frodo in the Shire (6.8:1019 "you have grown, Halfling").

[98] Cf. *Letters* 165:320[220] "The ennoblement of the ignoble I find especially moving". The whole historical trajectory of Tolkien's secondary world implies a similar process, featuring the "ennoblement of the Human Race", which includes the insertion of an Elven-strain into it. This will eventually culminate with Men replacing the Elves, as destined "from the beginning" (cf. *Letters* 153:289[194]).

II.2.1.4 Merging Myth into History:
The 'Symbolism' of the Hobbits

The Hobbito-centrism of the book, however, is important not only from a narrative, stylistic, and thematic point of view: it also has a crucial (meta-)literary function; that is, in Tolkien's words, merging myth into history:

> *The Hobbit*, which has much more essential life in it, was quite independently conceived: I did not know as I began it that it belonged [i.e. to the same mythological cycle of the Silmarillion]. But it proved to be the discovery of the completion of the whole, its mode of descent to earth, and merging into 'history'. (*Letters* 131:204[144])[99]

What does Tolkien mean by "descent to earth" and "merging into history"? A full answer to this question would probably require a book on its own.[100] Here I will simply say that the Hobbits introduce a point of view with which Tolkien and his readers can identify, an 'anthropocentric point of view', and more specifically the point of view of simple human beings living in a non-heroic (and non-Christian) age,

---

[99] Cf. *Letters* 131:160 "coming down [...] to the earth", quoted in n.95; *Letters* 163:314[215] "the value of Hobbits, in putting earth under the feet of 'romance', and in providing subjects for 'ennoblement'"; also in letter *TCG* 212 (22/10/1955) Tolkien noted that the *Silmarillion* stories were very high and Elvish and featured no hobbits that would "bring them down to common soil". Cf. also Christopher Tolkien's foreword to the posthumous *Silmarillion* material (*BLT* 1:1), noting that there is "no 'mediation' of the kind provided by the hobbits (so, in *The Hobbit*, 'Bilbo acts as the link between modern times and the archaic world of dwarves and dragons')"; in contrast in *The Lord of the Rings* Sam [...] "'mediates' (and engagingly 'Gamgifies') the 'high'" (ibid. 3).

[100] For a brief, but influential treatment see Shippey 2005:63–106; cf. also Shippey 2000:45–9; Klinger 2006; Klarner 2014; Korpua 2015, 2016; Brémont 2016.

such as that of Tolkien's twentieth-century modern England.[101] Tolkien himself often describes himself and (some of) his contemporaries as Hobbits.[102] The Hobbits are therefore the most 'symbolic' characters of *The Lord of the Rings* in the sense that they have a full life (a "more essential life") in both the primary and secondary worlds; they help the merging of myth and history because they link the secondary with the primary world, that is, the mythical universe of Middle-earth with its Elves, gods, and heroes, and Tolkien's real contemporary world. Tolkien would later gratefully acknowledge the key role played by the Hobbits in the development of his literary work, as well as his career as a writer in general.[103]

II.2.2 The 'Primary' Meaning of the Meta-textual Frame

This leads me to the final part of this chapter, in which I will try to decode the meanings of the meta-textual frame on the primary plane. In II.2.1, I only discussed 'internal' justifications for the meta-textual frame, which are related mainly to the need for realism and Tolkien's mythopoetic ambition. As I shall argue, however, this meta-textual frame is meaningful also from the perspective of the real world, by being a coded expression of Tolkien's primary experience

---

[101] Cf. Shippey 2000:3–11, noting that Bilbo is "incipiently vulgar" and "roughly Victorian to Edwardian".

[102] Cf. for instance *Letters* 205a, to Messrs. Voorhoeve en Dietrich, 18/03/1958:382 "I am a hobbit".

[103] Cf. *Letters* 187:357 "it was only as a sequel to *The Hobbit* that publication proved possible. Bless the little people!". Cf. also VI.2.1.

as a literary writer. This will thus help shed more light on Tolkien's conception of the "mystery of literary creation".

II.2.2.1 The Intrusion of the Hobbit

The starting point for this de-coding is again the Hobbits, or more precisely *The Hobbit*, a book that for Tolkien had a mysterious origin, and an 'independence' from his original authorial intentions. As already mentioned, Tolkien considered *The Hobbit* 'an unexpected discovery',[104] which "intruded" or "strayed" into its *legendarium* against his original intentions and literary preferences,[105] and yet eventually "modified it".[106] As

---

[104] Cf. *Letters* 163:314[215] "On a blank leaf I scrawled: 'In a hole in the ground there lived a hobbit'. I did not and do not know why." On the 'unexplained' inspiration of *The Hobbit* see esp. Carpenter 1977:230, Shippey 2005:65–70, Atherton 2012:1–2.

[105] Cf. *Letters* 17, to S. Unwin, 15/10/1937:29[24] "the world into which the hobbit **intruded**", *Letter to A. Ransom* (Hall and Kaislaniemi 2013:266) "the exact history of the world into which Mr Baggins **strayed**" (also ibid. on the epistemological of *The Hobbit*'s story "that is not the 'true tale' according to the history of the elves"). Cf. also a derogatory passage from a letter to G. E. Selby (*TCG* 84, published in *HDWM*), written only a few weeks after the publication of *The Hobbit*, in which Tolkien confesses that he doesn't much approve of *The Hobbit* himself, disparaging the "'rabble' of Eddaic-named dwarves [...], newfangled hobbits and gollums", preferring his own mythology with its consistent nomenclature.

[106] Cf. *Letters* 257:485[346] "*The Hobbit* **was not intended** to have anything to do with it"; *Letters* 31, to C. A. Furth, 24/07/1938:49[38] "the 'pure' fairy stories or mythologies of the *Silmarillion*, into which even Mr Baggins got **dragged against my original will**"; *Letters* 163:314[215] "*The Hobbit* was **originally quite unconnected**, though it inevitably got drawn in to the circumference of the greater construction; and **in the event modified it**". On the ways *The Hobbit* influenced Tolkien's *legendarium* see Rateliff 2014a, 2022; also Shippey 2000:1–3. On the history of composition of the text, and its subsequent revisions, Rateliff 2011 is fundamental.

Tolkien often stressed in his letters, the origin of the Hobbits and their following 'intrusion' into and 'modification' of his *legendarium* was unplanned. That is to say, Tolkien did not consciously invent the Hobbits, but the germ of *The Hobbit* story, suddenly and unexpectedly, was 'revealed' to him: it was a 'discovery', as unexpected as the discovery of a mysterious manuscript from a distant past (written by and about Hobbits).

The Hobbito-centrism of the meta-textual frame of *The Lord of the Rings* does not simply have narrative, thematic, and literary implications, but is thus connected to a fundamental experiential reality related to the writing of his stories: it is not Tolkien who decided to write about Hobbits, but it is, from his perspective, the Hobbits who were revealed to Tolkien as the object of his writing. As Tolkien put it in a letter: "I loved them [sc. Hobbits] myself, since I love the vulgar and simple as dearly as the noble. [...] I would build on the hobbits. And I saw that **I was meant to do it** (as Gandalf would say)" (*Letters* 180:337[232]).[107]

The passage alluded to by Tolkien is Gandalf's key dialogue with Frodo in chapter 1.2 of *The Lord of the Rings* (p.56), which, as will be shown in Chapter III, casts Frodo's whole mission as the response to a vocational call, ultimately of divine origin. Just as Frodo is 'chosen' and 'inspired' in *The Lord of the Rings*, so Tolkien was 'chosen' and 'inspired' to write about Hobbits: that is, Tolkien did not choose to be a writer of the Hobbits stories, but rather he discovered, in time, this

---

[107] Cf. also *TCG* 812 (to Maria Mroczkowska, 1969) in which Tolkien said that "he was born" to write his historic-myth.

particular and mysterious vocation. This also explains why Tolkien described his stories as 'given' to him, not the product of his inventiveness. As he put in a famous letter to Milton Waldman: "The mere stories were the thing. They arose in my mind **as 'given' things**, and as they came, separately, so too the links grew" (*Letters* 131:204[145]).

Tolkien's self-description as a 'discoverer' and 'compiler' of ancestral stories can thus be construed as an accurate, although 'secondary', expression of his experience as a writer of an 'unplanned', 'given' story, a story that he discovered rather than devised, and which eventually modified his *legendarium*. This is the first and main 'external' (or primary) function of the meta-textual frame: it expresses in secondary terms the actual origin of the works. Just as the fictional variant narrative of the finding of the Ring reflects real editorial variants, so the meta-textual notion of Tolkien's discovery of a Hobbits manuscript reflects the unplanned inspiration of his Hobbits stories.

II.2.2.2 Composition: The 'Self-Unfolding' of the Story

There are other 'real' features of Tolkien's writing history and practice that could be expressed through the meta-textual frame: the description of Bilbo's writing room in Rivendell, for instance, could equally describe the real Oxford study where Tolkien drafted his notes and books. Similarly, Bilbo's tendency to procrastinate in his writing and his obsession about the unfinished status of his diary is easily mirrored in real elements of

Tolkien's writing life.[108] Furthermore, the meta-textual frame, with Bilbo unable to go much beyond the drafting of the initial chapters of the 'new story', accurately reflects the actual chronology of *The Lord of the Rings*' composition, with Tolkien lingering over the first chapters of *The Fellowship of the Ring*.[109] However, the most important 'real' feature of the meta-textual frame is again related to the 'unexpectedness' of the stories, their 'unfolding' as unplanned, independent events.

That Tolkien considered his stories unplanned is true both at the level of the initial inspiration and at each stage of the writing process. Often Tolkien claimed, for instance, that "the story unfolded itself" (*Letters* 199:373[258]), with little help of sketches or synopses, and without "deliberately thinking out any episode" (ibid.), as we already saw in Chapter I (I.2.2.3). More specifically, Tolkien often declared that he did not have a (complete) knowledge

---

[108] Secondary entities are not always necessarily subsequent to their primary referents; there are cases in which meta-textual features seem to anticipate reality: for instance, Bilbo's handing over his unfinished notes to Frodo closely foreshadows the posthumous editorial history of the *Silmarillion*, compiled by his heir Christopher Tolkien (cf. Nagy 2022:99 "Christopher Tolkien inserted himself in the functional place of Bilbo, thus reinforcing the mythopoeic effect with the keystone that locks the whole into place. The 1977 *Silmarillion* does everything Bilbo's work is supposed to do, and ultimately in conception conforms to Tolkien's governing intention"). For an analysis of Christopher Tolkien's editorial work for the publication of *The Silmarillion*, and the nature and extent of his interventions on his father's manuscripts, see Kane 2009 and Ferré 2022.

[109] On the history of composition of *The Lord of the Rings* see Hammond and Scull 2005, Whittingham 2007, and in general *HME* volumes 6–9. For an overview of Tolkien's main 'discoveries' in the writing process see Scull 2006.

of characters and scenes before they were actually put in writing. Just like the general narrative idea, individual elements and characters were gradually 'discovered' rather than invented, and for this reason they are largely 'independent' for him and generate in him 'astonishment', including especially Faramir,[110] the Ents,[111] and several others.[112] As he explained in the same letter to Auden:

I had no conscious notion of what the Necromancer stood for [...] nor of his connexion with the Ring. [...] the essential Quest started at once. But I met a lot of things on the way that **astonished me.** [...] I had never been to Bree. Strider sitting in the corner at the inn was a shock, and **I had no more idea** who he was than had Frodo. [...] Fangorn Forest was an unforeseen adventure. [...] Saruman **had never been revealed to me**, and I was as mystified as Frodo at Gandalf's failure to appear on September 22. **I knew nothing** of the Palantiri though the moment the Orthanc-stone was cast from the window I recognized it, and knew the meaning of the 'rhyme of lore' that had been running in my mind. (*Letters* 163:315–16[215–17])

There is a specific image that Tolkien uses to express this experience of his narrative work as an organic, independent entity, 'unfolding' on its own. This is the image of

---

[110] Cf. *Letters* 66, to Christopher Tolkien, 6/05/1944:114[79] "A new character has come on the scene (I am sure I did not invent him, I did not even want him, though I like him, but there he came) [...]: Faramir, the brother of Boromir."

[111] Cf. *Letters* 247:470[334] "the Ents [...] only presented themselves to my sight, without premeditation or any previous conscious knowledge"; *Letters* 91, to Christopher Tolkien, 29/11/1944:147[104] "What happens to the Ents I don't yet know" (also *Letters* 163:310[211] with n.*, discussed at II.2.2.3).

[112] Cf. also *TCG* 464 (1961), in which Tolkien claimed that Tom Bombadil came into his mind independently.

the Tree, to which Tolkien often compared *The Lord of the Rings*, which was "growing out of hand" and "opening out in unexpected ways".[113] The image of the Tree was developed by Tolkien into the narrative of the short story *Leaf by Niggle*, a clearly meta-literary text that Tolkien allusively described as a "symbol of Tale-telling";[114] this can be considered as a symbolic manifesto of Tolkien's literary theory, and an expression of his experience while writing *The Lord of the Rings*, as will be demonstrated in detail in Chapter VI.

II.2.2.3 Writing as a 'Labour Pain': The 'Otherness' of the Story

An important implication of this conception of writing as discovery is Tolkien's paradoxical conviction that his own stories are in fact "written by someone else", "as if it were from a strange hand".[115] It should be clear by now

---

[113] Cf. *LotR Foreword*:352 "As the story grew it put down roots (into the past) and threw out unexpected branches"; *Letters* 64, to Christopher Tolkien, 30/04/1944:111[76] "'the Ring' [...] is growing and sprouting again [...] and **opening out in unexpected ways**"; *Letters* 91b, to Christopher Tolkien, 4/12/1944:148 "a germ of an idea is growing"; *Letters* 98, to S. Unwin, c. 18/03/1945:165[114], "a process of growth"; *Letters* 131:202[143] *Letters* 153 "the stuff has grown [...] growth and composition", and:284[189], "grown out of hand"; *Letters* 241:454[321] "[*The Lord of the Rings*] [...] was **growing out of hand**, and revealing endless new vistas"; *TCG* 231 (1956) "the story grew". Cf. VI.1.1.

[114] Cf. *Letters* 263, to the Houghton Mifflin Co., 10/09/1964:492[352]; cf. VI.1.4.

[115] *Letters* 211:398,400[278,280] "I read it now **as if it were from a strange hand**. [...] I have not named the colours [of the other Wizards] because I do not know them"; *Letters* 294, to C. and D. Plimmer, 8/02/1967:529[376] "passages that now move me most – written so long ago that I read them now as if they had been **written by someone else**". Also *Letters* 62, to Christopher Tolkien, April 1944:108[73] "this story takes me in charge".

that Tolkien's meta-textual self-representation as a decipherer and translator of someone's else story has thus a meaningful correlation with the way Tolkien perceived his real writing experience: in Tolkien's meta-textual frame, *The Lord of the Rings* and other works were *really* written by someone else.

Tolkien's conviction about the inherent otherness of his own stories also explains why he often declared a fundamental "ignorance" about many details of his narratives,[116] and also why he indulged in an apparently absurd self-exegesis of his own books, as we will see at length in the case-study discussed in Chapter V. This 'detached' attitude can be observed especially in the last years of his life, but can also be traced during the years when Tolkien was writing the book, which accordingly required "a lot of research".[117] In his letters, Tolkien develops his belief in the inherent 'otherness' of his own stories:

I had very little particular, conscious, intellectual, intention in mind at any point.* [*Take the Ents, for instance. I did not consciously invent them at all. The chapter called 'Treebeard' [...] was written off more or less as it stands, with an effect on my self (**except for labour pains**) almost like reading some one else's work. And I like Ents because they do not seem to have

---

[116] Cf. *Letters* 211:398[278] "I do not 'know' all the answers. Much of my own book puzzles me"; *Letters* 214:412[289] (quoted in n.62), *UT* 4.1:395 (quoted in Chapter III, n.37).

[117] *Letters* 59, to Christopher Tolkien, 5 April, 1944:102[70] "a lot of re-reading and research required [i.e. to finish *The Lord of the Rings*]". Cf. also *TCG* 116 (15/03/1942), to a young reader, in which Tolkien refers to narratives only alluded in the *Hobbit* as an obscure part of history that he had not yet "studied in detail", and *TCG* 688 (28/05/1965), where he claimed not to have certain knowledge about Merry's family and promised to "look into the matter".

anything to do with me. I daresay something had been going on in the 'unconscious' for some time, and that accounts for my feeling throughout, especially when stuck, that I was not inventing but reporting (imperfectly) and had at times to wait till '**what really happened**' came through.] (*Letters* 163:310[211] with n.*)

I have long ceased to invent [...] I wait till I seem to know **what really happened**. Or till it writes itself. [...] [I] wrote the 'Treebeard' chapter without any recollection of previous thought: just as it now is. (*Letters* 180:336[231])[118]

These passages condense all the points discussed earlier and integrates them into two poignant metaphors: for Tolkien, the experience of a writer is similar to that (1) of a woman in labour ("labour pains"), who is suffering in order to deliver a child, and (2) of someone trying to report imperfectly the truth about something that "really happened".[119]

II.2.2.4 Writing as Translation and Reporting: The Imperfectness and 'Partiality' of (Human) Stories

This second idea of writing as an imperfect report is crucial and introduces another important element of Tolkien's

---

[118] Cf. also Christopher Tolkien's comment on this letter, confirming on the basis of textual evidence that his father's claim "is fully borne out by the original text. [The chapter] 'Treebeard' did indeed very largely 'write itself'" (*TI* 22:411).

[119] In his commentary on the textual history of *The Lord of the Rings* Christopher Tolkien repeatedly refers to this formula ('what really happened') to describe the emergence, acceptance, or rejection of narrative elements; cf. for instance *TI* 10:200 "even before he had finished the initial draft of the chapter my father saw 'what really happened'", ibid. 20:390 "my father abandoned it, realising that the story as he was telling it was 'not what really happened'", ibid. 411; cf. VI.1.2.

writing experience, which is also expressed through the meta-textual frame. This is the inherent 'imperfection', 'approximateness', or 'incompleteness' of his writing.[120] As shown by the passages just quoted, Tolkien conceives his writing as originating in a true 'event', of which he only presents a 'report': Tolkien often points out in his letters that this report is 'imperfect' and incomplete, that he has a limited understanding "of the things revealed" to him,[121] and at times he explicitly connects this incompleteness with his pervasive meta-textual frames.[122] Similarly, on the linguistic side, Tolkien often remarks that the English language of his novels is an "approximate" and

[120] Brljak 2010 also highlights how the multi-layered nature of the metafiction contributes to the impression of a "distance between the narrative and its ultimate original", evoking in the reader an "unappeasable lack"; however, by doing so he associates the "radical mediation" of the metafiction with "an implacably anti-mimetic" stance, thereby positing a dichotomy between Tolkien's "promise of hyperrealism [...] verisimilitude and 'depth'" and the "premeditated and inevitable collapse" of the meta-textual structure. In contrast, I construe the sense of remoteness and incompleteness, which for Tolkien is inherent in any human artistic project, as the vertex of Tolkien's realistic project (epitomised in and bolstered by the meta-textual frame), rather than its deconstruction. For Tolkien's fascination with the fragmentary and incomplete cf. also Tolley 1993.

[121] *Letters* 187:357[248]. Also in letter *TCG* 209 (08/09/1955), Tolkien claims that he did not have any doubt about the events related to the final fate of the characters of *The Lord of the Rings*, but at the same time that he could not be sure that his "attempt to record them" had been successful; similarly, in letter *TCG* 815 (1906s), his assistant Joy Hill wrote that Tolkien did not have a clear knowledge of what happened to Frodo and the other characters after they crossed the sea.

[122] Cf. esp. *Letters* 115, to Katherine Farrer, 15/06/?1948:185[130] "The long tales out of which it [i.e. *The Silmarillion*] is drawn (by 'Pengolod' [i.e. the Elvish recorder who taught Ælfwine about the tales of the Elder Days]) are either incomplete or not up to date."

"not very accurate" rendering of the original (fictional) languages of his texts.[123]

This concept of 'approximation' could be related to Tolkien's philosophy of language, according to which modern languages of fallen men are no longer able to express the 'truth' of reality. For this reason, they are no longer beautiful, having lost the capacity to express with accuracy and precision the beauty of truth. I discussed this conception in I.2.1.2; here I will only stress how the meta-textual frame, which presents Tolkien as a compiler and translator, is perfectly coherent with his experience of writing as an incomplete and linguistically inaccurate report of events that remain inherently ineffable and mysterious.

Moreover, Tolkien's self-fashioning as an author with "limited understanding", using approximate language, echoes the description of the secondary authors of his *legendarium*, particularly Bilbo, whose narrative bias and imprecise language are often highlighted and are thematically significant (as discussed in II.2.1.2). One should also mention in this respect Tolkien's warnings on the inherent 'partiality' of any individual perspective embodied in his *legendarium*, whether specifically authorial or not, including that of particular characters or races. For instance, in a response to an objection to Treebeard's allegedly 'heterodox' remark on the making of Trolls and Orcs (cf. *LotR* 3.3:486), Tolkien stressed that Treebeard

---

[123] Cf. *Letter* 17, to S. Unwin, 15/10/1937:29[23] (on 'dwarf' and 'gnomes' being only translations of creatures with different names and functions); *Letters* 114, to H. Brogan, 7/04/1948:129 (on 'Elves' as a not accurate translation of 'Eldalië'); *Letters* 25:41[31] ('elf', 'gnome', 'goblin', and 'dwarf' as approximate translations).

was only a character in his story, and not himself, and that there was quite a lot "he does not know or understand" (*Letters* 153:285[190]).[124]

Limited understandings are accepted, cherished, and integrated into Tolkien's narrative framework (as iconically demonstrated by his enhancement of the Hobbits, arguably the characters with the most limited understanding of all). All perspectives remain limited (including his own), and for that reason they should never be taken as full reports of the actual 'events'.

II.2.2.5 Writing as Co-authoring: The 'Truth' of Human Stories and the Writer of the Story

But what kind of 'events' are we talking about? If for Tolkien writing is just an 'imperfect report' of what "really happened", what is the nature of this 'happening'? What happened? I will fully address these questions in Chapters IV and V, in which I discuss Tolkien's belief that all secondary creations have their own 'necessity' and 'reality' – they are all, as Tolkien says, episodes of History.[125] Here, I will only say, with a degree of simplification, that all these 'reported events' can be grouped together under

---

[124] Cf. also *MR Athr.*:337 in which the meta-textual frame is explicitly evoked ("The traditions here referred to have come down from the Eldar") to justify possible imprecisions and errors in the legends of the *Silmarillion* (especially of cosmogonic nature), and their discrepancy with human accounts.

[125] Tolkien himself asked these kinds of questions while reflecting on his own work: cf. in particular *Letters* 328:578–9[412], "that may explain to some extent why it [*The Lord of the Rings*] feels like 'history': it does not fully explain what has actually happened. [...] I feel as [...] if indeed the horns of Hope had been heard again, as Pippin heard them suddenly at the absolute nadir of the fortunes of the West. But How and Why?". See further IV.2.2.2.

one word: truth. For Tolkien, writing literature means to report (imperfectly) a true event, to *reflect* truth, as he says in a letter.[126] The idea of literature as a reflection of truth is at the core of Tolkien's meta-literary poem *Mythopoeia*, in which human sub-creation is described as a form of 'refracting' or 'splintering' a Single Light, a 'mirroring' of the likeness of a single Truth.[127] This image should also be related to Tolkien's self-description as a 'reporter', 'compiler', or 'translator' of a Story of which he was not the ultimate author.

In fact (and this is the ultimate meaning of the meta-textual frame), Tolkien never thought himself alone in his writing; he never considered himself as the only author of his stories. This belief is best epitomised in an anecdote, in which Tolkien reports his fortuitous encounter with an eccentric old fellow:

He had been much struck by the curious way in which many old pictures seemed to him to have been designed to illustrate *The Lord of the Rings* long before its time [...] Suddenly he said 'Of course you don't suppose, do you, that you wrote all that book yourself?' Pure Gandalf! [...] I think I said: 'No, I don't suppose so any longer'. An alarming conclusion [...]. But not one that should puff any one up who considers the imperfections of 'chosen instruments' and indeed what sometimes seems their lamentable unfitness for the purpose. (*Letters* 328:579[413])

---

[126] *Letters* 181:338[233], quoted in IV n.75.

[127] Cf. *Letters* 328:579[413], where Tolkien uses the imagery of Light in explicit reference to *LotR* "If sanctity inhabits his work [i.e. *The Lord of the Rings*, accordingly pervaded by a 'light from an invisible lamp'] or as a pervading light illumines it then it does not come from him but through him. And neither of you [readers] would perceive it in these terms unless it was with you also."

It is important to note that, for Tolkien, Gandalf is a divine entity and a sort of representation of divine grace "in mythological forms";[128] in this anecdote, it is thus as if God Himself, the source of Truth, were claiming co-authoriality of Tolkien's stories, reminding him of his purely instrumental role. This idea of instrumentality is important in Tolkien as a narrative theme,[129] and also illuminates his understanding of his literary vocation as a whole: as he wrote in 1916 to G. B. Smith (a close friend, one of the four members of the close-knit 'literary fellowship' TCBS, through which Tolkien discovered his literary ambition), he had sensed that he and his friends were meant for a particular kind of greatness, that is to say:

The greatness I meant was that of **a great instrument in God's hands** – a mover, a doer, even an achiever of great things, a beginner at the very least of large things. (*Letters* 5, to G. B. Smith, 12/08/1916:6[9])[130]

On a meta-literary level, Tolkien's self-perception as an 'instrument' implies the idea that the ultimate Author of Tolkien's stories is not Tolkien himself, but rather an Unnamed Person, "who is never absent and never named", as Tolkien puts it in a letter;[131] that is to say,

---

[128] This can be inferred in particular by a passage from *Letters* 109, to S. Unwin, 31/07/1947:174[120], clearly alluding to Gandalf's interaction with the hobbits: "there is no horror conceivable that such creatures [the Hobbits] cannot surmount, by **grace** (here appearing **in mythological forms**)".

[129] Cf. in particular Tolkien's description of Frodo's role as an 'instrument of divine providence', who was given 'grace', but only limited to what was sufficient for the accomplishment of his appointed task (*Letters* 246:461[326] with n.†).

[130] On this letter see further III.3.4. On the TCBS see I.1.5, n. 33.

[131] *Letters* 192:363[253], quoted in IV, n.103.

"the Writer of the Story". The 'otherness' of the stories, and the necessary imperfection of Tolkien's reports, are thus depending on their ultimate Divine (co-)Authorship. Tolkien's conviction that God is the ultimate source of his own stories, specifically of their 'otherness' and 'truth', can be traced throughout his fictional works. In the meta-literary short story *Leaf by Niggle*, for instance (on which I will focus closely in Chapter VI (VI.1.4)), it is not Niggle who gives life to his wonderful Tree – an image that (as we have seen) can be construed a 'symbol' of *The Lord of the Rings* itself: Niggle is only able to paint lifeless and disconnected leaves, with a longing for a vision that he can only imperfectly picture in his mind. The Divine powers that govern his world decide to bless and transfigure this desire, and create a wonderful, flourishing Tree out of it (cf. VI.2.1). The Tree thus has something divine in it, and yet it also has something of Niggle's individual artistic ambition. The birth of the Tree, and by analogy the birth of Tolkien's literary work, thereby originates in a mysterious interplay between human and divine forces.

This same mysterious interplay between sub-creator and Creator is at the centre of the *Ainulindalë*, the cosmogonic myth opening *The Silmarillion*, introduced in Chapter I (I.2.4). As will be demonstrated in detail in Chapters VI (VI.2.4) and VII, in Tolkien's vision, the Ainur's artistic freedom, and the contribution of their individual thoughts and desires, are fully cherished, enhanced and originally inspired by Eru, and eventually integrated into His Music: inspiration itself should be considered as a primeval pattern of creative collaboration. At the same time, Eru continues to participate in the Ainur's (sub)creation, by continuing to inspire and correct them, or by generously giving life and reality to their own (sub-)creations, as evident for instance in the case of Aulë's Dwarves;[132] above all, Eru is described as the ultimate source of the sub-creators themselves, and even of their own individual thoughts, which the Ainur are eventually called to recognise as originating from, and mysteriously contributing to His glory.[133] Indeed, within Tolkien's fiction, evil is always associated with the refusal to recognise the ultimate divine origin of an artistic (sub-)creation and the related attempt to create on one's own, which is what, for instance, Morgoth, Sauron, and Saruman try to do. Similarly, one of the main causes of the fall of the Noldor in *The Silmarillion* is the artificer Fëanor's prideful refusal to recognise the divine origin of the beauty of his fateful Silmarils (cf. V.1.7).

By contrast, Tolkien recognises his literary works, like Niggle's Tree or the Ainur's Music, to be 'other' and 'given'; they are the offspring of his artistic, sub-creative aspiration and the vitalising power of God, an offspring which Tolkien only "delivered" with "labour pains", which were revealed through him rather than by him.[134] Tolkien's stories are thus not only his own stories, just as a translation belongs to the translator but primarily to its original author. This is the reason why Tolkien

---

[132] See V.1.7, V.I.2.

[133] Cf. Saxton 2013a, esp. 167–8; 2013b: 51–3; see further VII.

[134] Cf. *Letters* 153:284[189] "parts seem (to me) rather revealed through me than by me"; also *Letters* 328:579[413] "through him" (quoted n.127). Cf. on this a passage from Michael G. Tolkien's St Andrews Lecture on his grandfather (available at www.michaeltolkien.com), noting that "all great writing transcends the writer himself; he writes as he does because of but also in spite of who he is".

considered literary creation as a "mystery": its occurrence and offspring cannot be fully explained, for Tolkien, in rational terms, as purely human activities autonomously performed by individual human beings.

II.2.3 Summing Up

In conclusion, the main functions of the meta-textual frame of *The Lord of the Rings* are related first of all to the realistic demands of Tolkien's secondary world, as construed especially as a collective mythopoetic corpus that is focalised through the particular perspective of the Hobbits – the missing link between the old tales of the *legendarium* and Tolkien's own post-heroic (and post-Christian) contemporary world. At the same time, the meta-textual frame also expresses, in secondary forms, some key aspects of Tolkien's 'primary' perception of his literary activity, and by reflection of his literary theory: the unplanned inspiration of his stories; their organic and independent development; and their inherent 'otherness' and 'truth', which ultimately derive from a Divine Authorship, and yet are necessarily mediated by a human co-author – the 'chosen instrument' who 'translates' and 'edits' these stories in imperfect, incomplete, and yet indispensable human language.

After discussing inspiration and aesthetic 'gratuitousness' in Chapter I, in this chapter I have thus introduced other central features of Tolkien's theory of sub-creation, which I will unfold in the following chapters: many questions remain unanswered. In particular, how exactly does Tolkien envisage the relationship between human author and divine Writer? How can artistic freedom be preserved if one posits an ultimate divine Authorship? How does the Divine Author participate and 'intrude' in human (sub-)creations? And, above all, why does the main, real Writer of the Story remain unnamed? Why did Tolkien eventually conceal his complex meta-textual frame, while leaving a large number of hints and traces? These are the main questions that I will explore in Chapter III.

III

The Lords of the West

Cloaking, Freedom, and the Hidden 'Divine' Narrative

~

In Chapter II, we introduced the 'hiding' or 'cloaking' of key themes and elements as an important and recurring feature of Tolkien's creative work. Such elements, despite their momentous relationship with the most pressing concerns of Tolkien's life and literary thought, are referred to only through allusions, hints, or glimpses (and especially so in his final texts). The relative concealment of the complex meta-textual frame underlying *The Lord of the Rings*, with its important meta-literary implications, is a typical example of such cloaking, but it is not the only one. The aim of this chapter is to explore Tolkien's pervasive 'poetics of cloaking' further, as well as its connection with his general views on the "mystery of literary creation". I will thus focus on what is arguably the most important of those 'hidings', namely the 'hiding' of 'God' in *The Lord of the Rings* and Tolkien's *legendarium* in general – "that one ever-present Person who is never absent and never named".[1] An important caveat: despite its 'divine' object, the aim and approach of this exploration are literary and not theological or philosophical in scope. As such, in this chapter I will principally

---

[1] *Letters* 192:363[253].

discuss the 'hiding of God' *within* Tolkien's secondary world; only subsequently will I explore the primary meta-literary implications relating to Tolkien's outlook on God as the ultimate Source of his narratives, that is, the primary "Writer of the Story" – an idea already introduced in Chapter II.

III.1 The Unnamed Authority in *The Lord of the Rings*

That 'God' has something to do with *The Lord of the Rings* is difficult to deny. Tolkien himself described *The Lord of the Rings* as having been "built on or out of certain 'religious' ideas",[2] focusing on a "conflict about God",[3] in sum as a "fundamentally religious and Catholic work".[4] And yet 'religion' is blatantly absent from the book: in *The Lord of the Rings*, there are apparently no references to cults, practices, or fully divine entities, praying or liturgy, temples or churches, priests or monks, and – above all – not a single overt mention of the name of God. This absence is an intentional authorial choice, as Tolkien often emphasised in his letters; in particular:

---

[2] *Letters* 211:404[283].
[3] *Letters* 183:350[243], in *LotR* "the conflict is [...] about God, and His sole right to divine honour".
[4] *Letters* 142:257[172]; cf. also *TCG* 341 (26/10/1958), in which Tolkien claims that the most powerful forces in *The Lord of the Rings* were the Christian religion and "on a lower plane" his linguistic interest; and *TCG* 711 (already mentioned in Chapter I, n. 79), in which Tolkien acknowledges that there is quite a lot of theology in *The Lord of the Rings*, but that this is perhaps made more "palatable by sugar coating"; also *Letters* 142:258, where Tolkien admits that he expects to get a large part of his support from Catholic circles.

I have not put in, or have cut out, practically all references to anything like 'religion', to cults or practices in the imaginary world. For the religious element is absorbed into the story and the symbolism. (*Letters* 142, to R. Murray, SJ, 2/12/1953:257[172])[5]

Following Tolkien's words, many readers and scholars have tried to 'distil' the religious element from the story and decode its Christian 'symbolism'. In doing so, they have often approached *The Lord of the Rings*, more or less intentionally, as a sort of religious allegory by focusing on the 'symbolic' meaning of events or characters or by reconstructing the moral or theological doctrine supposedly informing the narrative.[6] Many scholars have highlighted, for instance, the supposed Christ-type figure of characters such as Gandalf, Sam, Frodo, and Aragorn;[7] the Eucharistic symbolism of the Elvish way-bread

---

[5] Tolkien gives an analogous explanation of the absence of open religion in the short story *Smith of Wootton Major*, arguing that "in a story written by a religious man [...] religion is not absent but subsumed" (*SWM Ess.*:142). Tolkien commented on the apparent absence of God during his 1969 BBC documentary, noting that "as a matter of fact, there are references to God" (full transcript in Lee 2018:151) as well as in an unpublished letter to a reader (*TCG* 508, 21/10/1963). Cf. also Atherton 2012:139 on deletion of over-Christian references in the different stages of *The Hobbit*.

[6] Cf. Pearce 1998; Dickerson 2003; Wood 2003; Purtill 2003, 2006; Garbowski 2004; Rutledge 2004; Caldecott 2012; Dickerson 2012; Bernthal 2014; Pearce 2014; Mosley 2016; Kilby 2016 (esp. chapters 4 and 6, both reprints of old seminal articles). For analogous, but more theoretical investigations, cf. Hart and Khovacs 2007; Milbank 2009; Coutras 2016; Mosley 2016; McIntosh 2017; Halsall 2020. For a self-reflective overview of the fundamentals of such an approach see Dickerson 2007; for a criticism see for example Kerry 2011, esp. Introduction 17–56, Holmes 2011. On the thorny issue of Tolkien and (religious) allegory see IV.2.2.

[7] Cf. Kreeft 2005:221–6; Caldecott 2012:51–5, 59–62.

(*lembas*);[8] the chronological correspondences between the novel's timeframe and the liturgical year;[9] the Marian characterisation of Galadriel and Elbereth,[10] and so on.[11] More generally, a range of supposedly Christian 'values' or 'concepts' have been identified as figuratively embodied in the novel; these include friendship, self-sacrifice, redemption, mercy, metaphysical beliefs, and environmental concerns – to name a few. This approach is problematic and has rightly attracted the criticism of other scholars, especially those coming from a non-Christian background or those less inclined to read Tolkien as a catechism in disguise.[12] In any case, this is not the approach I

---

[8] Cf. Caldecott 2012:86.

[9] Cf. Shippey 2005:227–8; Caldecott 2012:81–3; Scarf 2013, esp. 164.

[10] Cf. already Fr Murray quoted by Tolkien in *Letters* 171–2; more recently Caldecott 2012:76–80; Kowalik 2013a.

[11] Cf. also Padley and Padley 2009 (on a number of "significant Christological loci"); Shoopman 2010 (identifying Christological figuration in every member of the Fellowship); Bernthal 2014:154, 239, etc.; Vassányi 2015; Pinsent 2022; Ordway 2023a, esp. 261–6, 290–3.

[12] Cf. Madsen 2003, 2011 (originally published in 1988); Hutton 2008 and 2011, arguing or assuming that Tolkien's secondary world does not (fully) conform to or express a Christian *Weltanschauung*, and in general that his literary work is not informed by, and not even compatible with his primary (Christian) beliefs, intentions, and statements. A different, more nuanced criticism comes from scholars such as Flieger (esp. 2014c, 2020) and Testi (2018) who consider inclusivity and paradox as the trademark of Tolkien's life and work, and perceive a blending or juxtaposition of opposite elements in his *legendarium* (pagan vs Christian, orthodox vs heterodox etc.) – an approach which can be traced back to Carpenter's influential description of Tolkien as "a man of antitheses" (Carpenter 1977:133). Cf. also the words of Fr Murray, a close acquaintance of Tolkien, from a recently published letter (West 2019:135) "Tolkien was a very complex and depressed man and my own opinion of his imaginative creation is that it projects his very depressed view of the universe at least as much as it reflects his Catholic faith". One of the aims of this

will take in this chapter (and in this book in general). My subject is neither the Christian God of Tolkien's 'primary reality', nor the theological or moral doctrines allegedly related to Him; instead, it is the 'God' within Tolkien's 'secondary plane', the 'God' of Middle-earth.

We know well that there is not just one divine entity in Middle-earth but several. A complex 'secondary' theology and cosmogony underpin Tolkien's imagined universe, which is openly and fully revealed in *The Silmarillion* and more so within related posthumous texts.[13] Although the cosmogonic origins of Tolkien's secondary world have already been introduced in the previous chapters, especially in the myth of the *Ainulindalë*,[14] a short overview is nonetheless necessary to pave the way for the following discussion.

According to Tolkien's 'secondary theology', a single, superior Being (Eru or Ilúvatar) created a number

book is to show that a *via media* is possible, and indeed necessary, which avoids both the idea of a 'schizophrenic' Tolkien (to a more or less degree), and the (even more un-Tolkienian) trap of apologetic or didactic allegoresis. This is the way opened by scholars such as Saxton (2013a, 2013b), who convincingly argues that (2013a: 170) "Middle-earth is [...] a remarkably dialogic space. But the presence of these diverse voices and dialects does not mean that they have equal weight. [...] Tolkien's word retains a privileged place throughout his mythology and, furthermore, that he places rhetorical approval behind those characters with whom he agrees". Cf. also Holmes 2011, who applies to Tolkien the ancient notion of *praeparatio evangelii*. I agree with his conclusions (141) that unless "the secularist misunderstanding of Christianity that Tolkien strove to correct in *Beowulf* criticism is [...] rooted out, no discussion of religion in his fiction will make much progress". Cf. also II.2.2.3, IV.2.2, IV.3.4, V.2.

[13] For an overview see Tolkien's own summary in *Letters* 131 and the extensive overview in McBride 2020; cf. also Flieger 2002:49–56, 2012; Caldecott 2014; Coutras 2016; Hammond and Scull 2017: *Reader's Guide* 1369–73; Pezzini 2021; Nagy 2022; Donovan 2022.

[14] Cf. I.2.4, II.2.2.5, and see Chapter VII for a full discussion.

of secondary divine powers (the Ainur, later Valar), with and through whom He subsequently brought into existence the World to which Middle-earth belongs (Arda). As explained in the *Ainulindalë*, the Valar eventually entered Arda together with a race of angelic assistants (the Maiar) and inhabited the Eden-like region of Valinor, situated in the Western side of the world; for this reason, they are normally known as the "Lords of the West". In Arda, the Valar "exercise delegated authority in their spheres" (*Letters* 131:206[146]), including dominion over water, earth, and wind in a fashion like the Greek gods.[15] From a narrative perspective, in *The Silmarillion* (and other works), the Valar are effectively characters: they speak, fight, deliberate, and interact with each other and the various anthropomorphic races inhabiting Arda.[16] The Valar interact especially with the Elves and Men, the special objects of the Valar's love and care because created by Eru alone, without the Valar's participation;[17] for this reason, Elves and Men are known as the 'Children of Ilúvatar'. Although Eru/Ilúvatar does not inhabit Arda (at least in the timeframe of the *legendarium*), He cares about it and, at times, intervenes in its

[15] Cf. *BLT1* 2:45, where the identity of the Valar is explicitly questioned ("are they the Gods?"). In early drafts of the *Silmarillion* (collected especially in *BLT1*) the Valar are normally referred to as 'gods'. See further Chapter VII. For a discussion of the nature the Valar (and their lower divine assistants, the Maiar), see Devaux 2003b.

[16] See Pezzini 2021 for an overview of the different patterns. The intervention of the Valar gradually becomes less open with the passing of time. In the Second Age for instance Manwë, although still a "vice-regent" of the creatures of Middle-earth, send messengers who intervene "in certain desperate events", "though in disguised form and issuing no commands" (*NME* 3.8:308).

[17] Cf. *Letters* 131:206[147] (on the Valar's special desire for the Children).

history, for instance, by causing the Atlantis-like catastrophe of Númenor that concludes *The Silmarillion*.[18] Eru/Ilúvatar and (secondarily) the Valar are also objects of religious veneration; most Elves know and are devoted to them, and many have lived together with them in Valinor following an ancestral summoning by the Valar themselves. Men, too, know about the existence of the Valar, although more vaguely and indirectly; some Men believe in and worship them, although few have seen them in person. The 'Elvenised' Númenórean Men in particular have a developed religious system dedicated to Eru and (secondarily) the Valar, which involves praying, temples, feasts, and sacrifices.[19] This is not the place to discuss all the implications of Tolkien's complex secondary theology and religion, but it is enough to show that in *The Silmarillion* 'the divine' is an important narrative presence, even (and perhaps especially) when it is rejected by anthropomorphic races. Indeed, the narrative core of the book, namely the quest for the ancestral jewels – the Silmarils – has itself a strong and explicit theological dimension: the Silmarils are creature-made artefacts, but their beauty derives from the divine light that they conserve; because of this, the Silmarils are catastrophic to all who try to possess them while forgetting or rejecting their divine origin.[20]

---

[18] In *NME* 1.6:39 where it is said that Eru, "independently of Manwë", sent messages and messengers to the first Men and Elves.

[19] Cf. for instance *UT* 2.1:165 (on the worship of Eru Ilúvatar on the sacred mount Meneltarma, where the Númenórean King went to pray on the occasion of three feasts dedicated to Eru).

[20] Cf.V.1.7. On the symbolism of the Silmarils see for example Caldecott 2012:110.

The Lord of the Rings is set in the same world as *The Silmarillion*, although a few millennia in the future and in a different geographical region; it also features several characters who originally appeared in *The Silmarillion*, including Sauron, Galadriel, and Elrond. The world is the same, and yet its 'religious' dimension, (explicitly) paraded in *The Silmarillion*, has almost completely been removed. Above all, in *The Lord of the Rings* there is no (open) interaction whatsoever between gods and humans – no 'theophanies' of any sort. If God and the gods are still alive, they have (apparently) ceased to care about Middle-earth, and vice versa. The qualifiers that I have used in brackets in the previous sentences are of course crucial, and I will dedicate the rest of the chapter to justifying their use and investigating their rationale in both the secondary and primary world, with the ultimate aim of shedding further light on Tolkien's complex views on "the mystery of literary creation" (and the nature of 'God').

III.1.1 Explicit References to 'Religion'

There are a small number of explicit references to 'religion' in *The Lord of the Rings*. The people of Gondor in particular, who descend from the Númenóreans, preserve vestiges of their ancient devotion to Eru and the Valar, although without full understanding.[21] During the battle

---

[21] A devotion that according to Tolkien should also be related to their refusal of idolatry (alluded to by Faramir at *LotR* 4.5:678 "the Nameless One was [never] [...] named in honour") – a "negative truth", signifying their 'absolute monotheism'; cf. *Letters* 156:303[206] "God (Eru) [...] had at the time of the War of the Ring no worship and no hallowed place. And that kind of **negative truth** was

against Eastern men, for instance, two Gondorian warriors openly invoke the Valar in battle with an apotropaic formula.[22] Moreover, Gondorians keep the practice of having a grace-like moment of silence before meals, with the head turned towards the West; that is, as Faramir explains to the "rustic and untutored" Frodo, "towards Númenor that was, and beyond to Elvenhome that is, and to that which is beyond Elvenhome and will ever be".[23] Finally, when Aragorn is enthroned as king, Gandalf appropriately associates his kingdom with that of the Valar.[24]

In addition to, and more consciously than the Gondorians, Elves also often invoke the protection of the Valar, and above all that of their Queen, named Varda or Elbereth.[25] One short hymn to Elbereth is recorded in *The Lord of the Rings*, in two versions,[26] as well as a song in which she is addressed nostalgically by

characteristic of the West [...] the refusal to worship any creature [...] They [the Gondorians] [...] preserved the vestige of thanksgiving. (Those under special Elvish influence might call on the angelic powers for help in immediate peril or fear of evil enemies)". Cf. also *Letters* 297:544[387] (on the memory of the One God Eru at the time of *The Lord of the Rings* events, in the (unspoken) prayer of those of Númenórean descent); *NME* 3.22:393–5 (on other instances of religious devotion in the history of Gondor, including Cirion's invocation of The One/God, possible because his people "were still permitted to address the One in thought and prayer direct").

[22] *LotR* 4.4:661 "May the Valar turn him aside".

[23] *LotR* 4.5:676; cf. also *Letters* 156:303[206] quoted in n.21.

[24] *LotR* 6.5:968 "may they [i.e. the days of King Aragorn/Elessar] be blessed while the thrones of the Valar endure!".

[25] Cf. *LotR* 1.3:85 "May Elbereth protect you!"; *LotR* 2.9:387 "'Elbereth Gilthoniel!' sighed Legolas as he looked up".

[26] *LotR* 1.3:79 "Snow-white! Snow-white! O Lady clear!" | [...] The starlight on the Western Seas"; *LotR* 6.9:1028 "A! Elbereth Gilthoniel!". See Shippey 2000:200–1 for a discussion.

Galadriel.[27] Galadriel's song is sung in Elvish and, crucially, is not immediately understood by Frodo but is
only interpreted by him "long afterwards" "as well as he
could".[28] The Hobbits' default unfamiliarity with 'religion' and 'religiosity', together with their gradual introduction to these throughout the course of the novel, is
an important feature of 'religion' in *The Lord of the Rings*.
In particular, Frodo and Sam gradually learn to cherish
the name of Elbereth and, in three key moments, successfully invoke her protection; in all cases, however, the
narrator emphasises a degree of unconsciousness in the
hobbits' act.[29]

Elbereth is the wife of the Jupiter-like deity Manwë,
the King of the Valar or 'Elder king', who is also mentioned once in *The Lord of the Rings* in another song sung
by Bilbo in Rivendell.[30] In *The Lord of the Rings* many of
the few references to the Valar or their land (Valinor, the
Blessed Realm, or the Uttermost West) are associated
with Elves or their songs and thus have an esoteric aura
to the hobbits.[31] To these references, one can add only

[27] *LotR* 2.8:377–8 "Ai! laurië lantar lassi súrine [...] Namárië!". On
Elbereth's characterisation cf. also Kowalik 2013a.

[28] *LotR* 2.8:377.

[29] *LotR* 1.11:195 "Frodo threw himself forward on the ground, and
he heard himself crying aloud: O Elbereth! Gilthoniel!"; *LotR*
4.10:730 (Sam's inspired Elvish hymn, quoted at I.2.4), *LotR* 6.1:914
"'Gilthoniel, A Elbereth!' Sam cried. For, **why he did not know**,
his thought sprang back suddenly to the Elves in the Shire." Cf. also
Letters 156:303[206] quoted in n.21, on those "under special Elvish
influence". See Shaeffer 2017 for a study of spiritual formation in
Tolkien's work.

[30] *LotR* 2.1:235 "the timeless halls where [...] endless reigns **the Elder
King** [...] on Mountain sheer".

[31] Cf. *LotR* 1.3:79 (the song of the Elves in the Shire, which shaped itself
in their thought "into words which they only partly understood");

a few other sparse examples,[32] including a simile comparing Théoden's ride to that of the Vala Oromë.[33] A few other cases are found in the appendix, mainly in connection with events recounted in *The Silmarillion*; a special case is a passing mention to Eru (the One), made by Arwen in her last dialogue with her husband Aragorn.[34] Interestingly, this mention occurs in an almost 'defiant' passage in which Arwen indirectly criticises Eru/Ilúvatar for demanding from Men a blind trust in accepting the bitter gift of death while He remains mute and distant. This is significant: all the explicit references to the divine in *The Lord of the Rings* belong to the human or elvish side of the relationship: Elves and Men may pray to the gods, but there is no explicit indication that the gods respond to them –that they are somehow 'active' in Middle-earth. God (or gods) remain silent.

These explicit 'religious' references are very few (fewer than twenty) and are scattered across *The Lord of the Rings*; given the size of the novel, they are like drops in the ocean, easily overlooked by the reader: and yet,

LotR 2.1:238 (Bilbo and Frodo's reaction to the Elbereth hymn and other songs of the Blessed Realm); *LotR* 6.6:974 (Queen Arwen singing a song of Valinor). On the 'mystic' power of poetry and poetic imagination in Tolkien see for example Caldecott 2012, esp. chapter 1; Eilmann 2011; Forest-Hill 2013. Cf. also Zimmerman 2013' insightful typology and analysis of poems in *LotR*, convincingly arguing that one of their main functions is to provide their audience with the momentary "glimmer of limitless extension in time" (cf. *Letters* 328:578[412]).

[32] *LotR* 2.1:238 "the stars of Elbereth"; *LotR* 2.2:245 "the Uttermost West".

[33] *LotR* 5.5:838 "he was borne up on Snowmane like a god of old, even as Oromë the Great in the battle of the Valar when the world was young".

[34] *LotR, Appendix A*:1063, cit. at V.1.5.

they are there, shining like 'glimpses' of a hidden light, to introduce a key Tolkienian analogy,[35] one that will be central in my following argument.

III.1.2 An Invisible Lamp: The Hidden 'Divine Narrative'

The light of the 'divine' (in a secondary sense) is much more present in *The Lord of the Rings*, however, than these sparse glimpses might suggest; nonetheless, it is a hidden and 'cloaked' presence. As an early reader put it, quoted with approval by Tolkien, in Middle-earth "some sort of faith seems to be everywhere without a visible source, like light from an invisible lamp".[36] I will now try to draw this lamp into the open, although not completely – not least because I believe that Tolkien would probably disapprove of the exercise.[37]

III.1.2.1 The Eagles of the Lords of the West

I will first focus on a passage that is perhaps the brightest glimpse of all, and, if correctly understood, the most explicit revelation of the hidden narrative running in the

---

[35] Cf. for instance *LotR Introduction*:xviii "This tale grew in the telling, until it [...] included **many glimpses** of the yet more ancient history that preceded it", *TOFS*:55=*TL*:41 "Fantasy, the making or **glimpsing** of Other-worlds" and the passages quoted in III.3.3 and III.3.4. See also IV.3.4, VI.1.5.

[36] Cited by Tolkien in *Letters* 328:578[413]. Cf. also Tolkien's response to this comment in the same letter (579[413]), quoted in Chapter II n.127.

[37] Cf. *UT* 4.1:395 "I do not (of course) know the truth of the matter [*i.e. about Gandalf's identity*], and if I did it would be a mistake to be more explicit than Gandalf".

background of *The Lord of the Rings* (what I will call 'the divine narrative'); at least to my knowledge, this reference has not been properly spotlighted.[38]

In the denouement of the story, after the Ring has been destroyed and Frodo and Sam have been rescued and celebrated in the Fields of Cormallen, the news of the unexpected victory has still to reach the city of Minas Tirith. But this is soon made up for:

> before the Sun had fallen [...] there came a great Eagle flying, and he bore tidings beyond hope from the Lords of the West: 'Sing now ye people of Minas Anor for the realm of Sauron is ended for ever and the Dark Tower is thrown down.' (*LotR* 6.5:963)

Who are the "Lords of the West", who send a winged messenger to announce "tidings beyond hope" to the city of men? Some readers have taken this epithet as referring to Aragorn and the other 'Captains of the West' who had victoriously led 'the host of the West' against Mordor. But this cannot be the case. As mentioned, the "Lords of the West" is the standard epithet in *The Silmarillion* of the Valar, and is attributable to no other being. In the Appendices to *The Lord of the Rings* and *Unfinished Tales*, it is explicitly stressed that appropriating that divine epithet (as done by the rebellious Númenórean king Ar-Adûnakhôr) is blasphemous.[39] The divine identity of the "Lords of the West" is further suggested by the standard association of the eagles with the Valar and especially with their king Manwë – from whose

---

[38] See however McBride 2020 chapter 4 for an extensive investigation of the Valar's hidden interventions in *LotR* (as well as *The Hobbit*).

[39] Cf. *LotR Appendix A*:1036 (only one of the Valar, and Manwë especially, can be named 'Lord of the West'); *UT* 1.2:222.

halls "hawks and eagles flew ever to and from".⁴⁰ In *The Silmarillion*, eagles are indeed described as divine entities, dispatched by Manwë to Middle-earth to act as emissaries of his pity, to guard,⁴¹ protect,⁴² and, in some cases, to rescue physically the beloved Elves or Men.⁴³ Although their divine identity is never revealed, eagles are also active in *The Hobbit* and *The Lord of the Rings* where they are characterised as bringers of hope in the most desperate circumstances: eagles rescue Bilbo and his companions from the fire of the Orcs in *The Hobbit* and later intervene to help secure the victory in the Battle of the Five Armies; an eagle rescues Gandalf twice in *The Lord of the Rings*, once from the prison of Isengard and later from the top of the mountains above Moria; above all, it is only thanks to the eagles that Sam and Frodo are rescued from the destruction of Mordor, just when the two hobbits are "stricken down by despair at last" (*LotR* 6.4:951).

In Tolkien's world, eagles are rescuers, sent by the Valar out of their love for Elves and Men (and Hobbits) to bring hope when all hope is lost.⁴⁴ There can be little

⁴⁰ *Sil* 1:40. Also *Sil* 13:110 (Manwë commanding eagles to keep watch upon Morgoth out of pity for the exiled Elves); *Sil Ak.*:277 (the Númenóreans frightened by the coming of the eagles of Manwë), *NME* 3.13:338 (eagles in Númenor). See further Caldecott 2012:44–5.
⁴¹ Cf. *UT* 2.1:166 (the Eagles as the 'Witnesses of Manwë, keeping watch upon Númenor).
⁴² For instance, the hidden city of Gondolin was preserved safe for many years only thanks to the eagles' surveillance of its borders.
⁴³ Cf. *Sil* 13:158 (Thorondor, King of Eagles preventing Fingon from killing Maedhros and later assisting him to rescue his friend, prisoner of Morgoth); *Sil* 18:110 (Thorondor sending two of his eagles to the aid of Huor and Húrin); *Sil* 23:243 (eagles assailing Orcs and driving them away, to protect the escape from the fallen Gondolin).
⁴⁴ Eagles have an important connection with one of the key notions of Tolkien's literary theory (and theology): eucatastrophe (see IV.3.4).

doubt, therefore, that the "Lords of the West" sending messengers of "tidings beyond hope" are the same Valar of *The Silmarillion*,[45] hidden presences who are also active in *The Lord of the Rings*, despite how things might appear to the inhabitants of Middle-earth, confounded by the lies of the Enemy.[46]

III.1.2.2 Dreams and Inspiration

The Valar (and Eru) still care for Middle-earth in the Third Age, and their activity in *The Lord of the Rings* is an important secret of the novel betokening the underlying 'divine narrative'.[47] This activity goes well beyond dispatching messengers. Another important way in which the Valar interact with the characters is through dreams. As we have already seen in Chapter I (I.2.4 and n.95), in *The Silmarillion* the Valar explicitly guide the history of Elves and Men by sending dreams with momentous implications. *The Lord of the Rings* similarly features several dreams, no less significant from a narrative perspective; these dreams have most likely the same divine

---

[45] The divine origin of eagles is also confirmed by nature of the song, which, as Shippey (2005:226–7) notes, is heavily based on Psalmic diction (cf. IV.2.2.1).

[46] Cf. *UT* 2.4:250 (Gandalf/Olórin reassuring a despondent Galadriel that the Valar are still giving thought to the people of Middle-earth, and that their hearts are not hardened); also *NME* 1.13:95 describing the notion that the Valar have abandoned Middle-earth as an ancient heresy. A more radical version of this heresy is maliciously promoted by Sauron, who denies the existence of Eru as a mere invention of the Valar (cf. *Letters* 131:216[155]).

[47] See for example Rutledge 2004 for a reconstruction of elements of a 'divine narrative' in *The Lord of the Rings*, although from a theological, rather than literary perspective; cf. also Garbowski 2004 and McBride 2020.

origin, although this is only declared allusively. The most important case is the dream sent to Faramir and Boromir, to summon them to Rivendell. This is how Boromir recalls the key dream during the Council of Elrond:

For on the eve of the sudden assault a dream came to my brother in a troubled sleep; [...] but in the West a pale light lingered, and out of it I heard a voice. (*LotR* 6.4:952)

Given the association between the Valar and the West, there is little doubt about the identity of the "pale light" in the West.[48] The same divine origin is alluded to in the important dreams of Frodo, as discussed (cf. I.2.5.1).

Moreover, the Valar also participate in the narratives of *The Lord of the Rings* through a pattern analogous to dreams, namely through what one might call 'inspiration'. If in *The Silmarillion* this form of intervention is explicitly attributed to the Valar, as we have seen,[49] in *The Lord of the Rings* this attribution is hidden and yet hinted at. There are several passages that could be quoted to illustrate this, but I will focus on two in particular:

At last with an effort he spoke, and wondered to hear his own words, as if some other will was using his small voice. 'I will take the Ring,' he said, 'though I do not know the way'. (*LotR* 2.2:270)

And then softly, to his own surprise, there at the vain end of his long journey and his grief, moved by what thought in his heart he could not tell, Sam began to sing. (*LotR* 6.1:908)[50]

---

[48] Cf. also *LotR* 2.8:368 (Aragorn's belief that the message of the dreams was a summons for him to go to Gondor).

[49] See I.2.4 and cf. also *Sil* 23:238–9 mentioned in I.2.5.1, n.114.

[50] Cf. also *LotR* 2.5:324 "Suddenly, and to his own surprise, Frodo felt a hot wrath blaze up in his heart"; 6.4:634 "Something warned him [Sam who has overheard Gollum's internal debate] to be careful"; *LotR*

The first passage is about Frodo's momentous decision to take the Ring at the end of the Council of Elrond, which Tolkien describes as a free individual choice, and yet involving the participation of "some other will", to the hobbit's own wonder. That this is the will of the Valar is suggested by Elrond's reaction to Frodo's words ("I think that this task is appointed for you, Frodo"), which evokes an important idea of the novel: that Frodo has been 'chosen' by the Valar (or perhaps Eru Himself) as the Ring-bearer (see III.1.2.5).[51] The second passage is from one of the most desperate moments of the story, when the hobbit Sam is locked out of the floor where Frodo is trapped in the dreadful tower of Cirith Ungol. Sam's act, which is 'surprising' to himself, will lead to a positive outcome: Frodo's rescue. That the Valar are behind Sam's 'musical inspiration' is suggested by the content of the song: a hymn about the permanence of Valinor and the divine light of the Silmarils.[52] Dreaming and inspiration are important forms of divine intervention in Tolkien's world,[53] and arguably have an ancestry in Greek and

6.1:902 "Then greatly daring [...] answering a sudden thought that came to him"; 908 "suddenly new strength rose in him"; *LotR* 6.3:942 "Suddenly a sense of urgency which he did not understand came to Sam"; and the passages quoted in n.29.

[51] Cf. also Tolkien's words in *Letters* 246, n.†:461[326]: "Frodo was given 'grace' to answer the call (at the end of the Council) after long resisting a complete surrender".

[52] Cf. Forest-Hill 2013, esp. 91, noting the spiritual significance of Sam's poetic interventions, and Zimmerman's (2013) insightful analysis of his "song of defiance" in particular. For similar moments of poetic or linguistic inspiration cf. *LotR* 1.7:124 (Frodo "overcome with surprise to hear himself" addressing Goldberry in verse).

[53] Tolkien offers further insights on the divine origin of dreams and inspirations in his secondary world in three posthumous texts now

Roman epic poems;[54] and yet the Valar's intervention in *The Lord of the Rings* does not consist only of sending messages or inspiring brave deeds.

III.1.2.3 The (West) Wind

The Valar also intervene through the natural powers of their competence.[55] As a case-study, I will here focus on wind, which is the element under the power of the "Elder King" of the Valar, Manwë. In *The Lord of the Rings*, the wind, often qualified as the Wind of the West, normally blows in concomitance with positive turns in the story. For instance, it is thanks to a "West Wind" that the hobbits survive their first encounter with the Black riders;[56] and it is the same West Wind that blows away the dark

published in *NME* (2.7 *Mind-Pictures*, 2.8 *Knowledge and Memory*, 2.10 *Notes on Órë*). Cf. esp. *NME* 2.8:199,201 (on dreams as the form in which Men and Elves receive visions from other minds, including "at the highest by 'inspiration' from Eru"), 2.10:221 ("on messages or influences on the mind – from other minds including the greater minds of the Valar and so indirectly from Eru"). Tolkien adds that this latter form of inspiration is normally denoted with the use of the phrase "my heart tells me", which appropriately in *LotR* 1.2:59 is used by Gandalf to refer to his momentous prevision that Gollum will have some important role play in the story (on which see n.83); cf. also *LotR* 2.2:251 "my heart misgave me"). Cf. also a note reported in *NME* 2.13:239 giving a physical explanation of inspiration, as triggered by the blowing of the wind of Manwë ("the spirit of Manwë blew forth and the hearts of the Eldar obeyed").

54 See Pezzini 2021:91–2.
55 Water (under the control of the Vala Ulmo) in particular plays an important role in Tolkien's universe, as a means to evoke in the Elves the desire for the Valar; cf. *Sil Ain.*:19 quoted in Chapter I n.115, *NME* 1.8:62 (on the Elves' love for water). On water in Tolkien see Dickerson 2011, Eilmann 2011, and Auer 2019.
56 *LotR* 1.3:71 "The wind's in the West"; 77 "The West wind was sighing in the branches. [...] the feeling of disquiet left them".

storm of Mordor, carries Aragorn's sails to the victory of Pelennor,[57] and later accompanies the march of the host of the West towards the gate of Mordor, clearing its foul air.[58] Conversely, it is a "great wind" that annihilates the crumbling power of Sauron,[59] and later carries away the spirit of Saruman after his death.[60]

All this wind-blowing should not be construed symbolically, but narratively: as revealed in *The Silmarillion*, the Vala Manwë is physically in control of the winds that blow over Middle-earth.[61] When the wind blows in *The Lord of the Rings*, and especially from the West, there is little doubt about its divine origin. This is further confirmed by the metaphorical association of the West Wind with the most important representative of the Valar's (hidden) power in Middle-earth: the wizard Gandalf, who is compared by Éomer and Théoden to "the breath of the West

---

[57] Cf. *LotR* 5.6:846 "a great wind blowing […] and the sun shining"; *LotR* 5.6:846 "black against the glittering stream they beheld a fleet borne up on the wind"; 847 "the wind that sped the ships blew all their clamour away".

[58] *LotR* 6.2:923 "The wind of the world blew now from the West, and the great clouds were lifted high"; 927 "A strong wind from the West was now driving the fumes of Mordor from the upper airs"; *LotR* 6.3:933 "in the high regions the West Wind still blew". Cf. also Aragorn's allusive song, wishing for a return of a blessed kingdom: *LotR* 3.2:423 "Shall Men behold the Silver Tree, | Or West Wind blow again between the Mountains and the Sea?".

[59] *LotR* 6.4:949, cf. V.1.8.   [60] *LotR* 6.8:1020, cf. V.1.8 with n.48.

[61] Cf. *Sil Ain.*:19 (Manwë pondering on airs and winds); *Sil Val.*:26 (Manwë's delight in all types of winds); *Sil* 1:36 "he heard the voice of Manwë as a mighty wind"; *Sil* 9:154 "the winds of Manwë had driven away the vapours of death"; *Sil* 18:154 (the wings of the eagle Thorondor as the winds of Manwë). Also *NME* 2.13:236 (on wind as emission of Manwë's power) and ibid. 239, quoted in n.52 (on wind-blowing and divine inspiration).

Wind", which has taken a visible form, and to "a west wind" that has "shaken the boughs" of Théoden's despondency.[62] Indeed, Gandalf himself is a (hidden) divine entity. A member of the Valar's people (the Maiar) and a sort of "incarnate angel" in Tolkien's definition,[63] Gandalf was sent at the Valar's orders from Valinor to Middle-earth and tasked with rekindling hope and bravery, leading the victory over Sauron, and, ultimately, communicating (although covertly) "the 'glad tidings' that the power of Ilúvatar is there and it endures", as well put by Nagy.[64]

III.1.2.4 Gandalf the Emissary

Gandalf's divine identity and his 'intermediary' mission are revealed openly in the posthumous *Unfinished Tales* through a number of incomplete narratives.[65] These narratives differ slightly from each other, as they provide different details, yet they all agree in presenting a 'hidden' narrative (the 'divine narrative'). According to this narrative, the "Valar under the One" (*UT* 4.1:391)[66] and Manwë in particular (who seemed remote but in fact was never "a mere observer"), had "designed" the victory against Sauron (i.e. the plot of *The Lord of the Rings*). This victory bore their design to

---

[62] *LotR* 3.6:524 and *LotR* 3.7:527.

[63] *Letters* 156:298[202] "I would venture to say that he [Gandalf] was an *incarnate* 'angel' – strictly an *aggelos*" (original italics). Cf. also *TI* 23:422 "Wizards=Angels".

[64] Nagy 2019:167.

[65] *UT* 4.1:389–90. Cf. also *NME* 2.6:192 on Gandalf's frail body as a "cloak for his power, wisdom, and compassion".

[66] On the Valar as intermediaries of Eru cf. also *UT* 2.2:184 "Such gifts […] come from the Valar, and through them from the One". On the Valar as sub-creators see further Chapter VII, and cf. Rosebury 2003:189; McIntosh 2017, esp. chapter 4 and *passim*; McBride 2020 esp. chapters 1–2; Pezzini and Spirito 2023.

fulfilment through their "emissaries" in Middle-earth, who include, above all, Gandalf, who "never turned aside from his appointed mission" (cf. *NME* 2.6:193) and "proved to be the director and coordinator both of attack and defence" (*UT* 4.1:395).[67] Crucially, these emissaries "were forbidden [...] to seek to rule the wills of Men or Elves by open display of power, but coming in shapes weak and humble were bidden to advise and persuade Men and Elves to good" (ibid. 389). With his joy, swift wrath, and "fire that kindles and succours in wanhope", Gandalf, in particular, was "veiled in garments grey as ash, so that only those that knew him well glimpsed the flame that was within" (ibid. 391). In the same way that the power of Gandalf is purposefully hidden, so too his role in the divine narrative is never revealed in open terms in *The Lord of the Rings*; and yet there are often allusions to this hidden role, such as in Gandalf's self-descriptions as a "servant of the Secret Fire", to the Balrog in Moria (*LotR* 2.5:330), and as "a steward", to the despondent and overbearing Denethor (*LotR* 5.1:758); and in his revelation of the name (Olórin) he had "in his youth in the West that is forgotten" (*LotR* 4.5:670). The elusiveness of these references is often explicitly remarked upon, especially through the insistence that Gandalf's "greater power" was "veiled" and "hidden under his grey mantle".[68]

---

[67] Cf. also *Letters* 156:304[207] "The *Istari* [...] are actually emissaries from the True West [i.e. Valinor, the land of the Valar] and so mediately from God, sent precisely to strengthen the resistance of the good".

[68] Cf. *LotR* 3.5:492 "a hidden power"; 4.5:501 "[Gandalf] shining now as if with some light kindled within"; *LotR* 5.1:757 "Gandalf had the **greater power** and the deeper wisdom, and a majesty that was **veiled**"; *LotR* 5.7,852 "Gandalf revealed the strength that lay hid in him, even as the light of his power was **hidden under his**

Gandalf's (divine) identity is also hidden to most characters and especially to the hobbits, who wonder: "What was Gandalf? In what far time and place did he come into the world, and when would he leave it?" (*LotR* 5.1:757). Elusiveness and allusiveness themselves are also important traits of Gandalf's characterisation: his speech and behaviour are full of riddles, hints, and omissions, often forcefully stressed,[69] and are perceived as such by characters, who describe Gandalf as 'close'.[70]

III.1.2.5 Chance, Fortune, and Fate

Gandalf's speech is allusive and elusive not just as regards his own identity, but also as regards his interpretation of the events unfolding in the narrative; his (divine) eyes recognise the events of Middle-earth as belonging to and being guided by the 'divine narrative' designed by his Masters. A recurring formula in this respect is Gandalf's allusive qualification of the notions of 'chance' or 'fortune'. Consider, for example, the following passages:

[Gandalf to Pippin after the Palantír episode] You have been saved, and all your friends too, mainly by good fortune, **as it is called**. (*LotR* 3.11:594)

grey mantle". Also *TI* 23:422 "[Gandalf] does not as a rule reveal himself"; *LotR* 1.1:34 (Gandalf's threat to Bilbo that he will see him "uncloaked"). Only at times Gandalf's power is (partially) "unveiled": cf. *LotR* 5.4:820 "Shadowfax bore him, shining, unveiled once more".

[69] Cf. *LotR* 1.2:56, original italics "But I am not going to give an account of all my doings to *you*"; *LotR* 3.5:502–3 "I wandered far on roads that I will not tell."

[70] Cf. also *LotR* 3.5:501 "I would not tell you all"; *LotR* 3.11:590 "Gandalf [...] [is] **closer** than ever"; *LotR* 4.5:671 "Mithrandir never [...] reveal his purpose"; *UT* 3.3:336 "'I do not really suppose that even now you are telling us all you know.' 'Of course not,' said Gandalf."

So it was 'by chance' **as Men call it (as Gandalf would have said)** that Peregrin, fumbling with the Stone, must have set it on the ground more or less 'upright'. (*UT* 3.3:326)

[Gandalf describing his momentous encounter with Thorin in the background of the Hobbit] A chance-meeting, **as we say** in Middle-earth. (ibid.)[71]

Gandalf often relates a positive turn of action in the narrative to 'chance' or 'fortune'; and yet he normally qualifies such relations with a remark such as "as it is called", or something similar. This kind of qualification can be construed as an allusive reference to the hidden 'divine narrative' described earlier: a divine entity such as Gandalf knows well that 'chance' and 'luck' are imprecise human words,[72] which are used by the unaware to refer to what is actually the providential plan of Eru and the Valar.[73] This is to say that Gandalf knows there are

[71] See further Tolkien's 'theological' exegesis of this passage at *NME* 2.11:229. Cf. also *LotR* 2.1:222 [Gandalf on Frodo's survival from the attack of the Black Knights] **"fortune or fate** have helped you"; 2.2:250 [Gandalf on the coincidence that the Ring was found by Bilbo in the same year as the White Council drove Sauron away from Mirkwood] "a **strange chance,** if chance it was; also, the use of inverted commas at *UT* 3.3:322 [Gandalf on the events of *The Hobbit*] "It was a strange business. I did no more than follow the lead of **'chance'** and made many mistakes on the way."

[72] On the imperfections or corruptions of language, and on Tolkien's philosophy of language in general see I.2.1.2; also Flieger 2002, esp. 33–44, 67–72.

[73] The word providence is never used in *The Lord of the Rings*, nor in *The Silmarillion*, or in other texts of the *legendarium* (such as *BLT1*, *BLT2*, *LB*, *SME* etc.), as expected for narratives set in a pre-Christian world, and written by non-Christian authors; in contrast, 'fate' and 'chance' are frequently found (56 and 12 tokens in *The Silmarillion*, about 40 and 120 occurrences in *LotR* respectively – a specular distribution that can be construed as reflecting the different register and imagined

hidden "powers at work" in Middle-earth, although he never openly reveals their identity. In particular, the finding of the Ring, which is (outwardly) described by human characters as a 'lucky' event,[74] is, instead, described by Gandalf to Frodo as the work of "something else":

It was the strangest event in the whole history of the Ring so far. [...] Behind that there was something else at work, beyond any design of the Ring-maker. I can put it no plainer than by saying that Bilbo was meant to find the Ring, and not by its maker. In which case you also were meant to have it. And that may be an encouraging thought. (*LotR* 1.2:56)

What, or, rather, who is this "something else at work", which chose Bilbo as the Ring-finder? This very question is put to Gandalf by his friends during the dialogue they have in Minas Tirith after the victory against Sauron, reported in *Unfinished Tales*. His answer, which explicitly

authorship of the two works (cf. II.2.1.2), with the higher term 'fate' more fitting to the language (and philosophy) of Elves, and the lower 'chance' to that of hobbits). It is thus incorrect to equate (Christian) providence and (Pre-Christian) fate/chance (as often done by apologetic scholars, such as e.g. Barrs 2013). At the same time, it would be also imprecise or at least misleading to oppose the two, as if they were denoting different referents. To put it in a nutshell, using linguistic terminology: Gandalf's linguistic approach to the notion of 'chance' implies that what is different for Tolkien is not the signified, but rather the signifier (a difference that is to be embraced and 'elevated', rather than patronised or belittled). This explains the need to accommodate a different degree of semantic precision and understanding in their different users, and ultimately may justify the whole enterprise of writing pre-Christian literature, and engaging with a non-Christian audience in general (cf. on this the sensible considerations of Holmes 2011, building on an analysis of Denethor's use of the anachronistic word *heathen*). Cf. also II.2.1.2 (on the use of the word 'luck').

[74] Cf. II.2.1.2.

cross-references the passage quoted here, is, of course, highly elusive:

> Gandalf did not answer at once. He stood up, and looked out of the window, west, seawards; […] 'In that far distant time I said to a small and frightened hobbit: Bilbo was meant to find the Ring, and not by its maker, and you therefore were meant to bear it. And I might have added: and I was meant to guide you both to those points. […] But what I knew in my heart, or knew before I stepped on these grey shores: that is another matter. Olórin I was in the West that is forgotten, and only to those who are there shall I speak more openly.' (*UT* 3.3:329)

Gandalf's answer remains unclear, but his act of looking "west, seawards" (i.e. to the Land of the Valar, who sent Him as their secret agent) is indicative enough, just as are his final words, referring to the "West that is forgotten", that is to say, the land of Valinor, from which he originally came, and whither he will return at the end of the story.

III.1.2.6 Narrative and Election

As the passage quoted here (*LotR* 1.2:56) reveals ("you also were meant to have it"), another key implication of the 'divine narrative' of which Gandalf is aware is that of 'election' or 'vocation'. Eru and the Valar are 'plotting' to overrule Sauron, but this involves the participation of human and elvish characters, who are called to identify and adhere to this plot. Gandalf is the perfect embodiment of this elective attitude towards the unfolding of the story, which is also revealed in his capacity to wonder at the 'strange' turns of the unfolding narrative as well as at the way apparent misfortunes are mysteriously transformed into positive events. These include his imprisonment by

Saruman and the resulting delay at the beginning of the story, which yet "might have been better so";[75] Pippin's incident with the Palantir, which eventually proved to be "strangely fortunate", as it saved Gandalf from the grave blunder of trying this perilous object himself;[76] and, above all, Merry and Pippin's kidnapping by the Orcs and the related betrayal of Saruman, which 'strangely' brought them to Fangorn "in the nick of time", where they played an important part in rousing the Ents to battle.[77]

These kinds of remarks are rooted in Gandalf's implicit awareness of the presence of a hidden providential narrative – one woven by "something else" and which he tries to acknowledge and interpret, so that he can facilitate and adhere to it. Thus, Gandalf has an almost meta-literary elective attitude to the story, with which he strives to familiarise the Hobbits:

'Why did it come to me? Why was I chosen?' 'Such questions cannot be answered,' said Gandalf. 'You may be sure that it was not for any merit that others do not possess: not for power or wisdom, at any rate. But you have been chosen, and you must therefore use such strength and heart and wits as you have.' (*LotR* 1.2:61)

Gandalf is not the only character who is aware of the 'divine narrative' hidden behind the events of *The Lord of the Rings*. The most enlightened characters of the story are

---

[75] Cf. *LotR*, 2.1:220.   [76] Cf. *LotR* 2.11:595.

[77] *LotR* 3.5:497; cf. also *LotR* 3.8:543 ("Better than my design") and 3.5:496, where Gandalf comments on Merry and Pippin's contribution to Boromir's redemption and on the 'other part' they still have to play, indirectly recalling his own foreboding regarding the importance of having them in the Fellowship (cf. *LotR* 2.3:276).

also aware of the importance of fate and, consequently, of adhering to their own 'vocation' in relation to that fate. These include 'high' characters such as Elrond,[78] Galadriel,[79] the 'Númenórean' Aragorn,[80] Faramir,[81] and others;[82] but also, eventually, the hobbits, who learn to interpret events as hints of a deeper, hidden narrative.[83] Even the narrator, at times, evokes the idea of a providential plan.[84] The more characters are aware of the activity of the Valar (under the One) within the story, the more they are aware of their life as a 'mission' or 'vocation', as seen in the case of Frodo going to Mordor ("I am commanded

---

[78] *LotR* 2.2:242 "That is the purpose for which **you are called hither.** Called, I say, [...] by chance as it may seem. Yet it is not so. Believe rather that **it is so ordered** that we [...] must now find counsel for the peril of the world".

[79] Cf. *LotR* 2.8:368 "Maybe the paths that you each shall tread are already laid before your feet, though you do not see them".

[80] Cf. *LotR* 2.9:390 (Aragorn going to Amon Hen in search for some sign to guide him), *LotR* 2.10:404 (Aragorn acknowledging that it is not his part to drive Frodo one way or the other, because "There are other powers at work far stronger").

[81] Cf. *LotR* 4.5:681 "If you seem to have stumbled, think that it was fated to be so".

[82] Cf. the words to the hobbits of the elf Gildor and Tom Bombadil respectively: *LotR* 1.3:84 "In this meeting there may be more than chance" and *LotR* 1.7:126 [Tom Bombadil speaking] "Just chance brought me then, if chance you call it".

[83] Cf. *LotR* 2.10:406 "I cannot tell you how glad. [...] It is plain that **we were meant** to go together". Also Gollum notes how "lucky" has been for the hobbits to have found him (*LotR* 4.1:619) – an allusive, and yet appropriate comment, both because the hobbits would never have been able to reach Mordor without him, and also more generally because their meeting was somehow fated, as perceived by Gandalf (*LotR* 5.4:815) and acknowledged by Frodo (*LotR* 4.3:640; 4.6:686).

[84] Cf. *LotR* 3.3:457 "It [i.e. the arrow killing the Orc Grishnákh and saving Merry and Pippin] was aimed with skill, or **guided by fate,** and it pierced his right hand." On this passage and its classical ancestry see Pezzini 2021:97–8.

to go"),[85] or Aragorn travelling the paths of the dead.[86] In particular, I can refer to Sam's interior dialogue with himself at a crucial moment of the story:

> But you haven't put yourself forward; you've been put forward. And as for not being the right and proper person, why, Mr. Frodo wasn't, as you might say, nor Mr. Bilbo. They didn't choose themselves. (*LotR* 4.10:732)

Again, this passage and other similar ones should be interpreted narratively – not symbolically or allegorically as if they were directly alluding to Christian Providence; in other words, they rather refer (almost meta-narratively) to the characters' growing awareness of the existence of an underlying narrative designed by a hidden, divine Author, to which the hobbits have been gradually introduced through their acquaintance with Gandalf. And yet all these references to the 'divine narrative' remain only allusive and elusive. Even the event that most patently betrays a divine intervention, Gandalf's 'resurrection' after his fall at Moria, remains unexplained in *The Lord of the Rings* (as will become clear in Chapter V). To be sure, the existence of this complex web of hidden narratives is fascinating per se from a literary point of view; yet an important question remains: why did Tolkien so patently hide the 'divine narrative', while leaving glimpses of it?

---

[85] *LotR* 4.3:638; also *LotR* 4.1:604 "It's my doom"; 4.3:638 "I must do so"; 4.5:668 "my doom"; 4.8:711 "so our path is laid".

[86] *LotR* 5.2:784 "'Aragorn. [...] Why will you go on this deadly road?' 'Because I must. [...] I do not choose paths of peril, Éowyn.'" Cf. also *LotR* 5.9:862, where Aragorn justifies his decision to use the Palantír on his belief that it had come to him "for just such a purpose".

III.2 Secondary Meanings: Cloaking and Freedom

As discussed in Chapter II, questions relating to Tolkien's poetics and theory must always be considered at two levels: one internal and the other external to his narrative universe. There are reasons belonging to the 'secondary' plane, that is, the world of Middle-earth, which express in a literary form Tolkien's own 'primary' understanding, more or less conscious, of literature, 'religion', and the relationship between the two.

III.2.1 Respect for Created Freedom

To begin, I will treat the stated question, 'why did Tolkien partially conceal a divine narrative within *The Lord of the Rings*?', on the level of the created 'secondary' or 'internal' reality – that is, according to the world of Tolkien's story itself. With this in mind, it is worth quoting at length a most illuminating passage from *Unfinished Tales* that begins to justify the hiding of God in *The Lord of the Rings*. The chapter on the mission of the wizards (*Istari*) states:

For with the consent of Eru they sent members of their own high order, but clad in bodies as of Men. […] And this the Valar did, desiring to amend **the errors of old**, especially that they had attempted to guard and seclude the Eldar by their own might and glory fully revealed; whereas now their emissaries were forbidden to reveal themselves in forms of majesty, or to seek to rule the wills of Men or Elves by open display of power. (*UT* 4.2:389)

The cloaking of the Valar's divine power is here revealed to be an intentional and momentous decision of the Valar, which seeks to amend the "errors of old".[87] These errors relate to one of the main events recounted in *The Silmarillion*; that is, the Valar's summoning of the Elves to an ancestral journey from Middle-earth to the blessed realm of Valinor.[88]

This summons originated in the Valar's love for the Elves, the first Children of Ilúvatar, and in their desire to share with the Elves their divine reality; the summons was thus made with good intentions and yet had disastrous effects (cf. *Sil* 3:52 "from this summons came many woes that afterwards befell"), resulting in the Elves' rebellion (allegedly motivated by a craving for freedom) and eventual ban from Valinor.[89] But in what exactly did the Valar's error consist? Simply put, in their failure, however unintentional, to respect Elvish freedom. By openly displaying their divine power to the Elves, the Valar effectively forced them to join them in Valinor; they 'dominated' the Elves, enforcing love on them out of fear or awe. In Tolkien's 'secondary theology' there is, thus, a strict association between 'cloaking' and 'freedom'. 'Cloaking' or 'veiling' is indeed the method chosen by the Valar (or rather ruled by Eru/Ilúvatar) to respect

[87] Cf. also *Letters* 156:302[202] "They were not allowed to destroy them, or coerce them with any 'divine' display"; *Letters* 200:375[260] "the Children of God must not be 'dominated', though they [the Valar] would be specially susceptible to it".

[88] Cf. esp. *Sil* 3:52 (the council of the Valar, eventually ruling against the advice of Ulmo, decides to summon the Elves to Valinor, out of fear for them in the dangerous world and the loving desire for their friendship). Also *NME* 1.12:89, 1.13:94–5.

[89] Cf. *Sil* 7:68 "Fiercest burned the new flame of **desire for freedom** [...] in the eager heart of Fëanor". Melkor/Morgoth is also deceivingly described as the "Giver of Freedom" (cf. *Sil Ak.*:272 "Melkor, Lord of All, Giver of Freedom, and he shall make you stronger than they").

the freedom of Elves (and Men) and oppose the Valar's temptation to domination.[90]

Cloaking does not, however, mean indifference or neglect: the Valar continue to care about the inhabitants of Middle-earth; despite appearances, they still guide, protect, and inspire the Elves in their resistance against Sauron, though not as openly as before. Moreover, the Valar still crave the love of the Elves and, ultimately, continue to wish for the Elves to join them in their Blessed Land in the west of Arda. However, this fellowship – the journey to the West – is no longer imposed by their open power, but discreetly proposed; after their ancestral 'mistake', the Valar have given up power and learnt to use a 'gentler' method more respectful of freedom, that is to say desire. In Tolkien's narratives, including *The Lord of the Rings*, desire for the divine is indeed a most important narrative element; and yet its true nature remains hidden from readers and often from the characters themselves.[91]

This desire is narratively expressed as a vague "latent desire for the Sea and for return into the West" (*UT* 2.4:237). All the 'high' Elves of the Noldorin race are characterised by this desire; but so too are 'lower' characters,[92] including the hobbit Frodo, who is gradually

---

[90] I will further discuss Eru's 'Rules' and their metaphysical implications in Chapter V, esp. V.1.2. On the freedom of the Children of Ilúvatar, and the Elves in particular, cf. also Flieger 2009 and Fornet-Ponse 2010. On the theme of the renunciation of (open) power in Tolkien's *legendarium* cf. further Rosebury 2003, esp. 178–86, and Saxton 2013b, esp. 54–6.

[91] Cf. *Sil Ain.*:19 ("the Children of Ilúvatar [...] **know not for what they listen**") quoted in Chapter I n.115.

[92] Among whom Legolas in particular; cf. Galadriel's prophecy to Legolas (*LotR* 3.5:503 "Beware of the Sea! If thou hearest the cry

introduced to this desire,[93] against the Hobbits' default indifference or fear for the Sea and the West in general,[94] and eventually yields to it, sailing out of Middle-earth towards the blessed West. The ending of *The Lord of the Rings*, which sees Frodo embarking on a journey to the West, is topical in this respect and effectively re-enacts the Elves' ancestral summons to Valinor. In contrast to *The Silmarillion*, however, Frodo's journey is not enforced through an open revelation of power but comes at the end of an 'education of desire' carried out by the Valar's secret agent in Middle-earth, Gandalf. In fact, Gandalf's task in Tolkien's narratives is not simply to guide the resistance again Sauron; rather, the Wizard seeks to "rekindle hearts" with the "memory of the high" and the knowledge of "greatness of the world" (cf. *UT* 3.3:331),[95] and, ultimately, the love for the divine (in a

of the gull on the shore, | Thy heart shall then rest in the forest no more") and its later fulfilment (*LotR* 5.9:873 "The Sea! Alas! [...] deep in the hearts of all my kindred lies the sea-longing, which it is perilous to stir"; also *LotR* 6.4:956). On this theme cf. Caldecott 2012:28–30.

[93] Cf. esp. Frodo's first dream: *LotR* 1.5:108 (quoted and discussed at I.2.5.1); also his longing words at *LotR* 6.6:986 "Yes, something of everything, Sam, except the Sea".

[94] Cf. *LotR* Prologue:7 (on the Sea as a word of fear and token of death for the hobbits, parallel to their fear for the Elves and mistrust for those who have dealings with them). Cf. also the clash between Sam and the mean Ted (*LotR* 1.2:45 "'They are sailing, sailing, sailing over the Sea, they are going into the West and leaving us," said Sam [...]. But Ted laughed. "[...] I don't see what it matters to me or you. Let them sail!')"; also, Ted's words of scorn on the way back (*LotR* 6.8:1017 "I thought you'd gone off in one o' them ships you used to prattle about, sailing, sailing").

[95] *LotR* Appendix B:1085 (Círdan giving the Ring of Fire to Gandalf, so that he may "rekindle hearts in a world that grows chill"). Cf. also *Mythopoeia* 88–9 "the legend-makers with their rhyme [...] kindled hearts with legendary fire", quoted in VI.2.3 (a parallel that confirms Gandalf's sub-creative identity, on which see V.1.7).

strictly secondary sense). This 'rekindling' begins with an act of election; that is, with Gandalf's decision to enrol Bilbo in the quest of Erebor, which soon reawakens within him the latent memory of his people of "the high and the perilous".[96] This desire is appropriately associated with natural entities, mountains and stars,[97] which in Tolkien have an important divine affiliation. As the mastermind behind Bilbo's adventure, Gandalf is thus implicitly characterised as the fire that rekindles the desire for the 'high' and, ultimately, for the world of the "Valar under the One"; and yet he does so in a discreet, veiled manner, always respectful of the characters' freedom.[98] In this way, Gandalf epitomises the Valar's attitude towards the inhabitants of Middle-earth: his 'cloaked' power goes hand in hand with his deep respect for the freedom of other creatures, as does his love for them in general, as will be demonstrated in detail in Chapter V (V.1.2).

---

[96] *UT* 3.3:331 "They [the Hobbits] had begun to forget: forget their own beginnings and legends, forget what little they had known about the greatness of the world. It was not yet gone, but it was getting buried: **the memory of the high and the perilous**. But you cannot teach that sort of thing to a whole people quickly. [...] And anyway you must begin at some point, with some one person. I dare say he [Bilbo] was 'chosen' and I was only chosen to choose him". Cf. also *LotR Prologue*, especially p.3, where Tolkien reveals that in ancient times some hobbits had friendly relationships with the Elves, and were skilled in language and song.

[97] *Hobbit* 1:19–20 "As they sang [...] something Tookish woke up inside him, and he wished to go and **see the great mountains**, [...] He looked out of the window. **The stars were out in a dark sky** above the trees".

[98] Gandalf's respect for freedom is also revealed in his "merciful" dealing with Saruman after his defeat (cf. *LotR* 3.1:579–84), which concludes with his statement that he will do nothing to him because he does not "wish for mastery" (ibid. 584).

III.2.2 The Freedom of the One

Human, Elvish, and Hobbit freedom is thus an important 'secondary' factor explaining the hiding of the 'divine narrative' in *The Lord of the Rings*; but there is more. That of Elves and Men is not the only kind of freedom that the Valar respect by cloaking their power. The deeper reason behind the Valar's respect for Elvish and Human freedom is the divine origin of this very freedom; that is, the fact that these beings are the Children of Ilúvatar, the fruit of the freedom of the Creator Eru. As explained in the *Ainulindalë*, the Valar had no part in the making of Elves and Men and were amazed at their coming, perceiving in them "the mind of Ilúvatar reflected anew" and learning "a little more of his wisdom".[99]

As Tolkien explains at length in an important letter, "the making, and nature of the Children of God" (Elves and Men) are "the two chief secrets" of the Creator; the creation of Elves and Men epitomises His retention of His Own creative freedom in the history of the world, which is closely related to a common narrative motive in Tolkien's *legendarium* ("the secret life in creation"):

The Knowledge of the Creation Drama was incomplete [...] the Creator had not revealed all. The making, and nature, of the Children of God, were the two chief secrets. [...] Here we meet among other things, the first example of the motive [...] that

---

[99] Cf. *Sil Ain.*:18 "And they saw with amazement the coming of the Children of Ilúvatar [...] For the Children of Ilúvatar were conceived by him alone; and [...] none of the Ainur had part in their making. Therefore when they beheld them, the more did they love them [...] wherein they saw the mind of Ilúvatar reflected anew, and learned yet a little more of his wisdom".

the great policies of world history, 'the wheels of the world', are often turned not by the Lords and Governors, even gods, but by the seemingly unknown and weak – **owing to the secret life in creation**, and the part unknowable to all wisdom but One, that resides in the **intrusions** of the Children of God into the Drama. (*Letters* 131:206–9[147–9])[100]

A key word in this passage is "intrusion", an important concept in Tolkien's 'secondary theology' with significant meta-literary implications. A passage from another illuminating letter deserves to be quoted in full to illustrate this:

the One retains all ultimate authority and […] reserves the right to **intrude** the finger of God into the story that is to produce realities which could not be deduced even from a complete knowledge of the previous past, but which being real become part of the effective past for all subsequent time (a possible definition of a 'miracle'). According to the fable Elves and Men were the first of these **intrusions**, made indeed while the 'story' was still only a story and not 'realized'; they were not therefore in any sense conceived or made by the gods, the Valar, and were called the Eruhíni or 'Children of God', and were for the Valar an incalculable element. (*Letters* 181:341[235])

The idea of 'intrusion' is thus strictly associated with the creative freedom of Eru/Ilúvatar, the "one wholly free Will and Agent" (*Letters* 156:301[204]), who intervenes in the story, introducing "new themes into the original design, which might therefore be unforeseen by many of the spirits in realization" (*Letters* 200:374[260]).[101] The Valar are the

---

[100] On this passage see further IV.3.4.
[101] Cf. also *Letters* 156:300[203] (the intrusion of Elves and Men into the story has nothing to do with the Ainur); ibid. 301[204], cit. in Chapter V n.56; *NME* 3.2:289–90 ("the signs of the finger of Eru", "intrusions into Eä from outside").

Lords of Arda and masterminds of its history, but they do not know (not even the most enlightened ones) the things "that lie still in the freedom of Ilúvatar" (*Sil. Val.*:28).[102]

By hiding His plans from the Valar, and, by analogy, every other creature, Eru/Ilúvatar affirms His own creative freedom that goes well beyond the creation of His (free) Children. God's freedom is also revealed in His free "intrusion" within the narrative; though he does so in ways that are always 'discrete', 'hidden', and 'secret', beyond the understanding of other beings, divine or otherwise. The already mentioned 'resurrection' of Gandalf is probably the most dramatic example of this kind of intrusion (as we will see in Chapter V), but there are arguably many others. From a narrative perspective, the freedom of God (the ultimate Author beyond the narratives) is enacted in His enhancement of the role played by seemingly irrelevant characters and events. As the important passage quoted earlier explicitly reveals, the Creation of Elves and Men is related to an important narrative motive; that is, that "the great policies of world history are turned by the seemingly unknown and weak". This motive (accordingly "owing to the secret life in creation") is at the core of the narrative of *The Lord of the Rings*; it is often highlighted in the story and associated, in particular, with Aragorn and the hobbits.[103] The Hobbits

---

[102] To these one should also add the "secrets of minds", which "are not readable even by the Valar", but are only knowable of Eru (*NME* 2.16:268).

[103] Cf. *LotR* 2.9:156 (Aragorn watching the hobbits in the inn at Bree, wearing a hood that "overshadowed his face" and a "travel-stained cloak"); *LotR* 2.2:270 "This is the hour of the Shire-folk, when they arise from their quiet fields to shake the towers and counsels of the Great". Cf. also Elrond's warning to Boromir that there are "other powers" that

are, of course, emblematic of this motive: iconically small and reserved, neglected or despised by the Wise and the Powerful, they will be revealed as heroes and saviours.

In this respect, it is not insignificant that the great lover of the Hobbits is the "incarnate angel" Gandalf, who – in contrast to Saruman, Sauron, and the "other powers" – holds them in high esteem.[104] Two features of the Hobbits, in particular, have attracted Gandalf's attention: their surprising unpredictability,[105] and their openness to pity and mercy for each other.[106] Tolkien explicitly associates both of these features with God;[107] this association

are hidden from him (*LotR* 2.2:268) and Gandalf's words to Aragorn on mount Mindolluin (*LotR* 6.5:971, urging him to turn his face "from the green world, and look where all seems barren and cold".

[104] Cf. on this Saruman's words of scorn for Gandalf's curiosity for the small, whereas he has no time for "simples of peasants" (*UT* 3.4:352).

[105] Cf. *LotR* 1.2:48 (Hobbit-lore as an "obscure branch of knowledge […] full of surprises"); 62 (Gandalf's reacting to Frodo's decision to take the Ring, noting that hobbits are "amazing creatures" that can "still surprise you at a pinch"). Also *LotR Prologue*:6 (on the Hobbits' capacity of survival "in a way that astonished"), Elrond's surprise at Frodo's tale ("most strange to me", *LotR* 2.2:265), and Treebeard's surprised reaction at his encounter with the hobbits (*LotR* 3.4:464) "What are you, I wonder? I cannot place you"; *LotR* 3.10:586 "they [the Hobbits] are the first new thing under Sun or Moon that I have seen for many a long, long day". On Hobbits as 'unforeseen characters' see II.2.2.1; cf. also Nagy 2019:165. Other aspects of the hobbits' attractiveness are their lack of greed (an antidote against the Dwarves' obsession in *The Hobbit*), and, as argued by Rosebury 2003:51, their "capacity for disinterested curiosity".

[106] Cf. *UT* 3.3:331 (Gandalf noting that it was also thanks to the Hobbits' pity for one another that they survived the Long Winter, thereby gaining "a warm place" in his heart).

[107] Cf. *Letters* 246:460[326], quoted in Chapter I n.129. Gandalf/Olórin himself, even before his mission to Middle-earth, was associated with pity (cf. *Sil Val.*:30–1 "Wisest of the Maiar was Olórin […] his ways took him often to the house of Nienna, and of her he learned pity and patience"). Cf. on this Caldecott 2012:55–9.

arguably confirms the Hobbits as the objects of a mysterious 'divine' preference recognised and embraced by Gandalf. His love for the Hobbits is not merely a narrative ornament: rather, Gandalf acknowledges that, by Eru's mysterious "wisdom", the Hobbits have been chosen as the instruments for the fulfilment of His narrative. From a narrative perspective, Gandalf thus understands that the Hobbits' apparent irrelevance is a powerful asset against Sauron. The weakness of the Hobbits is merely a 'cloaking' tactic of the divine design underlying *The Lord of the Rings* to confound the ways of the Powers. In general, 'cloaking' is an important narrative motive of *The Lord of the Rings* applied to many different characters and situations, including, in particular, Aragorn, the 'hidden' and 'cloaked' king of Gondor.[108] As a key element of the plot, 'cloaking' (i.e. the decision to entrust the Ring to Frodo to be destroyed in Mordor) is purposefully chosen by Gandalf during the Council of Elrond,[109] though this decision is counted as a "folly" according to the purely human wisdom of someone such as Denethor.[110] All of

[108] See n.103. Cloaking is also a key feature of the Fellowship of the Ring, especially after their stay at Lórien, where the Galadriel provides them with a hood and cloak (cf. *LotR* 2.8:370).
[109] Cf. *LotR* 2.2:268 "Well, let folly be our **cloak**, a **veil** before the eyes of the Enemy!"; also ibid. 267 "we must take a hard road, a road **unforeseen**. There lies our hope, if hope it be". The concept of 'folly' is also used by Tolkien to denote another important narrative element of *LotR*, that is, Frodo's sparing of Gollum (cf. *Letters* 181:234 "a piece of folly, or a mystical belief in the ultimate value-in-itself of pity").
[110] *LotR* 2.10:398 (Boromir venting out his frustration at the "folly" of sending a hobbit to walk blindly into Mordor). Cf. also *LotR* 2.7:356 (Celeborn rashly describing Gandalf's decision to enter Moria as his fall "from wisdom to folly").

this folly and cloaking in *The Lord of the Rings* is ultimately dependent on and analogous to Eru's operation in the history of Middle-earth: it is always secret, unforeseen, and baffling to the reasoning of the Wise.[111]

In conclusion, by hiding their power from Elves and Men, the Valar respect the freedom of Eru (God) in two different but related senses: they (1) respect His freedom as embedded in His Children, created free by Him; and they (2) abide with the 'methodology' of Eru in history, in accordance with the "life in creation", which is characterised by secrecy, unpredictability, and the enhancement of "the unknown and the weak".

III.3 Primary Meanings: Cloaking and Sub-creation

All these considerations pertain to the 'secondary' or 'internal' theology of Middle-earth, and yet they can also be construed as literarily expressing Tolkien's own 'primary' views. All the themes discussed so far are traceable in Tolkien's non-literary writings and in references to 'primary' entities, beliefs, and concerns. For instance, Tolkien often talks about the operation of God's freedom in human history as miraculous "intrusions";[112] he also states that God works in "the dark in some forgotten corner", and, for this reason, "no man can estimate what

---

[111] Cf. Gandalf's words to Frodo, *LotR* 1.2:59 (cited at VI.1.2), later recalled at 4.1:615; also, Elrond' statement during the Council of Elrond on the Hobbits 'shaking the counsels of the Great' (*LotR* 2.2:270 cit. n.103). On this motive see further Caldecott 2012:53.

[112] Cf. *Letters* 89:142[100] "miracles [...] are intrusions (as we say, erring) into real or ordinary life".

is really happening at the present *sub specie aeternitatis*".[113] Similarly, the notion of a God who embraces human weakness and reveals Himself through cloaked forms in order to respect human freedom and confound the plans of the Wise, is central to the Christian doctrine of Incarnation. It would be interesting to explore Tolkien's 'primary' theology in this respect; in this book, however, my focus will rather be on the (meta-)literary rather than doctrinal implications of Tolkien's 'poetics of cloaking'.

For Tolkien, 'cloaking' is not primarily a theological category but a literary one. For example, he consistently describes his literary work as a 'cloaking' or 'veiling' containing elements of truth and "allusions to the highest matters", which are not explicitly and openly expressed but are rather kept "under unexplained symbolic forms" or exemplified "in unfamiliar embodiments".[114] The category of 'cloaking' can thus be applied to Tolkien's literary work per se, which he explicitly describes as "mythical and legendary dress", cloaking his (imperfect) knowledge of life (and God):

> The author, the most modest [...] of men, whose instinct is **to cloak** such self-knowledge as he has, and such criticisms of life as he knows it, **under mythical and legendary dress**. (*Letters* 163:310[211])

---

[113] *Letters* 64:130[91], quoted in IV.3.4, and *Letters* 69:116[80] "One knows that there is always good: much more hidden, much less clearly discerned, seldom breaking out into recognizable, visible, beauties of word or deed or face". Cf. also *Letters* 250, to M. Tolkien, 1/11/1963:473[336] on the constant hiding of the greater part of truth, "in regions out of the reach of cynicism".

[114] Cf. *Letters* 156:297[201] "I have purposely kept all allusions to the highest matters down to mere hints [...] **or kept them under unexplained symbolic forms**"; also *Letters* 153:289[194] "unfamiliar embodiments" (quoted at the beginning of Chapter IV). See also III.3.2 with n.126.

This allows us to talk of a proper 'poetics of veiling' or 'cloaking', whose features and implications I will investigate in this final section of this chapter (III.3). Not surprisingly, one of the main traits of this poetics reflects something that is already found in Tolkien's secondary world, namely a high concern for freedom.

III.3.1 The Freedom of the Sub-creator: Cloaking as a Guarantee and Limit

As in the secondary world, in Tolkien's primary poetics 'cloaking' is associated with freedom, specifically that of the sub-creator, which is to say, the literary writer or human artist in general.[115] The following passage is from a draft letter (153) to a Catholic reader criticising Tolkien for having "over-stepped the mark in metaphysical matters" (*Letters*:281[187]), having created a world apparently incompatible with Catholic doctrine. Tolkien's response is a vigorous assertion of authorial and sub-creative freedom:

Are there any 'bounds to a writer's job' except those imposed by his own finiteness? **No bounds**, but the laws of contradiction, I should think. But, of course, **humility** and an awareness of peril is required. (*Letters* 153:289[194])

As shown by this important passage, the author's "right to freedom" is almost total in Tolkien's view, and yet requires "humility"; moreover, the sub-creator's freedom

---

[115] On the author's freedom in Tolkien, and its analogy with God's freedom, see Saxton 2013a and 2013b, comparing Tolkien and Bakhtin's positions on the topic. Saxton rightly points out that, in contrast to Bakhtin, for Tolkien, authorial freedom does not mean autonomy or insubordination. On this, and Tolkien's notion of sub-creation in general see Chapter VI.

is strictly related to the 'feigning' or 'cloaking' function of sub-creation, which has liberation "from the channels the creator is known to have used already" as its "fundamental function", as he says in the same letter.[116]

Therefore, Tolkien considers his literary activity as a form of sub-creation, whose aim is to express (and indeed 'discover') truth in artistically 'cloaked' forms. According to Tolkien, God continues His own free creation in history through the individual creative freedom of the artist,[117] who has "no bounds" within his own sub-created world. To impose bounds would be to limit the author's God-sanctioned freedom, as well as God's own freedom. To be sure, sub-creators do aim for truth (see III.3.2), but they present a truth that must be 'feigned' through myth or exemplified in "unfamiliar embodiments", just like Gandalf, for instance. The near total freedom of the artist resides in, depends on, and is restricted to this very act of 'cloaking'. Tolkien continues in the same letter to say: "Free Will is derivative, and is only operative within provided circumstances" (p.290[195]); this is to say that the 'sub-creative' plane,

in order that it may exist, it is necessary that the Author should guarantee it, whatever betides [...]. So in this myth, it is 'feigned' [...] that He [i.e. Eru] gave special 'sub-creative' powers to certain of His highest created beings [i.e. Melkor and the other Ainur]: that is a guarantee that what they devised and made should be given the reality of Creation. (*Letters* 153:290[195])

---

[116] *Letters* 153:283[188], quoted and discussed in VI.2.3.
[117] For a discussion of this idea from a theological perspective, see Hart 2013 (esp. chapter 5).

The possibility of sub-creative rebellion (here evoked through an indirect allusion to the reality of Melkor's sub-creations) is inherent to sub-creative freedom. In the same letter, Tolkien continues to say that the guaranteed "right to 'freedom'" does not grant that this freedom will not be used "wickedly".[118]

In conclusion, sub-creative 'cloaking' can be construed as both the guarantee and the limit of authorial freedom. Attempting to express truth in open, explicit, non-cloaked forms would be, in a sense, to betray the artist's mission and overstep his freedom by interfering with God's activity in the primary world, since "Myth and fairy-story must, as all art, reflect and contain in solution elements of moral and religious truth (or error), but not explicit, not in the known form of the primary 'real' world" (*Letters* 131:203[144]). To do so would, therefore, be an act of literary hubris, forgetting the inherent 'incompleteness', 'imprecision', and 'partiality' of any human authorial endeavour.

III.3.2 *Applicability and Fantastic Recovery: The Freedom of the Reader*

The author's artistic freedom is not the only freedom at stake in Tolkien's 'poetics of cloaking'. Another important freedom is that of the reader, in two related senses.

In the first place, 'cloaking' protects the reader's freedom from the author's 'domination'. A passage from

---

[118] *Letters* 153:290[195] "**The right to 'freedom'** of the sub-creator is no guarantee among fallen men that it will not be used as wickedly as is Free Will".

Tolkien's introduction to *The Lord of the Rings* is revealing in this respect:

> I cordially dislike allegory in all its manifestations [...]. I much
> prefer history, true or feigned, with its varied applicability to
> the thought and experience of readers. I think that many con-
> fuse 'applicability' with 'allegory'; but the one resides in **the
> freedom of the reader**, and the other in the **purposed domi-
> nation of the author**. (*LotR Introduction*:xx)

The dichotomy of "freedom" and "domination" is an
important motive in the secondary world of Tolkien's
novels, and is here associated with Tolkien's notorious
aversion to allegory. The distinction between 'allegory'
and the 'applicability' of 'myth' has confused many readers
and is, at times, also misunderstood in Tolkien scholarship: I will directly address this vexed question in Chapter
IV (IV.2.2). Here, I will only point out that one of the dis-
criminating factors between the two approaches is the different consideration of the reader's freedom. In allegory,
Tolkien contends, authors try to 'dominate' their readers
by tacitly indoctrinating them into their own 'truths', thus
treating literature as honey smeared on the brim of a med-
icine glass (to paraphrase an ancient analogy). By contrast,
the 'sub-creator' does not primarily aim to indoctrinate
their readers; for the sub-creator, literary 'cloaking' is
not a rhetorical strategy with an external purpose, but a
self-standing undertaking aimed at entertaining and moving the readers – not at preaching or catechising.[119]

---

[119] Cf. on this Tolkien's allusive criticism of George MacDonald's
"preaching", in his unfinished introduction to *The Golden Key* (*SWM
GK*:90 "I must warn you that he is a preacher"). A full discussion of
Tolkien's criticism of allegory is conducted in IV.2.2.

This does not mean that for Tolkien the sub-creator should not be concerned with truth and the edification of their readers: as he claims in the same letter, his work's purpose remains "didactic",[120] and one of his objects is "the elucidation of truth, and the encouragement of good morals in this real world" (*Letters* 153:289[194]). In fact, in order to be applicable to other people's lives, myth needs to contain elements of truth that are 'universal'; and yet its approach to truth is the approach of story, different from that of "priggish" allegory,[121] as will be demonstrated in detail in Chapter IV. Tolkien's 'actors' are not allegorical characters, but rather 'individuals'; their 'universality' is cloaked under the idiosyncrasies of fully imagined unique characters. In Tolkien's sub-creation, 'cloaking' is what distinguishes an allegory from a story: one could say that, for Tolkien, allegory has an open and intentional didactic purpose; whereas in story, 'truth' is fully embedded within the cloak of a literary code (the 'unfamiliar embodiment' of a sub-creation) and its primeval purpose remains aesthetic and 'gratuitous' (as we have seen in Chapter I). Sub-creation is not a rhetorical strategy but is related to Tolkien's deep respect for the freedom of the reader whom he discreetly invites to 'apply' to their own life the religious and ethical 'universals' embodied "under mythical and legendary dress".[122]

---

[120] *Letters* 153:284[189].

[121] Cf. *TCG* 214 (24/10/1955) in which Tolkien acknowledges that his books are indeed "moral" and "founded on Pity", but that to put it like that would sound "dreadfully priggish", while in a story it is better.

[122] On Tolkien's concern for the reader's freedom, especially as regards the interpretation of the meaning of a given text, see further the sophisticated discussion of Segura 2010.

The second important sense in which literary 'cloaking' enhances the reader's freedom is related to the notion of "recovery". As Tolkien explains at length in his essay 'On Fairy-Stories',[123] the greatest danger for (modern) humans is to become slaves of 'triteness', 'familiarity', or 'possessiveness'; that is, of an approach to reality that is possessive and devoid of wonder.[124] This, as Tolkien says, is not the way "we were meant to see" reality, and ultimately leads not only to a lack of beauty and enjoyment, but also to a lack of knowledge of reality as 'creation'. The purpose of 'creative Fantasy' (or sub-creation) is, instead, to recover all these by 'cloaking' them in unfamiliar and fantastic forms so that we "**may be freed** from the drab blur of triteness or familiarity – from possessiveness" (*TOFS*:67=*TL*:58).[125] This recovery is also equated by Tolkien to a liberation from the "slavery" of hard appearances,[126] and thus to an "escape of the prisoner";[127] the

---

[123] For an overview of this famous text, which can be properly considered Tolkien's literary manifesto, see in particular Flieger and Anderson's introduction in *TOFS* as well as Fornet-Ponse, Honegger, and Eilmann 2015, especially the chapters by Lothmann and Scholz, Hynes, Gut, and Nauman. Cf. also Rosenquist 2008; Shank 2013; Cook 2016.

[124] For embodiment of this theme in Tolkien's literary work cf. Simonson 2008b; Caldecott 2012:38–41.

[125] I will discuss this passage, and Tolkien's notion of recovery in general, in IV.3.3.

[126] *TOFS*:65=*TL*:55 "For creative Fantasy is founded upon the hard recognition that things are so in the world as it appears under the sun; on a recognition of fact, but **not a slavery** to it". Cf. also *SWM Ess.*:144 "Faery represents [...] a breaking out [...] from the iron ring of the familiar, still more from the adamantine ring of belief that it is known, possessed, controlled [...] a constant awareness of a world beyond these rings."

[127] See the whole section 88 of *On Fairy-Stories* (*TOFS*:69–70=*TL*:60–2).

reader is not only exposed to the intellectual domination of the author, but also to the slavery of their own intellectual biases, superficialities, and ideologies.

III.3.3 A Heart-Racking Desire

Literary 'cloaking' preserves the reader's freedom from both the author's and their own intellectual dominations through the enhancement of desire (the "Sea-longing" that I described in I.2.5). Thus, Tolkien's concern for the reader's freedom explains another important implication of his poetics of 'cloaking': the evocation of desire. As we have seen, in Tolkien's secondary world the Valar's 'cloaking' of their power goes hand in hand with the enhancement in the Elves of an unexplained, insatiate desire for the divine; this is how the Valar attract the Elves to their divine reality while respecting their freedom. The same connection between 'cloaking' and 'desire' is traceable in Tolkien's primary poetics, once more referring to the imagery of 'glimpsing' or 'glimmering' recurrent in Tolkien's criticism of his work. This can be illustrated by the following two passages:

A story must be told or there'll be no story, yet it is the untold stories that are most moving. I think you are moved by [a story about the Elves] [...] because it conveys a sudden sense of endless untold stories: mountains seen far away, never to be climbed, distant trees never to be approached – unless in Paradise. (*Letters* 96:160[110])

Part of the attraction of The L.R. is, I think, due to the **glimpses** of a large history in the background: an attraction like that of viewing far off an unvisited island, or seeing the towers of a distant city gleaming in a sunlit mist. To go there is to destroy the magic, unless new unattainable vistas are again revealed. (*Letters* 247:469[333])[128]

This experience of distances vaguely perceivable and yet 'veiled' evokes a heart-racking longing for something unattainable in the reader. This effect is at the heart of the attraction of *The Lord of the Rings* and it is achieved by revealing glimpses or fragments of light, but not its source; by cloaking but not preaching truth; by leaving stories incomplete; and by leaving the full picture implicit or unexplained, to paraphrase the various metaphors used by Tolkien.[129] From a literary-technical point of view, Tolkien achieves these effects by not saying everything;

---

[128] Cf. also *Letters* 328:578[412] "a brief episode [...] surrounded by the glimmer of limitless extensions in time and space". See on this important Tolkienian quality the recent monograph by Grybauskas 2021.

[129] Cf. *Letters* 268, to A. P. Northey, 19/01/1965:495[354] "I feel it is better not to state everything"; *Letters* 281, to R. Unwin, 15/12/1965:510[365] "if saying such things did not spoil what it tries to make explicit"; *Letters* 144:263[174] "As a story, I think it is good that there should be a lot of things unexplained"; *Letters* 151, to H. Brogan, 18/09/1954:279[185] "part of the "fascination" [of *The Lord of the Rings*] consists in the vistas of yet more legend and history, to which this work does not contain a full clue"; *Letters* 153:285[190] "exercising my sub-creator's right I have thought it best in this Tale to leave the question [about the identity of the wizards] a 'mystery' not without pointers to the solution"; *TCG 259* (5/11/1956) arguing that there should be something in a literary work that should be only suggested, and not fully explained. Cf. also *MC*:15 (on the poet of *Beowulf* "who feels rather than makes explicit what his theme portends" and presents it "incarnate"). On this motive, its embodiments in Tolkien's secondary world and associated literary techniques cf. Slack 2010; Grybauskas 2012; Izzo 2019; Hausmann 2019. For an example of narrative omission in *LotR* cf. *RS* 3:73, where Christopher Tolkien notes that his father "knew a good deal more about the Riders and the Ring than Bingo did, or than he permitted Gildor to tell".

making lavish use of omissions, lacunae, and allusions;[130] and, more specifically, omitting (almost) all explicit connections between *The Lord of the Rings* and the larger narrative.[131]

The attraction of incompleteness – of seeing things veiled or cloaked – is another important motive in *The Lord of the Rings*; this is embodied specifically in the hobbits' fascination and delight with the very "fragments" of the uncompleted Elvish songs, legends, and histories that Frodo (and Bilbo) will hear in full on the other side of the Sea.[132] Fragmentation and omission, which result in a tantalising tension between said and unsaid, are traditional tools of the literary craft, of course, which Tolkien certainly used in many cases, and with great mastery.[133] On one such case, Tom Shippey comments: "[w]hat Tolkien does in such passages is to satisfy the urge to know more (the urge he himself felt as an editor of texts so often infuriatingly incomplete), while retaining and even intensifying the counterbalancing pleasure of seeming always on

[130] In several cases omissions are explicitly flagged: cf. for instance *LotR* 1.9:158 "only a few words [...] are now [...] remembered"; *LotR* 2.2:240 "Not all that was spoken and debated in the Council need now be told"; *LotR* 2.6:341 "That is but a part, for I have forgotten much". Also *LotR* 2.7:359 (the "snatches" of Frodo's dirge for Gandalf, which faded "as a handful of withered leaves").

[131] Cf. *Letters* 247:469[334] "a lot of links between *The Hobbit* and *The L.R.* [...] were [...] cut out to lighten the boat".

[132] Cf. *Letters* 246:464[328] (on the completion of Frodo's life associated with the opportunity of "hearing the legends and histories in full the fragments of which had so delighted him").

[133] On 'fragmentation' or 'splintering' as a typical Tolkienian category cf. I.2.2.1, II.2.2.3 and see further Flieger 2012. On omission and lacuna as common literary techniques in Western literature see for example Gardini 2014.

the edge of further discovery, looking into a world that seems far fuller than the little at present known". And yet for Tolkien this is not just a literary technique or rhetorical strategy; as the passages quoted earlier demonstrate, there are important literary implications behind this idea of 'cloaked', 'glimpsed', or 'incomplete' literature; these implications are related to the freedom of another important 'free' Agent, God Himself, whose freedom is also respected and acknowledged in literary cloaking. This will be the final concern of this chapter.

III.3.4 Glimpsing the Light of God in Incomplete Stories

As we have seen, in Tolkien's secondary world, the notions of literary 'incompleteness', 'cloaking', 'hiding', or 'glimpsing' are strictly related to the divine in two important senses. First, according to Tolkien's meta-artistic cosmogony, the creation of the world is achieved through the Ainur/Valar (the Ur-artists); their 'artistic' individuality is cherished and enhanced, yet it ultimately derives from and belongs to God (Eru/Ilúvatar).[134] Though the Valar and all other rational beings, in different order, collaborate and play a part in God's musical drama, they do not have a full picture of it. Ilúvatar hid the fullness of His design even from the Valar, leaving their knowledge of His drama incomplete, so as to allow space for the free "intrusion of His finger" into the sub-created world, thus preserving His ongoing creative freedom. Secondly, the stories of Middle-earth are constantly described or

---

[134] Cf. I.2.4, II.2.2.5, and see Chapter VII for a full overview.

constructed by Tolkien as being inherently incomplete
and fragmentary: the complete fruition of these stories is
only possible in the Blessed Land of Valinor, where the
Elves live in full communion with the Valar, that is, with
the Divine as represented within Arda. The same view is
also affirmed by Tolkien on the primary level, who writes
in a letter to his son that there is a place where all the good
unfinished, the stories unwritten and the hopes unfulfilled will be continued and completed (*Letters* 45:76[55],
cited at VI.2.1).

What connects these two outlooks on narrative 'incompleteness' is the idea of God as the supreme Story-teller;
that is, as the only Author of a complete, accurate, and fully
satisfying Story.[135] The creative activity of human story-
tellers is analogous to God's (i.e. it is 'sub-creative'); however, given its non-divine, secondary nature, sub-creation
can only produce incomplete, fragmentary, and ultimately 'partial' stories – reflections of the Truth, but not
the Truth itself. On the secondary plane, this view is duly
reflected in the meta-textual frame according to which
the narratives are written by individual authors and only
present, in imperfect language, a partial and biased version of their story (as we have seen in Chapter II, II.2.1.2
and II.2.2.4). At the same time, these secondary stories
draw life (and 'Light') from and contribute to the One
Story of God: human stories are like fragments refracting
the divine light of the One Story, and in doing so they
become parts of the Whole and "tributary to its glory"
(*Sil Ain.*:17). Because of this, such human (or elvish) stories both evoke a heart-racking desire for the full vision of

---

135 Cf. II.2.2.4 and VI.2.1

the light of God and manage to convey "glimpses" of its truth – an image on which Tolkien insists in the powerful ending of *On Fairy-Stories*, dedicated to the concept of eucatastrophe;[136]

[The joy of the happy ending] denies [...] universal final defeat [...] giving **a fleeting glimpse** of Joy, Joy beyond the walls of the world, poignant as grief. [...] In such stories when the sudden 'turn' comes we get **a piercing glimpse** of joy, and heart's desire, that for a moment passes outside the frame, rends indeed the very web of story, and lets **a gleam** come through. [...] The peculiar quality of the 'joy' in successful Fantasy can thus be explained as **a sudden glimpse** of the underlying reality or truth. (*TOFS*:75–7=*TL*:69–71)

At the core of Tolkien's essay *On Fairy-Stories*,[137] and the related poem *Mythopoeia*,[138] is the view that human literature is a fragmented and partial reflection of the light of God's Literature, the Primary Creation. This view is also symbolically expressed in his myth, especially in the saga of the Silmarils, secondary artistic artefacts which yet contain a divine light (cf. V.1.7). This is why, for Tolkien, human stories are necessarily incomplete, for they can only be completed in Paradise (or Valinor); for this same reason, incompleteness is a powerful tool for evoking the human desire for the divine.

Bringing us back to the core question of this chapter are two important implications of this view: (1) human literature is, by its nature, unable to express fully and openly the divine; and (2) even the fragments of Truth contained in literature are not intentionally produced by the intellect of

---

[136] See IV.3.4.   [137] Cf. Flieger 2002:21–32.
[138] Cf. *TOFS*:64–5 (= *TL*:54–5)=*Myth*:87, quoted at VI.2.4.

the human author, but are rather external 'gifts', like the light of the divine Silmarils. That is, human sub-creation can glimpse God's nature through a process that remains primarily aesthetic and contemplative (as we have seen in Chapter I); it cannot, however, 'rationalise' truth and try to express it in open terms. For this reason, cloaking is inherent to the very nature of sub-creation. It follows that if literature tries to express Truth in uncloaked terms, it commits a hubristic act perhaps analogous to the one at the origin of Melkor's rebellion; this act consisted in "seeking the Imperishable Flame; for desire grew hot within him to bring into Being things of his own" (*Sil. Ain.*:16). Indeed, attempting to express Truth explicitly might be even construed as an offence against God's nature and creative freedom, which dictates that not everything be revealed to the human mind, and which gratuitously inspires in the sub-creators their very own literary thoughts and images. Moreover, to try to express Truth in open terms (rather than imperfectly and gradually discover it) would be a betrayal of the vocation of literature, when its task is to evoke that 'heart-racking' desire of things 'glimpsed' but not fully revealed. In fact, one might argue that, for Tolkien, trying to express Truth in literature would not just be an act of human hubris, but bad literature: to go to the top of the mountains is to destroy the 'magic' (cf. *Letters* 96:160[110], quoted in III.3.3) because the ultimate 'magic' is in the desire and its Object, not in the secondary, finite instrument (albeit valuable) which generates it.[139]

---

[139] On this paradoxical dynamic cf. also *Letters* 131:204[145] (quoted at I.2.1.3), referring to the passionate love of reality which is yet filled with the sense of mortality and unsatisfaction.

The desire evoked in Tolkien's works is a universal human seeking for something "beyond the world":[140] symbolically speaking, such desire is the nostalgia for a place and time where the relationship between God and man was immediate and uncloaked; that is, 'Eden'.[141] For Tolkien, any desire, longing, or nostalgia is ultimately an expression of the desire for 'Eden', as he explained to his son Christopher in a letter written during his service in the Second World War:

> Certainly there was an Eden on this very unhappy earth. We all long for it, and we are constantly glimpsing it: our whole nature at its best and least corrupted [...] is still soaked with the sense of 'exile'. If you come to think of it, your [...] obstinate memory

---

[140] Cf. *Sil* 1:41 "Therefore he willed that the hearts of Men should seek **beyond the world** and should find no rest therein"; on this idea see Caldecott 2012:12 and Vaninskaya 2020 (the latter relating it to Romantic *Sehnsucht*).

[141] This nostalgia for a lost Eden should be related with a 'narrative of decline' which certainly pervades Tolkien's works: this narrative construes history as a "long defeat" (cf. *Letters* 195, to A. Ronald, 15/12/1956:368[255]), from an idealised golden past to a grim present, and is traceable at many different levels, including the aesthetic, linguistic, moral, biological, and existential one (see e.g. Rateliff 2006; Fimi 2008; Caldecott 2012:1–3, 29–30, 119–20; Drout 2013; Pezzini 2022; also Fontenot 2019). At the same time, one should not equate the two, and infer that the 'nostalgia for Eden' (and the related desire for a relationship with the divine) necessarily implies Tolkien's full adherence to a 'narrative of decline': this is suggested first of all by the fact that the motive is 'focalised' within Tolkien's *legendarium*, and associated with a specific, and 'partial' perspective, that of the Elves (cf. in particular *Letters* 154, to N. Mitchison, 25/09/1954:293[197]), explaining that the Elves were not "wholly good or in the right" because they were 'embalmers' and tried to stop the change, history and growth of Middle-earth, thereby becoming "overburdened with sadness and nostalgic regret"; see further on this Pezzini 2022.

of this 'home' of yours in an idyllic hour (when often there is an illusion of the stay of time and decay and a sense of gentle peace) [...] are derived from Eden. (*Letters* 96:158–9[110])

For Tolkien, art and literature are supreme forms in which nostalgia for 'Eden' and seeking for the transcendent are expressed and re-awakened. In this and other respects, artistic sub-creations are analogous to (and continue) the Primary Creation of God, whose main function, as Tolkien suggests in a beautiful letter to a young friend,[142] is to generate in men the longing for a relationship with the Creator – who yet remains hidden and cloaked, in respect of the freedom of His creatures.

Tolkien's poetics of cloaking, and its technical implications such as omission, lacuna, and 'veiling', are thus also strictly related to his views on the nature of literature and of God. Literature evokes the longing for God by rekindling human desire with tantalising glimpses of infinite beauty; this is what gives literature its fascination and value. Although this is a literary strategy with many parallels in Western literature (and beyond), for Tolkien, it is more than that. Incompleteness and cloaking are means by which he acknowledges and expresses the ultimate sub-creative nature of his work, in the same way as in his secondary world the Valar (the secondary authors) respect Ilúvatar's ultimate Authority by recognising that their "knowledge of the drama" is incomplete and restraining from interfering with His intrusions ("the children of Ilúvatar"). For Tolkien, leaving matters incomplete, hidden, or cloaked is a way to leave the space

---

[142] *Letters* 310:560[399] quoted at I.3.

for God's Freedom to enter and transfigure human artistic creation, thus integrating it into His history of creation. The participation of God's freedom in sub-creation is another reason why literature must be 'cloaked' and why it should not be reduced to a doctrinal allegory. Literature is essentially a creative event, something that "has actually happened";[143] just as with any real event, it cannot be fully comprehended or expressed by human minds because God has participated in it. Removing the category of 'event' by trying to reveal or explain everything would simply mean to reduce literature to a purely human undertaking. This would result in a failure of the allure and mission of literature, which for Tolkien was to rekindle the desire for God by collaborating with His creative activity. This was Tolkien's life-long ambition and vocation, as he reveals in a letter he wrote to G. B. Smith in 1916, which was introduced earlier (II.2.2.5), where he describes his literary work in terms very similar to the mission of Gandalf in *The Lord of the Rings*, namely to "rekindle an old light" with a "spark of fire" that has been granted (and not independently conceived):

the TCBS had been granted some **spark of fire** [...] that was destined to kindle a new light, or, what is the same thing, **rekindle an old light** in the world; that the TCBS was destined to testify for God and Truth in a more direct way even than by laying down its several lives in this war. (*Letters* 5, to G.B. Smith, 12/08/1916:6[10])[144]

---

[143] *Letters* 328:578[412], quoted in Chapter II, n.125.

[144] Tolkien's experience with the friends of the TCBS had a seminal influence on his conception of literature, especially as a 'communal' event divinely inspired (cf. I.1.5, I.3). As noted by Atherton (2012) commenting on a poem by G.B. Smith himself, edited by Tolkien

III.3.5 Conclusions

In conclusion, Tolkien's poetics of cloaking, traceable above all in the hiding of the divine narrative in *The Lord of the Rings*, is related to (creative) freedom, "the secret life in creation": (1) the creative freedom of the writer, who is called to express truth in the cloaked dresses of sub-creation; (2) the freedom of the reader, whose dormant 'religiosity', just like that of the Hobbits, does not need preaching, but rather a 'rekindling' or 'recovery' of desire brought about by 'unfamiliar', 'artistic', and 'cloaked' forms; and finally (3) the creative freedom of God, the primary Writer of the Story, which the secondary writer respects, acknowledges, and evokes by purposefully declining to say all in 'primary' terms. Tolkien's creative work has certainly something to do with God, but not because it openly talks about Him or doctrines supposedly related to Him; rather, Tolkien considers his own sub-creation as an "instrument" and fruit of God's own creative power; in this way, God participates in the artistic event. This event ("the mystery of literary creation") involves a mysterious interplay between the freedom of the writer and the freedom of God, for the love of the freedom of the reader. This 'mystical' and collaborative conception of literature has momentous implications for the actual literary fabric of Tolkien's works, which I will discuss at length in Chapter IV, with a focus on internal parallelism and the relationship between particular and universal stories.

after Smith's death in the War: "Its authorial first person plural suggests a communal project, and one which is also divinely inspired. It confirms the sense that the reader, and more to the point Tolkien as editor and literary successor, is called upon to continue 'things undone' and take them further".

IV

Beren and Frodo

Intratextual Parallels and the Universality of the Particular

~

In my discussion of Tolkien's poetics of 'cloaking', I have referred a few times to the concept of 'allegory' and to Tolkien's notorious aversion to it. Unless construed as a mere authorial conceit, this aversion seems to contradict some key aspects of Tolkien's theory and practice of literature, at least as described in Chapters II and III; these aspects are epitomised by Tolkien's claim that his goal was "the elucidation of truth, and the encouragement of good morals in this real world, by the ancient device of exemplifying them in unfamiliar embodiments" (*Letters* 153:289[194]). Allegory – "the ancient device" – seems to describe precisely the kind of derivation and dependence of secondary creations on primary truths discussed in Chapter III. I will openly address this apparent contradiction – one of the great vexed questions of Tolkien scholarship – in this chapter. In so doing, I will again begin with a literary, rather than theoretical, discussion and focus on one of the most important and fascinating features of the fabric of Tolkien's *legendarium*: the hidden presence of a multitude of intratextual parallelism and what appears to be a kind of internal figuration. I will begin, that is, with the relationships between secondary entities, rather than the relationships between primary and secondary entities.

As I will show, the former type of relationship is analogous to the latter and thus may illuminate it.

IV.1 The 'Seamless Web of Story': Parallelism in the Secondary World

IV.1.1 Cross-Referencing to Elder Tales

My journey will begin *in medias res*, or rather *ultimas res* – at the very end of *The Lord of the Rings*. After the Ring has been 'providentially' destroyed, the hobbit Sam addresses his companion Frodo on the fiery slopes of Mount Doom, in a crucial passage:

> What a tale we have been in, Mr. Frodo, haven't we? [...] I wish I could hear it told! Do you think they'll say: Now comes the story of Nine-fingered Frodo and the Ring of Doom? And then everyone will hush, like we did, when in Rivendell they told us the tale of Beren One-hand and the Great Jewel. I wish I could hear it! And I wonder how it will go on after our part. (*LotR* 6.4:950)

Who is Beren One-hand? And why does Sam compare their own story to that of Beren, with a clear meta-narrative twist? As Tolkien readers know well, the tale of Beren and his lover Lúthien belongs to that large mythological corpus that Tolkien began to compose in 1917 during his convalescence after contracting trench fever at the battle of the Somme.[1] For Tolkien, the creation of this

---

[1] Although they were presumably in his mind before that, as he suggests for instance in *Letters* 115, to K. Farrer, 15/06/?1948:185[130], saying that he had laboured at his *legendarium* since about 1914. The early history of composition of Tolkien's *legendarium* is meticulously reconstructed by Christopher Tolkien in his notes and apparatus in *HML*, esp. *BLT1* and *BLT2*. See further Garth 2003, esp. 253–86, Garth 2014 and Garth 2022.

mythology was a response to a vocational call, as became particularly clear to him after the tragedies of the war; it remained his main literary ambition throughout his life,[2] and he continued to tinker with it until the very last days before his death. This mythology was also his greatest disappointment because he never saw it to completion and publication, in contrast with *The Hobbit* and *The Lord of the Rings*, which he had initially considered as unplanned 'intrusions' into this mythological cycle.[3] Preserved in different versions composed at different times, these mythological narratives were only posthumously published in a series of many volumes edited by his son Christopher. The first and best-known in the series is *The Silmarillion*, first published in 1977; the final volumes (at least in Christopher's vision) were published as recently as 2017 and 2018 and are titled *Beren and Lúthien* and *The Fall of Gondolin* – the last, but certainly not the least in the cycle.[4]

The tale of Beren and Lúthien, which dates back to 1917, is, in Tolkien's words, "the chief of the stories", the "fundamental link in the cycle", "the kernel of the mythology".[5] Moreover, as Christopher Tolkien points out in the preface to *Beren and Lúthien*, it is a myth that had a "deeply-rooted

---

[2] Cf. for instance *Letters* 98, to S. Unwin, *c.* 18/03/1945:165[113] "my only real desire is to publish 'The Silmarillion'". On Tolkien's failure to publish the *Silmarillion* tales see Rateliff 2020.

[3] See II.2.2.1 and cf. also *Letters* 124, to S. Unwin, 24/02/1950:193[136] "the Silmarillion and all that has refused to be suppressed. It has bubbled up, infiltrated, and probably spoiled everything."

[4] Two further volumes were published after Christopher's death, *The Nature of Middle-earth* (2021), edited by C. Hostetter, and *The Fall of Númenor* (2022), edited by B. Sibley.

[5] *Letters* 131:209[149] (quoted in IV.3.4); *Letters* 165:321[221].

presence in his [i.e. Tolkien's] own life".[6] The story is preserved in different variants, eventually superseded by the text printed as chapter 19 of *The Silmarillion*. The main narrative can be summarised in Tolkien's own words:

> It is Beren the outlawed mortal who succeeds (with the help of Lúthien, a mere maiden even if an elf of royalty) where all the armies and warriors have failed: he penetrates the stronghold of the Enemy [the Satanic-like Morgoth] and wrests one of the Silmarilli from the Iron Crown. Thus he wins the hand of Lúthien and the first marriage of mortal and immortal is achieved. [...] the capture of the Silmaril, a supreme victory, leads to disaster. The oath of the sons of Fëanor becomes operative, and lust for the Silmaril brings all the kingdoms of the Elves to ruin. (*Letters* 131:209[149])

Why, then, does Sam refer to this particular tale, comparing his own to it? To answer this question, we must first recall that Tolkien did (eventually) integrate the 'high' mythological narratives of the *Silmarillion* cycle into *The Hobbit* and *Lord of the Rings* as both historical and literary elements.

First, in *The Lord of the Rings*, these narratives are presented as actual historical, or semi-historical, events belonging to a very distant past ('the Elder Days'), which is nevertheless connected to the contemporary time (the 'Third Age'); this is accomplished especially through the presence of linking characters (Elrond, Galadriel, and Sauron in particular) and items that occur in both sets of stories (e.g. Frodo's ancestral sword Sting, forged in

---

[6] See IV.2.1, and cf. West 2003; Shippey 2005:292–6; Garth 2003:262–6; Beal 2014 (also discussing possible literary influences); cf. also duPlessis 2019, esp. 39–42.

Beleriand; the ring of Barahir, Beren's father, worn by Aragorn as a token of kingship; the *Palantíri*, perhaps wrought by the ancient artist Fëanor himself[7]).

Secondly, these 'Elder' narratives are often referred to or recounted by characters as pieces of a codified literature, oral and written. The integration of songs and narrative digressions is an important element of Tolkien's technique and contributes to create that "impression of depth" (cf. *MC Beow.*:27), which scholars such as Christopher Tolkien or Tom Shippey have identified as a core element of Tolkien's poetics.[8]

In one early episode of the novel (*LotR* 1.11:191–4), Sam and the other hobbits are introduced to the ancestral myth of Beren and Lúthien by listening to Aragorn who at Weathertop, before the Nazgul's attack, recounts parts of the story, first in verse and then in prose.[9] This story had been originally composed by Tolkien many years before quite independently from *The Lord of the Rings*, before he had even invented (or

---

[7] Cf. *LotR* 3.11:597.

[8] Cf. Christopher Tolkien in *BLT1*:1–11, Shippey 2005:257–67, and the rich investigation of Drout, Hitotsubashi, and Scavera 2014 as well as, more recently, Grybauskas 2021, Birns 2023. Cf. also Nagy 2004; Morrison 2005; Fornet-Ponse 2011; Butler 2013; and Kullman 2013 (the latter for an insightful, although at times speculative, discussion on the way poetic insertions relate with and illuminate their narrative context of performance, and the plot development of *The Lord of the Rings* in general). See further Chapter II, esp. II.2.1.1 on the contribution of the meta-textual frame to the 'impression of depth' in both *The Silmarillion* and *The Lord of the Rings*. See further Atherton 2012:25–38 on (Elvish) songs in *The Hobbit*.

[9] *LotR* 1.11:191 "I will tell you the tale of Tinúviel [...] in brief – for it is a long tale of which the end is not known." On Aragorn's song, and its following prose commentary see Zimmerman 2013.

rather 'discovered', cf. II.2.2.3) the hobbits. After this first sample, it is said that the Hobbits hear the full tale in Rivendell where it is told in its complete poetic version ("The Lay of Leithian");[10] in reality, Tolkien never managed to finalise this tale during his life, and it was made available in its most extended version only in 2017, as already noted.[11]

In the first place, therefore, Sam refers to Beren's tale because he has been repeatedly exposed to it during his journeys. This, however, is just a small part of the answer.

IV.1.2 Joining the Single Story: Narrative Constants

Sam does not simply refer to Beren's tale, he specifically associates his own story with it. This explicit association comes at the end of a journey of awareness, in which the hobbits have gradually discovered that their own story is just one chapter within a much greater and older story – a ring in a narrative chain that links back to Beren's ancestral tale and beyond.[12]

An important step in this journey of narrative awareness takes place during the dialogue between Elrond and Frodo, after the hobbit has finally chosen to accept

---

[10] *LotR* 2.3:277 (the hobbits hearing told in full the lay of Beren and Lúthien in the Hall of Fire at Rivendell).

[11] On the embedding of or allusion to *Silmarillion* material in Tolkien's published works see further Nagy 2003, esp. 241–2 (on allusions to Túrin's tale in *The Lord of the Rings*). Cf. also Hillman 2023b.

[12] Sepe 2008 rightly considers this narrative awareness as a distinctive feature of Tolkien's characters, and relates it to his valuing of stories per se and not as allegorical tools.

his mission to take the Ring to Mordor – a decision that according to Elrond places the hobbit among the "mighty Elf-friends of old" (including Beren himself).[13] Once Frodo has embraced his own (narrative) vocation, Elrond highlights to the small hobbit that he has now joined the great characters of the Elder Tales. Another step in this journey of narrative awareness takes place during Frodo's visions in the Mirror of Galadriel, when he watches some scenes of the "great history" and becomes conscious of his own involvement in it.[14] The most important and explicit step in this journey of awareness, however, is found in the meta-literary dialogue between Sam and Frodo on the stairs of Cirith Ungol; this passage of the book is one of the most dear to Tolkien, and he described it as the "disquisition on the seamless web of story":[15]

[Sam said] 'Beren now, he never thought he was going to get that Silmaril from the Iron Crown in Thangorodrim, and yet he did, and that was a worse place and a blacker danger than ours. But that's a long tale, of course, and goes on past the happiness and into grief and beyond it – and the Silmaril went on and came to Eärendil. And why, sir, I never thought of that before! We've got – you've got some of the light of it in that star-glass that the Lady gave you! **Why, to think of it, we're in the same tale still! It's going on.** Don't the great tales never end?' 'No, they never end as tales,' said Frodo. 'But the

---

[13] *LotR* 2.2:270–1 "if you take it freely, I will say that your choice is right; and though all the mighty Elf-friends of old, [...] and **Beren himself** were assembled together, your seat should be among them".

[14] *LotR* 2.7:364 "many swift scenes followed that Frodo in some way knew to be parts of a **great history in which he had become involved**".

[15] *Letters* 96:159[110].

people in them come, and go when their part's ended. Our part will end later – or sooner'. (*LotR* 4.8:711–12)[16]

In a sudden moment of epiphany, Sam understands that great tales such as that of Beren "never end", and that the hobbits themselves are within the same ongoing tale of Beren. This tale began before them, continues now through them, and, as acknowledged by Frodo's crucial remark, will go on after their part has ended. This meta-narrative dialogue also reveals that the narrative continuity between Beren and Frodo's tales is marked by the presence of some narrative constants that, in some cases, are supposed to be the very same entities. Among these, as Sam realises, is the light of the same Silmaril that was once recovered by Beren from Morgoth's crown, and which now shines in the phial of Galadriel.

Another important element of continuity is the identity of Frodo and Beren's enemies: Sauron, who appears in both stories, and the spider Shelob, who, as explicitly acknowledged by the narrator, was the same (kind of) monster that Beren fought during one of his journeys.[17] Tolkien himself highlights this connection in a letter, confirming that Frodo and Sam's "history is in a sense only a further continuation of" that Beren and Lúthien.[18]

---

[16] For an insightful analysis of this passage, and a discussion of meta-narrative elements in *The Lord of the Rings* in general, see the seminal work by Bowman 2006 (esp. 275–6), to which this section is especially indebted. Cf. also Hillman 2023b.

[17] *LotR* 4.9:723 "There agelong she [Shelob] had dwelt, an evil thing in spider-form, even such as once of old had lived [...] **such as Beren fought in the Mountains of Terror** in Doriath."

[18] *Letters* 144:270[180] "She is represented [...] as descendant of the giant spiders [...] which come into the legends of the First Age, especially into the chief of them, the tale of Beren and Lúthien. This

This continuity is evoked again a few pages later in *The Lord of the Rings*, when Beren's name is quoted during the fight with the monstrous spider.[19] There are many other elements of continuity between Beren and Frodo's respective tales that are less explicit but can be identified by narrative and, at times, even textual parallelism. I have listed the most evident ones in Table IV.1 (next page).

A full discussion of the parallelism of these passages and its literary implications falls outside the scope of this chapter. Here, I will focus on only one of these narrative parallels, a parallel that incorporates several of the others and is also particularly revealing from philological, literary, and 'theological' points of view. This is the scene (item b in the extracts that follow) in which Frodo and Sam are rescued by the eagles, which directly follows the meta-literary dialogue on the slopes of Mount Doom, quoted earlier. This passage has a clear parallel in an equivalent scene in the tale of Beren and Lúthien (item a):

a. Now Beren lay in a swoon within the perilous Gate, and **death drew nigh him** [...] Thus the quest of

is constantly referred to, since as Sam points out [...] **this history is in a sense only a further continuation of it.**" A (meta-literary) connection with the tale of Beren and Lúthien was also present in the original manuscript of *The Hobbit*, eventually deleted in the published version (cf. Rateliff 2011:73). In fact, as noted by Atherton (2012:29–30), "At first [...] Tolkien intended to use the story of Beren and Lúthien as a prequel to the events of *The Hobbit*)." See further Atherton 2012:31–6.

[19] *LotR* 4.10:728 "The blade scored it [...] but those hideous folds could not be pierced by any strength of men, not though [...] **the hand of Beren** or of Túrin wield it."

Table IV.1 Comparison between the tales of Beren and Frodo

	Beren (and Lúthien)	Frodo (and Sam)
Powerlessness and disproportion	"not all the power of the Noldor, […] had availed even to see from afar the shining Silmarils" (*Sil* 19:165) "Beren the outlawed mortal […] succeeds […] where all the armies and warriors have failed" (*Letters* 131:149)	"This is the hour of the Shire-folk, when they arise from their quiet fields to shake the towers and counsels of the Great" (*LotR* 2.2:270; also *LotR* 2.10:398 and 5.4:813 on the madness and folly of Frodo's mission)
(Apparent) hopelessness	"Lúthien […] must with you challenge the fate that lies before you – **hopeless**, yet not certain" (*Sil* 19:178); "**Hopeless** the quest, but not yet mad […] maybe backwards leads your path **beyond all hope** to Doriath" (*BL*:186–7); "**hopes we never had**" (*BL*:198)	"And after all he [Sam] **never had any real hope** in the affair from the beginning. […] Then he knew that the **hope** that had for one wild moment stirred in his heart **was vain**" (*LotR* 4.3:639) "The whole thing is quite **hopeless**" (*LotR* 6.1:914). (cf. V.1.5)
Inspired quest	"Beren looking up beheld the eyes of Lúthien […] **and it seemed to him that words were put into his mouth**" (*Sil* 19:164)	"At last with an effort he [Frodo] spoke, and wondered to hear his own words, **as if some other will was using his small voice**" (*LotR* 2.2:270)

Table IV.1 (cont.)

	Beren (and Lúthien)	Frodo (and Sam)
Defended by fate	"taking the hand and the ring he [Beren] **escaped**, being **defended by fate**" (*Sil* 19:160)	"'It is a marvel that I **escaped**!' 'Yes, **fortune or fate have helped** you'" (*LotR* 2.1:222)
Travelling disguised as Orcs	"they took their [the Orcs'] gear and their weapons [...] their own forms and faces were changed into the likeness of Orcs; and thus **disguised** they came far upon their northern road" (*Sil* 19:168)	"'As we're in Mordor, we'd best dress up Mordor-fashion' [...]. They picked up two shields to complete their **disguise** and then went on" (*LotR* 6.1:912,915)
Powerful ancestral blades	"Beren [...] took his knife, Angrist. That knife was made by **Telchar of Nogrod**, and hung sheathless by his side; **iron it would cleave as if it were green wood**" (*Sil* 19:175)	"'Sting [...] is an elven-blade. There were webs of horror **in the dark ravines of Beleriand where it was forged'**. [...] The blue-gleaming blade shore through them **like a scythe through grass**" (*LotR* 4.9:722)
'Magic' cloaks	"Lúthien climbed from her prison, and **shrouded in her shadowy cloak** she escaped from all eyes" (*Sil* 19:170); "Her **magic cloak** was hidden, and no prayer she spoke was heeded" (*BL*:151)	"'Are these **magic cloaks**?' asked Pippin, looking at them with wonder" (*LotR* 2.8:370); "Not even an eagle [...] would have marked the hobbits [...] **shrouded in their thin grey cloaks**" (*LotR* 4.3:644)

Table IV.1 (cont.)

	Beren (and Lúthien)	Frodo (and Sam)
Imprisonment in a tower, freedom through a star song[20]	"Lúthien […] sang a song that no walls of stone could hinder. **Beren heard, and he thought that he dreamed; for the stars shone above him** […]. And in answer he sang a song of challenge that he had made **in praise of the Seven Stars**" (*Sil* 19:172)	"suddenly new strength rose in him, and his voice rang out […] *beyond all towers strong and high*,	[…] *Stars for ever dwell*:	[…] **'I wasn't dreaming after all when I heard that singing** down below, and I tried to answer?" (*LotR* 6.1:908,910)
Stars and hope	"the **silver fire** that once Men named the Burning Briar, the Seven Stars […] were burning yet, **a light in darkness, hope in woe**, the emblem vast of Morgoth's foe" (*BL*:158)	"Sam saw a **white star** twinkle for a while. The beauty of it smote his heart, as he looked up out of the forsaken land, and **hope returned to him**" (*LotR* 6.2:922)
Holding a Silmarillion	"As he closed [the Silmaril] in his hand, the radiance welled through his living flesh, and **his hand became like a shining lamp**" (*Sil* 19:181)	"slowly he held aloft the Phial of Galadriel. […] it began to burn, and kindled to a silver flame […] as though Eärendil had himself come down […] with the last Silmaril upon his brow. […] **the hand that held it sparkled with white fire**" (*LotR* 4.9:720; also ibid. 730).

[20] Cf. Rosegrant 2019 for a comparison between the two songs.

Table IV.1 (cont.)

	Beren (and Lúthien)	Frodo (and Sam)
Travelling through places of terror	"Beren [...] climbing into the high regions of **Gorgoroth**, the Mountains of Terror, he descried afar the land of Doriath" (*Sil* 19:161)	"I was going to **Gorgoroth**. I must find the Mountain of Fire and cast the thing into the gulf of Doom" (*LotR* 6.2:922)
Mutilation, wounding and personal defeat	"Carcharoth [...] **took suddenly the hand within his jaws, and he bit off at the wrist.** [...] Thereafter Beren was **named Erchamion**, which is **the One-handed**; and suffering was graven in his face" (*Sil* 19:181)	"**Suddenly** Sam saw Gollum's long hands draw upwards to his mouth; **his white fangs gleamed, and then snapped as they bit**" (*LotR* 6.3:946); "I will sing to you of **Frodo of the Nine Fingers**" (*LotR* 6.4:954)
Bliss and grief	"there are yet some [tales] in which **amid weeping there is joy** [...] and of these histories most fair still [...] is the tale of Beren and Lúthien" (*Sil* 19:158); "Then Beren lay upon the ground in a swoon, as one slain at once by **bliss and grief**" (ibid. 163)	"all the host **laughed and wept** [...] in the midst of their merriment and tears [...] and they passed in thought out to regions where **pain and delight flow together** and tears are the very wine of blessedness" (*LotR* 6.4:954)

the Silmaril was like to have ended **in ruin and despair**; but in that hour above the wall of the valley **three mighty birds appeared**, flying northwards with wings **swifter than the wind**. [...] High above the realm of Morgoth Thorondor and his vassals soared, and [...] lifted up Lúthien and Beren from the earth, and bore them aloft into the clouds. Below them suddenly thunder rolled, lightings leaped upward, and **the mountains quaked. Fire and smoke** belched forth from Thangorodrim (*Sil* 19:181)

b. 'The North Wind blows, but **we shall outfly it**,' said Gwaihir. And he lifted up Gandalf and sped away south, and with him went Landroval, and Meneldor young and swift. [...] And so it was that Gwaihir saw them [...] two small dark figures, forlorn, hand in hand upon a little hill, while **the world shook** under them, and gasped, and **rivers of fire drew near**. And even as he espied them and came swooping down, he saw them fall, worn out, or choked with fumes and heat, or **stricken down by despair at last, hiding their eyes from death**. [...] the wanderers were lifted up and borne far away out of the darkness and the fire. (*LotR* 6.4:950–1)

The setting of the two scenes is similar: the fiery slopes of an active volcano, close to the impregnable fortress of a dreadful Enemy. The narrative context is the same: two improbable heroes, one of whom has just been indelibly maimed, have just performed an impossible quest – indeed the central, iconic quest of their age (the recovery of one of the Silmarils in the First Age of *The*

Silmarillion; the destruction of the Ring in the Third Age of *The Lord of the Rings*). In both cases, moreover, the fulfilment of the general quest has paradoxically involved a personal defeat: Frodo has 'fallen' at the very last stage, and the quest has been saved only thanks to the providential intervention of Gollum; Beren has recovered the Silmaril, but the hand holding it has been devoured by a werewolf.

Most importantly, the characters are unexpectedly rescued at the very moment they yield to despair: in both cases, the quest seemed hopeless from the beginning and yet, until the moment of despair, they clung to a slight thread of hope and persisted on their paths, confident that their quest was somehow 'desired' by some higher power. But, at the end of their respective missions, their confidence wanes, and they are at last overcome by despair. In both tales, this is the very moment that the three eagles appear, fighting against the wind and rescuing the protagonists, whose smallness, powerlessness, and mortality is more evident than ever.

The fact that this parallelism is not coincidental is further confirmed by the textual history of the narrative. First, the rescue of Beren and Lúthien by the three eagles does not occur in the earlier versions of the tale, as preserved in the oldest manuscripts. In these versions, little is told about their escape from the fortress of Angband, which they manage on their own or with the help of the hound Huan (cf. *BL*:77–8 and 138). The "radical change" in the manner of their escape (cf. *BL*:222) was inserted by Tolkien only at a later stage, after or at least at the same time as *The Hobbit* (with its eucatastrophic eagles scene) was completed in 1937, and perhaps later than that.[21] Second, and more importantly, in the original version of the eagles scene in *Beren and Lúthien*, regrettably abridged by Christopher Tolkien in the 1977 *Silmarillion*, the eagles accompanying Thorondor were named Lhandroval and Gwaewar, the very same eagles that rescue Frodo and Sam in *The Lord of the Rings*.[22] Later, in 1951, Tolkien emended the spelling of Gwaewar into Gwaihir, clearly in order to bring it in accord with *The Lord of the Rings*, as noted by Christopher Tolkien himself in his commentary to this text (*LR* 2.6:301). That Tolkien conceived a continuity between the eagles scenes in *Beren and Lúthien* and *The Lord of the Rings* (as well as with that in *The Hobbit*, arguably their common source) seems thus to be beyond doubt.

[21] It is difficult to reconstruct the textual history and exact dating of the *Beren and Tinúviel* tale in the manuscripts of the *Quenta Silmarillion*, which formed the basis of the *Beren and Lúthien* chapter in the published 1977 *Silmarillion*, and especially of its final part, after the monstruous wolf Carcharoth has bitten Beren's hand holding the *Silmaril* (see esp. Christopher's tentative reconstruction in *LR* 2.6:292–306). The first record with the eagles is apparently found in the text printed in *LB* 3:309–10 ("relatively late" according to Christopher); it appears in manuscripts QS(B) and QS(C) of the *Quenta Silmarillion* (cf. *LR* 2.6:294–5 and 301), tentatively dated by Christopher to 1937, about the same time *The Hobbit* was finalised and published (but I wonder whether this date is correct). In the *Later Annals of Beleriand*, dating to the late 1930s, the eagles do not yet appear (*LR* 2.3:135), in contrast to the version of the *Grey Annals* (*WJ* 1:63) dating to the 1950s, after the composition of *The Lord of the Rings*. It is also certain that the conclusion of the tale of Beren and Lúthien was added to the manuscript of *Quenta Silmarillion* by Tolkien only in 1951 (cf. *LR* 2.6:295). Cf. also *BL*:222–3.

[22] Cf. *LotR* 6.4:948 "Gwaihir the Windlord, and Landroval his brother […] mightiest of the descendants of old Thorondor".

IV.1.3 Bilbo and Aragorn: Genealogical Connections

The parallelism between Frodo and Beren is just one example within a large group of closely interconnected narrative patterns. In Tolkien's work, one can identify hundreds of constants and parallels of this kind; they join the different tales and characters of Middle-earth (and beyond) into a very complex 'web' of narrative units, all different and yet similar, as different leaves of the same tree (to introduce a key Tolkienian image).[23] I will here give just two further examples to illustrate that the parallelism between Frodo and Beren is not unique, but rather just one among many parallels between Tolkien's characters and tales.

First, Frodo is not just continuing or reliving Beren's story in a new form. Another important narrative

[23] On narrative parallelism in Tolkien's works see Hausmann 2015, noting, for example, the similarity between Glorfindel and Gandalf's respective duels against the Balrog, the David-and-Goliath-like battles of Fingolfin and Éowyn against Morgoth and the Witch-King, the parallel choices of mortality of Lúthien and Arwen. Hausmann also discusses another similar and yet different pattern of narrative parallelism ("distorting mirror"), which involves pairs of characters (such as Gandalf and Saruman) showing "strong similarities in their development but [...] direct oppositions in terms of their character disposition and their fates" (32). Cf. also Lewis 2007 (on Beorn and Tom Bombadil); Emerson 2008; Klinger 2009b; Atherton 2012, passim (on various connections between characters in *The Hobbit* and other characters and episodes in early drafts of Tolkien's *legendarium*, including Beren and Beorn, Tuor and Thorin); Caughey 2022. On intertextual parallelism in Tolkien beyond Middle-earth see Swank 2013 (on typological similarities between Gandalf and Father Christmas, the Polar Bear and Beorn); Long 2014 (on elements in *Smith of Wootton Major* paralleling elements of the *legendarium*, esp. Nokes // Gandalf, Faery Queen // Galadriel, etc.).

referent for Frodo is his cousin Bilbo: again and again, the narrator of *The Lord of the Rings* alludes to the notion that Frodo is reliving Bilbo's story, in a similar and yet different fashion.[24] For instance, Frodo's adventure begins with a song composed by his friends Merry and Pippin, which is described as having the same tune as the dwarf-song opening the *Hobbit*'s adventure, but (crucially) different words.[25] In his journey, Frodo will travel by the same roads and to the same places as Bilbo (e.g. Rivendell and the road leading there),[26] meet the same people (e.g. the Trolls), and, at times, explicitly recall "Bilbo's account of his journey" and their "family history".[27] Using Bilbo's own dagger, Sting, Frodo will also fight the same kind of enemies fought by his cousin, including especially the monstrous spiders of Mirkwood, which are likely the offspring of Shelob herself.[28] In some cases, the connection between Bilbo and Frodo (who also share the same birthday) is explicitly

[24] On the significance of Bilbo and Frodo's genealogical connections see Honegger 2020.

[25] Cf. *LotR* 1.5:106.

[26] *LotR* 1.12:208 (the hobbits and Aragorn following the very track used by Gandalf, Bilbo, and the dwarves; also *LotR* 2.1:225 (quoted in II.1.2).

[27] Cf. *LotR* 1.12:201 (Frodo recalling Bilbo's description of the towers on the hills north of the Road and the account of his first serious adventure with the Trolls):205 (Frodo recognising the Trolls as the characters of Bilbo's tale); 206 ("the reminder of Bilbo's first successful adventure was heartening"); 208 (Merry recognising the stone that marked the place where the dwarves had hidden the trolls' gold). Also *LotR* 1.8:140 (Frodo recalling "Bilbo Baggins and his stories" and thereby finding courage to fight the Barrow-wight; *LotR* 3.4:461 (Merry contrasting the forest of Fangorn with Bilbo's description of Mirkwood).

[28] Cf. *LotR* 4.9:723 (Shelob's broods spreading to the fastnesses of Mirkwood).

acknowledged by Gandalf: "'You take after Bilbo,' said Gandalf. 'There is more about you than meets the eye, as I said of him long ago'" (*LotR* 2.5:328).[29]

There are several other narrative elements – more covert, but no less important – pointing to a continuity between Frodo and Bilbo's stories. I am thinking, for instance, of the constant homesickness of the two hobbits;[30] the deciphering of secret signs by the light of the moon;[31] the journey under the mountains after an unsuccessful attempt at crossing them;[32] and, above all, the topical intervention of eagles. In *The Lord of the Rings*, the hobbit Pippin explicitly acknowledges this last point of continuity to Bilbo's story, commenting on the arrival of the eagles at the battle of the Morannon, which is announced with the very same words used by Bilbo during the Battle of the Five Armies ("The Eagles are

---

[29] Cf. also *LotR* 1.2:146, where Gandalf recalls the dramatic start of Bilbo's journey, which occurred at the same time of spring "nearly eighty years before", just before disclosing the Ring's origin to Frodo, and analogously initiating his adventure. This is followed a few pages later by Frodo's great desire ("which flamed up his heart") to follow Bilbo and run out the road "as Bilbo had done on a similar morning long ago" (*LotR* 1.1:62).

[30] Cf. *Hobbit* 2:38 "'I wish I was at home in my nice hole by the fire [...].' It was not the last time that he wished that!" // *LotR* 1.11:184 (the hobbits thinking of "sunset [...] through the cheerful windows of Bag End"); *LotR* 2.4:318 (Frodo wishing with all his heart to be back to Bag End).

[31] *LotR* 2.4:304 (moonlight revealing signs on the doors of Moria), which is analogous to the reading of Thorin's map by Elrond at the light of the moon in *Hobbit* 3:62–4.

[32] *LotR* 2.4, the fateful journey through Moria, undertaken after failing to reach the Redhorn pass, which parallels *Hobbit* 4 ("Over Hill and Under Hill"), where Bilbo and companions try to pass the mountains, but will eventually need to go under it).

coming", *LotR* 5.10:893 = *Hobbit* 17:330).[33] This identity
of phrasing makes Pippin recall Bilbo and his (fortunate)
tale (of "long long ago"), and yet this encouraging parallelism is immediately rejected by the hobbit on the basis
of a supposed difference ("This is my tale, and it is ended
now") before he loses consciousness (just as Bilbo did in
the parallel episode). In fact, Pippin's initial understanding of the coming of the eagles is correct despite his following despondency: his own tale is not different, in this
respect, from Bilbo's and will conclude, as in *The Hobbit*,
with an unexpected victory and a happy ending facilitated
by eagles.

As this passage also shows, narrative parallelism in
Tolkien's work often has meta-literary implications:
the characters compare the new story that is unfolding
through them to the 'literary' tales with which they are
familiar, and they discover – as unexpectedly as Sam
did in the passage quoted at IV.1.2 – that the 'literary'
tale uniquely continues through their own particular
story. Despite their kinship, Bilbo and Frodo remain
distinct, individual characters, as Tolkien remarked:
"Frodo is not intended to be another Bilbo" (*Letters*
151:279[186]). Whatever their similarities, their two
stories also have substantial differences and should not

---

[33] *Hobbit* 17:330 "'**The Eagles are coming!**' [...] 'The Eagles!' cried
Bilbo once more, but at that moment a stone hurtling from above
smote heavily on his helm, and he fell with a crash **and knew no
more**"; *LotR* 5.10:893 "'**The Eagles are coming! The Eagles are
coming!**' For one moment more Pippin's thought hovered. 'Bilbo!' it
said. 'But no! That came in his tale, **long long ago. This is my tale,
and it is ended now.** Good-bye!' And his thought fled far away and
his eyes saw no more." Tolkien highlights this momentous passage
in his letter to Milton Waldman (*Letters* 131:226).

be equated, as if one were a mere 'repetition' or 'allegory' of the other.[34]

The combination of likeness and unlikeness is key in another important narrative pair, namely Beren and Aragorn, and their related tales.[35] There are many similarities, often explicitly highlighted, between these two characters; this includes especially the topos of a marriage between a mortal man and an immortal Elvish queen who sacrifices her immortality for his sake. In particular, Aragorn's first encounter with his beloved Arwen is openly compared to the archetypal encounter between Beren and Lúthien, with Aragorn calling Arwen with the same epithet (Tinúviel) originally used by Beren for Lúthien:

For Aragorn had been singing a part of the Lay of Lúthien which tells of the meeting of Lúthien and Beren in the forest of Neldoreth. [...] he called to her crying, Tinúviel, Tinúviel! even as Beren had done in the Elder Days long ago. (*LotR Appendix A*:1058)[36]

This passage has strong meta-literary implications, with Aragorn re-enacting (or rather renewing) the very literary

[34] Frodo himself acknowledges the difference, noting that in contrast to Bilbo's 'there and back again' treasure quest, he had to lose a treasure "and not return" (*LotR* 1.2:66; the same point is repeated to his hobbit friends at *LotR* 1.5:104 "This is no treasure-hunt, no there-and-back journey"). On the differences between Bilbo and Frodo's adventure see for example Flieger 2014b; cf. also Holtz-Wodzak 2014, Klarner 2014.

[35] On the relation between the tales of Beren and Lúthien, and Aragorn and Arwen, see esp. West 2003, 2006, 2011. On Aragorn's character and its development see Nicholas 2012; Stephen 2012.

[36] Cf. also ibid. 1059 "I see [...] that I have turned my eyes to a treasure no less dear than the treasure of Thingol that Beren once desired"; *LotR* 6.6:974 "mine is the choice of Lúthien, and as she so have I chosen, both the sweet and the bitter".

tale that was the subject of his song.[37] Other, more covert, connections concern, for instance, the already mentioned "ring of Barahir", which plays an important part in Beren's tale;[38] or Aragorn's ancestral sword Narsil, which was first wrought by the smith Telchar "in the deeps of time",[39] that is, the same artificer of Beren's own blade Angrist.[40]

The similarity between Aragorn and Beren's tales is also justified in genealogical terms. Aragorn and Arwen are descendants of Beren and Lúthien, as pointed out by Tolkien in a letter.[41] In fact, Arwen is so similar to Lúthien that the Elves almost considered her as Lúthien's reincarnation: Arwen is she in whom "the likeness of Lúthien had come on earth again" (*LotR* 2.1:227). Again, Arwen and Lúthien are nonetheless different, unique individuals, as Tolkien himself explicitly stressed,[42] and yet there is a "likeness" between them, in all respects, which is linked to their genealogical ties.[43] The genealogical image is important and iconic in Tolkien,[44] and

[37] As also rightly highlighted by Barkley 1995:260; Bowman 2006:278–9.
[38] Cf. *LotR Appendix A*:1057 (the ring as a token of Elrond and Aragorn's kinship from afar).
[39] *LotR* 3.6:511.
[40] On parallel artefacts and their significance cf. Klinger 2009b (on similarly personified weapons) and Flieger 2014b (noting analogies between the Silmarils, the Arkenstone, and the Ring).
[41] *Letters* 144:270[180] "Both Elrond (and his daughter Arwen Undómiel, who resembles Lúthien closely in looks and fate) are descendants of Beren and Lúthien; and so at very many more removes is Aragorn."
[42] *Letters* 153:288[193] "Arwen is not a 're-incarnation' of Lúthien [...] but a descendant very like her in looks, character, and fate."
[43] On the similarity between Lúthien and Arwen cf. further Emerson 2008, Hausmann 2015, and the bibliography quoted in n.35.
[44] For an investigation of genealogical connections and their significance in Tolkien's works see Nicholas 2015.

is related to the aforementioned notion of a single ongoing Tale: there is only one Story; there is only one family tree, which sprouts again and again with different branches.

IV.1.4 Renewals and Tributaries

The motive of a genealogical revival is recurrent in Tolkien's works and is often evoked by the language and imagery of 'renewal'.[45] This is applied, for instance, to Aragorn's re-forged sword ("Renewed shall be blade that was broken", *LotR* 1.10:170)[46] and to Aragorn in general, also known as Envinyatar (the 'renewer'),[47] the one in whom the "dignity and kingship of the kings of old was renewed" (*LotR Appendix A*:1044).[48] Above all, the image of renewal is applied to the ancestral lineage of the trees of Gondor, which parallels Aragorn's own lineage. As the eagle of the Lords of the West sings in the psalmic hymn of victory discussed in Chapter III (III.1.2.1): "the Tree that was withered shall be renewed, | [...] and the City shall be blessed". (*LotR* 6.5:963). In the aftermath of the victory, Gandalf discovers a sapling of this ancestral tree preserved under the snow of Mount Mindolluin, whose life has been sleeping for many long years; the wizard then reminds Aragorn, the renewed king, of the ancient origin

[45] On 'renewal' as a key theme in *The Lord of the Rings* see for example Devine 2016.

[46] Cf. also *LotR* 2.3:276 (the Sword of Elendil forged anew); *LotR* 5.6:848 "Narsil re-forged as deadly as of old".

[47] Cf. *LotR* 5.8:86.

[48] Cf. also ibid. 1057 "the kingship was renewed". On Aragorn's role as a renewer cf. Gallant 2020b.

of the tree and of its future offspring, which "should be planted, lest the line die out of the world" (*LotR* 6.5:972–3).

The genealogical-botanic image of endless renewal is strictly related to another important image; that is, the motive of a single Road, which "goes on and on", and to which all individual paths lead and belong. This motive is associated with Bilbo in particular. The hobbit "used often to say there was only one Road; that it was like a great river: its springs were at every doorstep, and every path was its tributary" (*LotR* 1.3:73–4), and he, moreover, even composed an iconic poem about the Road:[49]

> The Road goes ever on and on
>> Down from the door where it began.
> Now far ahead the Road has gone,
>> And I must follow, if I can,
> Pursuing it with eager feet,
>> Until it joins some larger way
> Where many paths and errands meet.
>> And whither then? I cannot say. (*LotR* 1.1:35)[50]

These images, the renewal of the lineage, the many paths converging into one Road, the great river,[51] epitomise an important idea at the core of Tolkien's literary

---

[49] See Shippey 2000:288–92 for an analysis of the poem, in its different versions.

[50] The poem appears in another form at the end of the story (*LotR* 6.6:987), with important variations. For an insightful analysis of Bilbo's Walking Song see Zimmerman 2013.

[51] To these one should also add the image of the Tree and its branches (see IV.3.3). In a fragmentary text now included in *NME* (2.15:256) Tolkien explains that the use of the imagery of Rivers ("proceeding from a spring to their outflow into the Sea") to denote the relationship between Patterns and individuals is typical of Elves, whereas Men "often liken these things to Trees with branches".

theory. This is the notion of a single Story continuing "ever on and on" by being renewed in always different – yet always similar – individual stories. This idea of 'narrative renewal' is reflected by the parallels between Beren, Bilbo, Frodo, and Aragorn, and their respective stories, which are, I stress, only selected instances of a much more widespread phenomenon of Tolkien's literary fabric.[52]

IV.1.5 The Spring at Every Doorstep

An important implication of Tolkien's vision of narrative renewal is that its starting point is not the general Story but rather the individual story, the particular path. As Bilbo said to Frodo, the spring of the river-Road is "in every doorstep"; it is at the beginning of each personal story, however unimportant it might initially seem. Indeed, that each individual path is a tributary of the single 'Story' is neither the result of an original deduction nor is it the fulfilment of a project; rather, it is the surprise discovery that only emerges and at the end of a journey, as it does for Frodo and Sam. This is as true in literature as it is in life, as Tolkien stated in a letter: "Men do go, and have in history gone on

---

[52] Some explicit cases are for example *LotR* 5.4:828 "Grond they named it, in memory of the Hammer of the Underworld of old'"; *LotR* 3.6:522 "In him [Shadowfax] one of the mighty steeds of old has returned"; *LotR* 3.7:540 "Helm is arisen and comes back to war"; *LotR* 2.5:323 "Here we are, caught, just as they were before"; *NME* 3.16:348 (the elven smith Celebrimbor 'repeating' the story of the great Fëanor). Cf. also Tolkien's decision to reuse the illustration originally conceived for the forest of Taur-nu-Fuin for the forest of Mirkwood in *The Hobbit* (cf. *Letters* 14, to Allen & Unwin, 28/05/1937:22[18] "The Mirkwood picture is much the same as the plate in *The Hobbit*, but illustrates a different adventure", on which see further Hammond and Scull 1995:55, 58.

journeys and quests, without any intention of acting out allegories of life" (*Letters* 183:345[239]; see IV.2.2.2). The universal meaning of a narrative journey (i.e. its connection with the Story) is revealed to characters only once they have started 'walking' out of their doorstep and down the path that has been laid down for them.[53] As shown by Elrond's reaction to Frodo's decision to bear the Ring to Mordor (cf. IV.1.2), individual characters join the great River of Story, connecting themselves to the great heroes only once they have embraced their own particular story.

For this reason, the kind of narrative parallels discussed here should not be construed as 'internal allegories'. Frodo is not an 'allegorical' figure for Beren or Bilbo (or vice versa). Frodo's story is tightly connected with those of Beren and Bilbo, and many others,[54] but it has its own independent value, its particular "doorstep". The idiosyncratic features of Frodo, Bilbo, Beren, and Aragorn are not obliterated by their connection with a single, universal River-Story, but are, rather, enhanced and 'ennobled' by it. This is why one of the main themes of *The Lord of the Rings*, as Tolkien himself declared, is

---

[53] On the narrative significance of journeying cf. Tolkien's discussion in *Letters* 183:345-7[239-40], describing Bilbo's Walking Song as his attempt to express his observation that "even an afternoon-to-evening walk may have important effects". He also points out however that people change on journeys "without any high motive" or "need of symbolic explanation". Cf. also Bridgwater (2010, 2015), rightly arguing that the decision to travel (more or less reluctantly), versus staying home or in an 'insular realm' ('stasis'), has a momentous narrative significance in Tolkien, and is also charged with metaphysical implications. Cf. also Caughey 2022.

[54] Cf. also *Letters* 180:337[232] (on the analogous ennoblement of the ugly Duckling and Frodo).

the enhancement of the low and the humble and their integration into the high.[55]

At the end of our own journey into the "seamless Web of Story", it is time to address other fascinating questions: What is the meaning of this key feature of Tolkien's literary fabric, which we have seen epitomised in the narrative parallelism between the tales of Beren and Frodo? What has this to do with Tolkien's primary views on literature and life?

IV.2 Criss-crossing between Secondary and Primary Planes

IV.2.1 The Unfailing Line of Lúthien

To treat the questions raised at the end of IV.1.5, we must now start walking, as it were, towards the primary world, and directly address Tolkien's own views about the meaning of his tales and the relationship between fiction and reality. More specifically, to return to the case study already outlined, we need to address the issue of the relation between Beren's story and Tolkien's own personal, primary reality; that is, between literature and life, sub-creation and Creation. Tolkien strongly warned against this kind of exercise, claiming that only "one's guardian Angel, or indeed God Himself, could unravel the real relationship between personal facts and an author's works" (*Letters* 213, to D. Webster, 25/10/1958:411[288]).[56]

[55] Cf. *Letters* 131:220[159] "this is a study of simple ordinary man, neither artistic nor noble and heroic (but not without the undeveloped seeds of these things) against a high setting".
[56] Cf. also n.64.

And yet, as regards our particular case study, one should point out that Tolkien himself suggested that Beren's archetypal tale had a special relation with his own life story. This is iconically manifest in the inscription of the names of Beren and Lúthien upon his gravestone in Wolvercote cemetery in Oxford. In a letter commenting upon their grave inscription, he explicitly declared that his wife Edith was his own Lúthien and confessed that the inspiration for Lúthien's tale came from a crucial episode of their youthful love story. Although he never called her Lúthien, Edith was indeed for Tolkien "the source of the story that in time became the chief part of the Silmarillion" (*Letters* 340, to Christopher Tolkien, 11/07/1972:590[420]),[57] that is, the tale of Beren and Lúthien, through which he expressed "things deepest felt" such as "the dreadful sufferings of our childhoods [...] the sufferings that we endured after our love began" (ibid.). Continuing this line of interpretation, one could note the presence of many narrative parallels between Tolkien and Beren's story, including the existence of an initial ban; the unexpected survival after a battle; and the general fulfilment of an impossible hope, which is yet 'marred' by unhealed wounds.

Should we thus construe Beren and Lúthien as 'allegories' of Tolkien's own love story with Edith? I am sure that Tolkien would have strongly resisted this, while at the same time admitting that there was in fact some sort of relation between the two tales. The nature of this relation, I believe, can be inferred from a couple of passages

---

[57] Cf. also *Letters* 332, to M. Tolkien, 24/01/1972:417 "[then] I met the Lúthien Tinúviel of my own personal 'romance'". On the 'allegorical' significance of the tale of Beren and Lúthien see Maillet 2020.

in *The Lord of the Rings*, which introduce the notion that Lúthien's line "shall never fail", "though the years may lengthen beyond count".[58] To understand the implications of this phrasing, one must recall that in Tolkien's vision, the events of *The Silmarillion* and *The Lord of the Rings* took place in an imaginary past of our own world.[59] In fact, many of his tales were originally conceived within a time-travel framework, which Tolkien had agreed to write in tandem with C. S. Lewis' space-travel novels.[60] Within this framework, the idea that Lúthien's line shall never fail but will continue to sprout in distant future, "though all the world is changed",[61] implies the suggestion that there will always be new embodiments of Lúthien's tale, in different times and places. These include the timeframe of *The Silmarillion* and *The Lord of the Rings* as well as Tolkien's own twentieth-century England, which is supposed to be the same Middle-earth thousands of years and several tectonic changes later. Therefore, according to this framework, Tolkien's wife

---

[58] *LotR* 1.11:194 "There live still those of whom Lúthien was the foremother, and it is said that **her line shall never fail**"; *LotR* 5.9:876) "is he [Aragorn] not of the children of Lúthien? **Never shall that line fail, though the years may lengthen beyond count.**"

[59] Cf. for instance *LotR Prologue*:2 describing the regions where the Hobbits lived as "the Nord-West of the Old World", although "the shape of all lands has been changed", since those days are "long past". On this chronology and its gradual dimming (but not full obscuration) in the development of the *legendarium* cf. also II.1 with n.5; see further Rateliff 2006.

[60] Cf. *Letters* 24:39[29]; *Letters* 252:479[342]; *Letters* 257:487[347]; *Letters* 294:531[378].

[61] Cf. *Sil* 19:187 "Lúthien [...] is the forerunner of many in whom the Eldar see yet, **though all the world is changed**, the likeness of Lúthien the beloved, whom they have lost."

Edith could, in fact, be a descendant of Lúthien, alike to her as Arwen was.

There are many suggestive hints that in Tolkien's literary vision, the genealogical imagery discussed in the previous sections (and its related idea of renewal) crossed the dividing line between story and history.[62] Some posthumous texts from Tolkien's *legendarium* explicitly thematise the idea of a genealogical connection between fictional and real history. In particular, the Anglo-Saxon traveller Ælfwine, who acts as the frame narrator in many of Tolkien's early works (cf. II.1), is construed as a descendant of Eärendil (married to Beren's granddaughter Elwing). In the *Notion Club Papers*, Ælfwine or Alwin is cast as a twentieth-century Oxford English lecturer, belonging to a literary group very similar to the *Inklings*; he thus closely recalls Tolkien himself (as well as the Tolkien-inspired Elwin protagonist of C. S. Lewis' Space Trilogy). Alwin's 'secondary' ancestor is the Númenórean leader Elendil, himself another descendant of Eärendil.

These meta-literary genealogies imply the idea of a narrative continuity between the secondary and primary world; that is, the belief that the single Story identified in Tolkien's secondary world also extends into the primary world. But in what sense are Tolkien and Edith 'related' to Beren and Lúthien? How can those images

---

[62] Cf. Bowman 2006 (esp. 278–9) on Tolkien's blurring of the line between story and history, also thanks to a sophisticated use of meta-narrative comments. Bowman also discusses some literary precedents, including the episode of Paolo and Francesca in Dante's *Inferno*. On the concept of genealogy within a discourse on the relationship between individual and traditional/universal elements cf. also *SV*:24–5, quoted in IV.2.3.

of re-blossoming, re-forging, re-walking, re-singing, re-living, and, in sum, renewal apply to the relationship between literary works and real, primary entities? To fully address these questions, I finally need to address Tolkien's primary views on Allegory and how, for him, it is different from 'Story'.

IV.2.2 Allegory versus Story

It is tempting to describe the various forms of narrative parallelism discussed here in allegorical terms, as if Frodo were an allegorical type for Beren (or vice versa), Beren and Frodo for Tolkien, and so on, using the word 'allegory' in its basic etymological sense (*allos* + *agoreuein*, 'to speak/ refer to something else'). Because of this pervasive 'like-ness' of Tolkien's narratives (primary and secondary), it is natural to construe a particular character or episode in Tolkien's work as ultimately referring to something else (*allos*); such referents might include an event, char-acter, or situation of Tolkien's own life, or, more spe-cifically, an element somehow related to his (Christian) ideology. This kind of exegetical approach has permeated the reception of Tolkien's works from its very outset, and it seems almost unavoidable for scholars who seek to go beyond a mere encyclopaedic description of his *legendar-ium* in search of some sort of 'meaning' or 'source' of his works. And yet there is plenty of evidence to suggest that Tolkien objected to this kind of approach and its theoret-ical assumptions, just as he lamented source criticism,[63]

---

[63] Cf. *Letters* 297:536[379] "I remain puzzled, and indeed sometimes irritated, by many of the guesses at the 'sources' of the nomenclature,

or biographical criticism of his works.[64] Tolkien's relationship to allegory is, then, a thorny issue, a kind of gordian knot;[65] in many cases, Tolkien scholars cut the

and theories or fancies concerning hidden meanings"; *Letters* 337, to Mr Wrigley, 25/05/1972:587[418] "the search for the sources of The Lord of the Rings is going to occupy academics for a generation or two. I wish this need not be so"; *TCG* 812 (1969) where Tolkien calls for caution about identifying supposed sources of his work, since these are often things that he has never read nor wants to read, and inviting to consider that completely unrelated stories could feature the same things for no other reason that they are part of the same "human experiences and traditions". Cf. also Tolkien's famous words against the "desire to see the bones" in the soup of story (*TOFS*:39–40=*TL*:20) and his angry reply to a reader who had sent him a questionnaire including questions on the sources of his writing (*TCG* 566).

[64] Cf. *Letters* 183:345[239] "The story is not about JRRT at all, and is at no point an attempt to allegorize his experience of life"; *Letters* 199:371[257] "I do not feel inclined to go into biographical detail. I doubt its relevance to criticism"; *Letters* 329:580[414] "investigation of an author's biography [...] is an entirely vain and false approach to his works"; *Letters* 347a, to Miss T.R.C., ?January 1973;:599–600, "I have disliked intensely the dissection, source-hunting, interpretation, and biographical tunnelling and scavenging which are supposed [...] to assist in the dissection interpretation and 'understanding' of literary works"; *TCG* 812 (1969), arguing against those who try to "analyse" him; *SWM GK*:89 "do not pay any attention to me" [in a passage deploring the insertion of biographical introductions in books]. In (seemingly) contrast, in an unpublished letter (*TCG* 231, 1956) Tolkien claimed that he could not explain how his story grew "in anything less than an autobiography" (cf. also *TCG* 523 in which Tolkien discusses the influence of his long-lived grandfathers on the characterisation of the Old Took). And yet in another letter (*TCG* 717, 1966) he stressed that it is inevitable to be influenced by and to make use of personal events or life experiences, but this has nothing to do with allegory. For an example of a study explicitly aiming to investigate the interrelationship between Tolkien's biography and writing see Rosegrant 2021. Cf. also IV.2.1.

[65] On Tolkien and allegory see in particular the pithy overview by Petty 2007 with bibl.; cf. also Murray 1999; Shippey 2000:161–74; Flieger and Shippey 2001; Weidner 2002; Geier 2008; Segura 2010; Honegger 2011; Maillet 2020; Ordway 2023b (among many

knot by simply ignoring or rejecting Tolkien's warnings, regardless of whether they do so implicitly or explicitly.[66] Alternatively, they circumvent the issue, or settle uncomfortably with (vague) references to the notion of

others). As regards source criticism in Tolkien (which is another facet of the same exegetical problem, see *Letters* 347a quoted in the previous note) cf. Fisher 2011, esp. the editor's preface and the introductory discussion by Tom Shippey (2011b). An influential theoretical concept in this respect is that of 'calquing'; this concept was first used by Shippey (cf. esp. Shippey 2005:101–2, 234–7 and passim), and informs most of his works and many of its epigones. This concept, and its theoretical justification, are certainly more sophisticated and nuanced than those used by traditional source criticism, and have the merit to give the right emphasis to the individuality of the 'target language' (i.e. the literary code of Tolkien's secondary world): in my opinion they fail to fully explain Tolkien's opposition to any search for primary correspondences, his related claim of literary 'unconsciousness' (on this see I.2.2 and VI.1.3), and the implications of such positions as regards the kind of exegesis Tolkien would have probably wished for.

[66] Cf. the words of C. S. Kilby, a former collaborator of Tolkien, who openly challenged "the stone wall of Professor Tolkien's denial that the story has any direct or allegorical interpretations" (Kilby 2016:154, originally published in 1974), and spilled much ink on identifying Christian ideas and images hidden in Tolkien's works. For a response to Tolkien's objections to biographical criticism cf. Duriez 2012; Klinger 2012a: xi–xvi, and so on. For a more general warning against the use of Tolkien's own primary comments for the criticism of his secondary works see Drout 2005 and Martsch 2011. Their caution is legitimate, especially as regards the need for contextualisation, but one should also avoid throwing the baby out the bathwater, and also remember that in Tolkien's vision the author(ity) is hidden, but not absent (cf. Saxton 2013b, esp. 2013:57–8, convincingly addressing some of Drout's objections against reading too much in Tolkien's primary remarks), and that Tolkien himself suggested a deep connection between his primary and secondary texts (cf. *Letters* 234:440[310] where he describes *The Lord of the Rings* as "a practical demonstration of the views" that he had expressed in *On Fairy-Stories*; but of course by quoting this I am myself falling into a circular argument).

'applicability',[67] which, if not properly defined and understood, can be simply used as a disguised synonym for 'allegory'. In IV.2.2.1, I will confront this issue head-on because its solution, or at least its understanding, is closely related to the meaning of the complex web of narrative connections investigated in the previous sections.

IV.2.2.1 Tolkien and Allegory: An Unsolvable Contradiction?

As is well known, there is an apparent contradiction between Tolkien's theoretical and practical handling of allegory. On the one hand, Tolkien virulently opposed allegory and the allegorical hermeneutics of his works; he claimed, for instance, to have cordially disliked allegory "in all manifestations" ever since he grew "old and wary enough to detect its presence" (*LotR Preface*:xx);[68] he also stressed that *The Lord of the Rings*] "has *no* allegorical intentions, general, particular, or topical, moral, religious, or political" (*Letters* 165:319[220], original italics), since "conscious allegory [...] of the sort 'five wizards=five senses' is wholly foreign" to his way of thinking (*Letters* 203:377[262]), and he wrote in one of his final letters that it would have been enough for him if people enjoyed

---

[67] The term 'applicability' is found in two famous passages from Tolkien's letters: *Letters* 203:377[262] "That there is no allegory does not, of course, say there is no applicability"; *Letters* 215, to W. Allen (draft), April 1959:423[297]: "I do not like allegory (properly so called: most readers appear to confuse it with significance or applicability)". Cf. also *TCG* 199, quoted in n.86. On the concept of 'applicability' see esp. Segura 2007, 2010.

[68] Cf. also *Letters* 262, to M. di Capua, 7/09/1964:492[351] "I am not naturally attracted (in fact much the reverse) by allegory, mystical or moral".

his book "as a story without forming detailed comparisons between Middle-earth and the world today".[69] Yet, on the other hand, Tolkien's works are undeniably full of narrative elements that could easily be interpreted 'allegorically'; his work, that is, heavily features elements that can be, and have been, construed as conveying a hidden meaning, or, more specifically, as referring to corresponding 'primary' elements of Tolkien's life and thought, and especially to elements of Christian narratives, ethics, or doctrine.

Here, I will consider just two among many seemingly 'allegorical' moments in the *legendarium*. One of the central adventures in *The Hobbit* (chapters 4–6) involves the crossing of high mountains filled with unexpected and life-threatening experiences. This journey is somehow related to a momentous trip that Tolkien made in the summer of 1911 to the Swiss alps in the company of

---

[69] Quoted in Hammond and Scull 2017: *Chronology* 814. Cf. also *Letters* 211:404[283–4] "I have deliberately written a tale, which is built on or out of certain 'religious' ideas, but **is not an allegory** of them (or anything else)"; *Letters* 34, to S. Unwin, 13/10/1938:52[41] "The darkness of the present days has had some effect on it. Though **it is not an 'allegory'**"; *Letters* 144:263[174] "an imaginary mythical Age (mythical, not allegorical: **my mind does not work allegorically**)"; *TCG* 516 (16/12/1963), in which Tolkien stressed he never found attractive books on myths and symbolisms and that his story was in no way an allegory, in any sense of the word, but rather "mythical-historical"; also *Letters* 215:423[297], quoted in n. 67, and *TCG* 825 (24/12/1971), where he confessed his dislike for Lewis' Narnia stories since he "does not like 'allegory', and least of all religious allegory of this kind". There is also evidence that in the revision of *The Lord of the Rings* Tolkien deleted or toned down all passages that were more prone to allegorical interpretation, as referring to primary events and discourses; cf. for instance *TI* 11:212 (Saruman's reference to the "spheres of influence").

his aunt Jane Neave and some of her friends:[70] Tolkien himself makes it explicit in some letters, fully recounting the Swiss trip, and confirming that the adventure in *The Hobbit* "is based" on that 'primary' "adventure" in the Swiss Mountains.[71] In addition in one letter, Tolkien reveals that there is another important source for that 'secondary' adventure, this time not biographical but literary, a scene from the 1899 novel *The Black Douglas* by the Scottish author Samuel R. Crockett, which deeply impressed him as a young boy (*Letters* 306, n.*:550[391]). In other words, Tolkien seems to engage in, and also admit, just the kind of biographical and source criticism that he apparently disavows in other texts. Not surprisingly, some scholars have described this episode of *The Hobbit* in allegorical terms, as if Tolkien were referring, through it (consciously or not), to other 'primary' elements, whether biographical or literary.

The second example comes from a key passage already discussed in Chapter III. When the eagle of the Valar, the Lords of the West, flies to the city of Minas Tirith to announce the unexpected victory over Sauron, his song of joy apparently evokes the style and words of the Psalms, especially Psalms 24, 33, and 104:[72]

---

[70] See for example Morton and Hayes 2008:69–72, Hammond and Scull 2017: *Reader's Guide* 1275–8. Cf. also Currie and Lewis 2016:37–54, Garth 2020:82–99.

[71] Cf. *Letters* 232, to J. Reeves, 4/11/1961:438–9[308–9]; *Letters* 306, to M. Tolkien, 1967/8s:550[391].

[72] Cf. Psalm 24 (23):7–8 "Lift up your gates, O ye princes, and be ye lifted up, O eternal gates: and the King of Glory shall enter in"; Psalm 33 (32):1, 3 "Rejoice in the Lord, O ye just | [...] Sing to him a new canticle"; Psalm 104 (103):30, 33 "Thou shalt send forth thy spirit, and they shall be created: and thou shalt renew the face of the earth. | [...] I will sing to the Lord as long as I live."

> Sing and rejoice, ye people of the Tower of Guard,
> for your watch hath not been in vain
> [...] and your King hath passed through,
> and he is victorious [...]
> and he shall dwell among you all the days of your
> life. (*LotR* 6.5:963)

And as Tom Shippey points out, commenting on this passage: "[here] Revelation seems very close and allegory does all but break through [...] the first statement could very easily apply to Death and Hell (Matthew xvi, 18 'and the gates of hell shall not prevail'), the second to Christ and the Second Coming. This is a layer of double meaning" (Shippey 2005:200; cf. also Shippey 2000:209–10).

How can one deny that the eagle's song 'speaks about something else' (*all-egorein*)? That it conveys or at least refers to a hidden, 'ulterior' meaning, with all its implications as regards the general hermeneutics of *The Lord of the Rings*? This is just one of the many elements within Tolkien's works that could be, and indeed have been, construed as covertly related to 'other' elements in the primary world, as, that is, allegorical. In fact, Tolkien occasionally conceded in his letters that his tales could be 'made into allegories' and that *The Lord of the Rings* was, in fact, a sort of 'allegory' or 'exemplar'.[73]

---

[73] Cf. *Letters* 186:353[246] "my story is not an allegory of Atomic power, but of Power"; *Letters* 109:175[121] "You can make the Ring into an allegory of our own time"; *Letters* 153:284[190] (on the desire of the Elves of Eregion as an 'allegory' "of a love of machinery"); *Letters* 131:204[145] "I dislike Allegory [...] yet any attempt to explain the purport of myth or fairytale must use allegorical language"; *SWM Ess.*:111 denying that the short tale *Smith of Wootton* is an 'allegory', "though it is capable of course of allegorical interpretations" (also ibid. 141). Cf. also *Letters* 153:287[192] on Tom Bombadil being an

How can one explain this apparent contradiction? Does Tolkien have a split (literary) personality?[74] Or, to put it more generously, what exactly does Tolkien mean by allegory, why is he so against it, and what does he propose as his own alternative? I will address these questions in IV.2.2.2.

IV.2.2.2 The Allegorical Potential of Non-allegorical Stories

To understand Tolkien's problematic aversion to allegory, one must return to his belief in the existence of a "seamless web of Story": the criss-crossing between primary and secondary worlds described in IV.2.1. Tolkien explicitly puts 'Allegory' in opposition to this notion of 'Story', and there are several passages in his letters that allude to the contrast between them.[75] These are dense

'allegory' or an 'exemplar' of pure natural science (since "'allegory is the only mode of exhibiting certain functions'"); *TCG* 214 (24/10/1955) "an exemplary legend" (quoted in Chapter I n.128); *TCG* 211 (12/12/1955) on the Sammath Naur scene as a "'fairy-story' exemplum" of the Lord's Prayer.

[74] One might relate this contradiction to a general pattern of ambiguity and inconsistency, between different statements in his letters, different drafts of his theoretical essays, and between different views expressed in different texts; in one of her brilliant essays Flieger (2014c) identifies this as a typically Tolkienian feature, and explains as deriving from a general unresolved conflict between "faith and imagination" (cf. also recently Flieger 2020, arguing that (18) "oppositions are the sources of Tolkien's power and the tension between them is the energy that unites it"). Many readers of *The Lord of the Rings* and/or Tolkien's acquaintances would agree (cf. the words of Father Murray, quoted in Chapter III, n.12). I see the conflict and the coexistence of different views, but also their (non-dogmatic) resolution within an integrated, 'hierarchical' framework. Cf. nn.65–7, II.2.1.2.

[75] Cf. *Letters* 181:338[233] "There is no 'allegory', moral, political, or contemporary [...] **fairy story has its own mode of reflecting 'truth', different from allegory**, or (sustained) satire, or 'realism', and in some ways more powerful."

passages rather than lucid theoretical expositions. In what follows, I will try to establish some theoretical order.

First, the nature and goal of Tolkien's literary activity consists, quite simply, in writing beautiful 'Stories'. This is the task of the sub-creator, the artist storyteller. For Tolkien, 'Stories' thus have priority over everything else, as regards both composition and reception.[76] This is a point he often makes or alludes to in his letters; the priority of Story is, itself, related to that aesthetic and 'hedonic' primacy previously discussed in Chapter I (esp. I.2.3.1). Tolkien, for instance, claimed that his "stories come first", and that *The Lord of the Rings* was written primarily as an "exciting story", "to *amuse* (in the highest sense): to be readable", to be "enjoyed as such" and "be read with literary pleasure.[77] As he forcefully claimed in the *Foreword* to the second edition of *The Lord of the Rings*, his "prime motive" was simply the desire to write "a long story that would hold the attention of readers, amuse them, delight them, and at times maybe excite them or deeply move them", with no "inner meaning or 'message'" (at least in his intention).

Both the starting points and foci of 'Story' are thus individual, unique entities; they are "given things" that apparently came separately, as Tolkien says in a letter.[78] "[T]he unclassifiable individual details of a story" have an

---

[76] On this point cf. Sepe's (2008) insightful discussion, rightly contrasting Tolkien's approach with that of other writers such as Philip Pullman.

[77] *Letters* 200:375[260]; *Letters* 181:338[232]; and *Letters* 329:580[414] respectively. Cf. also *Letters* 165:319[219–20] (quoted at the beginning of Chapter I); *Letters* 208:385[267] "personally attractive", quoted at I.2.2.3, *Letters* 194a:369 "an exciting story", and *SWM GK*:93 "we should enjoy hearing [a Tale], before we even begin to think why".

[78] Cf. *Letters* 131:204[145], quoted at II.2.2.1.

independent value *per se*; they are what really count, "the most interesting thing to consider".[79] The individual details of a story, one might paraphrase, are the primary object of the love of the sub-creator, such as the Dwarves for Aulë in *The Silmarillion* or the leaves of Niggle in the eponymous story.[80] Therefore, the main literary goal of the sub-creator consists quite simply in the writing of a *particular* successful story – new and unique. At the same time, for Tolkien, the success of a story does not merely depend on its capacity to provide literary pleasure. Rather, in order to be attractive, exciting, or amusing, and thereby provide that very pleasure, a story needs to have "truth". Indeed, according to Tolkien, every secondary story has its own inner 'literary truth' that it is the task of the sub-creator to 'elucidate', like the figure of a statue being chiselled from a block of stone (to paraphrase a famous image of Michelangelo).[81] As we have already seen in Chapter II (II.2.2.5), in several passages, Tolkien associates the concept of 'truth' with storytelling and speaks of the "literary truth" of a story.[82]

[79] Cf. *TOFS*:39=*TL*:19 "It is precisely the colouring, the atmosphere, **the unclassifiable individual details of a story** [...] that really count"; *Letters* 337:587[418] "it is the particular use in a particular situation of any motive [...] **the most interesting thing to consider**".

[80] For Tolkien's concern for uniqueness, which is related to the "mystery of love" cf. *NME* 2.15:254–5 (quoted in Chapter IV, n.111). See further IV.3.3 and V.2.

[81] Cf. Michelangelo *Rime* 151 "Nothing the best of artists can conceive | but lies, potential, in a block of stone, superfluous matter round it. The hand alone | can free it that has intelligence for guide" (Transl. Nims).

[82] Cf. *Letters* 89:142[100] "It perceives – **if the story has literary 'truth'** on the second plane [...] – that this is indeed how things really do work in the Great World for which our nature is made"; also *Letters* 91, to Christopher Tolkien, 29/11/1944:147[104] "as if **the truth comes out then**, only imperfectly glimpsed in the preliminary sketch".

Crucially, however, the truth-bearing elements of a successful story are not 'planned' or 'invented', but, in Tolkien's words, arise "naturally (and almost inevitably) from the circumstances";[83] a story consists of 'inevitable events', which simply proceed from "the logic of the tale".[84] Consider, for instance, Tolkien's self-exegesis of Frodo's failure on Mount Doom:

The Quest was bound to fail as a piece of world-plan, and also was bound to end in disaster as the story of humble Frodo's development to the 'noble', his sanctification. Fail it would and did as far as Frodo considered alone was concerned. [...] Believe me, it was not until I read this that I had myself any idea how '**topical**' such a situation [i.e. Frodo's betrayal on Mount Doom] might appear. **It arose naturally** from my 'plot'. (*Letters* 181:339[248])

As this passage clarifies, the 'natural arising' of a given secondary element does not prevent a story from having a "topical" value; the exact opposite is true for Tolkien. This crucial and paradoxical passage shows that, for Tolkien, the life and truth of a particular story are proportional to the extent that they embody "universals". In one of his letters, Tolkien explained to a friend that individuals "would not live at all" if they did not "contain

---

[83] *Letters* 25:41[31] (on *Beowulf* being one of the most valued, and yet unconscious sources of *The Hobbit*).

[84] Cf. *Letters* 246:460[325] "From the point of view of the storyteller the events on Mt Doom **proceed simply from the logic of the tale** up to that time"; also ibid. 465[330] "This is due of course to the 'logic of the story'"; *Letters* 191, to J. Burns, 26/07/1956:362[252]) "I did not 'arrange' the deliverance in this case: it again **follows the logic of the story**"; *Letters* 192:363[252] (quoted in VI n.34) "**inevitable, as an event**".

universals" (*Letters* 109:174[121]). In other words, a particular, individual story or situation that does not contain or embody universals is simply not alive; when a story is not topical and thereby irrelevant to the "'human situation' (of all periods)", it is not "worth considering", and is neither pleasing nor exciting.[85] In fact, the literary, aesthetic, and even pleasurable quality of a story is, for Tolkien, directly proportional to its 'universality'. As Tolkien explains to Auden: "if one makes a good choice in what is 'good narrative' [...] at a given point, it will also be found to be the case that the event described will be the most 'significant'" (*Letters* 163:311[212]).[86] And he continues in another related letter to say: "it is precisely because I did not try, and have never thought of trying to 'objectify' my personal experience of life that the account of the Quest of the Ring is successful in giving pleasure to Auden (and others)" (*Letters* 183:345[239]).

A story that does not eventually reflect "universal truth" is, perforce, a story that has also failed from a narrative point of view: it is a 'bad' story, which has not been taken seriously in the first place and has thereby failed to achieve literary 'truth'. In contrast, a story that has been treated seriously cannot but help develop, unintentionally for its author, an inherent "morality", which is also, for

---

[85] Cf. *Letters* 181:338[233] "[adults] will not be pleased, excited, or moved unless the whole, or the incidents, seem to be about something **worth considering** [...] there must be some relevance to the **'human situation' (of all periods)**".

[86] Cf. also *TCG* 199 (2/3/1955) in which he stressed that his primary intention was simply to produce a good tale, and primarily for his own satisfaction, but at the same time that the more one puts into a story, the more it becomes capable of being "generally or particularly applied" to other matters.

Tolkien, at the foundation of its "realness": "the 'morality' [of *The Lord of the Rings*] [...] is that which gives the story its 'realness' and coherence which my critics seem to feel – rather than any pictorial vividness. It was not 'planned', of course, but arose naturally in the attempt to treat the matter seriously; but it is now the foundation" (*Letters* 148a, to K. Farrer, 18/08/1954:275).

This interconnection between universal and individual truth, between 'significance' and 'narrative quality', also explains why Story and Allegory can eventually 'converge':

Allegory and Story converge, meeting somewhere in Truth. So that the only perfectly consistent allegory is a real life; and the only fully intelligible story is an allegory. And one finds, even in imperfect human 'literature', that the better and more consistent an allegory is the more easily can it be read 'just as a story'; and the better and more closely woven a story is the more easily can those so minded find allegory in it. But the two start out from opposite ends. (*Letters* 109:174[121])

According to this famous passage, Allegory and Story start out from opposite ends.[87] Allegory begins in one's

---

[87] Cf. the perceptive words of Robert Murray, a close friend of Tolkien, quoting this very passage in his 1992 eulogy, in which he compared Tolkien's sub-creations and Jesus' parables: "'From opposite ends'. This exactly expresses the difference between, on the one hand, the development of natural symbolism by metaphor, simile or parable and, on the other, the artificiality of allegory. The one starts from things and human life in the actual world, seeing them as charged with natural symbolic potency; a flash of imaginative insight perceives how this potency can engender new meaning in another context, and so *meta-phora* occurs, the transference of a symbol's power so as to illuminate something else; but it is offered freely to whoever can respond" (Murray 1999:44–8).

own intellectual perception of primary Truth and is then consciously represented in secondary forms. In contrast, Story does not start from primary Truth, but *eventually* arrives at it 'unconsciously' by 'extracting' or 'revealing' the 'truth' of secondary entities.[88] This is why the recognition of the 'universal' Truth embodied in a particular story comes not as the expected fulfilment of an intellectual project. Rather, the recognition of the 'universal' value of a story is a discovery; it is an **"after-thought"**, which comes at the end of an narrative journey, driven by an aesthetic urge and aiming to report a "mere event", which really "happened" in a given period of time ("B.C. year X") and to actual "people who were like that", however fictional.[89]

The Ring is a good example of this paradoxical dynamic: the topical, 'allegorical', or 'universal' meanings of the motive (i.e. the "allegory of the inevitable fate that waits for all attempts to defeat evil power by power") "burst in", in Tolkien's words, as the inevitable

---

[88] On the 'unconsciousness' of the literary act see I.2.2.

[89] Cf. *Letters* 186:354[246] "But all that [the prominence of the themes of Death and the relationship between the small and the great in *The Lord of the Rings*] is rather '**after-thought**'. The story is really a story of **what happened in B.C. year X**, and it just **happened to people who were like that!**"; *Letters* 246:460[325] "Reflecting on the solution after it was arrived at (as **a mere event**)"; *TCG* 516 (16/12/1963) in which Tolkien claimed that the recognition of 'archetypal-motives' in *The Lord of the Rings* was just an "**afterthought**", and so it should be for any reader or critic: he did not set out to write with this in mind, as he was only to try to create an exciting and readable story, which would also give him scope for his personal pleasure in history, languages, and landscape. Cf. also *Letters* 69:116[80] (on *The Lord of the Rings* having "grown [...] large in significance") and see I.2.2.3.

result of his having taken the Ring "seriously" in the first place, by investing in the Ring's 'secondary' existence and making "things happen that would happen, if such a thing existed".[90] This is essentially the same dynamic by which Sam, on the stairs of Cirith Ungol, suddenly realises that his own story is connected to an ancestral story.

Because of their different endpoints, Story and Allegory are distinct; and yet they are potentially related: indeed, the truer a story is within its secondary plane, the more it reflects Primary Truth and thus 'converges' with a 'good' allegory. For this reason, every 'story' that has inner life and truth is potentially open – Tolkien admits – to an allegorical interpretation. For this reason, Tolkien admits in another important passage from his letter to Auden:

it is I suppose impossible to write any 'story' that is not allegorical in proportion as it 'comes to life'; since each of us is an allegory, embodying in a particular tale and clothed in the garments of time and place, universal truth and everlasting life. (*Letters* 163:310[212])

A crucial feature of this passage, also traceable in most of the previous quotes, is the blurring of the distinction between fictional and real individuals ("any 'story' [...] each of us"). A secondary story of fictional characters can be as potentially allegorical as the life of real people in the 'primary world'. This is to say that both secondary and primary individuals embody universals, if they are truly 'alive'.

---

[90] *Letters* 109:175[121].

IV.2.3 Modes and Motives, between Primary and Secondary Worlds

In Tolkien's 'organic' vision, Story and Allegory are categories that are valid not only in the secondary world but also in the primary world. Just as secondary narratives consist in the repetition and renewal of the same universal motives, in different forms or dresses, so too does human history and in fact every individual human life. This was clearly an important concern for Tolkien. In fact, as he writes in his essay *A Secret Vice*, in reference to an analogous dualistic tension between the 'personal' and the 'traditional':

Of great interest to me is the attempt to disentangle – if possible – [...] (1) the personal from (2) the traditional. The two are doubtless much interwoven – the personal being possibly (though it is not proven) linked to the traditional in normal lives by heredity, as well as by the immediate and daily pressure of the traditional upon the personal from earliest childhood. (*SV*:24–5=*MC*:211)[91]

In some cases, this notion of endless repetition of traditional or universal motives is given negative undertones, appearing in contexts that have been cited as evidence for Tolkien's supposed cosmic pessimism. These include dramatic letters written to Christopher in which he refers

---

[91] The tension between tradition and the personal was also a central concern of modernist poetry and criticism (and beyond), especially after T. S. Eliot's influential essay 1919 *Tradition and the Individual Talent* (see Cianci and Harding 2007 for an overview of its content and context, as well as sources and reception). Tolkien was apparently not a fan of Eliot (cf. *Letters* 261:490[267]), but he engaged with modernism more than has been traditionally believed (see on this Simonson 2008a; Hiley 2011).

to the "endless repetitive unchanging incurable wick-edness" of men who "(in spite of different dress) don't change at all" and bitterly points out that "it's always been going on in different terms".[92] But these kinds of passages do not reveal the full picture. The same belief in the never-ending re-embodiment of universals in different circumstances can also be seen in more positive terms. Such positivity is exemplified, for instance, in Tolkien's advice to the same Christopher, despondent at the senseless misery of the war, to start from the details and minor events of one's particular life, and, by going to their depth, find revealed their inner, universal values, which "often lurk under dreadful appearances".[93]

If one connects all the dots, one can see how Tolkien's primary views on Story and Allegory are reflected in the secondary world in the image of a "seamless Web of Story" and its related intratextual parallelism. Real people, as well as fictional characters, embody in different times and places the very same "universal truth and ever-lasting life" in various forms; in the same way, individual tales re-embody or renew the same motive in different modes, within Tolkien's own secondary world. Tolkien alludes to this idea of 'modes and motives' in several

---

[92] *Letters* 69:116[81] and *Letters* 77, to Christopher Tolkien, 31/07/1944:128[89] respectively; cf. also *Letters* 101, to Christopher Tolkien, 3/06/1945:168[116] "Wars are always lost, and **The War always goes on**."

[93] *Letters* 78, to Christopher Tolkien, 12/08/1944:129[90] "do not think that any detail of your exterior life, [...] or the most minor events, are not worth writing or of interest. And of course [...] one of the discoveries of the process is the realization of the values that **often lurk under dreadful appearances**." Also *Letters* 194a, to Michael Tolkien, 6/11/1956:367 (hidden Elvish interests under the head of an orc on a motorbike).

passages in his letters,[94] together with the related concept of difference within sameness, which explains why the most difficult task in a long tale is to maintain "a difference of quality and atmosphere in events that might easily become 'samey'" (*Letters* 96:159[110]).

IV.3 Conclusions: Tolkien and the Universality of the Particular

At the core of Tolkien's belief in the "seamless Web of Story" is the idea, widespread among literary traditions, that artistic creations embody ('exemplify') universal (and thereby traditional) ideas or 'archetypes'.[95] In the Western tradition, this idea can ultimately be traced back to ancient literary theory, and is present in both Plato and Aristotle, although with some important differences. For Plato, the literary artist represents his preconceived understanding of the world in his artistic creations; as

---

[94] Cf. *Letters* 131:204[145–7] "all this stuff is concerned [...] [w]ith Fall inevitably, and **that motive occurs in several modes**"; 209[149] "the first example of **the motive**" (quoted in IV.3.4).

[95] Tolkien is not fond of the word 'archetype', but he does use at least twice in his letters the adjective 'archetypal': *Letters* 276:505[361] (w. ref. to his Atlantis 'complex') "mythical or 'archetypal' images"; *TCG* 516 (16/12/1963) on *The Lord of the Rings* being founded on "deeply-rooted 'archetypal' motifs", which have put "into an entirely new setting, carefully devised", which produces a sense of reality. Cf. also *TCG* 340 (25/10/1958) in which Tolkien admits that no one can ever escape, (or could or should wish to) from the "ageing tradition or the ancestral voices and motifs"; *TCG* 341 (26/10/1958) in which he stresses that no one can invent or create in a void, but rather can only reconstruct ancestral material, perhaps impressing "a personal pattern" on it; also *Letters* 131:108[147] on "ancient wide-spread motives or elements" inevitably contained in his 'new' myths and legends.

such, the good artist must be a philosopher, with an accurate grasp of true universals (Ideas). For Aristotle and his followers (from Theophrastus down to the late antique commentator Donatus), the writer and, especially, the playwright is called to express the universal constants of human behaviour embodied in different characters.[96]

There are, however, four cardinal ideas of Tolkien's literary vision that appear peculiar to him or, at least, these ideas are renewed and integrated by him into an idiosyncratic and compelling framework. They are deeply related to his own 'commitment to creation' and, ultimately, to his particular Christian experience, and they are interrelated. While I have already partly introduced them in the previous discussion, in this final part of the chapter I will review and discuss them at length.

IV.3.1 The Endlessness of Story

The first notion, already mentioned in Chapter II (II.2.1.1), is the 'endlessness of Story' and the related 'partiality' of individual stories. These are both key related ideas in Tolkien's vision, often alluded to in both his secondary and primary works.[97] Here, I will focus on an important note from *On Fairy-Stories* that should be considered as

[96] See Halliwell 2011 for an overview of the main positions, from different perspectives; cf. also Pezzini 2020 with bibliography. For a holistic discussion of the discourse, and an original contribution to it, see Pickstock 2013.

[97] Cf. in particular *LotR* 2.1:232, quoted in II.2.1.1. Cf. also Gandalf's far-reaching and forward-looking words at the council of Elrond: *LotR* 2.2:266 "it is not our part here to take thought only for a season, or for a few lives of Men, or for a passing age of the world". Cf. also Walker 2009, chapter 3 and 4.

the theoretical intertext of the meta-narrative conversation on the Web of Story discussed earlier (*LotR* 4.8:711–12). In the passage, Tolkien explains that the opening and closures of individual stories are only apparent and artificial:

> The verbal ending [...] 'and they lived happily ever after' is an artificial device. [...] End-phrases of this kind are to be compared to the margins and frames of pictures, and are no more to be thought of as the real end of any particular fragment of the seamless Web of Story than the frame is of the visionary scene, or the casement of the Outer World.[98] (*TOFS Note H*:83–4=*TL*:80)

This important passage alludes to what Tolkien considered an "insuperable obstacle" in the early stage of writing of *The Lord of the Rings*, already discussed in Chapter II (II.2.1.1); this was the apparent closure of *The Hobbit* story, signposted by the formulaic sentence "Bilbo 'remained very happy to the end of his days.'" In the first redaction of the work, this ending was apparently construed as the actual *explicit* ending of the story, before the addition of the epilogue with Gandalf and Balin's visit.[99] As discussed already, Tolkien later found a solution to the conundrum

---

[98] In the same passage Tolkien also talks about "the endlessness of the World of Story" and the "endless tapestry", in relation to which a fairy story is like a "sharp cut" in it. Tolkien uses the same metaphor in his draft introduction to MacDonald's *Golden Key* (*SWN GK*:92–3 "the beginning and end of a story is to it like the edges of the canvas or an added frame to a picture") and also in an unpublished letter (*TCG* 471, 03/07/1961), in which he points out that although stories have no end, and pictures have no boundaries, one has to put small visions into a frame, because one cannot see anything clearly unless one concentrates on it.

[99] Cf. Rateliff 2011.

by integrating *The Hobbit* into a larger meta-textual frame
and presenting that ending formula as a mere reflection
of Bilbo's own unfulfilled desire for closure. In the passage quoted here, Tolkien offers an apparently different justification for that formula, which he construes as
a mere artificial device only acceptable in the genre of
fairy-stories because of their "greater sense and grasp
of the endlessness of the World of Story" (*TOFS Note
H*:84=*TL*:80). The theoretical assumptions are, in fact,
the same: as Bilbo acknowledges, reflecting on his unfulfilled closure, adventures never end (cf. *LotR* 2.1:232, in
II.2.1.1); every book has a sequel (and a prequel). This is
true because "roads go ever on",[100] and every individual
story is only a "particular fragment of the seamless Web
of Story" (*TOFS Note H*:83=*TL*:80). In what will eventually be the actual ending of the *Hobbit*, Gandalf's words to
Bilbo reveal the eponymous hobbit's 'partialness' within a
larger narrative horizon ("a little fellow in a wide world")
and its connection with the prophecies of the old songs
(cf. *Hobbit* 19:351, quoted at II.2.1.2).

Because of the 'partialness' of each individual story,
what may appear as narrative openings and closures are,
in fact, mere junctions of a larger, never-ending narrative
chain, which must eventually be acknowledged as such
by the individual characters.[101] As noted by Bowman

[100] In the manuscripts of *The Hobbit*, a version of Bilbo's poem, with the
plural title ("roads"), is placed at the very end of the story, after the
epilogue.
[101] The importance of acknowledging one's narrative 'partialness'
within a larger horizon (and its implications) is a theme that is often
embodied in Tolkien's works: cf. Gildor's words to the hobbits at
LotR 1.3:83 (the Shire does not belong to the Hobbits and the wide
world is all about them); also *LotR* 3.2:426 (Aragorn acknowledging

(2006:275–7), this is indeed the very discovery Sam made in his meta-narrative epiphany, analysed earlier.

IV.3.2 Narrative Continuity and
the Single Author

The second, related notion in Tolkien's literary vision is the conviction that there is a 'narrative continuity' between the primary and secondary worlds. Besides the 'secondary' hints discussed in the previous sections, there are many passages in his letters suggesting that, in his vision, the idea of a single endless Story, "ever going on and on" in similar yet different forms, also applies to the primary reality directly created by God. These include specific passages in which Tolkien uses (meta-)literary phraseology and imagery in reference to primary entities and events, using the words Story and History with capital S and H (as if to indicate its universal, multi-plane dimension). Consider in particular the following two passages:

Keep up your hobbitry in heart, and think that all stories feel like that when you are in them. You are **inside a very great Story!** (*Letters* 66, to Christopher Tolkien, 6/05/ 1944:113[78])[102]

to Gimli and Legolas that their quest is a small matter compared with the Quest of Frodo); *LotR* 6.6:982 (Aragorn reminding the Hobbits that also the Shire falls under the authority of his realm). This acknowledgement generates humility in the characters, and a spirit of self-sacrifice, but also hope and endurance, as epitomised in particular in a famous passage during the final stage of the journey to Mordor, in which Sam recovers hope after seeing a white star in the sky, shining for ever beyond the reach of darkness (cf. *LotR* 5.2:922).

[102] Bowman 2006 (esp. 286–7) rightly connects these words with Sam's meta-narrative considerations (cf. esp. *LotR* 6.4:950 "What a tale we have been in, Mr. Frodo, haven't we?"), which were in fact drafted

[The Lord of the Rings] was written slowly and with great care for detail, & finally emerged as a Frameless Picture: a searchlight, as it were, **on a brief episode in History**, and on a small part of **our Middle-earth**. (*Letters* 328:578[412])

As is particulary evident in the second passage, Tolkien often posits a conflation between the primary and secondary worlds that is both geographical ("our Middle-earth") and chronological/narrative ("a brief episode in History"). For Tolkien, the two great Stories of the primary and secondary worlds are not disconnected, but rather facets of the same Single Story, of the same narrative line that crosses from the primary to the secondary world and back.

The same conflation of and narrative continuity between the primary and secondary stories are also implied by Tolkien's meta-literary description of God as an "Author" or "Writer"; specifically, he expresses such continuity in his use of the concept of the "Writer of the Story" to refer to the single Authority, ruling over both primary and secondary worlds.[103] As Tolkien puts it, "in every world on every plane all must ultimately be under the Will of God" (*Letters* 153:285[191]). The idea of a continuity between primary and secondary stories, of one

in the very period that letter was written. For the idea of single Story (with capital S) cf. also *Letters* 94, to Christopher Tolkien, 28/12/1944:152[106] "we shall all doubtless survey our own story when we know it (and a great deal more of **the Whole Story)**".

[103] Cf. primary reference: "the author of it [the Gospel story] is the supreme Artist and the Author of Reality (*Letters* 89:143[101], cf. VI.2.2); "to speak in literary terms, we are all equal before **the Great Author**" (*Letters* 163:314[215]); "**the Writer of the Story** is not one of us" (*Letters* 191:362252); secondary reference: "The Other Power then took over: **the Writer of the Story** (by which I do not mean myself), that 'one ever-present Person who is never absent and never named'" (*Letters* 192:363[253]).

Story under a single Writer, is also embodied in Tolkien's literature in several other ways, apart from the genealogical imagery discussed in the above sections.

First, this idea can be traced in the cosmogonic myth opening *The Silmarillion*, according to which God creates the world through the agency of sub-creative entities (the Valar), bestowing 'life' and 'reality' to their secondary creations. And yet Eru repeatedly participates and intrudes in His mediated secondary creations, as we have seen (cf. III.2.2). He claims and retains an ultimate single 'Authority',[104] thereby preserving a narrative continuity between the different planes. In the same way, according to Tolkien, on the primary plane, God avails Himself of the gifts of the literary writer, which "He himself has bestowed" and of which He can be considered as the only "just literary critic" (*Letters* 113:183[128]). It is because of this narrative continuity between planes that, in Tolkien's organic meta-literary vision, God/Eru can be described as both the supreme Author and as a "literary critic". I will come back to this in Chapter VI (esp. VI.1.4).

Secondly, as noted by Bowman (2006:281–7), there are several meta-narrative passages in *The Lord of the Rings* that create a connection between the characters of *The Lord of the Rings* (the "folk inside a story") and its readers (those "outside it"). This is achieved, in particular, by casting Frodo and Sam in both roles, as both agents and recipients of the story, as, for instance, during the already mentioned dialogue on the stairs of Cirith Ungol:

---

[104] Cf. *Sil Ain.*:17 "nor can any alter the music in my despite"; *Letters* 181:341[235] "the One retains all ultimate authority". Cf. also *Letters* 156:299[202] "He [Gandalf] was handing over to the Authority." I will discuss this passage in V.1.1.

The brave things in the old tales and songs, Mr. Frodo: adventures, as I used to call them. [...] I expect they had lots of chances, like us, of turning back, only they didn't. And if they had, we shouldn't know, because they'd have been forgotten. We hear about those as just went on – and not all to a good end, mind you; at least not to what folk inside a story and not outside it call a good end [...] – like old Mr. Bilbo. But those aren't always the best tales to hear, though they may be the best tales to get landed in! I wonder what sort of a tale we've fallen into?' [...] I wonder if we shall ever be put into songs or tales. We're in one, of course; but I mean: put into words, you know, told by the fireside, or read out of a great big book with red and black letters, years and years afterwards. (*LotR* 4.8:711–12)[105]

In this passage, Sam acknowledges his transformation from audience/readership of "old tales" into a character of a new story ("we're in one, of course"); moreover, by alluding to the future readers of his own tale, he opens the possibility that the same dynamics of meta-narrative transformation will be repeated in the future. The readers of Sam's story, that is, will also be called to become characters of their own story, thereby continuing, "years and years afterwards", the very same Story. The fact that Sam's prophecy is verified at the very moment it is read adds further validity to the idea of a narrative continuity reaching out from the 'old tale' of Sam's secondary world to the primary world of the readers of his story.

This idea of a narrative continuity explains why Tolkien can implicitly suggest that his wife Edith is a descendant of Lúthien; more generally, it explains why the "seamless

---

[105] Cf. also *LotR* 6.4:950 (quoted in IV.1.1); 954 "I will sing to you of Frodo of the Nine Fingers and the Ring of Doom."

Web of Story" also extends to the primary world. Beren, Aragorn, Bilbo, Frodo, and Tolkien himself have different, individual stories that are yet linked, by virtue of their relation with the same universals, within a single, multi-planed Story. All these characters have a 'likeness' in common because they all embody, in different modes, the same "universal truth and everlasting life". For this reason, to return to the chapter's central question, Tolkien's literary sub-creations could, in theory, be read 'allegorically' (for those so minded); yet none of them originated as allegories, as we have seen, but rather as independent, self-standing, unique narrative entities, all with their own independent, and necessary, idiosyncrasies.

IV.3.3 Renewal and (Unique) Embodiment

The third feature of Tolkien's literary vision I will discuss in this chapter is related to the value and 'function' of sub-creation. Why does God advance His creation through sub-creators? Why should the "Great Author" cherish and embrace sub-created stories, integrating and assimilating them into His own Great Story?

The answer has to do with the ongoing, 'eventful' nature of the single Story of Creation and its constant renewal in new, different, and unfamiliar forms; as discussed, for Tolkien, Tales never end; the Road goes on and on; family lines "shall never fail"; and the Tree of Story is alive and keeps sprouting in unexpected places. The Story is *by its nature* always renewing itself; it is always ongoing. Renewal, as discussed earlier, is a key image in Tolkien's narratives: kingships, swords, trees, lineages, and stories are renewed because individual characters (usually humble and unexpected) carry on the one single Story by embracing their own particular tale (like Frodo).

Analogically, God's Creation is renewed in humble, secondary sub-creations, which thus have an important function and value, "to exhibit the infinity of His potential variety" (*Letters* 153:283[188]) and "assist in the effoliation and multiple enrichment of creation" (*TOFS*:79=*TL*:73).[106] Sub-created stories thus introduce 'variety' and 'enrichment'; as Tolkien explains, they 'exemplify' (and thereby revive) universal truths in new, "unfamiliar embodiments", as declared in a key passage from a letter (153:289[194]) quoted at the beginning of the chapter (cf. also III.3, with n.114). 'Variety', 'newness', and 'unfamiliarity' are important qualities of sub-creations also because they have healing and renewing effects on their recipients.[107] Tolkien explains this in a famous passage from *On Fairy-Stories*, already referred to in Chapter III (III.3.2), which here deserves to be quoted at length:

we need recovery. We should look at green again, and be startled anew (but not blinded) by blue and yellow and red. We should meet the centaur and the dragon, and then perhaps

---

[106] I will discuss at length the concept of effoliation (and its meta-literary implications) in VI.2.

[107] For a narratological investigation of Tolkien's penchant for variety see Honegger's (2018) study of "Tolkien's multi-faceted presentation of heroism", and its contribution to "make up a heroic music that is inclusive, wide, beautiful and harmonious". The introduction of a new, different hero does not mean however that the old ones are superseded: rather, as Honegger acutely points out, "The rise of the new type [...] provides rather an additional dimension and hallow the valiant deeds of the latter by setting them within the greater framework of divine Providence". Cf. also Kullman and Siepmann 2021.

suddenly behold, like the ancient shepherds, sheep, and dogs, and horses – and wolves. This recovery fairy-stories help us to make. [...] Recovery (which includes return and **renewal of health**) is a re-gaining – regaining of a clear view [...] 'seeing things as we are (or were) meant to see them' – as things apart from ourselves. We need, in any case, to clean our windows; so that the things seen clearly may be freed from the drab blur of triteness or familiarity – from possessiveness. [...] This triteness is really the penalty of 'appropriation': the things that are trite, or (in a bad sense) familiar, are the things that we have appropriated, legally or mentally. [...] Creative fantasy, because it is mainly trying to do something else (**make something new**), may open your hoard and let all the locked things fly away like cage-birds. (*TOFS*:67–8=*TL*:57–8)

Secondary creations, by trying to "make something new", produce in their audience a "renewal of health", a regaining of the original attitude of wonder in front of the 'otherness' of reality;[108] this is ultimately the wondrous recognition of the Presence of Reality as a given, as a Creation. Sub-creation renews and re-exhibits Creation in different, unfamiliar forms, and thus re-awakens in fallen humanity the perception of a Creator.[109] For this reason, one might say, the single, intertwined Story of Creation and sub-creation is the Creator's varied but

---

[108] In the same section of *TOFS* Tolkien refers to the concept of *Mooreeffoc* or Chestertonian Fantasy, a fantastic word that is able to "cause you to realise that England is an utterly alien land" (*TOFS*:68=*TL*:58). *Mooreeffoc* is a word popularised by Chesterton in his critical essay on Charles Dickens, to denote "the queerness of things that have become trite, when they are seen suddenly from a new angle" (ibid.).

[109] One can also note that in the *legendarium* the "desire to make things wonderful and new" is characteristic of the people of the Gnomes/ Noldor, the master sub-creators among the Elves (cf. *SME* 3:87).

seamless hymn of love begging for the awareness of the creature.

This idea can also be traced in Tolkien's secondary world. The renewal of Aragorn's kingship and the associated tree-lineage will not casually result, Tolkien declares in a letter, in a renewal of the worship of God, and His Name will "be again more often heard".[110] The other key quality associated with 'renewal' and 'newness' is that of 'uniqueness':[111] what each individual sub-creation makes, the content of each individual story, is unique, just as any individual leaf in the life of a tree is unique, as Tolkien suggests in another typical botanical imagery:

Who can design a new leaf? The patterns from bud to unfolding, and the colours from spring to autumn were all discovered by men long ago. But that is not true. [...] Spring is, of course, not really less beautiful because we have seen or heard of other like events: like events, never from world's beginning to world's end the same event. Each leaf, of oak and ash and thorn, is **a unique embodiment of the pattern**, and for some this very year may be the embodiment, the first ever seen and recognized, though oaks have put forth leaves for countless generations of men. (*TOFS*:66=*TL*:56–7)

At the same time, the newness and uniqueness produced by a particular sub-creation are not self-referential or autonomous, both because in Tolkien's vision these

---

[110] Cf. *Letters* 156:304[206].
[111] For Tolkien's concern for uniqueness cf. further a beautiful passage from *NME* (2.15:255), confirming that in Tolkien's vision all living things, such as trees, are "unique in history and according to the Tale of Arda", and this is related to the "mystery of love", "the singling out by love of one thing alone in its oneness and history unique" (ibid. 254).

qualities are inherently derivative as they only belong to the creative power of God/Eru,[112] and because each new sub-creation is an embodiment or a reflection of the same universal pattern of Truth, each ultimately belongs to the same Tree – to the same (divine) Creation, which can be described using Tolkien's allusive image of "The Tree of Tales" (cf. *TOFS*:66, quoted at VI.2.3) or "the King's Tree", which appears to Smith (the allegorical artist) in the eponymous story,[113] and whose main feature is the reconciliation of unity and diversity:

he [Smith] saw the King's Tree springing up, tower upon tower, into the sky, and its light was like the sun at noon; and it bore at once leaves and flowers and fruits uncounted, and **not one was the same as any other that grew on the Tree**. (*SWM*:24)[114]

The always new modes produced by sub-creations are, that is, in full continuity with their past embodiments or modes, just as Frodo is interconnected with Beren or an individual oak leaf with all its predecessors, present, past, and future, as individual examples of the same pattern;[115]

---

[112] Cf. *NME* 2.15:264 "Eru alone could create 'spirits' with independent, though secondary, being [...] individual and unique", and 3.3:294 (only Eru can make things "utterly new", in contrast to Melkor, whose fabrications "were never 'new'" but rather only "imitations or mockeries of works of others").

[113] On the allegorical significance of *Smith of Wootton Major* see Shippey 2000:296–304; also Shippey 2008.

[114] Cf. I.3.

[115] Cf. in this respect an illuminating passage from *NME* (2.15:250), where Tolkien, comparing the variety of Eru's Creation to that of the 'Art of the Incarnate', explains that in Eru's design members of one kind are not exactly alike but rather each "pattern conceived may be endlessly varied in individual examples", adding that "[t]o perceive the patterns, and their kinship, through living variation is a chief delight".

this is why Tolkien can claim, in one of his early letters, that "to kindle a new light" is the same as to "rekindle an old light in the world".[116]

Thus, in Tolkien's works there are different stories, unique examples or modes, but the underlying motive that they all embody is always the same. But what 'motive' or what 'pattern' are we referring to? What is the ultimate "universal truth" embodied in Tolkien's sub-creations that connects all the different stories into a single "seamless web"?

IV.3.4 Echoing the Evangelium

This question introduces a fourth important feature of Tolkien's literary theory that I will introduce in this final section, and further develop in the following chapters. This can be illustrated, again, by the interconnected tales of Beren and Frodo, which, as suggested by Tolkien, are two "examples" of the same "motive" :

The chief of the stories of *The Silmarillion*, and the one most fully treated is the Story of Beren and Lúthien the Elfmaiden. Here we meet [...] the first example of the motive (to become dominant in Hobbits) that the great policies of world history, 'the wheels of the world', are often turned [...] by the seemingly unknown and weak. (*Letters* 131:209[149])[117]

This archetypal motive in Tolkien's narratives not only applies to the secondary world, but also to the Primary as well. In fact, as Tolkien wrote to his son Christopher, in one of the darkest hours of the twentieth century:

[116] Cf. III.3.4.
[117] Full quotation and discussion of this passage in III.2.2.

No man can estimate what is really happening at the present *sub specie aeternitatis*. All we do know, and that to a large extent by direct experience, is that evil labours with vast power and perpetual success – in vain: preparing always only the soil for unexpected good to sprout in. So it is in general, and so it is in our own lives.

(*Letters* 64, to Christopher Tolkien, 22/08/1944:130[91])

what is really important is always hidden from contemporaries, and the seeds of what is to be are quietly germinating in the dark in some forgotten corner, while everyone is looking at Stalin or Hitler.

(*Letters* 79, to Christopher Tolkien, 30/04/1944:110[76])

There is one particular narrative, a primary story, in which this motive is best embodied in the Primary world; this is, of course, the Gospel Story, whose seed germinated in the forgotten corners of the Roman empire and which pivots on the unexpected narrative enhancement of the low and the weak. In fact, for Tolkien, the Gospel Story is the archetypal fairy-tale to which all stories ultimately refer. In Tolkien's literary vision, all sub-created stories (if they have true aesthetic value, that is, "life" and "reality") ultimately embody the "universal truth" that historically happened in the Gospel Story. This is not, as in Allegory, the result of an *intentional* and *intellectual* planning; rather, it happens *unconsciously* and '*eventually*' (in the etymological sense of 'in a manner dependent on and consequent to an event'); it happens, thus, through the discovery and revelation of the "truth" of idiosyncratic stories and within the context of the "mystery of literary creation".

Among the motives of the Gospel Story embodied (or rather renewed) in the tales of Beren and Frodo, there is one in particular that, for Tolkien, holds priority over all others; this is what Tolkien calls "eucatastrophe" – the unexpected happy turn of the story in a moment of despair.[118] Tolkien elaborates this view in the Epilogue of *On Fairy-Stories* (*TOFS*:75–9=*TL*:68–73) and returns to it in a passage from a letter to his son, which can here be quoted at length to conclude this chapter because it sums up all the points discussed here, as well as recalling some key moments of the stories of Beren and Frodo:

'eucatastrophe' [is] the sudden happy turn in a story which pierces you with a joy that brings tears (which [...] is the highest function of fairy-stories to produce). [...] [this] produces its peculiar effect because it is a sudden glimpse of Truth [...] It perceives – **if the story has literary 'truth' on the second plane** [...] – that this is indeed how things really do work in the Great World for which our nature is made. [...] the Resurrection [is] the greatest 'eucatastrophe' possible in the greatest Fairy Story – and produces that essential emotion: Christian joy which produces tears because it is qualitatively so like sorrow, **because it comes from those places where Joy and Sorrow are at one**, reconciled, as selfishness and altruism are lost in Love. [...] I knew I had written a story of worth in 'The Hobbit' when reading it [...] I had suddenly in a fairly strong measure the 'eucatastrophic' emotion at Bilbo's

[118] There are several other cases of micro-eucatastrophes in *The Lord of the Rings*, such as for instance Aragorn's finding of Gollum, which happened "by fortune", just after he "despaired at last" (*LotR* 2.2:253) or the timely rescue of the disguised Sam and Frodo from the Orcs in Mordor, which occurs just as Sam is about to draw his sword and disclose his identity (*LotR* 6.2:931). Cf. also the iconic Elvish proverb "Oft hope is born, when all is forlorn", quoted by Legolas at *LotR* 5.9:877. On the concept of 'eucatastrophe' see esp. Garbowski 2007; cf. also Shippey 2000:206–12; Moulin 2008; Shank 2013 (esp. 158–60); Neubauer 2016; Thayer 2016b, esp. chapters 2 and 5.

exclamation: 'The Eagles! The Eagles are coming!' [...] And in the last chapter of The Ring [...] Frodo's face goes livid and convinces Sam that he's dead, just when Sam gives up *hope*. (*Letters* 89:142–3[101])

As seen earlier (IV.1.2), the rescue by the Eagles is one of the most important narrative motives in Tolkien's works, connecting the narratives of Beren, Bilbo, Frodo, and several other characters.[119] This motive embodies, in different forms, what Tolkien defines as "eucatastrophe" – the narrative experience that is "the highest function of fairy-stories to produce", a "glimpse or echo", a reflection of the same, single Truth.[120] This motive can be described as a 'secondary miracle' correlating with many other 'miraculous' events in both primary and secondary worlds and forming a narrative chain that ultimately has its central, master ring in the Resurrection, the 'Primary Miracle'.

For Tolkien, the Resurrection is the eucatastrophe of the eucatastrophe,[121] the focal point of History, and

[119] On the association between eagles and eucatastrophe cf. Flieger 2002:21–32; Shippey 2000:206–11; Caldecott 2012:45; also Neubauer 2016 (on the possible Germanic origin of the trope and its transformation by Tolkien into a Christian figurative framework). Eagles are also associated allusively with the members of the Fellowship of the Ring: for instance, the silver brooch given to all the members of the Fellowship by Galadriel was wrought in the likeness of an eagle. On eagles as creatures 'with a suggestion of transcendence' cf. Rutledge 2004:29–43, 340–1.

[120] Cf. also *Letters* 131:227 where Tolkien describes more specifically the celebration of Frodo and Sam at the Field of Cormallen as the eucatastrophe of the whole romance, "a supreme moment of its kind" that brought tears to his eyes when he wrote it.

[121] Cf. *TOFS*:77–8=*TL*:71–2 "in the 'eucatastrophe' we see in a brief vision that the answer may be greater – it may be a far-off gleam or echo of evangelium in the real world. [...] The Birth of Christ is the eucatastrophe of Man's history. The Resurrection is the eucatastrophe of the story of the Incarnation."

the perfect embodiment of the "secret life in creation" glimpsed unconsciously in the best of all sub-creations. All sub-created stories ultimately refer to this 'master eucatastrophe': they are unique stories, but all interconnected within the same "seamless Web of Story". All sub-created stories are new and different; all have their own individual, particular uniqueness and value, but they are also always similar and always ancient because they embody and renew, although imperfectly and in different modes, the same "universal truth and everlasting life". This, ultimately, is the 'good news' with which God 'renews the face of the earth' (cf. *Psalm* 104); this recalls the announcement that "your King shall come again [...] and the Tree that was withered shall be renewed" (*LotR* 6.5:962), as the Eagle of the Valar sings in its song of victory (cf. III.1.2.1, IV.2.2.1). Tolkien's 'theory', in conclusion, articulates complex beliefs of organic narrative interconnectedness within and between secondary and primary realities; of the combination of particularity and universality; and of the prophetic potential inherent in any successful, 'living' narrative. These beliefs are all rooted and epitomised in Tolkien's description of literature as the "mystery of literary creation". This will be the direct focus of my final Chapter VI, in which all the themes and images discussed in the previous chapters will be briefly recapitulated and brought together into a single vision. To pave the way to that, however, I still need to discuss another important episode from *The Lord of the Rings*, which is related to the eucatastrophic stories of Beren and Frodo and is yet exceptional in many respects.

V

Gandalf's Fall and Return

Sub-creative Humility and the 'Arising' of Prophecy

~

In Chapters III and IV, I discussed two important features of Tolkien's literary work: namely (1) the existence of a secret, 'divine narrative' featuring the participation or intrusion of higher creative beings in lower planes of creation in a manner that is discreet and respectful of the freedom of lower creatures; and (2) the interrelationship between different narrative entities (characters, storylines, etc.), implying a pattern of difference and uniqueness within similarity and interconnection, and underpinning a theoretical framework that is distinctively non-allegorical.

In this chapter, I will bring the two topics together and discuss more extensively their meta-literary significance, in relationship with Tolkien's theory of sub-creation (or "the mystery of literary creation"). To do so, I will turn to the narrative episode that Tolkien suggested was the most extensive intrusion of the "Great Author" within his own literary work. This intrusion has momentous meta-literary importance and helps to illuminate

This chapter originates from a conversation (or dispute) with Prof. Paolo Prosperi, whom I thank for the inspiration: after a lot of thought and ink, I think I have succeeded in demonstrating that he was right (Gandalf really did die and resurrect, in some sense), but I hope that he (and other readers) will still appreciate the fruits of the journey that I had to travel in order to get there.

Tolkien's paradoxical conviction that, on the one hand, any accomplished secondary story cannot help but have a connection with other texts, stories, and events of the primary world (and with the Gospel Story above all); but on the other hand, that any such extra-textual meaning ('allegorical', 'symbolical', 'prophetic') potentially identifiable within his narratives is completely unintentional. In fact, the introduction of primary figuration within a secondary creation could be described as the consequence (and indeed the mark) of God's intervention within the "mystery of literary Creation". This divine intervention and its unexpected implications can even be in tension with the author's own intentions, resistances, and creative idiosyncrasies, as we will see.

As before, I will begin my journey from within the secondary world, offering a close reading of the episode of 'Gandalf's Fall and Return' in *The Lord of the Rings*. I am sure that many readers are familiar with it, but it will be good to recall briefly its context and content.

V.1 Gandalf's Fall and the Loss of Hope

During their journey through the dark mines of Moria, the fellowship of the Ring is attacked by a great host of Orcs led by a monstrous, mysterious figure known as a Balrog – an ancient demon belonging to a race of fallen angels. Gandalf and his companions initially manage to flee, but just after they cross the last perilous bridge of Moria, they are assaulted by the Balrog, with no hope of escape. Knowing the power of his enemy, Gandalf decides to confront him alone, in one of the most epic and famous scenes of the book:

'You cannot pass!' he [Gandalf] said. With a bound the Balrog leaped full upon the bridge. Its whip whirled and hissed. At that moment Gandalf lifted his staff, and crying aloud he smote the bridge before him. The staff broke asunder and fell from his hand. A blinding sheet of white flame sprang up. The bridge cracked. Right at the Balrog's feet it broke, and the stone upon which it stood crashed into the gulf, […]. With a terrible cry the Balrog fell forward, and its shadow plunged down and vanished. But even as it fell it swung its whip, and the thongs lashed and curled about the wizard's knees, dragging him to the brink. He staggered and fell, grasped vainly at the stone, and slid into the abyss. 'Fly, you fools!' he cried, and was gone. (*LotR* 1.5:330–1)

Gandalf disappears into the abyss: the fellows of the Ring manage to escape the darkness of Moria, but are left to continue their journey on their own, dismayed, despondent, and indeed almost desperate. As Aragorn, taking on the role of the new leader, says to his companions "Farewell Gandalf. […] What hope have we without you? […] We must do without hope" (*LotR* 1.6:333). I will come back to these words in a later section. Gandalf's bereaved companions will later report his fall to the Elves of Lórien, to their great distress, and the Elves will make "songs of lamentation for his fall" (*LotR* 1.7:358). In Lórien, Frodo and Sam will also mourn the death of their friend, composing for him a dirge, which ends with a gloomy couplet: "his staff was broken on the stone, | in Khazad-dûm his wisdom died" (*LotR* 1.7:359–60).

But Gandalf's departure is, of course, only temporary. After a few chapters he will re-enter the narrative, unexpectedly appearing to Aragorn, Legolas, and Gimli in the forest of Fangorn, with a new white robe and a new staff.

Later, Gandalf will lead the armies of Rohan and Gondor to the victories of Isengard and Minas Tirith, revealing a much greater power than that of his previous self, as noted by Tolkien in an important letter in which the new Gandalf is even compared to the angel rescuing St Peter from prison.[1] Gandalf's change is repeatedly highlighted in the book,[2] and is especially noted by the hobbit Merry, who points out that "[Gandalf] has grown, or something. [...] He has changed" (*LotR* 3.11:590). And Gandalf himself proclaims to Saruman, in the confrontation after the battle of Isengard, that he is no longer Gandalf the Grey, but rather "Gandalf the White, who has returned from death" (*LotR* 3.10:583). What is the origin, nature, and consequence of Gandalf's change, which is clearly closely related to his 'return from death' in Moria? What exactly happened to Gandalf after he fell into the abyss of Moria?

V.1.1 A Reticent Account and Unclear Exegesis

In Fangorn, the new Gandalf reluctantly gives his eager friends a brief recount of the events between his fall and return (*LotR* 3.5:501–3); he describes his underground

---

[1] Cf. *Letters* 156:299[203 "[Gandalf] remains similar in personality and idiosyncrasy, but both his wisdom and power are much greater. [...] where the physical powers of the Enemy are too great for the good will of the opposers to be effective he can act in emergency as an 'angel' – no more violently than the release of St Peter from prison."

[2] Cf. for instance *LotR* 6.4:949, with Gandalf referring to his "old life burned away". Also during his first conversation with Aragorn and friends Gandalf behaves in peculiar ways: he appears to have forgotten his name, collects light in his hands, and looks straight at the sun (cf. *LotR* 3.5:494–5, 500). I owe this point to Edmund Weiner.

duel and chase with the Balrog; his victory on the peak of the mountains; and his eventual rescue by the eagle Gwaihir, who carries him to Lórien where he is healed and clothed by Galadriel. On one crucial passage, however, Gandalf is altogether reticent, explicitly refusing to elaborate:

I threw down my enemy, and he fell from the high place and broke the mountain-side where he smote it in his ruin. Then darkness took me, and I strayed out of thought and time, and I wandered far on roads that I will not tell. Naked I was sent back – for a brief time, until my task is done. And naked I lay upon the mountain-top. (*LotR* 3.5:502)

This passage is purposefully cryptic and yet extremely important.[3] What I will do for most of the rest of the chapter is to try to clarify this passage, filling Gandalf's gaps, reconstructing what happened on the mountain's peak, and offering an exegesis of this mysterious event, which has a momentous thematic significance for the understanding of *The Lord of the Rings* as well as crucial meta-literary implications.

To this purpose, I am fortunate enough to be able to rely on Tolkien's own commentary on this passage, which, however short, dense, and allusive, provides an enlightening and essential springboard for any discussion. Tolkien speaks about Gandalf's fall and return in a section from a draft letter to his friend Robert Murray (I have highlighted in bold passages which I will refer to in the following discussion):

---

[3] Cf. also an authorial note collected in *TI* 23:422 "How did he [Gandalf] escape? This might never be fully explained."

in his condition it was for him [Gandalf] a sacrifice to perish on the Bridge in defence of his companions, less perhaps than for a mortal Man or Hobbit, since he had a far greater inner power than they; but also more, since it was **a humbling and abnegation of himself** in conformity to 'the Rules': for all he could know at that moment he was the only person who could direct the resistance to Sauron successfully, and all his mission was vain. He was **handing over to the Authority** that ordained the Rules, and **giving up personal hope of success**. That I should say is what the Authority wished, as a set-off to Saruman. [...] He was sent by a mere prudent plan of the angelic Valar or governors; but **Authority had taken up this plan and enlarged it, at the moment of its failure**. 'Naked I was sent back – for a brief time, until my task is done'. Sent back **by whom, and whence?** Not by the 'gods' whose business is only with this embodied world and its time; for he passed 'out of thought and time'. Naked is alas! unclear. It was meant just literally, 'unclothed like a child' (not discarnate), and so ready to receive the white robes of the highest. (*Letters* 156:298–9[202–3])

I will now try to unpack Tolkien's dense and allusive prose and make some first important considerations.

V.1.2 A Self-Sacrifice

First of all, Tolkien describes Gandalf's fall in Moria as a sacrifice for the sake of his companions: although Gandalf does not exactly throw himself into the deadly abyss, by putting himself forward on the bridge to confront the Balrog, he is implicitly offering his life to protect that of his friends. This is also revealed in the text visually by Gandalf's act of smashing his iconic staff (the symbol of his power and authority) in order to demolish the rock of the bridge – an act that is significantly recalled by Frodo in his dirge (as seen earlier).

V.1.3 Obedience to 'The Rules'

Secondly, Gandalf's sacrifice is described as an act of obedience – the climax and epitome of a general attitude required from him ('The Rules'), involving a personal "humbling and abnegation" ordained by some unnamed "Authority". Tolkien is here alluding to a key narrative element of *The Lord of the Rings*, which remains implicit in the book itself but is disclosed in other posthumous texts.[4] This has to do with Gandalf's identity as a Maia, as an angelic being belonging to a race of immortal, spiritual entities governed by seven major Valar – the Lords of the West, the 'gods' of Middle-earth.

As discussed in Chapter III (III.1), all of these angelic beings existed before the genesis of the physical world (Arda); indeed, they participated in its creation, later entering it to complete their 'sub-creative' work, which nonetheless remained under the authority of a single, higher transcendent being known as Eru/Ilúvatar. Eru is clearly the 'Authority' to which Tolkien alludes in his letter; He is the single divine 'Creator' who empowered the Valar with their sub-creative mission, but who also created, independently from the Valar, all other rational creatures of Middle-earth, including especially Elves and Men. The 'Rules' ordained by Eru, which Gandalf abides by through his sacrifice, concern the relationship

---

[4] Cf. also *Letters* 156:297[201] "I have severely cut G's account of himself." Cf. III.3, with n.114.

between Valar/Maiar and Elves/Men – between spiritual, 'higher' creatures and incarnate, 'lower' ones.

I have already discussed some of these 'Rules' in Chapter III (esp. III.2.1) in relation to Gandalf's cloaked identity and veiled power. I will here briefly recall and delve further into this set of Rules and their rationale with a quotation from the recently published *The Nature of Middle-earth* (2021) – a fascinating volume that collects Tolkien's later reflections on the metaphysics of his secondary world:

> With regard to Elves and Men Eru had made one absolute prohibition: the Valar were not to attempt to dominate the Children [...]. The minds of the Children were not open to the Valar (except by the free will of the Children), and could not be invaded or violated by the Valar except with disastrous consequences: their breaking and enslaving, and the substitution in them of the dominating Vala as a God in place of Eru. It was for this reason that the Valar adopted the *fanar* [i.e. the physical form taken on by the Valar in Arda]; but they did this also out of the love and reverence for the Children that they conceived when Eru first revealed to them His idea of them. The Valar – all save one, Melkor – obeyed this prohibition by Eru, according to their wisdom. (*NME* 2.12:233)

As explained in this passage, Eru's prohibition is closely related to the preservation of his Authority in His Children's minds against any deceitful manipulation and idolatry. Despite the 'absoluteness' of the prohibition, as Tolkien explains later in the same text and as we discussed in Chapter III, the Valar had not fully abided with it in the past, and, more than once, they had forced their will on the Children of Ilúvatar.[5] The Valar had

---

[5] Cf. III.2.1.

also failed to abide with Eru's Rules in another, opposite way: by withdrawing into the West and temporarily ceasing to care about Middle-earth, they failed in their sub-creative task of fostering and protecting the lives of Elves and Men (the prohibition of domination does not justify neglect and indifference for other creatures). Tolkien points out that this complementary failure to obey the Rules of Eru was not an act of full rebellion, and yet "revealed a failure in understanding of His purposes and in confidence in Him" (*NME* 2.12:235). The sending of the secret envoy of disguised Maiar – including Gandalf – is closely related, then, to the Valar's desire to make amends for their "error of old" and fully to obey Eru's Rules, without revealing themselves "in forms of majesty" and without "an open display of power" in general (cf. *UT* 4.2:389) – as already discussed in Chapter III (III.2.1).

Tolkien further elaborates on the relationship between Gandalf's identity and Eru's prohibition in an important letter:

since in the view of this tale & mythology Power – when it dominates or seeks to dominate other wills and minds [...] – is evil, these 'wizards' were **incarnated** in the life-forms of Middle-earth, and so suffered the pains both of mind and body. They were also, for the same reason, thus involved in the peril of the **incarnate**: the possibility of 'fall', of sin, if you will. (*Letters* 181:342–3[237])

With its insistence on the notion of 'incarnation', this passage introduces another important element to consider in Gandalf's fall in Moria, concerning his problematic ontological status.

V.1.4 Gandalf's Problematic Ontology and His Assimilation to 'Lower' Creatures

According to Tolkien's complex secondary metaphysics, there are three main types of rational beings in Arda, each one of which has a different ontological status regarding, in particular, the relationship between its soul/spirit and body (*fëa* and *hröa* in Elvish) and its permanence within the physical world (Arda):[6]

a) Valar and Maiar are immortal, 'divine' beings whose primary nature is spiritual but who can 'clothe' or 'clad' themselves in bodily forms so that they can interact with lesser beings – forms which are corporeal but remain, for them, as a mere 'raiment' or 'garment'.[7] The Valar and their people are, thus, 'discarnate'; and yet, crucially, they cannot escape the boundaries of the physical world, both Space and Time. As explained in *The Silmarillion*, "this condition Ilúvatar made [...] that their power should thenceforward be contained and bounded in the World, to be within it for ever, until it is complete" (*Sil Ain.*:8). These boundaries are spatial and also temporal: as Tolkien remarks in a text now printed in *The Nature of Middle-earth*: "The Valar entered into Eä and Time of free will, and they are now in Time, so long as it endures. They can perceive nothing outside Time" (*NME* 2.9:207).[8]

---

[6] See further on this McBride 2020, chapter 6.

[7] Cf. *NME* 2.13:238, also *Sil Ain.*:21 (on the Valar's shape compared with a raiment for human creatures, without which one does not suffer loss of their being).

[8] Cf. also *Letters* 200:374[259], stressing that the Valar would have to remain within Arda (the realised world) "until the Story was finished".

b) Elves are 'incarnate' beings, and thus "consisted naturally of the union of a fëa (spirit) and a hröa (body)" (*NME* 1.3:14–15); at the same time, they are "immortal within Arda". Their doom (as Tolkien explains in his letters) is to "last while it [the world] lasts, never leaving it even when 'slain'" (*Letters* 131:206[147]), and "[w]hen 'killed', by the injury or destruction of their incarnate form, they do not escape from time, but remain in the world, either discarnate, or being re-born" (*Letters* 181:342[235]). The inverted commas ('slain', 'killed') are Tolkien's original, and confirm that, to his mind, the violent death of an Elf is not fully equivalent to a human 'death' – it is, rather, a 'seeming death' (cf. *Sil* 1:42). The Elves' immortal spirit is clearly 'dominant' over its body, which can be repaired or substituted in case of violent death, or even "discarded to dissolution" (*NME* 1.3:15); in sum, Elves – as the envious Númenórean Men point out – "do not die" (*Sil Ak.*:274).

c) Finally, human beings ('Men') are weak, mortal, and 'bodily' to the highest degree: their spirits cannot subsist without a symbiotic relationship with their own bodies, and, once the body is destroyed or decayed, they are doomed to leave Arda forever, suffering death in its full sense. Humans are, in this sense, 'lowest' in the spiritual hierarchy, and yet they are also the only ones who can escape the physical world; their "freedom for the circles of the world" (*Letters* 131:206[147]) is often remarked upon in Tolkien's texts.[9] For this

---

[9] Cf. the dramatic confrontation between the Valar's Elvish emissaries and the rebellious Númenóreans (*Sil Ak.*:264–5), in which the former remind the latter that death is the gift of Ilúvatar, and not a punishment, and in fact it is a gift that they themselves envy, since

reason, death – the Gift of Ilúvatar to men – is something that Elves and even the Valar eventually come
to envy.[10] It is because of their mortal nature and their
escape from the "circles of the world" that men will
eventually have the important task of 'redeeming' the
marred Arda, in some mysterious way.[11]

There are some apparent exceptions to this tripartite
framework, such as Ents and Dwarves (sub-created by the
Valar Yavanna and Aulë) as well as Orcs and Hobbits,
all of which, however, should probably be considered as
variations of the second and third type (the latter is certainly the case for Hobbits). The real exception in this
framework is the case of the Istari, or 'incarnate' Maiar,
such as Saruman and Gandalf. In Tolkien's conflicting
descriptions, the wizards' ontological status is fluid and
ambiguous, but clearly (and crucially) there is some sort
of 'lowering' of ontological status from their originally
spiritual nature to "approach the state of 'incarnation'"

---

thanks to it Men "can escape, and leave the world, and are not bound
to it". Cf. also *LR* 1.2:18 (on Men's fate being "not within the world").
[10] Cf. *Letters* 131:206[147] "it is a mystery of God [...] a grief and **an
envy** to the immortal Elves"; *Sil* 1:29–30, "the sons of Men die indeed,
and leave the world [...] the gift of Ilúvatar, which as Time wears even
the Powers **shall envy**"; *BLT1* 2:59 ("envy and amazement").
[11] Cf. *MR Athr.*:343, "[the Elves] still believe that Eru's healing of all the
griefs of Arda will come now by or through Men; [...] By the holiness
of good men – their direct attachment to Eru, before and above all
Eru's works – the Elves may be delivered from the last of their griefs:
sadness; the sadness that must come even from the unselfish love of
anything less than Eru"; *SME* 2:50 (on Ulmo's foretelling and the
Elves' prophecy about Men's eventual role in rekindling the Two
Trees and the glory of old). Cf. also *BLT1* 2:59 on Men's gift of
freedom, and their power to 'turn things' "despite Gods and Fairies"
and "fashion and design their life beyond even the original Music of
the Ainur" (ibid. 92). See further VI.2.5.

(*NME* 2.9:209). As is also evident in the Moria episode, Gandalf's body, and its relationship with his spirit, is markedly different from the temporary 'self-arraying' of the Valar.

This ontological lowering is another important aspect of the wizards' "humbling and abnegation" devised by the Valar to avoid the risk of the domination of lesser beings (cf. III.2.1). Such a lowering is also a radicalisation of the wizards' "love and reverence" for humbler creatures, through a sympathetic sharing of their likenesses and weaknesses that becomes greater and more effective than their original "raiment", which was already an expression of their love for the Children of Ilúvatar.[12]

As Tolkien explains, the Istari "suffered the pains both of mind and body" (*Letters* 181:343[237], just like Elves and especially Men. It seems clear that the Istari – or at least some of them – are assimilated more to men ("in bodies as of men") rather than to Elves, and that men are supposed to be their main object of concern; this is certainly true in the case of Gandalf, who dedicated his life to the edification and empowering of Men, including those of the lowest nature – the Hobbits, whose idiosyncratic habits (including, for example, smoking) he even deigns to take up himself.[13]

We can thus point out how, on the bridge of Khazad-Dûm, Gandalf takes an even greater step in his process of 'lowering' and sympathetic assimilation with human beings in that he voluntarily faces what is, in Tolkien's

---

[12] Cf. *Sil Ain.*:21 (on the Valar taking shape after that of the Children out of love for them).

[13] Cf. *Letters* 131, n.*:220[159] on Gandalf especially watching human affairs, of Men and Hobbits.

mythology, the most characteristic drama of human nature: the acceptance of death.

V.1.5 Accepting the Gift of Ilúvatar

Accepting death is indeed *the* problem of Men in Tolkien's imagining. If Elves are more concerned with deathlessness,[14] Death is, instead, "the doom of Man" – the specific "gift" given by Eru/Ilúvatar to men, according to Tolkien's mythology. And yet, because of its apparent opposition to the human love for life and its mysterious nature and purpose, humans find it very difficult to accept this Gift. As Tolkien explains in a footnote to his letter to Murray:

the view of the myth is that Death [...] is not a punishment for the Fall, but a biologically (and therefore also spiritually, since body and spirit are integrated) inherent part of Man's nature. The attempt to escape it is wicked because 'unnatural', and silly because Death in that sense is the Gift of God (envied by the Elves), release from the weariness of Time. **Death, in the penal sense, is viewed as a change in attitude to it: fear, reluctance**. A good Númenórean died of free will when he felt it to be time to do so. (*Letters* 156, n.†:302[205])

"Fear" and "reluctance" to accept death are closely related to the problem of the relationship between Eru and his human children, who are called to accept out of mere trust a "gift" that they do not understand; for this reason, they are always tempted to delay or prevent it, ultimately rebelling against the faceless Giver of that undesirable gift. This is a crucial temptation or test, which must

---

[14] Cf. *Letters* 131:146 (on the Elves' concern for the burdens of deathlessness in time and change).

eventually be faced by all humans and 'humanised' Elves, such as Arwen, Aragorn's wife. This is indeed the focus of their final dialogue, before Aragorn dies of free will (as a "good Númenórean"), in what Tolkien considered as the most important Appendix of *The Lord of the Rings*:[15]

'I say to you, King of the Númenóreans, not till now have I understood the tale of your people and their fall. As wicked fools I scorned them, but I pity them at last. For if this is indeed, as the Eldar say, the gift of the One to Men, it is bitter to receive.' 'So it seems,' he said. 'But let us not be overthrown at the final test, who of old renounced the Shadow and the Ring. **In sorrow we must go, but not in despair.** Behold! **we are not bound for ever to the circles of the world**, and beyond them is more than memory. Farewell' 'Estel, Estel!' she cried, and with that even as he took her hand and kissed it, he fell into sleep. (*LotR*, Appendix A:1063)

The problem of death, of its acceptance or refusal, is crucial in all of Tolkien's work, and this theme is especially pertinent in the tale of Númenor's fall, of which the death of Aragorn represents a sort of epilogue. It is also central in *The Lord of the Rings*, as Tolkien himself acknowledged in several letters, in which he notes that the "real theme" of *The Lord of the Rings* was "something much more permanent and difficult: Death and Immortality" (*Letters* 186:353[246]).[16] The "dominance" of the problem of death is reflected, for instance, in the

---

[15] Cf. *Letters* 181:343[237].

[16] Cf. also *Letters* 203:378[262] "the tale is not really about Power and Dominion [...] it is about Death and the desire for deathlessness"; *Letters* 208:385[267] "the dominance of the theme of Death" (quoted in Chapter VI n.32). See on this Vaninskaya 2020; also the collection of essays in Arduini and Testi 2012.

narrative prominence of the Rings, and the One Ring in particular, whose main functions are to delay death (as is clear in the cases of Bilbo and Gollum, as well as of the Nazgûl), and to control the will of other creatures.

With its double power, the Ring iconically reveals that, in Tolkien's mytho-theology, trying to prevent death and to exert Power on the wills of others (even for their own good) are two facets of the same error; they betray the same human temptation to rebel against the Rules of Ilúvatar and thus ultimately to contest and rebel against his Authority. By contrast, it is an attitude of submission to Ilúvatar's authority that demands and compels the acceptance of death and the refusal of Power. Submission requires 'lowering' oneself, assimilating oneself to lower creatures, to the point of embracing human 'Doom' and freely embracing death for other creatures' sake.

We can start to see how Gandalf's sacrifice in Moria is just the final step of a process of 'lowering', beginning from his original spiritual status as Maia, down to taking on the "Doom of Men" (which, as we will see later on, is for Gandalf a genuine death, not just a disembodiment) in conformity with the Rules and wishes of Ilúvatar; this is a process that Ilúvatar himself triggered and will soon bring to completion.

Before proceeding to this final point, we must consider yet another important factor at play in Gandalf's fall, which again is closely related to Eru's Authority: hope.

V.1.6 Hoping beyond Hope: Amdir versus Estel

Returning to Tolkien's exegesis of Gandalf's fall, it is clear that in Moria Gandalf is not merely sacrificing his life (for however good a cause). In his death, he is also giving up his "personal hope of success" (*Letters* 156:299[202]). Gandalf accepts and indeed provokes the failure of the main 'plot' of *The Lord of the Rings* devised by the Valar and carried out by himself: the plan to lead the people of Middle-earth to victory against Sauron. This plan pivots on Gandalf's own role as leader of the resistance, and as Frodo's personal guide on his journey to Mordor. Gandalf is the "enemy of Sauron" because he is the only one who has the power and wisdom to lead the fellowship to the victory against Sauron, as is often highlighted in the story. Without Gandalf, there is no real hope that the mission of the Fellowship of the Ring can be fulfilled, as Aragorn immediately acknowledges after Gandalf's fall ("what hope have we without you?", *LotR* 1.6:333). And yet, despite his recognition of the 'hopelessness' of the situation, Aragorn does not give in to despair, as Denethor will do in a similar situation; rather, Aragorn decides to press on, flagging his paradoxical resolution with the statement "We must do without hope" (ibid.).[17]

This apparent paradox of 'hoping beyond hope' is another central theme in *The Lord of the Rings* and in Tolkien's work in general.[18] This theme is related to an important distinction that Tolkien makes between two radically different kinds of hope. This distinction underlies *The Lord of the Rings*,[19] and is explicitly thematised in a

[17] Frodo will express the same attitude again and again during his journey to Mordor; cf. esp. *LotR* 6.2:918 "I haven't a hope left. But I have to go on trying to get to the Mountain"; also ibid. 924.

[18] The archetypical hero Eärendil himself is described as the "longed for that cometh beyond hope" (*Sil* 24:248–9). See I.2.5.2.

[19] Cf. Elrond's programmatic words in Rivendell "we must take a hard road, a road unforeseen. There lies our hope, if hope it be" (*LotR* 2.2:267); later, Gandalf's revealing advice during the council after

posthumous text known as the 'Dialogue between Finrod and Andreth' or *Athrabeth* (published in *MR*, part 4). In this text, the Elvish king Finrod explains to his human interlocutor that Elves have two different terms to refer to two notions that humans merge under the single term 'hope'.

On the one hand, there is 'hope' initially defined as "[a]n expectation of good, which though uncertain has some foundation in what is known" (*MR Athr.*:320). The Elves call this 'Amdir'.[20] This is a kind of 'rationalistic' hope, a hope founded on a human assessment or personal analysis of current circumstances and their implications. This is the hope that Gandalf is 'sacrificing' on the bridge of Moria when he accepts the destruction of the most important 'foundation' of his own "expectation of good"– his own life.

But, Finrod continues, there is another kind of hope called 'Estel' by the Elves; it is "founded deeper" and has a quite different meaning:

But there is another which is **founded deeper**. Estel we call it, that is "trust". It is not defeated by the ways of the world, for it does not come from experience, but from our nature and first being. If we are indeed the Eruhin, the Children of the One, then He will not suffer Himself to be deprived of His own, not by any Enemy, not even by ourselves. This is the last foundation of Estel, which we keep even when we contemplate the

---

the victory of Minas Tirith: "This war then is without final hope, as Denethor perceived. [...] I still hope for victory, but not by arms. For into the midst of all these policies comes the Ring of Power [...] the hope of Sauron" (*LotR* 5.9:878).

[20] Devaux (2023) notes, however, that this definition of *amdir* is unstable and develops throughout the dialogue, also encompassing the concept of dream.

End: of all His designs the issue must be **for His Children's joy**. (*MR Athr.*:320)

According to this second definition, hope is founded on nothing else except the belief in Eru's higher benevolent Authority; it is based on the trust that His designs are ultimately "for His children's joy". In this sense, as explained in later passages of the same dialogue, Estel can be properly defined as 'trust in Eru', which is one of the two things demanded by Eru from his Children (together with "belief in him"); this complete trust ("naked Estel") consists in the confidence that "whatever He designed beyond the End would be recognized [...] as wholly satisfying" (*MR Athr.*:332).[21] Crucially, this kind of hope ('Estel') is the very thing specifically required from Men so that they may face and embrace death, the "gift of Ilúvatar", and which they often fail to uphold, to the Elves' surprise (and disapproval).[22]

It is no coincidence, then, that one of Aragorn's other names is Estel – eponymously indicating his destiny as the man who will restore human trust in Eru and amend the sins of his Númenórean ancestors.[23] Aragorn's

---

[21] Cf. also *MR Athr.*:338 "Eru [...] appears in the Elvish tradition to demand two things from His Children (of either Kindred): belief in Him, and proceeding from that, hope or **trust in Him** (called by the Eldar *estel*)."

[22] Cf. *MR Athr.*:332 "the Elves were less sympathetic than Men expected to the lack of hope (or **estel**) in Men faced by death". Also, the Númenóreans' justification of their envy for the immortal Elves: "'Why should we not envy [...] the least of the deathless? For of us is required the greater trust and **hope without assurance**'" (*SD*:365).

[23] In an unpublished letter (*TCG* 201, 12/05/1955) Tolkien appropriately described the final scene of the tale of Aragorn and Arwen as "an allegory of naked hope". Cf. the recent study by Whitmire (2023), appropriately discussing the tale as 'a Narrative of Hope Beyond Hope'.

destiny of hope is shown again and again in *The Lord of the Rings*, from his initial decision to trust the "fool's hope" of Gandalf (whose identity and mission are known to him), against the 'wisdom' of Sauron, to the willingness to look after the kidnapped hobbits Merry and Pippin, "hoping against hope";[24] and from his hopeless descent to the paths of the dead (repeating in a sense Gandalf's descent to Moria),[25] and his later journey to the Gate of Morannon,[26] to his final discovery of the new sapling of the Tree.[27] In all these cases, Tolkien alludes to the same contrast of hopes and thereby confirms Aragorn's hope (Estel) beyond hope (Amdir), revealed in his decision to always follow the path "laid out for him" (by Eru) without despairing, even when the path seems hopeless. Aragorn's *Estel* will reach its acme at the moment of his death, as retold in the scene to which I have already referred. After renewing his final trust in Eru by pithily saying that he must go "in sorrow [...] but not in despair" (*LotR* Appendix A:1063), Aragorn is addressed by Arwen with his iconic name of Estel at the very moment when his destiny of hope (qua Estel) is fulfilled.

[24] Cf. *LotR* 3.1:415 "I will take these things, **hoping against hope**, to give them back"; 420 "With hope or without hope we will follow the trail of our enemies"; also *LotR* 3.2:427 "'This is a bitter end to our hope and to all our toil!' [...] 'To hope, maybe, but not to toil'"; 429 "but this endless chase began to tell on him, as all hope failed in his heart". Cf. also Gandalf's later words to Aragorn, confirming that his choice of what seemed the right path has been rewarded (*LotR* 3.5:500).

[25] Cf. *LotR* 3.2:783 (Éowyn begging Aragorn not to go on the Paths of the Dead, so that "our hope be the brighter", and Aragorn replying to her that it is not madness to go on a path appointed).

[26] Where the reader will see "the hopeless defeat of the forlorn hope" (*Letters* 131:226).

[27] Cf. IV.1.4.

It is therefore this second type of hope – Estel – that Gandalf upholds on the bridge of Moria, while sacrificing Amdir, "giving up personal hope of success" and embracing death, the Doom of Man. In Tolkien's vision, therefore, 'hope as human calculation' is not the same as 'hope without guarantees, hope as trust in Eru'; in fact, human hope is normally inversely proportional to trust in Eru: it is when one fully gives up the former type of hope (Amdir), in obedience to Eru's wishes, that the latter type (Estel) can be realised to the fullest (a 'naked trust').[28]

This dynamic is thematised again and again in *The Lord of the Rings*, and is central to its plot, which focuses on a clash between Gandalf's "fool's hope" and the despair of the Wise (such as Saruman and Denethor).[29] But it is not just Gandalf and Aragorn who are called to give up 'Amdir' and uphold 'Estel' by obeying what they perceive to be their duty in a particular situation. Frodo will also live the same paradoxical drama, especially when trudging along towards Mount Doom.[30] The hobbit's implicit trust

---

[28] One could perhaps trace a figurative representation of this dynamic in the Elvish bread Lembas, which is given to serve "when all else fails" (*LotR* 2.7:370) and has a potency that increases when one relies on it alone (*LotR* 6.3:936), as well as in the phial of Galadriel, filled with the light of Eärendil, which is "a light […] in dark places, when all other lights go out" (*LotR* 2.8:376). Cf. also Aragorn's words before embarking on his desperate journey to Morannon: "We come now to the very brink, where hope and despair are akin" (*LotR* 5.9:880).

[29] Cf. esp. the tense exchange between Gandalf and Denethor at *LotR* 5.4:813, followed by Gandalf's words at 815, and later by Denethor's desperate sarcasm against him ("the Grey Fool", 823); also, their final confrontation at *LotR* 5.7:853 ("thy hope is but ignorance").

[30] Cf. esp. *LotR* 6.2:918 "I haven't a hope left. But I have to go on trying to get to the Mountain." The desperateness of his mission is acknowledged from its very start (cf. *LotR* 1.5:107 "[it] sounds very desperate") and is reiterated again and again in the course of

in Eru is revealed by his stubborn obedience to continue in his appointed mission, despite having no personal hope of success. Indeed, in an early draft of *The Lord of the Rings*, Frodo was given the new name of "Endurance beyond Hope" (*SD* 1.7:62) at the end of his journey. Sam also undergoes the same process, gaining new strength exactly "as hope died in Sam, or seemed to die" (*LotR* 6.3:934). By contrast, Denethor fails to uphold Estel by putting trust in Gandalf's plan; with the fading of his Amdir, he eventually yields to despair and suffers a 'heathen death'.

This Tolkienian paradox of hope also explains why, in *The Lord of the Rings*, all the good turns of the story follow moments of apparent hopeless failure; such moments are consistently pinpointed with the label "without hope" or the like, and include the Fellowship's escape from Moria;[31] Gandalf's return as a White Rider after his fall in Moria;[32] the destruction of the Witch King,[33] and the following return of the sun after the battle of Minas Tirith;[34] and, indeed, the whole victory against Sauron in general (i.e. the plot goal of *The Lord of the Rings*).[35]

---

the book (e.g. *LotR* 3.5:500 "a peril near despair"; 4.3:638–9; *LotR* 5.4:813 "There never was much hope"; *LotR* 6.1:914 "The whole thing is quite hopeless", etc.).

[31] *LotR* 2.5:331 "they came **beyond hope** under the sky and felt the wind on their faces"; *LotR* 2.7:355 "when our escape **seemed beyond hope** he [Gandalf] saved us, and he fell".

[32] *LotR* 3.5:495 "**Beyond all hope** you return to us in our need!".

[33] *LotR* 5.7:856 "**Beyond hope** the Captain of our foes has been destroyed".

[34] *LotR* 6.6:976 "the Sun, **returning beyond hope**, gleamed [...] in the morning".

[35] *LotR* 6.5:963 "he bore tidings **beyond hope** from the Lords of the West"; *LotR*, Appendix A:1062 "**hope beyond hope** was fulfilled". Cf. also *LotR* 3.1:415, quoted in n.24. In his early review of *The Lord of the*

Crucially, this kind of radical upholding of 'Estel' is required so that, eventually, even human hope can be fulfilled and Gandalf's plan can succeed. As Tolkien explains in a passage that – to come full circle – explicitly connects Gandalf's fall with the problem of death and hope:

> the situation became so much the worse by the fall of Saruman, that the 'good' were obliged to greater effort and sacrifice. Gandalf faced and suffered death; and came back or was sent back, as he says, with enhanced power. [...] Here I am only concerned with Death as part of the nature, physical and spiritual, of Man, and with **Hope without guarantees**. (*Letters* 181:343[237])

If Gandalf had not given up his "personal hope of success" (Amdir) and upheld his "Hope without guarantees" (Estel) by embracing death – the "nature, physical and spiritual, of Man" (*Letters* 181:343[237]) – he would not have obtained his "enhanced" power, and the victory over Sauron would not have been achieved. In other words, it is only by accepting the failure of his own plan and by "handing over to the Authority" (see V.1.1), that his own plan is eventually fulfilled, having been taken over and enlarged by that very Authority.

But why is the problem of Death and Hope related to a 'handing over of authorities', and why it is so important and necessary? This leads to another important aspect of Gandalf's fall, with momentous meta-literary implications.

Rings, C. S. Lewis allusively acknowledged the centrality of this theme, concluding that readers of the book "will know that this is good news, **good beyond hope**" (in *On Stories and Other Essays on Literature*, New York 1966/1982:84).

V.1.7 Sub-creative Co-operation and the
Sacrifice of the Sub-creator

In Tolkien's commentary on the Moria episode, one can also trace implicit allusions to a meta-literary metaphor that underlies the whole of his mythology. This metaphor is indirectly introduced in the *Ainulindalë* – Tolkien's cosmogonic myth – and is spelled out in more explicit terms in other texts, especially in a short text known as *Fate and Free Will*, now included in *The Nature of Middle-earth*, which I will quote at length in Chapter VI (VI.1.2). This is a difficult text, typical of Tolkien's mytho-theological concerns of his later years, which would take too long to discuss in full. It will be enough for me here to point out how this text spells out a meta-literary metaphor that likens Eru to a literary author ("the Author of the Great Tale") and the world (Arda) to his literary work – his own Tale or Drama (the "Tale of Arda" is a common phrase in Tolkien's later works). At the same time, the "actors" or "characters" created by Eru, who act within his Tale, are not mere puppets; rather, they are somehow independent from him; they have free will, and can also, crucially, alter the 'plot' of this drama in ways originally 'unforeseen' by Eru. By doing so, these characters become themselves 'co-authors' of the Tale, although with a lower authorial authority – using Tolkien's terminology, one should call them "sub-creators".[36]

---

[36] Cf. also Finrod's words in the *Athrabeth*, comparing Eru to a "master in the telling of tales", and himself and other creatures as characters and co-authors of His story: "In no wise is the surprise and wonder of his art thus diminished, for thus **we share**, as it were, **in his authorship**" (*MR Athr.*:319). Cf. also ibid. 322 ("the author without", "the singer [...] the designer").

As mentioned earlier, the most important sub-creators of Tolkien's mythology are the Ainur or Valar, who were called by Eru to assist him in the world-building of Arda (i.e. Eru's Tale) with their own "plots and devices". For this reason, the Tale of Arda can be described, in a sense, as also the Valar's artwork, not least because, at a certain point, the Valar directly enter into it to complete their sub-creative work as the "angelic Powers of the World" (cf. *Letters* 156:298[202]). With an ambivalent, collaborative, and yet hierarchical concept of authoriality, Eru "retains all ultimate authority" over his Tale. This is demonstrated by the co-existence of Rules (which cannot be altered by the Valar) and Eru's freedom to 'intrude' at any time in the Tale (breaking those very Rules), and also by the presence within the Tale of other characters that have been created by Eru without the Valar's assistance. Above all, these include Elves and Humans – the Children of Ilúvatar, whom the Valar are called to love and help to develop according to Eru's plan, just as a gardener would do with the plants entrusted to them by the master of the house, to introduce an important Tolkienian metaphor to which I will return. Like all of Eru's creatures, Elves and Humans have been endowed with the same sub-creative power as the Valar; as a result, they also have the freedom to alter Eru's (and the Valar's) Tale and enrich it with their own artistic works: such sub-created enrichment includes, for instance, the iconic Silmarils, in which eventually "the fate of Arda lie locked" (*Sil* 15:121).[37] Elves

---

[37] Cf. also *BLT1* 2:58, stressing that the Silmarils, finest of all gems, "were not in the world before the Eldar" and *Letters* 131:207[148] on the making of gems (and the *Silmarilli* above all) as the main symbol of the "sub-creative function of the Elves".

and Men, however, are called to abide within the Rules of the higher 'authorial' authority of the Valar and, ultimately, of Eru.

To sum up: according to this complex meta-literary metaphor, Tolkien's secondary world is construed as a literary creation that involves the 'co-operation' of different authors.[38] This work of creation is founded on a hierarchy of authorships and related works, which are interconnected in a complex relationship that can be described using the concept of Chinese box or *mise-en-abyme*:[39] each primary author within a lower tale (e.g. a Vala within Arda) is also originally a character within a higher one (e.g. Eru's Tale) and has entered the 'lower' tale to serve the secondary authors that Eru has added within that tale (i.e. the Children of Ilúvatar incarnate in Arda). The nature of the Creation is both co-operative and hierarchical, and it is ultimately dependent on Eru, who is the only One who can create secondary 'authors' and bestow life and reality on artistic works, and who thus retains primary authority over all Tales. For this reason, all authors are called to interact with each other and to embed their tale within a larger, pluralistic framework; it is incumbent upon sub-creators to respect and foster the sub-creative power of 'lower' authors and submit to the authority of 'higher' authors, and ultimately to that of Eru Ilúvatar – who participates in all creations and integrates them into a single, cohesive Tale.

---

[38] On the "joys of cooperation" cf. *Letters* 113:182[127], quoted and discussed in VI.2.4.

[39] Cf. Baldick 2008 s.v. 'mise-en-abyme': "A term coined by the French writer André Gide, supposedly from the language of heraldry, to refer to an internal reduplication of a literary work or part of a work".

This call to accept and embrace dependence on a Creator is never painless or automatic for the sub-creator. Instead, as Tolkien explains,

the sub-creator wishes to be the Lord and God of his private creation. He will rebel against the laws of the Creator – especially against mortality [...] [This] will lead to the desire for Power [...] the use of these talents with the corrupted motive of dominating: bulldozing the real world, or coercing other wills. (*Letters* 131:205[146])

Here, Tolkien is clearly alluding to the acts of Morgoth and, later, to those of Sauron; their sub-creative rebellions against Eru epitomise a more general temptation of all sub-creators with which Gandalf is also confronted and eventually overcomes. Indeed, Gandalf in Moria does exactly the opposite of the rebellious acts mentioned in the letter (refusing death, dominating other wills, etc.); as noted, such acts are all the main powers of the One Ring, whose renunciation and destruction is, of course, the main plot event of *The Lord of the Rings*.

Sub-creative humility (and its related temptation of possession) is a central theme in Tolkien's work, and it is significant that Tolkien concludes in a letter that "the whole matter from beginning to end is mainly concerned with the relation of Creation to making and sub-creation (and subsidiarily with the related matter of 'mortality')" (*Letters* 153:282[188]).[40] Important manifestations of this theme include the rebellion against Eru's rules (Death and Time in particular); the domination of lower

---

[40] Sub-creative submission is not in contrast of authorial freedom (on which see III.3.1).

sub-creators (instead of looking after them); and the possessive impatience that prevents sub-creators from seeing their own creation as something ultimately 'other', independent, with its own inherent powers or talents. Eru regards His own created sub-creators, as we have seen, with a non-possessive gaze; by analogy with the Creator, sub-creators are called to develop this manner when they look at their own sub-creations and therefore to engage in a complex *mise-en-abyme* ultimately aimed at assimilating all sub-creators to their Creator and integrating all their works into a single Tale – like a book written by innumerable co-authors.

The most extreme embodiment of this Tolkienian theme of sub-creative humility consists in the call for the sub-creator to destroy their own work at the request of a higher Authority – a sort of meta-literary sacrifice of Isaac. A negative embodiment of this motive is the story of the elf Fëanor – the greatest of Elvish sub-creators and maker of the Silmarils, who "seldom remembered now that the light within them [i.e. the Silmarils] was not his own" (*Sil* 7:69) and was "wound about the things he himself had made" (*SME* 3:88). Fëanor ultimately refused the destruction of his artistic work, as requested by higher sub-creators (the Valar), for the greater good of healing Arda, despite having been reminded that the Light of his iconic jewels did not originally come from him.[41]

On the positive side, we find the sub-creative humility of the Vala Aulë, who is ready to destroy his own artistic work – the Dwarves – to uphold his filial, sub-creative dependence upon Eru. As recounted in one of the most

[41] Cf. *Sil* 9:78–9.

beautiful scenes of *The Silmarillion* (2:43–4), Aulë made the
Dwarves in secret, desiring to create something other than
himself and yet attempting a task beyond his power and
authority, since only Eru can give the gift of being – as
He himself reminds the Vala in a dramatic dialogue. Aulë
acknowledges his presumption and decides to destroy his
creatures, offering them to Eru as a child to his father.
Crucially, Aulë's submission to Eru's authority moves Eru
to compassion and to the embrace of Aulë's original desire
for things other than himself "to love and to teach" (*Sil*
2:43); indeed, Eru enhances and fulfils Aulë's desire, endowing his creatures with a life that they would not have otherwise possessed. Again, these new living characters – the
Dwarves – will themselves become important sub-creators
in Tolkien's mythology, because, as Aulë points out, children imitate their creative father: "the making of things is
in the heart from my own making by thee" (*Sil* 2:43).

The same narrative pattern can be traced in *The Lord
of the Rings* within the story of Galadriel, another master-
ful sub-creator. With the help of her ring, Galadriel has
created a beautiful enclosed 'artistic garden' – Lórien –
where she exerts almost absolute dominion and where the
decay of Time is prevented, partly against the Rules of
Eru.[42] Her sub-creative redemption is accomplished by

---

[42] Cf. *Letters* 131:212[151] (on the Elves' obsessions for 'fading', the
mode they perceived "the changes of times (the law of the world under
the sun)". However, (*Letters* 181:342[236]) "mere change as such is not
represented as 'evil': it is the unfolding of the story and to refuse this is
of course against the design of God. But the Elvish weakness is […] to
become unwilling to face change." Also *NME* 1.21:162 (on the Elvish
conception of future as decay and retrogression), 3.16:350–1 (on
Galadriel's regret and awareness that her "golden dream" was doomed
to fade).

her willingness to lose her ring, accept to be 'diminished' (just like Gandalf), and thus to permit the destruction of her sub-creation. As she says to Frodo in a crucial dialogue: "I pass the test [...] I will diminish, and go into the West, and remain Galadriel" (*LotR* 2.7:366). And yet her work will not be destroyed completely; her gift to Sam, the nut of a majestic Mallorn tree, will continue to live and sprout in the gardens of the Shire.[43]

Coming back to my focus, Gandalf's fall in Moria can be thus construed as just another embodiment of this pattern of sub-creativity submission, although with a narrative rather than artistic semantics. Gandalf's sub-creative identity is more similar to that of the author of a tale or a play rather than to that of an artisan. His plans and choices in *The Lord of the Rings* are analogous to those of a writer devising a story, and his dealings with other characters are like those of a director instructing their actors.[44] Gandalf is an emissary of the Valar, and he acts on their behalf to bring forward the 'plan' they have devised, which is essentially the plot of *The Lord of the Rings* – the victory

---

[43] The theme of sub-creative humility can also be traced in the short story *Smith of Wootton Major*, in which the eponymous artisan Smith (like all his predecessors and successors) must eventually part with the magical star that gives him his artistic talent and the ability to enter the world of Fairy (cf. *SWM*:38–40 with Tolkien's notes at 108, observing that this parting was induced by a mysterious 'King', "without the use of command or authority, as an act of generosity").

[44] Cf. also the chess metaphor at *LotR* 5.1:759–60 ("The board is set, and the pieces are moving [...] the Enemy has the move, and he is about to open his full game"), which compares Gandalf and Sauron as two players moving their pieces on the board. Also ibid. 767 (Pippin's feeling on "the wrong chessboard") and *LotR* 6.8:1018, "When his [i.e. Gandalf's] tools have done their task he drops them." On Gandalf's sub-creative identity as a rekindler of hearts cf. also III.2.1 with n. 95.

against Sauron achieved through the destruction of the One Ring of Power. Indeed, as Aragorn will acknowledge during his coronation, Gandalf "has been the mover of all that has been accomplished, and this is his victory" (*LotR* 6.5:968).[45]

Gandalf's acceptance of his plan's failure in Moria is thus analogous to the destruction of the Dwarves for Aulë and to what the breaking of the Silmarils would have meant for Fëanor. Gandalf's acceptance of death and commitment to hope without guarantees are expressions of the same sub-creative humility that Aulë originally displayed to Eru. And, just as Eru accepted Aulë's sacrifice and fulfilled his desire, so Eru will accept Gandalf's sacrifice and take up and enlarge the plan of Gandalf and the Valar.

We can see how Gandalf's "handing over to the Authority" is an act with important meta-literary implications that can only be understood within Tolkien's complex *mise-en-abyme* of creative authorities: the authority at stake on the bridge of Moria is an 'authorial' one; it is the authority of Eru as the ultimate Author of the Great Tale to whom all sub-authors – such as Gandalf – should ultimately submit with "naked trust". The most extreme form of this submission is the acceptance to destroy one's work (the Dwarves, the Silmarils, Lórien, and Gandalf's plot) for the sake of other creatures.

Gandalf's fall is, therefore, an embodiment of a common Tolkienian motive of sub-creative submission; and yet there is something arguably exceptional and enhanced compared with previous embodiments; in his case, Gandalf does not only accept the destruction

---

[45] Cf. also Faramir's words at *LotR* 4.5:671 ("a great mover").

of his own work by embracing and indeed provoking the failure of his plot, but he also goes to the point of accepting his own destruction. His sub-creative authority is handed over in an extreme way, through a paradoxical fulfilment of his sub-creative vocation, which, as seen, ultimately consists in the fostering of other, lower creatures (the Children of Ilúvatar). Gandalf's act is one of extreme sub-creative humility and Estel; as in other embodiments of the pattern, it will also result in a miraculous intervention of Eru, similar to the preservation of Aulë's Dwarves, but arguably of even greater ontological significance.

So far, I have focused my attention only on Gandalf's decision to face the Balrog, 'lowering' himself for the sake of his friends in conforming with "the Rules"; accepting death; giving up hope; and handing over his sub-creative authority in an extreme way. These very interconnected things are all related to the upholding of Eru's Authority, as we have seen. But I still need to discuss what is perhaps the most mysterious aspect of all; that is, the actual outcome of Gandalf's decision. What happens after his fall, underground chase with the Balrog, and final victory on the peak of the mountains of Moria? Which roads did Gandalf wander far on, after 'darkness took him', before he "was sent back"? What does it mean that the Authority took up and enlarged the plan?

V.1.8 Eru's Intrusion and the Death of Gandalf

The most important textual hint that helps solve the riddle that has been posed is Gandalf's allusive statement that he "strayed out of […] time" (cf. V.1.1).[46] This is, for Gandalf, a very peculiar thing to say. As we have seen, according to Tolkien's mytho-theology, most creatures of Arda cannot 'go out of time'; this includes both the Valar, who are "in Time, so long as it endures" and cannot perceive anything outside Time (cf. *NME* 2.9:207), as well as the Elves, who "do not escape from time" (*Letters* 181:342[236]). The impossibility of escaping time is closely related to the spiritual nature of both Valar and Elves, who can remain in the world even 'discarnate', as discussed earlier. The Maiar share the same ontological status as the Valar, as members of the same order, but they are lower in ranking; although they are "capable of self-incarnation", the Maiar primarily remain 'spirits', whose outward form is "especially Elvish" (*UT* 4.2:378).

The principally spiritual nature of the Maiar is also shown by the fact that their spirit survives the occasional destruction of its body. Thus, they can even reincarnate themselves, as in the case of Sauron; after his first two defeats in the Second Age, his spirit was vanquished but gradually took shape again after many years.[47] Like the 'seeming death' of the Elves, the 'vanquishing' of an incarnate Maia cannot be

---

[46] I have preferred not to analyse the second formula ("out of thought"), as its exegesis would necessitate another lengthy and complex discussion. I am grateful to Michaël Devaux for sharing his view with me, suggesting that the "thought" referred to is not solely that of Gandalf (who indeed loses consciousness and memory), but also that of Eru, since the Valar (and Maiar) are the "offspring of [Eru's] thought" (cf. *Sil. Ain.*:15). This may suggest that after his death, Gandalf is approaching Eru as closely as possible, in a sort of pre-creational dimension.

[47] Cf. *LotR* 1.2:52 (Sauron's spirit taking shape again in Mirkwood after remaining hidden for long years).

considered, therefore, a death in its full sense. And indeed, when Gandalf foresees Sauron's future after the destruction of the Ring, he does not talk about his 'death' but rather of his becoming "a spirit of malice gnawing itself in the shadows", which "cannot again grow or take shape" (*LotR* 5.9:879). The description of Sauron's eventual demise fits in with this ontological framework, with its focus on a "huge shape of shadow", which was blown away by a great wind and eventually "passed" (*LotR* 6.4:949).

Like Sauron, the Istari – such as Gandalf and Saruman – are incarnate Maiar and are also primarily spiritual beings who do not die in the full sense. Indeed, as Tolkien explains in *Unfinished Tales*, the Istari "did not die, and aged only by the cares and labours of many long years" (*UT* 4.2:372). It is thus not surprising that Tolkien describes Saruman's 'death' in very similar terms to that of Sauron: as "a grey mist" rising "to a great height", but soon dissolved by a Cold Wind from the West.[48] This appears to suggest that Saruman's spirit was doomed to the same destiny of discarnate impotence, far from Middle-earth, but still within the physical boundaries of Arda.

For all these reasons, 'death' does not seem to be an appropriate word to describe the fate of a spiritual being such as Gandalf. Tolkien himself seems to confirm this view in some of his letters by occasionally putting the word 'death' (and its derivatives) in inverted commas when referring to Gandalf's fate on the top of the mountain.[49]

---

[48] *LotR* 6.8:1020; cf. also *UT* 4.2:391 "[Saruman's] spirit went whithersoever it was doomed to go, and to Middle-earth, whether naked or embodied, came never back."

[49] *Letters* 156:298,300[201,203] "Gandalf really 'died', and was changed: [...] 'I am G. the White, who has returned from death'. [...] if it is

Within this framework, Gandalf's destruction on the top of the Moria mountains should not be different from that of Sauron or Saruman; it should consist in a mere disembodiment of a spiritual entity, and his return should be a reincarnation rather than a resurrection.

And yet in the very same letter, Tolkien cannot help but observe how the text he had written and published, perhaps without fully understanding it, was pointing in a different direction ("by whom, and whence?", *Letters* 156:299[203], see V.1.1). Tolkien implies that, by going 'out of time', Gandalf's spirit leaves the "embodied world and time" of Arda and goes somewhere beyond it and to Someone other than the Valar, who are in fact only concerned with the world's time. One can infer, then, that Gandalf's spirit is going directly to Eru, "beyond the circles of the world", and this is nothing other than to say that Gandalf *dies*. Therefore, on the top of Moria, Gandalf is not just undergoing the same kind of spiritual disembodiment as an Elf or a Maia; rather, he is dying a human death in the full sense. Tolkien describes human death as "going beyond time", 'passing out of Eä', as well as 'a direct return to Eru' or even a 'surrender to Eru';[50] this is essentially what befalls Gandalf on Moria.

'cheating' to treat 'death' as making no difference, embodiment must not be ignored"; also ibid. 298[202] (on the incarnate status of the Istari, which make them capable even of being 'killed').

[50] Cf. *MR Athr.*:340 "the fëar of dead Men also went to Mandos [...]. There they waited until they were **surrendered to Eru**"; *NME* 2.17:273 "The wisest of Men [...] believe that they are **surrendered to Eru** and pass out of Eä"; *MR*:429 "[the] nature and doom [of the human soul] under the will of Eru that it should not endure Arda for long, but should depart and go elsewhither, **returning maybe direct to Eru** for another fate or purpose".

Connecting all the dots, we can conclude that the outcome of Gandalf's sacrifice in Moria is a human death in its full sense. Different as it is from that of Sauron (and of Saruman), Gandalf's death is a quite exceptional, 'miraculous', event. Since Gandalf is, by nature, a higher spiritual being, his miraculous death must necessarily involve a transformation of his ontological status from that of a Maia (a spiritual being, bound to the time of Arda) to that of a man (fully incarnate, and able to escape Time and return to Eru) – or, perhaps more precisely, he becomes an 'angel' fully incarnated into a human body. We find a revealing, concise description of all this in a scrap of paper preserved in a signed copy of *The Lord of the Rings* together with a brief letter of Tolkien to Antony D. Wood (*TCG* 22/2/1958). The note reads:

Gandalf really did die, it was sacrificial. He is rather like an angel. It is very important that he should not dominate people's wills. That is why he was an old man.

This note was probably written by the author David Smith, and apparently records Tolkien's answers during a conversation he had with Wood and Smith at Merton College. Although tantalisingly uncertain in content and origin, this note seems to confirm that my reconstruction accurately captures Tolkien's thoughts on the matter.

Therefore, the first and perhaps most important 'miracle' does not really concern Gandalf's return (any Maia on their own has, in principle, the power to reincarnate themselves); rather, the miracle consists in his death in its full sense, which involves a level of 'incarnation' unparalleled before in the previous history of Arda, as well as an escalation in the process of the lowering assimilation of a Maia. This first miracle, Gandalf's human death, also clarifies and enhances the second one – his unexpected return. In light of his death, his return should not be considered a 'reincarnation' but rather a 'resurrection' in its full sense, involving some further ontological enhancement.[51]

There are precedents in Tolkien's mythology for this sort of ontological transformation. A very close and intriguing parallel is reported in a posthumous text written by Tolkien in his final years (*PME* 13:379–82). The text concerns the elf-lord Glorfindel who, during the destruction of the city of Gondolin, faced a Balrog alone and sacrificed himself to allow the escape of a few survivors, and was thereby rewarded with an enhancement of his spiritual power and ontological status, which became close to that of a Maia.[52] Other important parallels for Gandalf's change of ontology specifically involve mortality and immortality, the most radical breaking of Eru's Rules: these include, in particular, the brief return from the dead of the man Beren,[53] the 'mortalisation' of his spouse Lúthien, and her eventual death out of love for him, which Tolkien describes as one of the exceptions

---

[51] The "enhanced power" that Tolkien refers to in his letters. Nothing certain, however, can be further said on what this means exactly, and I will not speculate further, at least in this book.

[52] Cf. *PME* 13:381 (on Glorfindel's spiritual power having been "greatly enhanced by his self-sacrifice" and himself having become almost an equal to a Maia). On Glorfindel's character and his sacrifice see the perceptive study by Vink 2020a.

[53] Cf. *NME* 1.19:156 "by special permission of Eru". Cf. ibid. 1.11:78 on the ontological status of Eärendil's descendants – a special grace obtained "from Eru via Manwë".

owing to the "freedom of Eru".[54] Another interesting similarity between the case of Beren and Gandalf is the fact that their return from death to Middle-earth is only temporary ("for a short time" (*MR Athr.*:341); "for a brief time" (*LotR* 3.5:502)); this may further suggest that Gandalf's final destiny may well be another human death, beyond the circles of the world, just as in the case of Beren – another 'irregular' event according to Tolkien's secondary ontology.

What is crucial is that, in all these exceptional 'breakings of the Rules', one can clearly trace the intrusion of Eru into Middle-earth, more or less explicitly.[55] As already discussed in Chapter III (III.2.2), and as Tolkien often explained, the freedom to break his own Rules is an important prerogative of Eru and a sign of His meta-literary ability to intrude directly into the "Tale of Arda". This especially includes the alteration of the "fundamental kind" of His creatures, "the biological and spiritual nature of the Children of God", namely the immortality of Elves and the mortality of Men:

[The Valar] called upon the One in the crisis of the rebellion of Númenor [...] which necessitated a catastrophic change in the shape of Earth. Immortality and Mortality being the special gifts of God [...] it must be assumed that no alteration of their

---

[54] *MR Athr.* pp. 340–1 "No fëa of a dead Man ever returned to life in Middle-earth. To all such statements and decrees there are always some exceptions (because of the '**freedom of Eru**'). [...] Beren returned to actual life, for a short time"; cf. also *Sil* 19:187 (on Manwë's decision to allow Lúthien to choose to die together with Beren, after their brief return to Middle-earth – a decision taken after seeking counsel in his inmost thought, "where the will of Ilúvatar was revealed").

[55] On the concept of 'intrusion' see III.2.2.

fundamental kind could be effected by the Valar even in one case: the cases of Lúthien (and Túor) and the position of their descendants was a direct act of God. (*Letters* 153:289[194])[56]

That Gandalf's human death should be construed as one of Eru's exceptional intrusions into his Tale is also confirmed by comparison with another important episode in Tolkien's mythology, which is mentioned in the passage just quoted and with which Gandalf's death has also a strong analogy. I am referring to the Valar's decision to "call upon" the One when the rebellious Númenóreans invade their land of Valinor. At that moment: "the Valar laid down their government of Arda. But Ilúvatar showed forth his power, and he changed the fashion of the world" (*Sil Ak.*:278). This decision of the Valar to 'lay down' their sub-creative authority to Eru resulted in the "great Catastrophe" of the Second Age, as Tolkien calls it in a posthumous text:

at the end of the Second Age came the great Catastrophe (by an intervention of Eru that **foreshadowed**, as it were, the End of Arda): the annihilation of Númenor, and the 'removal' of Aman from the physical world. (*MR Athr.*:341)

The expression used by Tolkien to describe the sub-creative submission of the Valar closely recalls the one used to describe Gandalf's "handing over to the Authority that ordained the Rules" (see V.1.1). What is also interesting to note in this passage is that this

---

[56] Cf. also *Letters* 156:301[204] "'mortality' [of Men] [...] and 'immortality' [of Elves] [...] could not be altered [...] except perhaps by one of those strange exceptions to all rules and ordinances which seem to crop up in the history of the Universe, and show the Finger of God, as the one wholly free Will and Agent".

intervention of Eru has some sort of prophetic power, as it 'foreshadows' some future event in the history of Arda ("the End of Arda").[57]

This leads me to the final and most interesting implication to consider in Gandalf's death and return.

V.2 The Arising of Prophecy

With regard to Gandalf's fall in Moria, we can sum up now what we have discussed so far: Gandalf is a higher spiritual being who has taken up a human body and assimilated himself to lower mortal beings out of love; he eventually sacrifices himself for their sake; he mysteriously suffers a human death and is eventually sent back by God to Earth, for a brief time, with enhanced power. If this all rings a bell and reminds you of the death and resurrection of Jesus Christ, you are not alone; plenty of scholars and readers have identified this parallel, including Tolkien himself, who suggested that in Gandalf's death and return one could be "reminded of the Gospels" (*Letters* 181:343[237]). It would take another book to explore and discuss all the possible implications of Gandalf's Paschal similitude, from the white robes worn by Gandalf after his resurrection to his later dealings with Aragorn and friends, but this is not my primary focus.[58]

What I am concerned about here is how Tolkien himself frames the undeniable resemblance between these two events; it is a parallel most readers would probably

---

[57] Cf. also *NME* 3.15:344 "a foretaste of the End of Arda".

[58] On Christ's acceptance of death as an epitome of his humility cf. Philippians 2 "humbler yet, even to accepting death".

recognise, but which becomes even more striking once the nature of Gandalf's sacrifice and the ontological implications of his death and resurrection are understood more fully. And yet, although ready to admit the parallel, Tolkien was also keen to stress that the two events were radically different:

Gandalf faced and suffered death; and came back or was sent back, as he says, with enhanced power. But though one may be in this reminded of the Gospels, it is not really the same thing at all. The Incarnation of God is an infinitely greater thing than anything I would dare to write. (*Letters* 181:343[237])

The category that Tolkien would probably have used to explain this apparent paradox of similitude within difference is that of 'prophecy'; this is suggested by a passage found in an unpublished section of what is now *Letters* 226, written on 31 December 1960 to L. W. Forster, Professor of German at University College London, and later at the University of Cambridge.

At Forster's request, Tolkien provided feedback on a draft of an encyclopaedic lemma dedicated to him (eventually published in Forster 1961), which mentioned his 'Fabulierlust' ('love for storytelling') and also discussed religious elements (and the lack of them) in *The Lord of the Rings*.[59] In his response, Tolkien made

[59] In the original draft Forster noted that "Although Tolkien is a Catholic, his mythical world lacks specific Christian features (e.g. the Trinity, the Blessed Virgin, the Fall of Man, redemption by a Saviour) and there is hardly any mention of a God or divine service, but in the background an inscrutable unfathomable providence is palpable and the intense preoccupation with good and evil rather than right and wrong betrays a theological significance" (my translation). The final version (Forster 1961), after Tolkien's comments, instead only read:

an explicit connection between the death of Gandalf (Olórin's "voluntary sacrifice and death") and Christ's Incarnation, but at the same time stressed that he was not making use of this "specifically Christian myth" in his "very minor work". In Tolkien's view the two events could not be equated (as per an allegorical framework), not least because the events of *The Lord of the Rings* were supposed to be historical events taking place thousands of years *before* the birth of Christ. For Tolkien, Gandalf and Christ's deaths and resurrections are thus historically separate events that are, nonetheless, somehow related. The literary concept used by Tolkien in his letter to Forster to frame their relation is that of 'prophecy'. Indeed, as Tolkien writes, in sub-creative works, Christian matters can "only arise in the form of prophecy".[60] Tolkien thereby implies that he considered Gandalf's death and resurrection to be prophetic of the incarnation and resurrection of Christ – one miraculous event foreshadowing another similar yet more

"Although Tolkien is a Catholic, his mythical world lacks specific Christian traits; however, an inscrutable providence can be felt in the background" (my translation). I am very much indebted to Oronzo Cilli for pointing me to this correspondence and for sharing with me a reproduction.

[60] It is also worth quoting in this respect a letter to C. S. Kilby (excerpted in Kilby 1976:55–6), in which Tolkien commented on an essay appropriately titled "Kingship, Priesthood and Prophecy in *The Lord of the Rings*", which claimed, among other things, that Gandalf was "the major prophet figure" and that "[at] every point, the human dynamics of *The Lord of the Rings* are drawn from the tradition ascribed to Christ's redemptive activity". In reading the essay Tolkien acknowledged that much of that interpretation was "true enough", except, of course, "the general impression given [...] that I had any such 'schema' in my conscious mind before the writing".

miraculous event, which would take place thousands of years in the future.[61]

Indeed, Gandalf's story is not the only 'prophecy' of the Paschal mystery within the secondary world of Arda. The Valar's original 'embodiment' into Arda and their gradual 'lowering' to the level of humbler creatures could also be construed as prophetic; as could the incarnation of the Maiar. This chain of analogous and yet distinct events moves according to a linear progression of even greater assimilation to lower beings (which Tolkien himself suggests). But this is not all. As Tolkien explains in the powerful epilogue of *On Fairy-Stories*, every successful Story and indeed every successful narrative micro-episode, cannot help but be connected indirectly to the Gospel story and, more specifically, to the Incarnation and Resurrection of Christ. This is because such stories are a "sudden glimpse" or a "far-off gleam or echo of it", a secondary 'eucatastrophe' that "looks forward (or backward: the direction in this regard is unimportant) to the Great Eucatastrophe" (*TOFS*:78=*TL*:73), namely the Resurrection of Christ.[62]

Therefore, according to Tolkien, the joy of any narratively successful human story is prophetic of the Great

---

[61] One could also introduce here the concept of 'typology', a notion developed in ancient Christian exegesis, which frames characters or events in the Old Testament as 'types' or figurations (*figurae*), foreshadowing and anticipating Christ and His story in an imperfect manner (see esp. Daniélou 2018[1950]). Despite its (partial) appropriateness, I have not used this terminology because apparently Tolkien never employed it. For typology and figuration in literary criticism, see especially the influential essay *Figura* by Auerbach 2016[1938]; for a study of typology in Tolkien see Honegger 2023: 120–6 with bibliography.

[62] On Tolkien's conception of eucatastrophe see III.3.4, IV.3.4, VI.2.5.

Story to which all human stories point. As a matter of prophetic aspiration, a human story becomes similar to the Divine story, and yet remains different from it: as imperfect and 'secondary' as any human event, a human story remains valuable as a unique event within the History of the World (real or feigned), which foreshadows the Great Event. This concern for historicity, uniqueness, and 'narrative secondariness' (cf. IV.3.3) also explains why Tolkien was so keen to stress the radical difference between the two deaths and resurrections (Gandalf is not God, but a mere 'angel');[63] this is why prophecy is the only category Tolkien could accept as a way to frame the relationship between his secondary world and the primary Christian event.

Later in his life, Tolkien introduced within his secondary mythology a very clear reference to the Gospel Story, apparently breaking the divide between primary and secondary worlds in an open way. However, this apparent break is achieved through the means of a prophecy of the Incarnation of God into Arda – the final intrusion of Eru into his narrative foreshadowed by all His previous intrusions, analogous and yet imperfect, including the death and resurrection of Gandalf. It is no coincidence that this explicit prophecy ("the Old Hope") is found in the already mentioned posthumous *Athrabeth* just after Finrod's discussion of the meaning and importance of Estel:

'What then was this hope, if you know?' Finrod asked. 'They say,' answered Andreth: 'they say that the One will himself

---

[63] In a letter Tolkien makes an analogous distinction between the resurrection of Christ and the raising of Lazarus (*Letters* 212, n.†:408[286]).

enter into Arda, and heal Men and all the Marring from the beginning to the end'. (*MR Athr.*:321)

As noted by Christopher Tolkien in his perceptive commentary on this passage (p.356, quote follows), here his father seems to challenge his own restrictions on the use of Christian elements within his mythology. And yet, as Christopher also points out with great honesty and critical lucidity, Tolkien's integration of the prophecy of the "old hope" is just a natural extension of the 'theology' of Arda – but, crucially, "represented as vision, hope, or prophecy".

Was he referring then to the astonishing conception in the Athrabeth of 'the Great Hope of Men', as it is called in the draft A (p.352), 'the Old Hope' as it is called in the final text (p.321), that Eru himself will enter into Arda to oppose the evil of Melkor? In the Commentary (p.335) this was further defined: 'Finrod … probably proceeded to the expectation that "the coming of Eru", if it took place, would be specially and primarily concerned with Men: that is to an imaginative guess or vision that Eru would come incarnated in human form' — though my father noted that 'This does not appear in the Athrabeth'. But this surely is not parody, nor even parallel, but the extension — **if only represented as vision, hope, or prophecy** — of the 'theology' of Arda into specifically, and of course centrally, Christian belief; and a manifest challenge to my father's view in his letter of 1951 on the necessary limitations of the expression of 'moral and religious truth (or error)' in a 'Secondary World'. (*MR Athr.*:356)

This is to say that the prophecy of Andreth is only making explicit something that is already implicit within the mytho-theology of Arda, from the *Ainulindalë* down to *The Lord of the Rings*. Eru fixes the scars and dissonances of the sub-creators, from Melkor's rebellion to Sauron's wars, by 'intruding' into their artistic work (which is their work, but also, and above all, His own Tale). He does so according to a sequence of different 'intrusions' of greater ontological value, all unique and yet all sharing the same 'eucatastrophic' narrative motive, featuring hope beyond hope, the sprouting of unexpected new life, the assimilation with and enhancement of lower creatures – that is, the "secret life in creation", as Tolkien calls it (*Letters* 131, quoted in III.2.2). For this reason, all these secondary 'intrusions' ultimately foreshadow the definitive, and most extreme intrusion of all: Eru's own Incarnation and eucatastrophic Resurrection.

This is a crucial implication that should be stressed: the prophetic value of secondary eucatastrophic events, such as Gandalf's death and resurrection, is not the intentional product of the sub-creator's craft (Gandalf or Tolkien); rather, they are 'collaborative miracles' – miraculous intrusions of Eru into the sub-creator's work (the Valar's world, Gandalf's plan). And yet this is only possible because of the sub-creator's free submission to Eru's authority and 'Rules', as seen in the Valar's handing over of authority to respect the freedom of the Númenóreans, and Gandalf's hopeless sacrifice for the sake of lower creatures. This explains why, in the passage quoted from his letter to Prof. Forster, Tolkien uses the verb "arise" to describe the emergence of prophecy within the secondary world; this is a verb favoured by Tolkien and which is also used in another illuminating passage from a draft letter to Peter Hastings:

the things I have scribbled about [i.e. the deep philosophical-theological meaning of his stories including God's tolerance of evil], **arise** in some form or another from all writing (or art) that is not careful to dwell within the walls of 'observed fact'. (*Letters* 153:291[195])

The 'similitude' of Tolkien's Tale with Christian doctrine (i.e. by extension its prophetic value) is not just the product of mere craft, but rather cannot but 'arise' when a sub-creator does not dwell within the walls of observed fact (cf. IV.3.4); this occurs, as can be glossed with a passage from *On Fairy-Stories*,[64] when human Imagination is allowed to break free from the domination of partial and reductive conceptions of the world, especially the sub-creator's own. To allow the 'arising of prophecy' and the related enhancement (and enchantment) of their work, the sub-creator needs to 'die' first; they must submit to God's higher authoriality, just as Gandalf needs to accept his hopeless death first on the bridge of Moria so that Eru can "[take] up this plan and [enlarge] it, at the moment of its failure" (cf. V.1.1).

What does it mean exactly for a 'primary' author such as Tolkien to submit to God's Authority and His Rules? Is there a 'death of an author' in the primary sense? Can there be a 'resurrection' of the author and what would this entail? How could God 'intrude' into the artworks and plans of a human author such as Tolkien? And in what sense can these be 'taken up' and 'enhanced'?

[64] *TOFS*:60=*TL*:47 "I propose [...] to use Fantasy [...] in a sense [...] which combines with its older and higher use as an equivalent of Imagination the derived notions of 'unreality' (that is, of unlikeness to the Primary World, of **freedom from the domination of observed 'fact.'**"

Fragments of an answer to these questions are already scattered in the 'secondary' analysis I have given so far in this and the previous chapters. But I think it is now time to move firmly to the primary world, to Tolkien's primary literary 'theory'. I will address these questions directly in Chapter VI, trying to give a comprehensive answer, in what will be the final, and perhaps most difficult, leg of my journey.

VI

The Next Stage

The Death of the Author and the Effoliation of Creation

⁓

In this chapter, I will discuss Tolkien's literary theory in primary terms, building on the secondary analysis conducted in Chapter V, in which I considered the meta-literary significance of Gandalf's fall and return. In doing so, I will incorporate all of the topics discussed in the previous chapters – artistic 'gratuitousness' (Chapter I), authorial detachment (Chapter II), literary cloaking (Chapter III), and narrative parallelism (Chapter IV) – in order to bring them together into a single comprehensive framework.

The aim of this chapter is to present, then, a primary overview of Tolkien's 'self-reflections' on the nature of sub-creation. In other words, I hope to formulate, to reveal at last, what Tolkien may mean by the "mystery of literary creation".[1] This overview will be systematic and yet, necessarily, partial and imperfect. The word "mystery" contains *in nuce* everything that I am going to say in

---

[1] For an introduction to the notion of sub-creation see esp. Phelpstead 2022 with bibliography; also Flieger 2012, part 1; Hynes 2016 (on precedents and parallels); Fimi and Honegger 2019, esp. the chapters by Izzo, Nagy, and Vink; for a discussion of the notion from a theological and/or philosophical perspective see in particular Hart 2007; Testi 2016; Coutras 2016; McIntosh 2017; Halsall 2020.

this chapter and that I have already introduced in the previous ones. For Tolkien, literature – its origin, processes, and purpose – cannot be reduced to something that can be fully described in analytical terms, as if it were merely the product of a human mind. Instead, literature is a "mystery", which involves the participation of another mysterious Entity, who inspires the sub-creator in the first place (Chapter I); continues 'editing', 'correcting', and 'enhancing' their work, generating characters and stories that do not derive from the author's intention (Chapter II); assists the author's efforts in a discrete manner (Chapter III); connects and enriches the story's secondary, human elements with primary, divine significance (Chapter IV); and, ultimately, invites the human author to acknowledge and submit to His ultimate authorial authority (Chapter V). Arguably, the participation of 'God' in this mystery also explains why literary creations and human stories share many analogies with primary Creation and primary History (since they are both (co)authored by the same Writer). Such analogies between primary and secondary creations include their beauty and 'gratuitousness'; their inherent 'otherness'; their propaedeutic potential, 'introductory' to higher planes and truths; and other common themes and features (including, above all, the idea of authorial submission). It would take another book to discuss the many parallels and possible sources of this 'mystic' conception of artistic creation, from classical literature and medieval mysticism to romantic and modernist literature. This is not, however, the aim of this chapter (nor of the book in general); rather, in this chapter, I will put together all the tesserae that I have collected during my journey and try to offer a unified vision of the mosaic of

Tolkien's literary 'theory' – while remaining aware of its ultimate incompleteness and artificiality (Tolkien was a self-reflective artist, not a systematic theoretician).

As always, my approach will be exegetical and inductive, rather than theoretical and deductive. Following Tolkien's footsteps, I will present the results of a critical "observation" on the primary significance of the secondary event discussed in Chapter V (Gandalf's death and resurrection); this episode, as we will see, truly epitomises the dramatic relationship between Creator and sub-creator within "the mystery of literary creation". To accept and acknowledge this mysterious relationship is the core drama for the human sub-creator, as such recognition requires a form of authorial self-denial – a 'death'.

VI.1 The Death of the Sub-creator

The starting point of my discussion returns to Gandalf's fall in Moria, which I will now analyse from a 'primary' point of view, as meta-literary evidence for the reconstruction of Tolkien's views (or self-perceptions) on sub-creation. I will begin by discussing possible 'primary' meanings of the first part of his story (the 'fall'), focusing on Gandalf's acceptance of death. As seen in Chapter V, this is the apex and epitome of a general attitude required from the sub-creator towards their own artwork, which must be approached as something that they do not possess. Possession is the great temptation of the sub-creator, as Tolkien explains in a key passage from his letter to Milton Waldman:

This [sub-creative] desire [...] may become possessive, clinging to the things made as 'its own', the sub-creator wishes to be the Lord and God of his private creation. He will rebel against the laws of the Creator – especially against mortality. Both of these (alone or together) will lead to the desire for Power, for making the will more quickly effective, – and so to the Machine (or Magic). By the last I intend all use of external plans or devices (apparatus) instead of development of the inherent inner powers or talents. (*Letters* 131:205[145])

To accept or rebel "against mortality" is thus a choice closely related to the sub-creator's acceptance of not being "the God of his private creation", of resisting "possessiveness" and the related temptation of power,[2] and thus of acknowledging the mysterious origin and nature of their own sub-creations. One could argue that disowning the evidence that one's own literary work is a "mystery" is itself an act of rebellion and a paradoxical result of sub-creative desire – a noble and yet naturally corruptible instinct. But what does all this mean, in primary terms, for the literary sub-creator?

VI.1.1 Abiding by the Rules and Developing Inner Powers: Writing as Gardening

In the first place, and as the passage just quoted already suggests, sub-creative 'unpossessiveness' has to do with the decision to abide by some 'laws' or 'rules', which, to decode the meta-literary metaphor, are also narrative, poetic, and

[2] Cf. *Letters* 131:208 and 215[148, 154] (on the "possessive attitude" of Fëanor and the Númenóreans) with n.*; ibid. 205[146] "[the Elves'] Fall is into possessiveness and (to a less degree) into perversion of their art to power". See I.2.1.3.

artistic. A passage from his essay *A Secret Vice* confirms that, for Tolkien, the "courage" to abide by artistic rules is the same as "resisting the temptation of the supreme despot", who alters the rules using some sort of "technical object". True poetry, in contrast, is only possible for people who have the courage to resist this temptation.[3] In this passage, Tolkien is referring to the construction of a fictional language specifically, but one can assume that his words could be extended to any aspect of the creative endeavour, including 'narrative rules'.[4] Strikingly, the return of Gandalf in *The Lord of the Rings*, as well as his cryptic account of his death, are explicitly related by Tolkien to the "compulsions of narrative technique", which apparently went against his own preferences.[5]

As Tolkien also explains in the passage from *Letters* 131 quoted earlier, resisting the temptation of possessiveness also consists of avoiding the "use of external plans or devices" "instead of development of the inherent inner powers or talents" (*Letters* 131:205[145]). The fostering and development of "inherent powers" is indeed the opposite of sub-creative domination. There is one metaphor

---

[3] *SV*:33=*MC*:218–19 "if you construct your art-language on chosen principles, and in so far as you fix it, and courageously abide by your own rules, **resisting the temptation of the supreme despot** to alter them for the assistance of this or that **technical object** on any given occasion, so far you may write poetry of a sort".

[4] Tolkien makes a similar point, describing metrical rules as a stimulus for poetic imagination, in a series of letters to future writer Paula Coston, which were published by the addressee in the August 2014 issue of the American magazine *Writing Magazine* (pp.12–14). On the whole issue cf. Fimi 2018.

[5] *Letters* 156:297[201] "I think the way in which Gandalf's return is presented is a defect [...] partly due to the ever-present **compulsions of narrative technique**."

often used by Tolkien, also underlying this passage, that epitomises this correct attitude of sub-creative fostering. This is the metaphor of gardening, which Tolkien uses often in his letters to refer to a range of different, but analogous, kinds of "husbandry". These include the relationship of ecclesiastic authorities ("the keepers of the Tree") with their Church, which Tolkien describes as "a living organism (likened to a plant), which develops and changes in externals" and which must be looked after "with trepidation, knowing how little their knowledge of growth is!".[6] Individual humans should have the same attitude when dealing both with their neighbours (whose development must not be interfered with) and with their "own inner talents" and their "innate vitality and heredity", which must be developed "without waste or misuse", because "a man is both a seed and in some degree also a gardener".[7]

Similarly, the sub-creative task of the Valar in Tolkien's mythology is often described in garden-related terms, with the same emphasis on the need for active – but not "meddling" – fostering, as well as for a humility founded on the awareness of not knowing everything about the creatures that have been entrusted to their care. The Valar are not supposed to "meddle with the Children" (*NME* 1.12:89; 2.15:248) but only "guard them so that they can develop as they should" (*NME* 1.6:39).[8] In Tolkien's

---

[6] *Letters* 306, to M. Tolkien, 1967/8:533[394].

[7] *Letters* 183:346[240] (on "man" compared to a seed with its capacity to grow and develop, as well as to a gardener, "for good or ill"); also *Letters* 310:561[399] (quoted in n.9). Cf. also *NME* 2.15:251 on 'growing in Time' as the distinctive mark of the living.

[8] Cf. also *NME* 2.12:232–3, connecting the Valar's 'gardening' task to the 'mystery of free will': "The Valar were themselves 'on trial' – an aspect of the mystery of 'free will' in created intelligences. They had

vision, sub-creators are called to approach their creations in the same way that gardeners would look after the plants growing in their gardens; they grow and develop each plant, with its own inner patterns and powers. The gardening metaphor also clarifies why sub-creators cannot just be passive observers, but rather are called to protect and foster the development of creatures entrusted to them; this is what Gandalf does in *The Lord of the Rings*, eventually sacrificing himself for love of them, which, as Tolkien suggests in a letter, is the highest form and culmination of the 'gardening'.[9]

That Tolkien conceived his own process of writing as another form of gardening is suggested by the use of the same language of growth and development.[10] This is especially evident in his consistent reference to the 'botanic' metaphor that he uses to describe *The Lord of the Rings*, his own "internal Tree" that "was growing out of hand" (*Letters* 241:454[321]);[11] this metaphor also captures his

---

a sufficient knowledge of the will of Eru and his 'design' to undertake **the responsibility of guiding its development**".

[9] Cf. *Letters* 310, to C. Unwin, 20/05/1969:561[399] "morals should be a guide to our human purposes [...] (a) the ways in which our individual **talents can be developed** without waste or misuse; and (b) **without** injuring our kindred or **interfering with their development** (Beyond this and **higher lies self-sacrifice for love**)."

[10] E.g. *Letters* 70, to Christopher Tolkien, 21/05/1944:117[81] "Gollum **continues to develop** into a most intriguing character", and cf. II.2.2.2 with n.113.

[11] See II.2.2.2, with n.113. Cf. also a passage quoted by Carpenter (1977:171) in which Tolkien uses an extended botanic metaphor to describe the writing of *The Lord of the Rings*, which grew "like a seed [...] out of the leaf-mould of the mind [...]. No doubt there is much selection, as with a gardener: what one throws on one's personal compost-heap; and my mould is evidently made largely of linguistic matter."

perception of his stories and characters as being something inherently 'other'. Indeed, the gardening metaphor is particularly useful for highlighting the ultimate 'otherness' of artistic creation and especially of the "life" contained in it. This introduces a second aspect of sub-creative humility in a primary sense.

VI.1.2 The 'Other' and Unforeseen Life of Literature

Recalling my previous discussion (V.1.3), one should stress that Gandalf's sacrifice for his companions is closely related to and springs from the Valar's commitment to nurturing and fostering the life of other 'lower' creatures, inhabiting the very world that the Valar sub-created. The adjective 'other' is crucial. The original sub-creative humility that blossoms in Gandalf's acceptance of death resides in the paradoxical acknowledgement that the ultimate source of one's creative endeavours is external to the sub-creator himself – it is 'other' than him. It is the paradox of the Silmarils, created by Fëanor, and yet independent "living things", which derive their 'life' and 'beauty' from the light of Aman embedded within them.[12] This paradoxical yet original 'otherness' of sub-created entities is especially true in the case of other living beings insofar as they are the 'characters' enacting the drama of the sub-creators.

---

[12] Cf. *Sil* 7:67 "crystal was to the Silmarils but as is the body to the Children of Ilúvatar: the house of its inner fire, that is within it and yet in all parts of it, and is its life. And the inner fire of the Silmarils Fëanor made of the blended light of the Trees of Valinor [...] as were they indeed **living things**."

In Tolkien's literary vision, as we have seen in Chapter II,[13] there is always some 'life' within sub-creation that does not derive from the sub-creators themselves, but, rather, from a higher Creative Authority. For the Valar, the *Ur-Artists*, this 'other life' consists in the Elves and Men, the Children of Ilúvatar, who, because they do not proceed from the creative mind of the Valar, fill them with wonder ("as though they were beings sudden and marvellous and unforeseen" *Sil* 3:49). For the co-authors of the Tale of Arda, Elves and Men are thus similar to characters within a play that they have written; yet these characters remain independent from the Valar, who do not know everything about them because they remain ultimately free.

More broadly, however, the whole life and reality of the sub-creation, however foreseen or "forethought" by the Valar, remains for them a great source of wonder. As told in *The Silmarillion*, apropos of the first encounter of the Vala Oromë with the Elves: "[f]rom without the World, though all things may be forethought in music or foreshown in vision from afar, to those who enter verily into Eä each in its time shall be met at unawares as something new and unforetold" (*Sil* 3:49).

Similarly, in a beautiful passage now printed in *NME* (3.3:292), Tolkien explains that the Valar experience their making "as a new thing", "just like the makers or artists among the Incarnate".

This attitude of detachment towards one's own creation is not just required from the sub-creators; instead, it reflects the attitude of the Creator Himself – the perfect

---

[13] Cf. esp. II.2.2.3.

Author – Whom all sub-authors are called to imitate. Indeed, Eru Himself is like an "author of a tale": he has "certain general designs" about plot and characters, and yet he does not know everything about the 'actors' within it. These characters 'come alive' in "the process of the tale" and are free to modify it in ways unforeseen. Tolkien elaborates on all this in a meta-literary passage from the posthumous text *Fate and Free Will*, already referred to in Chapter V (V.1.7):

> the ultimate problem of Free Will in its relation to the Foreknowledge of a Designer [...], **Eru, "the Author of the Great Tale"**, was of course not resolved by the Eldar. it is the continual clash of *umbar*, the 'chances' of *ambar*[14] as a fixed arrangement which continues to work out inevitably (except only for "miracle": a direct or mediate intervention of Eru, from outside *umbar* and *ambar*), and purposeful will **that [?ramifies] a story or tale (as an excerpt from the total drama of which Eru is the Author or as that Drama itself)**. [...] though this likeness is only a "likeness", not an equation, the nearest experience of the Incarnates to this problem is to be found **in the author of a tale**. The author is not in the tale in one sense, yet it all proceeds from him (and what was in him), so that he is present all the time. Now while composing the tale he may have certain general designs (the plot for instance), and he may have a clear conception of the character (independent of the particular tale) of each feigned actor. But those are **the limits of his 'foreknowledge'**. Many authors have recorded the feeling that one of their actors 'comes alive' as it were,

---

[14] In Tolkien's secondary theology *umbar* ('chance, fate') refers to "the net-work of 'chances' (largely physical) that is, or is not, used by rational persons with 'free will'"; *ambar* ('world') to "the conditions and established (physical) processes of the Earth (as established at its Creation directly or mediately by Eru)"; cf. *NME* 2.11:226–31.

and does things that were not foreseen at all at the outset and may modify in a small or even large way the process of the tale thereafter. All such unforeseen actions or events are, however, taken up to become integral parts of the tale when finally concluded. Now when that has been done, then the author's 'foreknowledge' is complete, and nothing can happen, be said, or done, that he does not know of and will or allow to be. Even so, some of the Eldarin philosophers ventured to say, it was with Eru. (*NME* 2.11:229–30)

The idea of a 'God' holding back his omniscience for the love of free will (at least in some metaphorical sense) is theologically intriguing, but this is not the place to discuss it further. Here, I will only focus on the meta-literary implications of such restrained omniscience, which are certainly important for Tolkien. We have already noted that, for Tolkien, being aware of having only incomplete 'foreknowledge' of their own artwork (including a book's plot) is a required trait of wisdom on the part of the sub-creator, whether this is a Vala or a Church Authority. The same idea is also present in *The Lord of the Rings* and is indeed at the very core of its plot. As Gandalf and Elrond explain in relationship to two momentous plot elements of *The Lord of the Rings* (the sparing of Gollum and the destruction of the Ring):

Many that live deserve death. And some that die deserve life. Can you give it to them? Then do not be too eager to deal out death in judgement. For even the very wise cannot see all ends. (*LotR* 1.2:59)

Who of all the Wise could have foreseen it? Or, if they are wise, why should they expect to know it, until the hour has struck? (*LotR* 2.2:270)

The biblical contrast between divine foolishness and human wisdom is an important subtext, of course, for understanding the contrast here between sub-creative foreknowledge and ignorance. This dichotomy is also crucial in order to grasp the contrast between Gandalf and Elrond's 'foolish hope' and the 'wisdom' of characters such as Saruman and Denethor, which is itself just another embodiment of the contrast between *Amdir* and *Estel* discussed in Chapter V (it is no coincidence that, in his dirge, Frodo described Gandalf's fall in Moria as the moment when Gandalf's "wisdom died" (*LotR* 1.7:360). What is fascinating, though, is how this biblical contrast is embodied in Tolkien's work within a meta-literary discourse. As the passage from *Fate and Free Will* quoted earlier implies, Tolkien is not talking about 'imperfect foreknowledge' and 'coming alive' only in theoretical terms; rather, he is referring to his own experience as a literary writer, implicitly comparing his relationship with his characters to that of God with his creatures, as well as his own process of creative writing to God's 'primary' creative activity in general.

Just as the Valar wondered at the Children of Ilúvatar, so Tolkien clearly perceived his own literary work and, in particular, his characters as something 'other' than himself, which 'came alive' in the act of writing and filled him with love and wonder.[15] The complex web of meta-textual frames that construct Tolkien's work as an approximate translation or report of something written or retold by

---

[15] Cf. *Letters* 163, n.*:310[211] (the Ents), quoted at II.2.2.3; *Letters* 66:114[79] (quoted in Chapter II n.110). Also *TOFS*:35=*TL*:14 on the existence in fantasy of "real wills and powers, independent of the minds and purposes of men".

other authors (as we have seen in Chapter II, esp. II.2.2) is further evidence of Tolkien's perception of the otherness of his work. In particular, the relationship between Tolkien and *The Hobbit* (and its eponymous characters) is framed in very similar terms to the sub-creative relationship between the Valar and the Elves in *The Silmarillion* or the (related and analogous) relationship between Gandalf and the Hobbits in *The Lord of the Rings*: like the presence of Elves (and Men) in the Valar's work, so too is *The Hobbit* described by Tolkien as an 'intrusion' having "essential life" in it (cf. *Letters* 131) and which eventually modified (and completed) his mythology (cf. II.2.1.4, II.2.2.1). Indeed, just as Gandalf "was meant" to look after Bilbo and the Hobbits,[16] for whom he developed great love (a love analogical to that of the Valar for the Children of Ilúvatar), so too was Tolkien meant to "build on the hobbits" and eventually love them (cf. II.2.2.1).[17]

More generally, there is plenty of direct textual evidence confirming that Tolkien's characters and stories emerged and developed in ways that were unforeseen, as something 'other' than him. This evidence can be found especially in the central volumes of the monumental *History of Middle-Earth*, where Christopher Tolkien collects the early drafts of the individual chapters of *The Lord of the Rings*. I could quote many examples to document this,[18] but here I will focus on two passages only. These

---

[16] Cf. *UT* 3.3:329 (quoted and discussed at III.1.2.5) and *TI* 6:114 "my fate seems much entangled with hobbits".

[17] *Letters* 109:175[121] "I had to have hobbits (whom I love)."

[18] Cf. for instance Tolkien's typical questions and comments preserved in manuscripts of *The Lord of the Rings* querying the development of the narrative (*TI* 1:6 "Who is Trotter?"; 11:210 "How does Gandalf

passages are, in fact, written by Christopher and not his father, and they consist in two editorial notes that sum up two 'prime marks' of his father's writing – which closely recall Tolkien's secondary description of (sub-)creation, as already discussed:

> it is deeply characteristic that these scenes [i.e. of the Black Riders] **emerged at once** in the clear and memorable form that was never changed, but that their **bearing and significance would afterwards be enormously enlarged**. [...] The 'event' (one might say) was fixed, but **its meaning capable of indefinite extension**; and this is seen, over and over again, as a prime mark of my father's writing. (*RS* 2:71)

> There is of course no question that **the story was coming into being in these pages**, and the handwriting is so fast as to be practically a code. (*TI* 10:195)

With their allusive phrasing, these passages arguably sum up Tolkien's experience of sub-creative detachment – an experience that is insightfully reconstructed by Christopher through a painstaking analysis of the editorial history of his father's work, to which I refer for the discussion of individual cases.[19] Each individual scene or

---

reappear?"; 26:451 "shall Lórien be left slowly to fade? Yes [...] and Elrond? No", and the material collected in *RS* 13 'Queries and Alterations' and *RS* 22 'New Uncertainties and New Projections'). See further Shippey 2000:50–6 for a brief overview of the early textual history of *The Lord of the Rings*, where Tolkien's general lack of direction and unplanned approach to writing are especially evident, despite the occasional use of sketches and outlines (on which see n.22).

[19] Cf. for instance Christopher's comments at *RS* 1:18 "my father had no idea [about Bilbo's intentions]", 26 "a beginning without a destination", 44 "an unpremeditated turn" [i.e. the appearance of the Black Riders]; *TI* 2:30 "'Pippin' appears for the first time as the text was written"; 4:72 "my father was still quite uncertain what happened

chapter of *The Lord of the Rings* has a "clear and memorable form" from the beginning, and yet they 'emerge' and 'come into being' as something 'other', just like the vision given to the Ainur by Ilúvatar at the beginning of Arda, or the 'plot' of Ilúvatar mentioned in the quoted passage (*NME* 2.11:229–30).[20]

As noted by Christopher Tolkien, the "bearing and significance" of a particular narrative event is not something that Tolkien possessed from the beginning, or in full, because this was "capable of indefinite extension".[21] It is as if, after a preliminary 'vision' or 'foresight' of

to Gandalf"; 8:168 "it was at this point that my father 'realised' that it was Trotter and not Gandalf who especially feared Moria, and at once changed the text of the passage accordingly"; 11:207 "ideas were emerging and evolving as my father wrote it"; *WR* 2.1:86 "my father [...] struggled (in increasingly impossible handwriting) to discover just how Sam and Frodo did in the end get down"; *MR* 5:386 "my father was beginning a new story, working it out as he went". See further II.2.2.3 with n.119.

[20] Cf. also *TI* 10:199 "this chapter [i.e. that relating Gandalf's fight against the Balrog] was very fully formed from its first emergence". The verb 'emerge' is common in Christopher's reconstruction of his father's narratives, used more than 150 times in the central volumes of the *History of Middle-earth* (6–9), which record the textual history of *The Lord of the Rings*.

[21] Cf. Tolkien's words in the *Foreword* to the second edition of *The Lord of the Rings*, referring to "glimpses that had arisen unbidden" in *The Hobbit*, whose significance was only later 'discovered', and "revealed" the Third Age and its culmination in the War of the Rings; also Christopher Tolkien's comments on the development of the characters of Saruman and Wormtongue, who did not originate from a clear authorial intention: in the former's case a remark of Gandalf to Frodo during their initial dialogue prepared "the place that Saruman would fill when he had arisen – although, characteristically, he did not arise in order to fill that place" (*TI* 2:23); in the latter's case, Tolkien "did not introduce him [i.e. Wormtongue] into Théoden's household with the conscious intent that he should play the rôle that he did in fact come to play" (*TI* 26:445).

the event, the act of writing is conceived by Tolkien as already being exegetical in nature and thus inherently "partial" and "incomplete". Each revision of the preliminary text of a given chapter is a sort of 'interpretation' discovering and enlarging the significance of the literary event, only partially 'glimpsed' in the first draft (just as the Ainur's initial vision of Arda will be later enfolded *in actu* through its history).[22] Again and again, Christopher Tolkien highlights this "mark" of his father's writing in his commentary notes on the textual history of *The Lord of the Rings*, even identifying different types of script associated with different stages of composition.[23] To a certain extent, it is as if Christopher's own exegetical work could be considered as a mere prosecution of his own's father work. Indeed, as Randel Helmes has pointed out, in a passage quoted by Christopher himself in his introduction to the first volume of the *History of Middle-Earth*, *The Silmarillion* provides "a classic example of a long-standing problem in literary criticism: what, really,

---

[22] Cf. for instance *Letters* 247a, to Austin Olney, 31/07/1965:500, explaining that a revision of the text for the second edition of *The Lord of the Rings* was meant "to make my vision of the scene clearer: if I did not (as I do) retain a clear picture of what I was trying to describe, I should not get one from the present text". Important moments of 'foresight' are *TI* 11 ("The Story Foreseen from Moria"), 16 ("The Story Foreseen from Lórien") and 25 ("The Story Foreseen from Fangorn"). Cf. also *SWM*:106 (on the fading "vision" of artists, quoted in Chapter I n.102), and Tolkien's words in the *Foreword* to the second edition of *The Lord of the Rings* ("Foresight had failed").

[23] Cf. for instance *WR* 2.5:147 "at this point my father's handwriting speeded up markedly and becomes very difficult, often a sign that a new conception had entered that would entail the rewriting and rejection of what had preceded".

is a literary work? Is it what the author intended (or may have intended) it to be, or is it what a later editor makes of it?" (R. Helmes, quoted in *BLT1 Foreword*:6).

And, in a sense, Tolkien's conscious decision to entrust his son Christopher with the finalising and publication of *The Silmarillion* (recalling Bilbo's handing over to Frodo in *The Lord of the Rings*) was an extreme form of the non-possessive attitude the sub-creator can take towards his work (arguably a form of sub-creative death).[24] Indeed, there is evidence suggesting that Tolkien conceived his work as a collective, open-ended project, not bound by his literary intention.[25] This introduces a third important aspect to discuss, and brings us even closer to the notion of the 'death of the author' in a full Barthesian sense.

VI.1.3 Writing as Imperfect Interpreting: Giving Up Intention and Domination

Tolkien's emphasis on the 'otherness' of his stories is complemented by his constant downplaying of the role of his conscious intention in the writing of his books, as I have noted throughout;[26] this applies especially to *The Lord of the Rings*. This book accordingly featured characters that had nothing to do with Tolkien (cf. *Letters* 163 n.*),[27] and whom he "did not even want" (*Letters* 66:114[79]),[28]

---

[24] *LotR* 6.6:988, discussed in II.1.4.

[25] Cf. *Letters* 131:203[145] "I would draw some of the great tales in fullness, and leave many only placed in the scheme, and [...] leave scope for other minds and hands, wielding paint and music and drama."

[26] See in particular I.2.2.3, II.2.2.2 and II.2.2.3, IV.2.2.2.

[27] Quoted in II.2.2.3.   [28] Quoted in II n.110.

together with narratives elements that "arose naturally" (*Letters* 181:339[234]),[29] at times "against [...] [his] original will" (*Letters* 31:49[38]).[30] Returning to a passage already introduced in Chapter IV (IV.2.2.2), Tolkien's most forceful words in this respect are found in his letter to W. H. Auden:

The Lord of the Rings as a story was finished so long ago now that **I can take a largely impersonal view of it, and find 'interpretations' quite amusing; even those that I might make myself,** which are mostly post scriptum: **I had very little particular, conscious, intellectual, intention in mind at any point.** [...] Except for a few deliberately disparaging reviews [...] what appreciative readers have got out of the work or seen in it has seemed fair enough, **even when I do not agree with it.** Always excepting, of course, any 'interpretations' in the mode of simple allegory: that is, the particular and topical. In a larger sense, it is I suppose impossible to write **any 'story' that is not allegorical in proportion as it 'comes to life';** since each of us is an allegory, embodying in a particular tale and clothed in the garments of time and place, universal truth and everlasting life. (*Letters* 163:310[211–12])

It would be tempting to construe Tolkien's rejection of authorial intentionality as a rhetorical strategy or a mere literary pretence (still interesting in its own right); however, there is plenty of textual evidence confirming that his self-perceptions did reflect his writing practice. Similarly, one should be wary of discounting too easily Tolkien's claim that he "was not inventing but reporting (imperfectly)", as he put it in a footnote to this

---

[29] Quoted in IV.2.2.2.   [30] Quoted in II n.106.

passage.[31] A further confirmation in this respect comes from Tolkien's intriguing self-fashioning as an 'interpreter' of his own work, retaining "a largely impersonal view of it", which can be traced in many other letters.[32] We have already seen in Chapter V (V.1.1), for instance, how Tolkien engaged in an exegesis of Gandalf's fall and return, whose meaning was not fully articulated even by himself ("Naked it is alas! unclear", *Letters* 156:299[203]). Similarly, Tolkien claimed that he was discovering, rather than imposing, the 'meaning' of narrative elements that naturally and unconsciously emerged in the process of writing.[33] Interestingly, Tolkien's self-exegesis also concerns the interpretation of the significance of key situations: these include, for instance, Frodo's 'apostasy' on Mount Doom, whose 'topicality' he had no idea of until he had read the episode, as he claims in a letter.[34]

Tolkien's self-fashioning as the first reader and interpreter of his work has important implications regarding his conception of authorial control of the meaning or significance of a literary text. In the passage quoted earlier, Tolkien appears to give up his authorial position of dominance and presents himself instead as providing but one of many possible ("amusing") interpretations; his

---

[31] Quoted and discussed in II.2.2.3.

[32] Cf. *Letters* 208:385[267] "it is only in reading the work myself (with criticisms in mind) that I become aware of the dominance of the theme of Death". Cf. I.1.2, V.1.5.

[33] Cf. *Letters* 163:315–16[216–17] (quoted and discussed in II.2.2.2).

[34] *Letters* 181:339[234], quoted and discussed in IV.2.2.2). Cf. also *Letters* 192:363[252] "following the logic of the plot, it was clearly inevitable, as an event. And surely it is a more significant and real event than a mere 'fairy-story' ending."

interpretation, in other words, is not necessarily more valid than others (even those that Tolkien did "not agree" with).[35] With its tolerant attitude towards other readers' interpretations (except those in the "mode of simple allegory"), this passage exemplifies Tolkien's non-possessive attitude towards his work; at the same time, it clarifies at last how the concept of the 'death of the author', in its specific Barthesian sense, appropriately describes this attitude. The meaning of Tolkien's work is not 'owned' by the author himself – it does not even derive from the author's conscious intention; rather, it is the author himself (qua first reader) who 'discovers' the meaning while editing and interpreting his text, gradually, and always in a way that is limited and incomplete.[36] As discussed in Chapter II (II.2.2.4) and III (III.2.2), "limited understanding" (*Letters* 187:357[248]) and "incompleteness of information" (*Letters* 214:412[289]) are important features of Tolkien's authorial self-fashioning and are reflected, within his sub-creative mythology, in the Valar's incomplete "knowledge of the Creation Drama" (*Letters* 131:206[147]). The Valar's incomplete

---

[35] Tolkien expresses the same view, from the perspective of a reader, in his unfinished introduction to George MacDonald's *Golden Key*, in which he claims not to be troubled by the fact that other readers found different 'meanings' in this story, since "these pictures or visions that come in such tales are large and alive and no one who sees them, not even the writer himself, understands the whole of them" (*SWM* GK:91–92).

[36] Cf. also Tolkien's qualification about his understanding of the meaning of his work (*Letters*:202[143] "what (he thinks) he means or is trying to represent") and his words of gratitude to his friend Robert Murray, to whom he had sent a copy of *The Lord of the Rings* for comments and criticism, noting that he had even revealed to him "more clearly" some things about his work (*Letters* 142:257[172]).

knowledge is closely related to their understanding of being only co-authors of their creation, which ultimately depends on Eru; it also correlates with the Valar's surrender of sub-creative domination over the children of Ilúvatar and their respect for the "secret life" embedded within the world that they themselves helped to create. That for Tolkien this surrender had meta-literary implications is also confirmed by his rejection of conscious allegory as residing in the "purposed domination of the author" and as violating the "freedom of the reader" (*LotR Introduction*:xx), as discussed in Chapter III (III.3.2). Since, for Tolkien, allegory has a close relationship with the primary 'topicality' and 'meaning' of a given secondary entity, one can conclude that Tolkien's rejection of allegory is just another facet of his non-possessive attitude towards the interpretation of his work.

At the same time, sub-creative surrender of the desire for domination over the 'meaning' of one's work (i.e. the acceptance of a Barthesian 'death') does not prevent the author or any other reader from recognising the 'universal', prophetic significance of any story that retains "life", as Tolkien does while interpreting *The Lord of the Rings* post scriptum. In fact, the exact opposite of this is true, because, as Tolkien writes in the same passage quoted earlier (*Letters* 163:310[211–12]), the more a story "comes to life", the more it becomes "allegorical". It would be the ultimate act of domination for the author or any other interpreter to deny that within a well-made story, whether primary or secondary and regardless of the author's intentions or the characters' awareness, there might be hidden "universal truth and everlasting life", just as in the case of Gandalf's death and resurrection.

To refuse to acknowledge and accept the universal significance of a secondary story would be, for the author, to impose their original intention upon the story; in so doing, they would impede the story's 'natural' development and refuse to allow in it unexpected (or unwanted) characters, situations, or links (in the case of Tolkien, this would have been to refuse to write about the Ents, Faramir, or the Hobbit, as he was "meant to").

To sum up Tolkien's non-possessive attitude towards his work, I would like to quote a final passage that comes from Tolkien's 'Introductory Note' to the volume *Tree and Leaf*, which collects two texts specifically dealing "in different ways" with sub-creation, *On Fairy-Stories* and *Leaf by Niggle*:

> Though one is an 'essay' and the other a 'story', they are related: by the symbols of Tree and Leaf, and by both touching in different ways on what is called in the essay 'sub-creation'. Also they were written in the same period (1938–9), when The Lord of the Rings was **beginning to unroll itself** and to **unfold prospects of labour and exploration in yet unknown country** as daunting to me as to the hobbits. At about that time we had reached Bree, and I had then no more notion than they had of what had become of Gandalf or who Strider was; and **I had begun to despair of surviving to find out**. (quoted by Christopher Tolkien in *TL Preface*:v–vi)

Here we see another good description of that non-possessive attitude of sub-creation: *The Lord of the Rings* was not the realisation of Tolkien's intention, but rather was 'unrolling' itself; writing it, for Tolkien, was "an exploration" into an "unknown country". Tolkien's experience is analogous to that of the Valar entering into Arda, their own sub-creative work of which they have only an imperfect fore-knowledge and which is also inhabited by creatures other than themselves. Besides demonstrating the meta-literary significance of the short story *Leaf by Niggle*, this passage also helps to introduce yet another important 'primary' dimension of authorial experience, which is, just as in the case of Gandalf, closely related to hope and death ("I had begun to despair of surviving to find out").

VI.1.4 *The Hopeful Despair of the Writer and Christ as the Only 'Literary Critic'*

To discuss the fourth aspect of 'authorial death', and develop my overall argument in the rest of this chapter, I will henceforth focus more closely on the short story *Leaf by Niggle*.[37] As noted by critics such as Tom Shippey (2000:266–77), this is a text with a clear allegorical resonance, and more specifically (one might add) a strong meta-literary significance, crucial to understanding Tolkien's theory and experience of creative writing. In fact, as Tolkien acknowledged, this short story "arose from my own preoccupation with *The Lord of the Rings*, the knowledge that it would be finished in great detail or not at all, and the fear (near certainty) that it would be 'not at all'. The war had arisen to darken all horizons" (*Letters* 199:257[372]).[38]

---

[37] On *Leaf by Niggle* see in particular Ellison 1991; Shippey 2000:266–77; Segura 2007; Geier 2008; Shippey 2008; Saxton 2013b, esp. 50–1; also, for a general introduction, Hammond and Scull 2017: *Reader's Guide* 658–63.

[38] Tolkien's perception that he would have died a premature death, before he had "said his word", originated early in his life during the time of the First World War. It persisted with him for many years, as recalled in a footnote to a letter he wrote to his son Michael (*Letters* 43, n.*:71), in which he also explained that his urge to write poetry stemmed from the perception that "Death was near".

To contextualise Tolkien's authorial preoccupation, one must recall that the writing and publication of *The Lord of the Rings* was a very long and difficult process for him, taking almost two decades of work, from its original conception in 1937 to its publication in 1954–5. Before its eventual publication, Tolkien was anything but a recognised author. Published in 1937, *The Hobbit* had certainly been an unexpected success, relatively speaking, with 1,500 copies sold out after a few months of publication and an American edition produced soon after; and yet it had not given Tolkien the fame and success that would come with the publication of *The Lord of the Rings*, not least because paper shortages prevented the wider circulation of the work until the late 1940s. Moreover, Tolkien's long-standing aspiration was not to become a writer of children stories (as *The Hobbit* was still perceived to be), but rather to finalise and publish his mythological magnum opus, the *Silmarillion*, on which he had been working for many years.[39] In fact, after the publication of the *Hobbit*, Tolkien submitted an early draft of the *Silmarillion* material to his publishers (the *Quenta Silmarillion*); but, after an unfavourable review, they rejected it and urged him to write a sequel to *The Hobbit* instead, "encouraged by requests from readers for more information concerning hobbits" (*LotR Foreword* xviiii). Tolkien alludes to this authorial failure in the *Foreword* to the second edition of *The Lord of the Rings*, connecting his decision to write *The Lord of the Rings* with his loss of hope that the *Silmarillion* would ever find an interested readership.[40]

[39] See Shippey 2000:226–36 for an overview.
[40] Cf. *LotR Foreword* xviiii "[*The Lord of the Rings*] was begun soon after The Hobbit was written [...] but [...] I wished first to complete and set in order the mythology and legends of the Elder Days [...]. I

Strikingly, then, Tolkien's 'despair' did not result in him giving up writing completely; rather, it led him to take on a different project, following the requests of others. In an analogous fashion, perhaps, Aragorn did not abandon the journey after the death of Gandalf but decided to go on and eventually take a different route, despite having, like Tolkien, "no hope". This is a recurrent pattern in Tolkien's experience as an author. Even the writing of the 'sequel' proved to be difficult, and in 1938–9, with the start of the Second World War, Tolkien almost lost hope of ever finishing *The Lord of the Rings* and of ever accomplishing his juvenile literary aspirations.[41] Not by chance does the writing of *Leaf by Niggle* date to these years of 'despair' and anxiety, under the dark shadow of the war, when the "world was threatening".[42] Nevertheless, 'authorial despair' was not the journey's end, and a new way was again opened first of all through an act of literary 'altruism', a concern for

---

desired to do this for my own satisfaction, and **I had little hope** that other people would be interested in this work [...]. When those whose advice and opinion I sought corrected **little hope to no hope**, I went back to the sequel, encouraged by requests from readers for more information concerning hobbits and their adventures."

[41] We can trace the inception of these ambitions to the momentous 'Council of London' of the TCBS in 1914 (cf. Hammond and Scull 2017: *Chronology* 65). Cf. *Letters* 5:6[10] "I cannot abandon yet the hope and ambitions (inchoate and cloudy I know) that first became conscious at the Council of London."

[42] Cf. *Letters* 241:454[321] "I was anxious about my own internal Tree, *The Lord of the Rings*. [...] I wanted to finish it, but **the world was threatening**. And I was dead stuck [...] It was not until Christopher was carried off to S. Africa that I forced myself to write Book IV, which was sent out to him bit by bit." Cf. also *Letters* 56a, to Christopher Tolkien, 27/03/1944, "It seems **beyond hope** that I shd. do any Hobbit."

others: Tolkien forced himself to continue to write for the sake of his son Christopher, who, as a despondent soldier, needed the comforting beauty of his father's writing, and, as a reader, was keen to see how *The Lord of the Rings* would develop.

Tolkien's preoccupation with his work did not end with the end of the war; as late as 1948, only a year before the completion of *The Lord of the Rings*, we find traces in his letters of his authorial frustration. This is indicated in the following excerpt from a letter to C. S. Lewis – another man who had played a crucial role in encouraging Tolkien to keep writing.[43] The letter refers to a discussion between the poets G. M. Hopkins (H.) and R. W. Dixon about whether literary recognition in this world was an essential part of authorship, at least as a future aspiration (in this respect Hopkins quoted a sentence by E. Burne-Jones who said that "one works really for the one man who may rise to understand one"); or, to paraphrase, whether it might be appropriate and fulfilling for an author to work without the hope of eventually receiving literary recognition. Tolkien writes:

I have something that I deeply desire to make, and which it is the (largely frustrated) bent of my nature to make. [...] H. seems clearly to have seen that 'recognition' with some understanding is in this world an essential part of authorship, and the want of it a suffering to be distinguished from (even when mixed with) mere desire for the pleasures of

[43] As Tolkien acknowledged in *Letters* 282, to C. S. Kilby, 18/12/1955:511[366] "But for the encouragement of C.S.L. I do not think that I should ever have completed or offered for publication The Lord of the Rings"; also *Letters* 276, to D. Plotz, 12/09/1965:506[362]. Cf. on this Poe 2021:192.

fame and praise. [...] But H. then demurred, perceiving that Burne-Jones' **hope can also in this world be frustrated**, as easily as general fame: a painter (**like Niggle**) may work for what the burning of his picture, or an accident of death to the admirer, may wholly destroy. He summed up: The only just literary critic is Christ, **who admires more than does any man the gifts He Himself has bestowed**. Then let us 'bekenne either other to Crist'. (*Letters* 113 to C. S. Lewis, early 1948:181–3[126–8])

This crucial passage shows Tolkien's deep understanding of authorial frustration, as well as his Christian response to authorial despair; his response consists, just as in the case of Gandalf, in giving up *Amdir*, a human hope that can be frustrated in this world, and taking up *Estel*,[44] the hope of being 'recognised' by Christ, the only one "who admires more than does any man the gifts He Himself has bestowed". 'Let's entrust each other to Christ ("bekenne either other to Crist"), Tolkien wrote to his fellow sub-creator C. S. Lewis; this resolution is essentially the same as Gandalf's "handing over to the Authority" (cf. V.1.1), the ultimate content of his sub-creative death.

The fourth aspect of authorial death consists, therefore, in an author's acceptance of the apparent failure of his artistic vocation. The acceptance that one's work may not be completed or admired and that one may fail to receive recognition in this world can be construed as another form of sub-creative submission to a higher literary Authority ("the only just literary critic"). An author can continue to write out of obedience to his vocation, as revealed through

---

[44] Cf. V.1.6.

circumstances,[45] even without the hope of being one day recognised by fellow human beings. As Tolkien suggests to C. S. Lewis, an author should embrace the possibility of dying without having seen the completion of his work; indeed, this is how Tolkien felt in the 1940s regarding *The Lord of the Rings* and it is how he would feel several years later regarding the *Silmarillion*, which he never saw to publication.[46] An author should be ready to die even with the knowledge that their work may be neglected or destroyed after their death; such was, one might observe, the fate of Tolkien's closest school friends – the TCBS – poets and artists swept away by the horror of the First World War; this is also the fate of Niggle, the protagonist of the 'allegorical' story written by Tolkien at the very time when the completion of *The Lord of the Rings* (not to mention the fulfilment and recognition of his literary vocation in general) was "beyond hope".

As Tolkien explicitly alludes to in the passage quoted earlier ("like Niggle"), Niggle's authorial destiny will indeed be to die an unrecognised death: in the story, Niggle does not manage to finish his painting, and its scattered fragments are eventually destroyed after his death, with his fellow townsfolk scorning him because

---

[45] Circumstances are indeed for Tolkien the "instruments" or "appearances" of God (cf. *Letters* 43:70[51] "life and circumstance do most of it [i.e. the choosing] (though if there is a God these must be His instruments, or His appearances)". Cf. also *Letters* 38a, to M. Tolkien, 12/07/1940, "the chances of life (or God)".

[46] Cf. also a correspondence with the Polish scholar Przemyslaw Mroczkowski (*TCG* 326, 9–10/11/1957), in which Tolkien showed a keen awareness of literary incompleteness, discussing the disordered status of Chaucer's works resulting from the premature death of their author. On Tolkien's relationship with Mroczkowski see Neubauer 2020.

"he never finished anything" (*LN*:117); eventually, "the Museum was burnt down, and the leaf, and Niggle, were entirely forgotten in his old country" (*LN*:118) – the very opposite of worldly recognition. Of course, this is not the true end of Niggle's story, because, after his death, his artwork will be completed and 'realised' thanks to the intervention of some mysterious Divine voices, as we will see; crucially, however, this artwork will be realised not as Niggle's own possession, but rather as the redeemed fruit of the co-operation between him and his neighbour Parish. This introduces the fifth and last aspect of authorial death in the primary sense.

VI.1.5 Dying for Parish and the Co-operation with Modernity

To explain this final aspect, I need to return to *Leaf by Niggle* and recall the reasons why Niggle the artist never manages to finish his artwork. Apart from being naturally indolent and inconclusive (like Tolkien himself), Niggle is constantly interrupted by the requests of his neighbour Parish, who can be described as the prototype of the non-artistic (modern) man. Parish is completely uninterested in Niggle's work and is unable to catch the "glimpse" of a higher reality contained in it;[47] he is a bit like a reader unable or unwilling to recognise the higher significance glimpsed in a sub-creative work (cf. III.3.4). And yet it is to this very non-artistic, materialistic man, whom "he did not

---

[47] Cf. *LN*:115 "'But it did not look like this then, not *real*,' said Parish. 'No, it was only a **glimpse** then,' said the man; 'but you might have caught the **glimpse**, if you had ever thought it worth while to try.'"

like very much", that Niggle devotes himself, performing "a good many odd jobs", although begrudgingly; it is for Parish's sake that Niggle neglects his artistic duties, compelled by his "kind heart" and his feeling "uncomfortable" at other people's troubles (cf. *LN*:93–4).

Eventually, Niggle decides to attend to an annoying, petty request of Parish, which results in his fatal illness and complete artistic failure; tending to this request impedes Niggle's final chance to finish his painting and especially to treat "the shining spray which framed the distant vision of the mountain" (*LN*:99); this is a failure that Niggle perceived with "a sinking feeling in his heart". After the return from his chore for Parish, Niggle goes to bed, destitute, and wakes up only to embark on a final "wretched journey", which is clearly meant to represent death. In *Leaf by Niggle* the eponymous artist literally dies for the sake of his non-artistic, prosaic, and mundane neighbour.

The final aspect of authorial death, then, consists in the openness to offer one's life for the sake of what is apparently banal or trivial; it is to accept collaborating with the mundane, which may reach the point of assenting to sacrifice one's literary vocation to attend the needs of other (non-artistic) people. In Tolkien's case, this would be his family, friends, colleagues, students, and so on. This tension between literary vocation and social duties is central to understanding Tolkien's creative personality. Tolkien was not, after all, just a writer, but a father of four and a busy academic, among other things. As rightly observed by his grandson Michael G. Tolkien:

Niggle's conflict between absorption in his art (the status of which he is unsure) and his kindly sociable heart was something

I noticed in my grandfather's conflict between the life of the study and other unavoidable daily distractions. [...] Tolkien's ability to achieve some kind of resolution of the conflicts between his inner life, his professional duties, family demands and other sociable activities is part of his stature as a man and reflects the humanity we find in the most endearing of his fictional heroes. (*Autobiographical essay on my grandfather, J.R.R. Tolkien, from* www.michaeltolkien.com)

The conflict and resolution between high art and mundane life are not just biographical elements; they are also thematised in Tolkien's work on a secondary level, being especially evident in the lives of the Hobbits, who are described by Tolkien as exhibiting the "plain, unimaginative parochial man".[48] As discussed in III.2.2, and V.1, it is significant that Gandalf – the great lover of hobbits and the fosterer of their heroism – will accept death in Moria for the sake of this kind of "parochial man". Gandalf's self-sacrifice in Moria can be related to Niggle's death after attending to Parish's needs – another sacrifice that will later be acknowledged and rewarded by some mysterious divine Voices. It is only because of his 'gratuitous' acts of love for Parish, culminating in his own death for his neighbour's sake, that these Voices grant Niggle the chance "go to the next stage", that is, allegorically, to leave Purgatory for Paradise, as retold in a crucial passage of the story:

'[Niggle] was a painter by nature. [...] **He took a great deal of pains with leaves, just for their own sake**. But he never thought

---

[48] Cf. *Letters* 131 n.†:219[454*] "The Hobbits [...] are made small [...] partly to exhibit the pettiness of man, **plain unimaginative parochial man**."

349

that that made him important. [...]. There is the Parish case, the one that came in later. He was Niggle's neighbour, never did a stroke for him, and seldom showed any gratitude at all. But there is **no note** in the Records **that Niggle expected Parish's gratitude**; he does not seem to have thought about it. [...] that wet bicycle-ride. I rather lay stress on that. It seems plain that this was a genuine sacrifice: Niggle guessed that he was throwing away his last chance with his picture, and he guessed, too, that Parish was worrying unnecessarily.' [...] 'Well, what have you to say?' 'Could you tell me about Parish?' said Niggle. '**I should like to see him again**. [...] He was a very good neighbour, and let me have excellent potatoes very cheap, which **saved me a lot of time**.' 'Did he?' said the First Voice. 'I am glad to hear it.' There was another silence. Niggle heard the Voices receding. 'Well, I agree,' he heard the First Voice say in the distance. 'Let him go on **to the next stage**'. (*LN*:106–8)

There are two elements of Niggle's relationship with Parish (and other people in general) that are crucial from the perspective of the Voices, and which also deserve to be highlighted because of their meta-literary implications.

First, complete 'gratuitousness' (Niggle did not expect "Parish's gratitude"), which is akin to and complements the 'gratuitousness' of his artistic work ("He took a great deal of pains with leaves, just for their own sake"). As discussed in Chapter I (esp. I.3), 'gratuitousness' is a key feature of artistic sub-creation; it is analogical to the 'gratuitousness' of primary Creation and is, ultimately, related to the 'gratuitousness' of divine Mercy (which is reflected in Niggle's love for his neighbour, and thereby acknowledged by the Voices).

Second, the reciprocity of the relationship: Niggle is not just worrying about Parish out of sheer altruism, but he is also ready to acknowledge his own gratitude to his neighbour (he "saved me a lot of time") and express his personal need for him ("I should like to see him again"); it is only after this acknowledgement that the First Voice is persuaded to let Niggle go "to the next stage". This notion that the parochial characters (like Parish and the hobbits) are themselves necessary to more artistic and 'enlightened' characters (such as Niggle and Gandalf) is crucial also in Tolkien's secondary world. In *The Lord of the Rings*, for instance, the 'high' Gandalf instructs the 'lower' hobbits and sacrifices himself for them; yet without the hobbits there would be no final victory (cf. III.2.2). In *The Silmarillion*, the divine Valar guard and help the Children of Ilúvatar, and yet their Arda is salvaged from Melkor's evil and eventually redeemed only thanks to the Children's contribution and mediation (cf. V.1.4).

Moving to the primary world in meta-literary terms, Tolkien might have originally belittled the literary value of *The Hobbit* in contrast to his beloved higher mythology, but it is only thanks to the *Hobbit*'s intrusion into Tolkien's *legendarium* and the related success of *The Lord of the Rings* that his mythology was 'completed' and managed to 'descend to earth' (cf. *Letters* 131:204[144], discussed in II.2.1.4); it is on account of these 'lower' works that *The Silmarillion* was eventually published. One could even take a step further and construe this reciprocal relationship between Niggle and Parish, and Gandalf and the hobbits, as reflecting for Tolkien that of Christian Art and secular modernity. Parish is also, in many respects, the 'symbol' of the modern non-religious man, incapable of imagining the 'mountains' of divine transcendence (just as the Victorian-like hobbits, before Gandalf's 'education', have forgotten the "memory of the high").[49] In contrast to some apologetic Christian art, Tolkien's mythology does not ignore or oppose modernity, but rather works with it, builds upon it, learns from it, enhances it, and re-integrates it into a higher vision.[50]

The common element between all these possible interpretations is the recognition and acceptance of the need of reciprocal co-operation with other sub-creators. This even includes the apparently lower sub-creator, who has limited understanding (not coincidentally, Parish, just like the hobbits, is a gardener like Sam). Embracing co-operation can be considered the ultimate content of the 'death of the author' and the main form of acknowledging the mysterious nature of literary creation. To refuse the necessarily co-operative nature of sub-creation on the basis of a supposed creative superiority – artistic, intellectual, or spiritual – is clearly, for Tolkien, a temptation that any sub-creator needs to overcome. It is no coincidence that, in his mythology, this refusal is a distinctive trait of rebellious sub-creators such as Melkor, who, "being alone [...] had begun to conceive thoughts of his own unlike those of his brethren" (*Sil Ain.*:16); and Fëanor, who, living apart from his brothers, "was driven by the fire of his own heart only" (*Sil* 6:65) and "asked the aid and sought the counsel of none [...] great or small".[51] By contrast, a sub-creator such as Gandalf does

---

[49] Cf. III.2.1. At the beginning of *The Lord of the Rings*, Bilbo's decision to leave the Shire and embark on a new journey is connected to his desire to see mountains again (cf. *LotR* 1.1:32–33).

[50] On Tolkien's (complicated) relationship with modernity see esp. Curry 2004, Weinreich and Honegger 2006, Wood 2015.

[51] Cf. V.1.7. Also the fall of Saruman, another sub-creator corrupted by his desire of power, goes hand in hand with his decision to withdraw from Gandalf and the other members of the Council.

not work in isolation, but thrives in co-operation with other characters, such as the 'low' hobbits, recognising, embracing and enhancing the necessity of their contribution for the fulfilment of his own sub-creative mission.

A final, important point: embracing the co-operative nature of sub-creation ("the mystery of literary creation") is not a mere moral requirement, a sort of 'pass' to acquire the favour of some divine entities such as the Voices in Niggle's story; rather, co-operation is an intrinsic mark of artistic creation per se, with important aesthetic implications and even an eschatological dimension. Indeed, when Niggle finally reaches the Paradise-like region where he will spend the rest of his existence and sees his Tree miraculously completed and realised, he is surprised to observe that "some of the most beautiful – and the most characteristic, the most perfect examples of the Niggle style – were seen to have been produced in collaboration with Mr. Parish" (*LN*:110). With this final point on the transcendental beauty of co-operation, it is time to move away from the 'death of the author' and on to the second part of Gandalf's story: the 'resurrection of the author'.

VI.2 The Resurrection of the Author: Taking Up to the Primary Plane

Just as in the case of Gandalf and Niggle, the death of the author is not the end of the story in Tolkien's vision, even in a primary sense. Although sub-creative death is an unavoidable and ubiquitous presence in Tolkien's secondary world, it remains only a passage – a passage leading to some other purpose; that is, to a sort of 'sub-creative resurrection', instrumental "in devising things more wonderful", to quote Eru's words to Melkor in the *Ainulindalë* (*Sil Ain.*:17).[52] Niggle the artist dies, and his art is forlorn and neglected, but his artistic vocation is eventually fulfilled by the Voices who decide to integrate his sub-creation into Their plan. Gandalf the sub-creator dies, but he eventually comes back to life to fulfil his sub-creative vocation: his sacrifice has been accepted, and his plan is eventually "taken up and enlarged" by Eru, who sends him back with "enhanced power" (cf. V.1.6, V.1.8).

We find the same phrasing and metaphor of 'taking up' in other key texts explicitly or allusively dealing with Tolkien's 'theory' of sub-creation. In particular, these include the meta-artistic dialogue between Eru and Aulë in *The Silmarillion*, in all its different textual versions: after Aulë's humble offer to destroy the Dwarves (itself a form of sub-creative death), Eru announces his decision to bestow life on them, declaring to Aulë: "I have taken up thy desire and given to it a place therein" (*Sil* 2:44); or, in another version, Eru states that "Thy making I have taken up into my design" (*Letters* 212:409[287]), having seen Aulë's humility and taken pity on his impatience.[53] Of course, the same idea of 'taking up' is also central in *Leaf by Niggle*, as Tolkien acknowledges in a draft letter to P. Hastings: "I tried to show allegorically how that might come to be **taken up into Creation** in some plane in my 'purgatorial' story Leaf by Niggle" (*Letters* 153:290[195]).

'Taking up into Creation' is the essential content of what I have called 'sub-creative resurrection', the supreme

---

[52] Cf. VII.2.
[53] Cf. also *Letters* 247:470[335], where Tolkien describes Eru's dealing with Aulë's dwarves as an act of mercy (which led the Vala Yavanna to ask Him for the same grace in the matter of Ents).

sign of God's "intrusion" in the "mystery of literary creation" and the ultimate mark of its collaborative nature. Just like Eru with Gandalf or Aulë, for Tolkien, God does not repress, dispose of, or even amend the sub-creative desires and endeavours of human sub-creations.[54] Rather, He hallows them, redeems them and, ultimately, integrates them into His Creation, just as Niggle's leaves are eventually integrated by the Voices into a single Tree, planted in a large Forest within sight of the Mountains. However, this 'sub-creative resurrection' is only possible after the sub-creator has allowed the supreme Creator to partake in their sub-creations, entrusting themselves and their works to Him with filial humility and a non-possessive attitude. This is, in essence, what sub-creative humility and authorial death are about: from Aulë to Fëanor and from Gandalf to Tolkien (cf. V.1.7).[55] But what exactly are the nature and effects of this 'taking up' into Creation, in a primary sense? The allegorical, meta-literary story *Leaf by Niggle* will help us to unfold the different aspects of Tolkien's vision on the primary level – different gifts bestowed by the same Author.

VI.2.1 The Gift of Completion and the Enhancement of Imagination

The first gift that follows the death of the author is the completion and fulfilment of their sub-creative work, which, as already discussed in Chapter II (II.2.2.3 and

---

[54] Cf. Eru's final words to Aulë: "in no other way will I amend thy handiwork, and as thou hast made it, so shall it be" (*Sil* 2:44).
[55] On this point, and the similarity between Aulë's Dwarves and Niggle's Tree cf. also Holloway 2011 and Saxton 2013a, esp. 169, 172.

II.2.2.4),[56] inevitably remains fragmentary and imperfect in their own life. This is the fate of Niggle, who, on arriving to 'Paradise', encounters his Tree finally completed, blossoming with all the leaves and branches that he had imagined, "felt or guessed" in his life, but had "so often failed to catch":

Before him stood the Tree, his Tree, finished. If you could say that of a Tree that was alive, its leaves opening, its branches growing and bending in the wind that Niggle had so often felt or guessed, and had so often failed to catch. He gazed at the Tree, and slowly he lifted his arms and opened them wide. 'It's a gift!' he said. He was referring to his art, and also to the result; but he was using the word quite literally. He went on looking at the Tree. All the leaves he had ever laboured at were there, as he had imagined them rather than as he had made them; and there were others that had only budded in his mind, and many that might have budded, if only he had had time. (*LN*:109–10)

That Tolkien conceived Paradise as the place where God completes all human stories and where human imagination and sub-creative desire find complete fulfilment and recognition is also suggested by passages from his letters. Tolkien explains to his son Christopher that "There is a place called 'heaven' where the good here unfinished is completed; and where the stories unwritten, and the hopes unfulfilled, are continued" (*Letters* 45, to M. Tolkien, 9/06/1941:76[55]), and that "untold stories" are like "mountains seen far away, never to be climbed, distant trees (like Niggle's) never to be approached [...] unless in Paradise or N's Parish" (*Letters* 96:160[111]).

[56] Cf. also III.3.1.

Should one infer from these words that Tolkien conceived literary completion as a mere eschatological event, impossible in this world? We should recall, as noted earlier (VI.1.4), that Tolkien wrote *Leaf by Niggle* at a time when he had almost despaired of finishing *The Lord of the Rings*; this might explain why, at that time, he could seriously contemplate the possibility of artistic failure (i.e. Niggle's worldly fate) and see completion as only a future, eschatological event. Even when *The Lord of the Rings* was finally published, Tolkien still did not think of it as a fully completed work; indeed, even years after its publication, he continued to find defects in it, as if the full completion had not yet been achieved. Tolkien never saw the completion of his magnum opus and goal of his juvenile ambition, his beloved *Silmarillion*, and he struggled to complete his work in his final years, with great frustration,[57] for it to be published only after his death. In a sense, Tolkien died, as Niggle did, without having seen the completion of his Art. This apparent contradiction between completion and incompletion is corroborated by a paradoxical remark found in a letter written a few months before the finalisation of *The Lord of the Rings* (*Letters* 109, to S. Unwin, 31/07/1947). Tolkien comments on the urge to bring his work to completion ("The thing is to finish the thing as devised [...] the chief thing is to complete one's work"), and yet he immediately qualifies the very concept ("as far as completion has any real sense").[58]

---

[57] Cf. for instance *Letters* 311, to Christopher Tolkien, 31/07/1969:562[401]) "I begin to feel a bit desperate: endlessly frustrated. [...] I cannot get anything of my real work finished."

[58] *Letters* 109:176[122].

At the same time, it would be incorrect to assume that Tolkien thought of completion only in eschatological terms. *The Lord of the Rings* (his internal Tree) was eventually completed in this world, and yet in a manner still mysteriously analogical to (and somehow prophesied by) the completion of Niggle's Tree. In fact, Tolkien would later refer to the completion of *The Lord of the Rings* as a sort of miracle, a truly astonishing fact, beyond hope; this was especially true, considering his characteristic ineffectiveness (again, recalling that of Niggle):

The chief biographical fact to me is the completion of The Lord of the Rings, which still astonishes me. A notorious beginner of enterprises and non-finisher [...] I still wonder how and why I managed to peg away at this thing year after year, often under real difficulties, and bring it to a conclusion. (*Letters* 199:371–2[257])

No less astounding for Tolkien was the enormous success of the book, which was completely unexpected, and this is a point made many times in his letters.[59] In a passage from one letter in particular (*Letters* 328:578–9[413]), already discussed in Chapter II (II.2.2.5), Tolkien is even more explicit, stating that *The Lord of the Rings* "does not belong" to him (as a child does not belong to his parents) and that any "light" within it does not come "from him but through him", also hinting that the literary fulfilment

[59] Cf. *Letters* 347a, to Miss T.R.C. (draft), January 1973:600 "to my delight, but still more to my great amazement"; Tolkien uses the words 'astonishing' and 'surprise' and derivatives in many other unpublished letters, referring to the success of *The Lord of the Rings*, as for instance in *TCG* 205 (28/07/55), *TCG* 212 (22/10/1955), *TCG* 341 (26/10/1958), *TCG* 511 (25/12/1963), *TCG* 691(10/10/1968), *TCG* 1528 (16/04/1956).

and relevance of his book had only been possible thanks to the intervention of a divine co-Author who chose him as an 'imperfect instrument' to sound "the horns of Hope"– the same authorial Entity Who bestows to the reader the receptiveness needed to appreciate all this.[60] That Tolkien conceived the completion and success of *The Lord of the Rings* as a miracle somehow equivalent to the completion of Niggle's Tree is also suggested by the witness of his daughter Priscilla, who, in a letter sent for a Tolkien conference in 2004, made the explicit connection:

The history of how this book has become world famous is well known but as J.R.R. Tolkien's daughter I can only repeat my father's own awed comment at its success in his lifetime and his gratitude for his having touched so many people's lives through the power of his writing. How much of his own gratitude may be seen in the words of Niggle in 'Leaf by Niggle' when he contemplates his picture complete and made part of his landscape: **'It's a gift'**. (*Letter by Priscilla Tolkien to Members of the Conference 'Tolkien's Fifty Years' organised by Oronzo Cilli*)

Thus, the completion of *The Lord of the Rings* can be construed as the first miracle, the first facet of the 'resurrection', following Tolkien's authorial death; this betrays the same sort of intrusion and co-authoriality of the Divine Author that we have seen in the case of Gandalf. At the same time, this literary fulfilment is not definitive;

---

[60] Cf. *Letters* 328:578–9[413] "Looking back on the wholly unexpected things that have followed its publication – […] I feel as if […] the horns of Hope had been heard again […] But How? and Why? […]. Of course *The L.R.* **does not belong to me**. It has been brought forth and must now go its appointed way in the world, though naturally I take a deep interest in its fortunes, **as a parent would of a child**." Cf. II.2.2.5 with n.125.

being in this world, it is a fleeting yet meaningful and miraculous 'glimpse' of the final eschatological fulfilment ('already and not yet').[61]

A final important note: for Tolkien, the completion of Niggle's Tree (and any sub-creation in general) also involves the fulfilment and enhancement of all of his imaginative aspirations. As seen in the passage quoted earlier, not only did the Voices complete Niggle's work, but They also fulfilled and enhanced all that "he had imagined", as Eru enhances the sub-creations of His creatures, including Gandalf's plan and power after his death and resurrection. That Tolkien conceived God's creative work as also involving the merciful embracing and enhancement of human imagination is confirmed in the *Ainulindalë*, in which the Valar, entering into the reality of Arda, contemplate the full realisation and fulfilments of the things that they had originally imagined (cf. Ulmo's words to Eru "Truly, Water is become now fairer than my heart imagined", *Sil. Ain.*:19). This leads to the second aspect of sub-creative Resurrection: the gift of reality.

VI.2.2 The Gift of Realisation and (Sub-)creative Mise-en-abyme

God's bestowal of Reality ("being") to sub-creation is a second important gift resulting from His intervention in the "mystery of literary creation"; it is also a central tenet of Tolkien's mythology. As Tolkien explains in open meta-literary terms:

[61] Cf. III.3.3 and III.3.4.

[The Valar] shared in its 'making' – but only on the same terms as we 'make' a work of art or story. The realization of it, the gift to it of a created reality of the same grade as their own, was the act of the One God. (*Letters* 181, n.*:341[235])[62]

Just as in the *Ainulindalë* Eru provides reality to the thoughts and songs of the Ainur through the Imperishable Flame,[63] and grants the gift of life to Aulë's Dwarves, fulfilling their sub-creative desire for a "realised art",[64] so Niggle's imagined tree is bestowed life and reality in Paradise (it "was alive", the leaves "were there"). As Parish points out in contemplating it, the Tree that now lives in Paradise ("Niggle's Parish") is no longer 'unreal' as was the tree that Niggle vainly tried to finish during his lifetime (*LN*:115 "'Niggle's Picture!' said Parish in astonishment. [...] it did not look like this then, **not *real***").

Again, that Tolkien does not formulate this realisation of the artistic project in purely eschatological terms is suggested in *On Fairy-Stories*, where he describes the "inner consistency of reality" to be a typical mark of successful Art (qua "the operative link between the Imagination and sub-creation").[65] Tolkien especially elaborates on this point in the epilogue of *On Fairy-Stories*, where he clarifies the substance and origin of the "inner consistency of reality". In contrast to some of his contemporaries,

---

[62] Cf. also *Letters* 153:290[185] "[God] gave special 'sub-creative' powers to certain of His highest created beings: that is a guarantee that what they devised and made should be given the reality of Creation."

[63] Cf. *MR Athr.*:345, and see I.2.4, VII.2.

[64] Cf. *TOFS*:64=*TL*:53 "the desire for a living, realised sub-creative art" and see V.I.7 on the Ainur's sub-creative desire.

[65] *TOFS*:59=*TL*:46–7 "The achievement of the expression, which gives (or seems to give) 'the inner consistency of reality', is [...] Art, the operative link between Imagination and the final result, Sub-creation."

Tolkien does not consider this quality to be the result of a successful magical trick or the mere product of human imagination; rather, this quality, the wish and hope of every sub-creative writer,[66] would be impossible if the work did not "partake of reality":

every sub-creator, wishes in some measure to be a real maker, or hopes that he is drawing on reality: hopes that the peculiar quality of this secondary world (if not all the details) are derived from Reality, or are flowing into it. If he indeed achieves a quality that can fairly be described by the dictionary definition: 'inner consistency of reality', it is difficult to conceive how this can be, if the work does not in some way partake of reality. (*TOFS*:77=*TL*:73)

Moreover, as Tolkien further elaborates in a letter to his son Christopher commenting on this very passage, this 'partaking' is only possible because God himself – the only One who can bestow reality – has decided to make real and verify human stories by becoming the protagonist of a Primary fairy-story, thereby redeeming his corrupt creatures "in a manner consonant" with their strange nature of story-tellers, that is to say "by a moving story".[67] In so doing, He 'raises' their sub-creative desires and aspirations (indeed, an 'authorial raising'), as Tolkien explains:

the Gospels contain a fairy-story, or a story of a larger kind which embraces all the essence of fairy-stories [...] this story has entered History and the primary world; **the desire and aspiration of sub-creation has been raised** to the fulfilment

---

[66] Including Tolkien himself, of course, whose original desire was to create a world in which his invented languages, "might seem real" (cf. *Letters* 205, 382[264–5], quoted at the beginning of Chapter I).

[67] *Letters* 89:142[101].

of Creation. [...] This story begins and ends in joy. It has pre-eminently the 'inner consistency of reality'. [...] For the Art of it has the supremely convincing tone of Primary Art, that is, of Creation. (*TOFS*:78=*TL*:72)

The Gospel story is, for Tolkien, the 'greatest fairy-story'; it is the one that "was also made to Be, to be true on the Primary Plane", "since the author of it is the supreme Artist and the Author of Reality" (*Letters* 89, 143[101]). Since all human stories are somehow connected to the Gospel 'fairy' story (just as glimpses of light are connected to the source of the light), the Gospel story (which is real in the primary sense) bestows reality upon all other human fairy-stories, past and future; it makes them capable of offering the perception of "how things really do work" and enables them to provide a "far-off gleam or echo of evangelium in the real world", to produce a joy that "has the very taste of primary truth" (*TOFS*:77–8=*TL*:71–3).[68] Therefore, through the Gospel story, God partakes of other human stories, integrating all of them in the single, multi-plane reality of Creation and His (shared) Authoriality. As Tolkien concludes: "Art has been verified. God is the Lord, of angels, and of men – and of elves. Legend and History have met and fused" (*TOFS*:78=*TL*:73).

An important consequence of the miracle of realisation is that, because sub-creations are given the same ontological status as the sub-creator, sub-creators can actually enter into their works, with a sort of meta-artistic *mise-en-abyme*, which is itself a robust description of the storyline of the Gospel story (God's incarnation within His creation) and which is an important theme of Tolkien's mythology, as

[68] Cf. IV.3.4.

we have seen (cf. V.1.7). This *mise-en-abyme* is the experience of the Valar, who desired to enter the reality Arda stunned by the wonder of its beauty;[69] it is also the experience of Niggle, who literally enters his artwork to contemplate his Tree. This is also the experience of Tolkien, who hinted his wish that the Creator would give Reality to his secondary world ("on any plane"),[70] and who approached it, especially in his final years, as a real world to study, love, and contemplate.[71] This is also the experience of his son and editor Christopher, who confessed that he found his father's mythology (which he himself was editing) to be no less real than primary tales and indeed real events; as put in an interview, he "grew up in Middle-earth and found the cities of *The Silmarillion* 'more real than Babylon'".[72] This leads me to consider another aspect of God's intervention in sub-creation: the gift of ramification.

VI.2.3 The Gift of Ramification and the Transcending Vocation of the Sub-creator

Niggle's Tree is not 'realised' in a vacuum – it is not an autonomous or self-referential entity; rather, its realisation coincides with its integration within a larger

---

[69] Cf. *Letters* 200:374[259] "Those who became most involved in this work of Art [...] became so engrossed with it, that when the Creator made it real [...] they **desired to enter into it**, from the beginning of its 'realization.'"

[70] Cf. *Letters* 153:284[189] "It is only [...] an incompletely imagined world, a rudimentary 'secondary'; but if it pleased the Creator to give it (in a corrected form) Reality on any plane, then **you would just have to enter it.**"

[71] Cf. II.2.2.2, II.2.2.3, V.1.1.

[72] As quoted by John Garth in his obituary for Christopher Tolkien (*The Guardian*, 20/01/2020).

landscape that is inhabited by other creatures that enjoy its presence:

The birds were building in the Tree. Astonishing birds: how they sang! They were mating, hatching, growing wings, and flying away singing into the Forest, even while he looked at them. For now he saw that the Forest was there too, opening out on either side, and marching away into the distance. The Mountains were glimmering far away. (*LN*:110)

Niggle's Tree is only one Tree within a buzzing Forest surrounded by Mountains "glimmering far away" or one Tale within the "seamless Web of Story" (cf. IV.3.2), only one Leaf within the single Tree of Tales (cf. IV.3.3). In a letter (248) commenting on the origin of the volume *Tree and Leaf* (collecting *Leaf by Niggle* and *On Fairy-Stories*), Tolkien acknowledges that this latter image, which refers to the single but variously revived Creation of God, is closely related to Niggle's story. Tolkien explains that the decision to put these works together under the title *Tree and Leaf* derived from the relationship of *Leaf by Niggle* with two key passages of *On Fairy-Stories* (and the "keyword effoliation", in particular):

It is easy for the student to feel that with all his labour he is collecting only a few leaves […] from the countless foliage of the Tree of Tales, with which the Forest of Days is carpeted. (*TOFS*:66=*TL*:56)

The Christian. […] may now, perhaps, fairly dare to guess that in Fantasy he may actually assist in the effoliation and multiple enrichment of creation. (*TOFS*:79=*TL*:73)

The third important gift bestowed by God to sub-creators is that he integrates their imagined Trees into his Own creative Forest. God grafts sub-created Leaves into His own Tree of Tales or, as Tolkien (apparently) puts it in a passage from *Fate and Free Will* quoted earlier (VI.1.2), he "ramifies" (if the text is correct) "a story or tale as an excerpt from the total drama of which Eru is the Author or as that Drama itself" (*NME* 2.11:230). The outcome of God's grafting or ramification is that the sub-creator's artistic endeavour is no longer a 'private vice', but is rather 'hallowed' and 'enhanced' into an important task, namely to "assist in the effoliation and multiple enrichment of creation" (*TOFS*:79=*TL*:73) and to pay tribute "to the infinity of God's potential variety", making "things not found within recorded time" (to use other analogous expression used by Tolkien in *Letters* 153 and his meta-literary poem *Mythopoeia*):

I should have said that liberation 'from the channels the creator is known to have used already' is the fundamental function of 'sub-creation', a tribute **to the infinity of His potential variety**, one of the ways in which indeed it is exhibited (*Letters* 153:283[188])[73]

> Blessed are the legend-makers with their rhyme
> **of things not found within recorded time.**
> They **have seen Death and ultimate defeat,**
> and yet **they would not in despair retreat,**
> but oft to victory have turned the lyre
> and kindled hearts with legendary fire,
> illuminating Now and dark Hath-been
> with light of suns **as yet by no man seen.** (*Myth*:88–9)

---

[73] Cf. IV.3.3. For the idea that God's Creation is inherently incomplete to accommodate the participation of sub-creators and related theological debates, see Hart 2013:chapter 5.

As these passages also imply, the enhancement of human sub-creations implies and results in a criss-crossing of ontological planes (cf. IV.2), since human sub-creators are capable of breaking (and indeed are called to break) the boundaries of the plane to which they belong (the 'primary' one) and of crossing into another one, "breaking free from the channels already used [...] in this world", where they find things beyond "recorded time", "as yet by no man seen". Human sub-creations, therefore, are sites of ontological intersection, pathways or joints that connect one plane to another.[74] This can be a lower plane (e.g. the sub-creative plane of Tolkien's world), but also, arguably, a higher one (the transcendent reality of God).

There are a few hints in Tolkien's texts that suggest that human sub-creators are also capable of crossing (and are called to cross) into higher realities (i.e. to transcend their own ontological plane). These include, for instance, the idea of a human vocation driven by insatiable desire "to cross the Sea", which is a capital motive in Tolkien's mythology,[75] and has important meta-literary implications (given that sub-creations originate from and express

[74] In an important letter to his Polish friend Professor Przemysław Mroczkowski, still unpublished (*TCG* 543, 20–26/1/1964), Tolkien explicitly talks of a "simultaneity of different planes of reality touching one another", in relation to his idea that literature can never express everything in open terms (what I called the 'poetics of cloaking' in Chapter III). This is because, as Tolkien argues in the same letter, no construction of the human mind can englobe "all that there is". On this see further III.3.3 and cf. also a passage from *TCG* 464 (1961) in which Tolkien discusses the 'mystery' of Tom Bombadil as an example of an element opening as "window into some other system", which always must exist in any imagined world.

[75] Cf. esp. I.2.5.2, III.3.3.

this sort of desire). Another suggestion of human ability to cross to the higher plane is the notion that Eru's redemption of Arda will ultimately require the mysterious involvement of Men, through their acceptance of death. As we have seen (V.1.4, V.1.5), death is the specific gift given by Eru that allows Men only to "escape the circle of the world" (i.e. the boundaries of their lower plane).[76] Death allows humankind to join Him in another, higher Reality and eventually helps Him to heal "all the griefs of Arda"; this is a process that somehow recalls the sub-creative trajectory of the legend-makers of *Mythopoeia*, who turn their lyre to victory having seen "death and ultimate defeat".

Moreover, since the healing of this secondary plane is also closely related to the death and resurrection of Christ, and since all human fairy stories are somehow connected to this primary and yet 'higher' event, one can infer that, for Tolkien, the ontological criss-crossing of sub-creations has a double, paradoxical and yet complementary, direction. It is indeed by creating new secondary planes that human sub-creators are also able to transcend their primary reality and glimpse the higher Reality of God, thereby casting out branches (a 'ramification') that connect the different planes – different and yet all belonging to the same multi-plane Creation (cf. III.3.4).

In conclusion, Tolkien envisages Creation as an ongoing collaborative process, a 'ramification' or 'effoliation'

---

[76] Cf. also *Letters* 131:206[147], *Letters* 245:459[325] (freedom and liberation from the circle of the world). See Vaninskaya 2020, also referring to the Romantic concept of *Sehnsucht*.

criss-crossing different planes, through which God involves human sub-creators in His ongoing Story of Creativity and Redemption – a single Story that yet needs to be continuously renewed in the individual stories of human sub-creators (cf. IV.3.2 and IV.3.3).[77] As Tolkien explains in the epilogue of *Tolkien on Fairy-Stories*, the incarnation of God has not abrogated legends; rather, He has redeemed and hallowed the task and aspiration of the sub-creators, provided that they are ready to "work, [...] hope and die":

The Evangelium has not abrogated legends; it has hallowed them, especially the 'happy ending'. The Christian has still **to work**, with mind as well as body, to suffer, **hope, and die**; but he may now perceive that all his bents and faculties have a purpose, which can be redeemed. (*TOFS*:78–9=*TL*:73)

But with this emphasis on 'assistance', I will proceed to the next gift bestowed to Niggle's Tree.

VI.2.4 The Gift of Harmony and the Healing Power of Literature

A fourth gift concerns what one could call "the joys and healing of cooperation". Tolkien uses this expression to refer to the exercise of the power of mercy, which "is only delegated" and ideally "exercised [...] with cooperation of a Higher Authority" (*Letters* 131:182[127]). One of the most distinctive features of Niggle's Tree is that

---

[77] Some theologians have used the concept of 'participation' to refer to this Tolkienian idea; e.g. Hart 2013:chapter 5, Del Rincón Yohn 2021.

it is a collaborative work, a fruit of the unwitting cooperation between Niggle and Parish in their previous life
and also of their ongoing co-operation in Paradise, finally
acknowledged and harmonised:

'Of course!' he [Niggle] said. 'What I need is Parish. There
are lots of things about earth, plants, and trees that he knows
and I don't. This place cannot be left just as my private park.
I need help and advice: I ought to have got it sooner.' [...] As
they worked together, it became plain that Niggle was now the
better of the two at ordering his time and getting things done
[...] while Parish often wandered about looking at trees, and
especially at the Tree. [...] They went on living and working
together: I do not know how long. (*LN*:111–13)

The never-ending work on the Tree in "Niggle's
Parish" allows its sub-creators to communicate with each
other; it allows them to recognise each other's merits
and rejoice in the healing beauty of cooperation, which
is further extended to all the "astonishing birds" building
and singing on the Tree (cf. VI.2.3) as well as to those
visitors who are sent to "Niggle's Parish" by the Voices
for "refreshment". For Tolkien, another great gift of God
to human Art is that He transforms it into a space for
harmonious collaboration between creatures as different
as Niggle the (spiritual) Artist and Parish the (modern)
everyman for the benefit of all its recipients (the singing
birds, the convalescent visitors). If the miracle of artistic harmony has an eschatological dimension (cf. VI.2.5),
this is as a foretaste or glimpse in this world of the world
to come. Human literature, however imperfect, displays
a miraculous power of connecting different people and
providing them with a common space for healing; this

healing, as explained in *On Fairy-Stories*, is closely related to the idea of escaping from the prison of the self and regaining a relationship with 'otherness' (cf. III.3.2). As exemplified by the reception of *The Lord of the Rings*, literature can connect different authors with each other and with a multitude of readers. This is indeed the content of the 'gift' mentioned by Priscilla Tolkien in the passage quoted earlier in which she refers to her father's awed "gratitude for his having touched so many people's lives through the power of his writing".[78]

This connecting power of literature, however, is not just the fruit of an individual talent; rather, it also derives from a shared nature and a single origin, as Tolkien sings in *Mythopoeia*:

> man, sub-creator, the refracted light
> through whom is splintered from a single White
> to many hues, and endlessly combined
> in living shapes that move **from mind to mind**.
> (*TOFS*:64–5=*TL*:54–5=*Myth*:87)[79]

The shared derivative nature of all sub-creators allows them to connect with each other in harmony, just as, in the case of Niggle, the co-operation between him and Parish is only possible thanks to the intervention of the Voices. In this sense, "Niggle's Parish" is analogous to the Music of

---

[78] Cf. also *Letters* 87, to Christopher Tolkien, 25/10/1944:139[98] (expressing his gratitude for the "grace and fortune" that have allowed him, with *The Hobbit*, to provide 'a drop of water' to the "barren stony ground" of humanity) and *TCG* 756 (18/09/1967), in which Tolkien mentions his great pleasure and surprise to find out that many readers had the same feelings as him about what is appealing or moving.

[79] Cf. also *TOFS*:82 (=*TL*:78) "Literature works **from mind to mind** and is thus more progenitive."

the Ainur because it also features the co-operation of many different sub-creators under the authority of a Master Creator, whose creative power is primarily revealed in His miraculous power to connect them in harmony with each other, and ultimately with Himself.[80]

The harmony of collaboration bestowed to human sub-creators not only concerns their reciprocal relationship, but also their individual relationship with the Creator. As discussed (cf. esp. I.2.4 and II.2.2.5), literature, for Tolkien, already has an inherent collaborative, dialogic dimension in this world, since, as Eru says to the rebellious Melkor, "no theme may be played that hath not its uttermost source in me" (*Sil Ain.*:17).[81] Human sub-creators are never alone in their sub-creative work, but are always co-authors. Sub-creators already experience in their sub-creating activity (whatever the degree of their acceptance or awareness), "the joys and healing of cooperation". Already in this life, then, the experience of any (humble) sub-creator can be enlightened with the gift

[80] Cf. *Sil Ain.*:15 "as they listened they [...] increased **in unison and harmony** [...] 'I will now that ye make **in harmony together** a Great Music'".

[81] On the "dialogic and collaborative" nature of sub-creation according to Tolkien cf. the essays by Saxton 2013a and 2013b, comparing and contrasting Tolkien's and Bakhtin's positions, especially as regards the different views on God and the Sub-Creator, and their implications. In particular, as eloquently noted by Saxton (2013a:172) "While Barthes's Author-God is monologic *by definition*—he always issues "a single 'theological' meaning"—Tolkien breaks down the causal relationship between omnipotence and domination and, in its place, presents God as an omnipotent force that leaves space for the creativity and agency of his subjects". As a consequence, (ibid. 170–1) "Tolkien's fiction is not polyphonic in the strong sense". To put it in a different way, for Bakthin the Author-God is dead, for Tolkien He is alive, but His 'authority' is hidden, 'collaborative', and mediated.

of harmony with their Creator – a foretaste of the perfect harmony of eschatological collaboration.

In Niggle's story, we see traces of God's power of never-ending collaboration. Niggle and Parish are not just co-operating with each other, but also with the divine Voices who have bestowed reality to the Great Tree and summoned its authors to what will eventually be called "Niggle's Parish". As the Second Voice declares, "Niggle's Parish" is used as a holiday place for their 'healing project', in preparation for the Mountains of transcendence:

It is proving very useful indeed [...] [a]s a holiday, and a refreshment. It is splendid for convalescence; and not only for that, for many it is the best introduction to the Mountains. It works wonders in some cases. (*LN*:118)

With this idea of hallowed Art as "an introduction to the Mountains", I can move to the last gift bestowed by the Voices to Niggle's Tree, the final section of this chapter.

VI.2.5 The Gift of Prophecy and the Final Music

The final gift to human sub-creations proceeding from God's hallowing intervention in the mystery of literary creation consists in their transformation into "an introduction to the Mountains". In Niggle's story and Tolkien's literary works in general,[82] Mountains have a clear divine affiliation; to describe Niggle's Tree as an introduction to the Mountains is also to suggest that, for Tolkien, human

---

[82] Cf. III.2.1, III.3.3.

literature and art can become a propaedeutic anticipation of some form of divine reality or truth, an anticipation that can be described as a 'prophecy'. God's final gift to human sub-creators is thus the gift of prophecy, which mysteriously "arises" from imperfect sub-creations (cf. V.2). For Tolkien, any (successful) human story, if written with the non-possessive openness of Niggle, can become a prophecy of Divine Truth and, thereby, an imperfect yet significant 'foretaste' or 'glimpse' of Divine Reality – as in the case of Gandalf's Death and Resurrection.

Among these Truths and Realities, the Gospel story and especially the Resurrection have a primary place, as we have seen (cf. IV.3.4, V.2, VI.2.2). The Gospel story is, for Tolkien, the main object of literature's prophetic potential, the participation in which affords human stories their beauty, truth, and (one might add) redemptive value. For Tolkien, this is the Primary Fairy Story to which all other stories "look forward or backward" as prophecies *pre-* and *post-eventum*, secondary miracles, as it were, that are like echoes and glimpses of the primary Miracle.

The Gospel story and the Eucatastrophe of the Resurrection are certainly central for Tolkien but they are not the only elements of the Divine History glimpsed in human sub-creations. I think we can here attempt a final step and briefly mention another Divine Truth that Tolkien likely perceived as being anticipated and prophesied in his experience of sub-creation. This Truth has a meta-literary significance and is closely related to the "mystery of literary creation", of which it can be considered an eschatological fulfilment; this is the light glimpsed in the experience of worldly human sub-creations, the

Mountain to which Tolkien's Tree has offered an introduction. I am here referring to the eschatological vision
of Paradise, which, in several places, Tolkien describes in
meta-literary terms. Leaving to one side *Leaf by Niggle*, it
is said in the *Ainulindalë* that the primordial Music of the
Ainur (the archetypal sub-creation in Tolkien's mythology) is just the 'rough draft' of another perfect musical
event, which will take place at the end of time (cf. VII.2):

it has been said that a greater [music] still shall be made before
Ilúvatar by the choirs of the Ainur and the Children of Ilúvatar
after the end of days. Then the themes of Ilúvatar shall be
played aright, and take Being in the moment of their utterance,
for all shall then understand fully his intent in their part, and
each shall know the comprehension of each, and Ilúvatar shall
give to their thoughts the secret fire, being well pleased. (*Sil
Ain.*:15–16)

Similarly, in *Mythopoeia*, Tolkien explicitly describes
Paradise as a never-ending artistic event in which human
sub-creative activity will not cease, but will rather be perfected and will continue for ever its 'renewing' contribution:

> In Paradise perchance the eye may stray
> from gazing upon everlasting Day
> to see the day-illumined, and renew
> from mirrored truth the likeness of the True. [...]
> In Paradise they look no more awry;
> and though they make anew, they make no lie.
> Be sure they still will make, not being dead,
> and poets shall have flames upon their head,
> and harps whereon their faultless fingers fall:
> there each shall choose for ever from the All.
>
> (*Myth*:90)

375

In contrast to more static conceptions of Paradise (on which I will not elaborate here), Tolkien's vision of Paradise appears to be dynamic and meta-literary in nature; this vision consists a perfect artistic event, featuring the joyful, creative co-operation of all sub-creators under the one Great Author and – I dare to say – in the definitive 'fulfilment' and 'realisation' of all imaginative efforts of all human beings across history. This is because, as we have seen, for Tolkien "God is the Lord of angels, of men, and of elves". The Greatest Prophecy of human Sub-Creation is thus related to its very nature: Tolkien's self-reflected theory of literature, as a whole, can be considered as a prophecy of its eschatological redemption and enhancement, because

all tales may come true; and yet, at the last, redeemed, they may be as like and as unlike the forms that we give them as Man, finally redeemed, will be like and unlike the fallen that we know. (*TOFS*:79=*TL*:73)

VI.3 Explicit

I would like to end this long journey with a short quote from a dramatic letter written in the midst of the Second World War. In this letter, written in March 1941 and addressed to his son Michael, Tolkien does not talk about sub-creation, art, or literature. And yet I think this passage provides the best summary of all that I have tried to say in this last chapter, while also revealing how, for Tolkien, the dynamics of sub-creative 'death and resurrection' do not only apply to the Mystery of Literary Creation, but also to any human endeavour, of any kind and at any time. In Tolkien's vision, the possibility to 'graft' one's life into the Great Tale of Redemption, with its death and resurrection, is offered to any human being and especially to those (according to Tolkien) who accept the invitation to be guests at His Feast already in this world:

Out of the darkness of my life, so much frustrated, I put before you the one great thing to love on earth: the Blessed Sacrament […] There you will find romance, glory, honour, fidelity, and the true way of all your loves upon earth, and more than that: Death: by the Divine paradox, that which ends life, and demands the surrender of all, and yet by the taste (or foretaste) of which alone can what you seek in your earthly relationships (love, faithfulness, joy) be maintained, or take on that complexion of reality, of eternal endurance, which everyman's heart desires. (*Letters* 43:74[53])

VII

Epilogue

A Short Introduction to the Ainulindalë

∼

In conclusion to this book, I will not offer a summary, but rather a short introduction to a text that, in my view, encapsulates Tolkien's theory of literary sub-creation with power and beauty. This text is the *Ainulindalë*, Tolkien's cosmogonic myth opening *The Silmarillion*. It presents the narrative of the creation of Tolkien's secondary world, framed as an artistic event – a polyphonic concert with God as its composer and director. Given the *Ainulindalë*'s obvious meta-literary significance, often acknowledged by Tolkien, this text has already been referred to several times in the book, but I now invite readers to (re)read it for themselves. I believe that the *Ainulindalë* provides the best conclusion possible for my investigation, as it encapsulates all of Tolkien's experiences, intuitions, and views about literary (sub-)creation in a single beautiful story. Here, I only provide a short presentation of the textual history of this myth (VII.1) and a brief overview of its content (VII.2), highlighting some key passages useful for recalling all six chapters of *Tolkien and the Mystery of Literary Creation*.

VII.1 Textual History

The *Ainulindalë* (the Music of the Ainur in Quenya, the language of the high Elves) is the creation myth that frames and sets in motion the history of Tolkien's secondary world, Eä or Arda. It survives in several versions of different length and textual sophistication. The myth's inception can be traced back to the 1910s,[1] and Tolkien continued to tinker with it until at least the late 1950s. Five main redactions of the text are preserved: the first (A) was originally written between 1918 and 1920, while Tolkien was working for the Oxford English Dictionary, and was incorporated in the *Book of the Lost Tales (BLT1* 2:52–63); another (B) is preserved in a manuscript dating to the mid-1930s (*LR*:155–66); this text was heavily rewritten (C) in the late 1940s (*MR Ain.*:8–29), on the basis of a previous redaction of the myth, now almost completely lost (cf. *MR Ain.*:39–44); this revised text (B + C) was then copied into a beautiful illuminated manuscript, partly written in Old English script (D) (*MR Ain.*:29–39), which was subsequently emended in several layers. The text (E) eventually printed by Christopher Tolkien in the 1977 *Silmarillion* (pp.15–22) reflects these later emendations, with only minor editing interventions. Because of its 'canonical' nature, this is the textual version on which the following analysis is based and from which I will quote, without providing page numbers for each citation, given the relative brevity of the text (less than eight pages).

There are many and often major divergences between these different redactions; in particular, these include

---

[1] John Garth (2022) compellingly dates the composition of the first version of the *Ainulindalë* to 1917 (i.e. around the same time when the other early stories in Tolkien's *legendarium*, particularly the *Fall of Gondolin*, were composed), two years earlier than was normally believed (including by both J. R. R. and Christopher Tolkien).

the shape of the world (flat versus round) and the time of Melkor's arrival into it (together with or before the other Valar). These divergences are related to some of Tolkien's deep concerns about life and literature, and they reveal the development of his literary 'theory' and theological views. The main elements of the myth are, however, present in the earliest draft and are developed in the following versions. Besides the general notion of a musical cosmogony, these consistent elements include the myth's primal concern for "the relation of the One, the transcendental Creator, to the Valar [...] and their part in ordering and carrying out the Primeval Design" (*Letters* 257:485[345]). The complex and dramatic relationship between Creator and sub-creators is at the heart of Tolkien's 'theory', and the *Ainulindalë*, with its meta-literary implications, is a crucial text in which he investigated and reflected on this question.

VII.2 Structure and Content

The *Ainulindalë* can be described as an incomplete symphony in three movements, introduced by a double Prelude and containing a prophecy of a final, definitive movement "after the end of the days".[2] Each movement

---

2 At *MR Athr.*:336 Tolkien describes what I call Prelude as a double event, and thereby distinguishes five stages in the *Ainulindalë*: a. The Creation of the Ainur (= Prelude 1); b. The communication of Eru's Design to the Ainur (= Prelude 2); c. The Great Music ("a rehearsal" that remained in the stage of thought and imagination) (= first movement); d. The 'Vision' of Eru ("a foreshadowing of possibility") (= second movement); e. The Achievement, still ongoing (= third movement).

corresponds to a different instantiation of the same sub-creative event, with some important differences.

The Prelude gives immediate prominence to the Ainur, the "offspring of Eru's thought" and the Ur-Artists with and through whom Eru will bring about his Creation.[3] Upon their primordial creation (Prelude 1), the Ainur are called by Eru to sing on the musical themes He propounds to them (Prelude 2). At first, they sing individually, without clearly comprehending the music of their brothers. However, by listening to each other, they gradually come to a "deeper understanding" and increase "in unison and harmony". From the very beginning, the Ainur's art (in analogy with Eru's Creation) is presented as an ongoing co-operative activity, with the music of each Ainu called to harmonise gradually with that of his brothers and, ultimately, in accordance with Eru's over-arching theme. After this initial 'tuning-up', Eru calls the Ainur to participate in a single Music, whose "mighty theme" He declares to them, to their great amazement, and which they will 'perform' in three stages.

The first stage (or movement of the 'symphony') is purely aural: the Ainur participate in a majestic polyphonic concert; under Eru's inspiration, they are invited to "show forth their powers in adorning", making "in harmony together a Great Music". Through the echo of the voices of the Ainur, Eru begins to fill the Void with Being; in Tolkien's vision, this act is immediately associated with a musical metaphor: the harmonious Sound

---

[3] In meaningful contrast with the biblical Genesis, Tolkien's cosmogonic myth is distinctively sub-creative, and thus meta-artistic, framing divine Creation as a multi-plane collaborative artwork.

of Creation, whose power of attraction will eventually also affect Elves and Men. However, the harmony of the Music is soon broken. Three times, Ilúvatar proposes a theme, and three times, Melkor, the most powerful of the Ainur, introduces "matters of his own imagining that were not in accord with the theme of Ilúvatar", desiring to add greater glory and power to his part. This sows discord among the Ainur and disharmony into the Music. The first and second time, Melkor's cacophony is corrected by Eru, who introduces in turn a new theme into the Music that strives with Melkor's sound by taking its notes and weaving them "into its own solemn pattern". The third cacophony is concluded by Eru's direct intervention; he interrupts the Music with "one chord, deeper than the Abyss, higher than the Firmament" and warns Melkor that no one can alter the music against his will.

In the second movement, once the Music has finished, Eru shows the Ainur a visual rendition of their sub-creation ("giving them sight where before was only hearing"); he therefore provides a sort of expanded, explicated reiteration of what they have sung ("that ye may see what ye have done"). Essentially, this vision is a cinematic projection of the history of Tolkien's secondary world, and is aided by Eru's commentary. In his description of the vision, Eru directs the Ainur's attention to the visual renditions of their musical imaginations (e.g. water); shows how these have been affected by Melkor's cacophonic interventions (e.g. "bitter cold immoderate"); and reveals how they have eventually been amended creatively by Himself, in collaboration with the other Ainur ("the cunning work of frost", the clouds, which result from the co-operation of the Ainur Manwë and Ulmo). Yet this vision remains incomplete, both because Eru interrupts the projection before it reaches its conclusion, and, more importantly, because "in every age there come forth things that are new and have no foretelling". The Children of Ilúvatar are among these new creations; indeed, the Ainur "saw with amazement" their coming into Arda and perceived them as "things other than themselves, strange and free, wherein they saw the mind of Ilúvatar reflected anew". In their contemplation, the Ainur are filled with love for the Children and "become enamoured of the beauty of the vision and engrossed in the unfolding of the World".

At this point, Eru ceases to provide the vision and the third movement begins, in which Eru acknowledges and fulfils the hidden desire of the Ainur. He thus decides to give being to the Ainur's Music, "even as ye yourselves and yet other", and the history of the world (*Eä*) properly begins, not merely as an aural event or vision, but as a proper reality. In a meta-literary move, some of the Ainur decide to enter this new world and become the Valar: their sub-creative work restarts from the very beginning, since they perceive "that the World had been but fore-shadowed and foresung, and they must achieve it". Thus, the sub-creative event of the Ainur is repeated for the third time, but this time they are no longer external to it: as spiritual beings yet forever bounded in their World, the Valar continue their work of sub-creation with more awareness and understanding than in the previous instantiations; while resisting the ongoing corruptions of Melkor, they assist with the growth and development of their world in an effort to prepare a habitation for the coming of the Children of Ilúvatar. Because of Melkor, even this third realised sub-creation of the Ainur is not perfect, and "nowhere and in no work was their will and purpose wholly fulfilled". It is prophesied that the full realisation of the Music will be achieved in a future eschatological sub-creative event "after the end of days", when the "choirs of the Ainur and the Children of Ilúvatar" will make an even great music and the original themes of Ilúvatar "shall be played aright".

The meta-literary significance of this myth is self-evident and often acknowledged by Tolkien. There are even some hints that suggest a specific, overarching reference to his own sub-creative work: in particular, the moment in which Eru ceases to provide the vision at the end of the second movement clearly corresponds to the beginning of the Fourth Age, when *The Lord of the Rings* ends;[4] it is as if Tolkien had the same (fore)knowledge of the Ainur and could likewise not see through his sub-creation to "the Later Ages or the ending of the World". More generally, the myth encapsulates all key features of Tolkien's vision of "the mystery of literary sub-creation". I briefly present them here, roughly following the same structure of this book.

First, the Music is primarily described as an aesthetic event, filled with themes gradually gathering "new beauty". This pleases Eru, who is "glad that through [the Valar] great beauty has been wakened into song"; it also pleases the Ainur, who eventually become "enamoured with its beauty". The Ainur initially approach the Music as only a 'gratuitous' aesthetic event, without knowing

---

[4] *Sil Ain.*:20 "the vision ceased ere the fulfilment of the Dominion of Men and the fading of the Firstborn [...] the Valar have not seen as with sight the Later Ages or the ending of the World".

"that it had any purpose beyond its own beauty". The Ainur's creativity is thus not primarily for any utilitarian purpose, but simply results from the joy and beauty of making itself – which fills the Void with Being. Together with this aesthetic primacy, the myth also places great emphasis on the individual sub-creative desires of the Ainur, which are cherished and integrated by Eru into His purposes.

Second, this Music has a (hidden) purpose, for the benefit of the Children of Ilúvatar, whose unexpected arrival the Ainur contemplate "with amazement"; in fact, the Ainur eventually perceive that "[i]n the labour of their music [they] had been busy" in the preparation of "the habitation of the Children of Ilúvatar". Thus, the purpose of the Music is to assist Eru in His Creation, providing a dwelling for other creatures that Eru will embed within it (and this is what is also alluded to, arguably, in the description of the Ainu Manwë as "the chief instrument of the second theme"). The Valar's sub-creation channels and hosts the new life directly created by Eru; for this reason, this new life is, for the Ainur, something inherently 'other', which fills them with wonder – it is, as Tolkien glosses in a letter, like "a story composed by some-one else".[5] This 'otherness' becomes especially clear to the Ainur in the second and third movements, when "this World began to unfold its history, and it seemed to them that it lived and grew". Another important facet of this 'otherness' is the Ainur's incomplete knowledge of it,

---

[5] *Letters* 131:206[146] "[*the Valar*] perceived [*the cosmogonical drama*] first as a drama (that is as in a fashion we perceive a story composed by some-one else), and later as a 'reality'".

since "to none but himself has Ilúvatar revealed all that he has in store".

Third, the Ainur's sub-creation develops into and is fully realised as a proper fostering of the Children inhabiting it, "things other than themselves, strange and free". This fostering is the main content and goal of the third movement, in which some of the Ainur decide to enter covertly into the created world and be bound for ever to it. There, they are "drawn [...] by love of the Children of Ilúvatar" and aim to "achieve", in Time, what they had foreshadowed and foresung; there, they labour "together in the ordering of the Earth" and "prepare it for the coming of the Firstborn". In doing so, they must protect the freedom of the Children and thereby resist Melkor's desire "to subdue to his will both Elves and Men [...] and to be a master over other wills". In contrast, "the delight and pride" of Ainur such as Aulë is "in the deed of making and the thing made, and neither in possession nor in his own mastery".

Fourth, the *Ainulindalë* articulates a complex web of interlacing planes of sub-creation; each plane has a different ontological status and degree of perfection and enacts a different role and level of awareness on the part of the sub-creators. The Music of the Ainur is repeated three times; to this, one should add the initial proposition of the theme by Ilúvatar in the prelude and the final perfected music. The Ainur grow to understand the significance of their relationship with sub-creation. At first, the Ainur sing without fully understanding what they are doing; they are unaware of the independent nature of their music. Gradually, they begin to perceive the 'otherness' of their sub-creation and its purpose; despite lacking full knowledge, they wonder at the life of the Children and at the mind of Ilúvatar "reflected anew" in them. Finally, with a sort of sub-creative *mis-en-abyme*, the Ainur directly enter their sub-creation, understanding that their sub-creative vocation is inherently collaborative and that it consists in fostering the Children of Ilúvatar (themselves Created sub-creators). This sub-creative project (Arda) will then be completed at the end of time; transcending their own plane, the Children of Ilúvatar will join to perfect the choirs of the Ainur, and Eru's themes will "take Being in the moment of their utterance". Thus, each single instantiation of the sub-creation is prophetic of the next and provides an exegesis of the previous. Indeed, Eru participates in and connects all of these planes, and His creatures are called to move between these planes for their mutual benefit, eventually joining Him for the final Music, when "all shall understand fully his [Eru's] intent in their part, and each shall know the comprehension of each, and Ilúvatar shall give to their thoughts the secret fire, being well pleased".

Finally, nearing the core of the "mystery of literary creation", Eru maintains supreme Authority over the sub-creation and the Ainur initially acknowledge this supremacy with a primordial act of sub-creative humility ("the glory of its beginning and the splendour of its end amazed the Ainur, so that they bowed before Ilúvatar and were silent"). The Music of the Ainur is an 'inspired' event in which Eru participates in all of its stages. In fact, Eru creates the Ainur in the first place, endowing them with their sub-creative powers and enkindling them with the "Imperishable Flame"; he invites them to sing about the themes that He propounds, and, most notably,

He continues to interfere with their Music, adding new themes to it (i.e. "things that do not proceed from the past"), enhancing it with a new layer of ontology (first visual, and then real), and continually supporting the Ainur's ongoing sub-creative activity. Eru does not simply grant the Ainur a share in His creative power, sending them forth and remaining Himself removed from the outcome. The Ainur's gift of creativity is not autonomous or isolated; rather, it requires collaboration with similarly inspired sub-creators in mutual enrichment; creativity ultimately depends on Eru's thought as the source and inspiration for the Ainur's creativity, as Eru explicitly says to Melkor at the end of the first 'movement': "no theme may be played that hath not its uttermost source in me". Eru is the ultimate source of all sub-creation in the same way that a spring is the source of a water's continuous flow. This explains why even the Ainur's most secret, individual thoughts – "all those things which it may seem he himself devised or added" – are revealed as "a part of the whole and tributary to its glory".[6]

The Creative Power through which Eru participates in sub-creation, and integrates the different parts into the whole, is the Imperishable Flame or Secret Fire. Indeed, this is precisely what Melkor tries to seize by endeavouring to "interweave matters of his own imagining that were not in accord with the theme of Ilúvatar" and "to conceive thoughts of his own unlike those of his brethren". But since the Fire "is with Ilúvatar", Melkor could

---

[6] Cf. also *BLT1* 2:59 where similar words are used by Eru to refer to the evil deeds and works of Men, which eventually will only 'redound to His glory', and be a tributary to the beauty of His world.

not find it. The sub-creator's attempt to separate himself from his creative source and thereby "bring into Being things of his own" coincides with the refusal to hearken to other sub-creators and to be "a part of the whole"; the desire to master other wills and "increase the power and glory of the party assigned to himself" is bound to fail. The mystery of literary creation will always remain a mystery of collaboration and integration, for, as Eru says to Melkor, whoever tries to alter the music against His wishes "shall prove but mine instrument in the devising of things more wonderful, which he himself hath not imagined".

BIBLIOGRAPHY

Primary Sources and Abbreviations

Primary texts are cited by page number from the given edition (e.g. LN:111–13 = Leaf by Niggle pp.111–13), unless otherwise indicated.

All texts by J. R. R. Tolkien are reprinted by permission of HarperCollins Publishers Ltd © (year as per the following list).

ATB	*The Adventures of Tom Bombadil and Other Verses from the Red Book.* With illustrations by P. Baynes. Edited by C. Scull and Wayne G. Hammond. London: HarperCollins, 2014.
BL	*Beren and Lúthien.* Edited by Christopher Tolkien. London: HarperCollins, 2017.
BLT1	*The Book of Lost Tales, Part One.* (*HME* 1, 1983). Cited by chapter and page.
BLT2	*The Book of Lost Tales, Part Two.* (*HME* 2, 1984). Cited by chapter and page.
FG	*The Fall of Gondolin.* Edited by Christopher Tolkien. London: HarperCollins, 2018.
FN	*The Fall of Númenor.* Edited by Brian Sibley. London: HarperCollins, 2022.
HDWM	*J.R.R. Tolkien: The Hobbit: Drawings, Watercolors, and Manuscripts.* Exhibition Catalogue. Marquette University, 1987.
HME	*The History of Middle-earth.* Twelve volumes. Edited by Christopher Tolkien. London: HarperCollins, 1983–96.

Hobbit   *The Hobbit*. 5th edn. London: HarperCollins, 1995 [1st edition 1937, 2nd revised edition 1951]. Cited by chapter and page.

LB   *The Lays of Beleriand*. (*HME* 3, 1985). Edited by Christopher Tolkien. London: Allen & Unwin 1985. Cited by chapter and page.

Letters   *The Letters of J.R.R. Tolkien: Expanded and Revised Edition*. Edited by Humphrey Carpenter, with the assistance of Christopher Tolkien. London: HarperCollins 2023 [1st edition 1981: Allen & Unwin]. Cited by number of letter and page, with page of the 1981 edition in square brackets (e.g. *Letters* 180:336[231] = *Letters* no. 180, p.336 in 2023 edition = p.231 in 1981 edition). Addressees and date of the letter are normally indicated, except for the following letters that are cited several times in the book:

Letters 25, to the Editor of the 'Observer', February 1938

Letters 43, to Michael Tolkien, 6–8/03/1941

Letters 69, to Christopher Tolkien, 14/05/1944

Letters 89, to Christopher Tolkien, 7–8/11/1944

Letters 96, to Christopher Tolkien, 30/01/1945

Letters 109, to S. Unwin, 31/07/1947

Letters 131, to Milton Waldman, late 1951

Letters 144, to N. Mitchison, 25/04/1954

Letters 153, to Peter Hastings (draft), September 1954

Letters 156, to R. Murray SJ, 4/11/1954

Letters 163, to W. H. Auden, 7/06/1955

Letters 165, to the Houghton Mifflin Co. June 1955

Letters 180, to Mr Thompson, 14/01/1956

Letters 181, to M. Straight, January or February (?) 1956

Letters 183, Notes on W. H. Auden's review of The Return of the King, 1956

Letters 186, to Joanna de Bortadano (draft), April 1956

Letters 187, to H. Cotton Minchin, April 1956,

Letters 192, to A. Ronald, 27/07/1956

Letters 199, to C. Everett, 24/06/1957

Letters 200, to R. Bowen, 25/06/1957

Letters 203, to H. Schiro, 17/11/1957

Letters 205, to Christopher Tolkien, 21/02/1958

Letters 208, to C. Ouboter, 10/04/1958

Letters 211, to R. Beare, 14/10/1958

Letters 212, Draft of a continuation to the above letter (not sent)

Letters 241, to J. Neave, 8–9/09/1962

Letters 246, to E. Elgar (draft), September 1963

Letters 247, to Colonel Worskett, 20/09/1963

Letters 297, to Mr. Rang (draft), August 1967

Letters 257, to C. Bretherton, 16/07/1964

Letters 328, to C. Batten-Phelps (draft), Autumn 1971

Letters 329, to P. Szabó Szentmihályi (draft), October 1971

Unpublished letters are referred to according to the numbering of the *Tolkien's Collector Guide* (*TCG*, see below).

LN   *Leaf by Niggle*, originally published in *Dublin Review* (January 1945): pp.46–61. Cited from *TL* (pp.93–118).

LotR   *The Lord of the Rings*. 50th anniversary edition. London: HarperCollins, 2004. Cited by book, chapter and page.

LR   *The Lost Road and Other Writings* (*HME* 5, 1987). Cited by part, chapter and page.

MC   *The Monsters and the Critics and Other Essays*. London: Allen & Unwin, 1983. *Beow.*=*Beowulf: The Monsters and the Critics*

MR	*Morgoth's Ring* (*HME* 10, 1993). *Ain.=Ainulindalë* (pp.3–44); *Athr.=Athrabeth Finrod Ah Andreth* (pp.303–66).
Myth	*Mythopoeia*. Cited from *TL* (pp.85–90).
NME	*The Nature of Middle-earth*. Edited by Carl F. Hostetter. London: HarperCollins, 2021. Cited by part, chapter and page.
NN	*The Name Nodens*. First published as an Appendix (pp.132–7) in *Report on the Excavation of the Prehistoric, Roman, and Post-Roman Site in Lydney Park, Gloucestershire*, by R.E.M. and T.V. Wheeler (London 1932). Reprinted in *Tolkien Studies* 4 (2007), 177–83.
PME	*The Peoples of Middle-earth*. (*HME* 12, 1996). Cited by chapter and page.
RS	*The Return of the Shadow* (*HME* 6, 1988). Cited by chapter and page.
SD	*Sauron Defeated* (*HME* 9, 1992). *Not.=The Notion Club Papers* (pp.145–327). Cited by part, chapter (except *Not.*) and page.
Sil	*The Silmarillion*. Edited by Christopher Tolkien. London: Allen & Unwin, 1977. *Ain.=Ainulindalë*; *Val.=Valaquenta*; *Ak.=Akallabêth*; *Ring.=Of the Rings of Power and the Third age*. Cited by chapter (except *Ain.*, *Val.*, *Ak.*, *Ring.*) and page.
SME	*The Shaping of Middle-earth*. (*HME* 4, 1986). Cited by chapter and page.
SWM	*Smith of Wootton Major*. Extended edition prepared by Verlyn Flieger. London: HarperCollins, 2005. [1st edition 1967]. *GK=Draft introduction to the Golden Key* (pp.89–96), *Ess.=Smith of Wootton Major Essay* (pp.111–45).
SV	*A Secret Vice: Tolkien on Invented Languages*. Edited by Dimitra Fimi and Andrew Higgins. Revised edition. London: HarperCollins, 2020 [1st edition 2016].

TCG	*Tolkien's Collector Guide* (www.tolkienguide.com/guide/letters/), used as a reference database for unpublished letters.
TCP	*The Collected Poems of J. R. R. Tolkien*, edited by C. Scull and Wayne G. Hammond. London: HarperCollins, 2024.
TI	*The Treason of Isengard* (*HME* 7, 1989). Cited by chapter and page.
TL	*Tree and Leaf.* Second edition. Including *On Fairy-Stories, Mythopoeia, Leaf by Niggle*, and *The Homecoming of Beorhtnoth*. London: Unwin Hyman, 1988.
TOFS	*Tolkien On Fairy-Stories*. Edited by Verlyn Flieger and Douglas A. Anderson. London: HarperCollins, 2008. [1st edition 1947, 2nd edition 1964].
TPR	*Tales from the Perilous Realm*. 2nd edition. London: HarperCollins, 2008.
UT	*Unfinished Tales of Númenor and Middle-earth*. Edited by Christopher Tolkien. London: Allen & Unwin, 1980. Cited by part, chapter, and page.
WJ	*The War of the Jewels* (*HME* 11, 1994). Cited by part and page.
WR	*The War of the Ring* (*HME* 8, 1990). Cited by part, chapter and page.

Secondary Sources

Adams, M. (2011a), 'Introduction', in Adams 2011b, 1–16.

Adams, M. (ed.) (2011b), *From Elvish to Klingon: Exploring Invented Languages*. Oxford and New York: Oxford University Press.

Agøy, N. I. (2007), 'Viewpoints, Audiences and Lost Texts in *The Silmarillion*', in Turner 2007a, 139–63.

Alfaiz, N. (2015), 'The Preservation of National Unity by [Dis]remembering the Past in Tolkien's The Hobbit and

The Lord of the Rings', in Croft, J. B. (ed.), *Baptism of Fire: The Birth of the Modern British Fantastic in World War I* (Altadena, CA: The Mythopoeic Press), 80–91.

Amendt-Raduege, A. M. (2006), 'Dream Visions in J.R.R. Tolkien's The Lord of the Rings', *Tolkien Studies* 3, 45–55.

Amendt-Raduege, A. M. (2018), *The Sweet and the Bitter': Death and Dying in J.R.R. Tolkien's The Lord of the Rings*. Kent, OH; The Kent State University Press.

Anderson, D. A. (2002), *The Annotated Hobbit: Revised and Expanded Edition*. Boston: Houghton Mifflin.

Anderson, D. A. (2005), 'Tom Shippey on J.R.R. Tolkien: A Checklist', *Tolkien Studies* 1, 17–20.

Arduini, R. and Testi, C. A. (eds.) (2012), *The Broken Scythe: Death and Immortality in the Works of J.R.R. Tolkien*. Zurich and Jena: Walking Tree.

Arduini, R. and Testi, C. A. (eds.) (2014), *Tolkien and Philosophy*. Zurich and Jena: Walking Tree.

Atherton, M. (2012), *There and Back Again: J. R. R. Tolkien and the Origins of The Hobbit*. London and New York: I.B. Tauris.

Auer, R. M. (2019), 'Sundering Seas and Watchers in the Water: Water as a Subversive Element in Middle-earth', in Fimi and Honegger 2019, 237–59.

Auerbach, E. (2016), 'Figura', in Porter, J. I. (ed.), *Time, History, and Literature: Selected Essays of Erich Auerbach* (Princeton: Princeton University Press), 65–113.

Baldick, C. (2008), *The Oxford Dictionary of Literary Terms*. 3rd ed. Oxford: Oxford University Press.

Barkley, C. (1995), 'Point of View in Tolkien', in Reynolds, P. and Goodnight, G. H. (eds.), *Proceedings of the J. R. R. Tolkien Centenary Conference 1992* (Milton Keynes and Altadena, CA: The Mythopoeic Press), 256–62.

Barrs, J. (2013), *Echoes of Eden: Reflections on Christianity, Literature, and the Arts*. Wheaton, IL: Crossway.

Bassham, G. and Bronson, E. (eds.) (2013), *The Lord of the Rings and Philosophy*. Chicago and La Salle, IL: Open Court.

Battarbee, K. J. (ed.) (1993), *Scholarship and Fantasy*. Anglicana Turkuensia 12. Turku: University of Turku.

Beal, J. (2014), 'Orphic Powers in J.R.R. Tolkien's Legend of Beren and Lúthien', *Journal of Tolkien Research* 1, 1–25.

Beare, R. (2007), 'A Mythology for England', in Turner 2007a, 1–31.

Bennett, M. Y. (ed.) (2017), *Philosophy and Oscar Wilde*. Basingstoke: Palgrave Macmillan.

Bernthal, C. (2014), *Tolkien's Sacramental Vision: Discerning the Holy in Middle-earth*. Kettering, OH: Second Spring Books.

Bertoglio, C. (2021), *Musical Scores and the Eternal Present: Theology, Time, and Tolkien*. Eugene, OR: Pickwick Publications.

Birns, N. (2015), 'Authorship and the Vita Contemplativa: Tolkien's Self-depiction in The Lord of the Rings', in Burke and Burdge 2015, 153–82.

Birns, N. (2023), *Literary Role of History in the Fiction of J. R. R. Tolkien*. London: Routledge.

Birzer, B. J. (2002), *J. R. R. Tolkien's Sanctifying Myth: Understanding Middle-earth*. Wilmington, DC: ISI Books.

Blackham, R. S. (2008), *Tolkien's Oxford*. Cheltenham: The History Press.

Blackham, R. S. (2011), *Tolkien and the Peril of War*. Cheltenham: The History Press.

Błaszkiewicz, B. (2013), 'Orality and Literacy in Middle-earth', in Kowalik 2013b, 29–46.

Bloom, H. (ed.) (2008), *J.R.R. Tolkien*. New York: Infobase.

Bogstad, J. M. and Kaveny, P. E. (eds.) (2011), *Picturing Tolkien: Essays on Peter Jackson's The Lord of the Rings Film Trilogy*. Jefferson, NC: McFarland.

Bowers, J. M. (2019), *Tolkien's Lost Chaucer*. Oxford: Oxford University Press.

Bowers, J. M. and Steffensen, P. (2024), *Tolkien on Chaucer, 1913–1959*. Oxford: Oxford University Press.

Bowman, M. R. (2006), 'The Story Was Already Written: Narrative Theory in *The Lord of the Rings*', *Narrative* 14, 272–93.

Bratman, D. (2006), 'The Artistry of Omissions and Revisions in *The Lord of the Rings*', in Hammond and Scull 2006a, 113–38.

Bratman, D. (2023), *Gifted Amateurs and Other Essays: On Tolkien, the Inklings, and Fantasy Literature*. Altadena, CA: The Mythopoeic Press.

Bray, S., Gavin, A. E., and Merchant, P. (eds.) (2008), *Re-Embroidering the Robe: Faith, Myth and Literary Creation Since 1850*. Newcastle: Cambridge Scholars.

Brémont, A. (2016), 'How to Slay a Dragon When You Are Only Three Feet Tall', in Pott 2016, 187–200.

Brljak, V. (2010), '*The Book of Lost Tales*: Tolkien as Metafictionist', *Tolkien Studies* 7, 1–34.

Bridgwater, S. (2010), 'Staying Home and Travelling: Stasis Versus Movement in Tolkien's Mythos', in Dubs and Kaščáková 2010, 19–40.

Bridgwater, S. (2015), 'Stay or Go: Some Reflections upon Stasis and Travelling in Tolkien's Mythos', in Collier 2015, 37–41.

Brückner, P. A. (2012), 'One Author to Rule Them All', in Klinger 2012a, 127–72.

Bueno Alonso, J. L. (ed.) (2022), *Tolkien in the 21st Century: Reading, Reception, and Reinterpretation*. Newcastle: Cambridge Scholars.

Bugajska, A. (2014), 'Scottish Ghosts, English Wraiths: The Supernatural Imagination of Macpherson and Tolkien', in Walczuk, A. and Witalisz, W. (eds.), *Old Challenges and New Horizons in English and American Studies* (Frankfurt: Peter Lang), 159–68.

Burke, J. and Burdge, A. (eds.) (2015), *Forgotten Leaves: Essays from a Smial*. Staten Island, NY: Myth Ink.

Burns, M. (2017), *Perilous Realms: Celtic and Norse in Tolkien's Middle-earth*, 2nd ed. Toronto: Toronto University Press [1st edition 2005].

Butler, C. (2013), 'Tolkien and Worldbuilding', in Hunt 2013, 106–20.

Caldecott, S. and Honegger, T. (eds.) (2008), *Tolkien's The Lord of the Rings: Sources of Inspiration*. Zurich and Jena: Walking Tree.

Caldecott, S. (2012), *The Power of the Ring: The Spiritual Vision Behind The Lord of the Rings*. 2nd ed. New York: Crossroad.

Caldecott, S. (2014), 'A New Light: Tolkien's Philosophy of Creation in The Silmarillion', *The Journal of Inklings Studies* 4, 67–85.

Campbell, L. (2011), *The Ecological Augury in the Works of JRR Tolkien*. Zurich and Jena: Walking Tree.

Carpenter, H. (1977), *J. R. R. Tolkien – A Biography*. London: HarperCollins.

Casagrande, C. (2022), *Friendship in the Lord of the Rings*. Edinburgh: Luna Press.

Caughey, A. (2022), 'The Hero's Journey', in Lee 2022a, 386–98.

Chance, J. (ed.) (2003), *Tolkien the Medievalist*. London and New York: Routledge.

Chance, J. (ed.) (2004), *Tolkien and the Invention of Myth: A Reader*. Lexington, KY: University Press of Kentucky.

Chance, J. and Siewers, A. (eds.) (2005), *Tolkien's Modern Middle Ages*. London: Palgrave Macmillan.

Chance, J. (2016), *Tolkien, Self and Other: "This Queer Creature"*. Basingstoke: Palgrave Macmillan.

Chandler, W. A. and Fry, C. L. (2017), 'Tolkien's Allusive Backstory: Immortality and Belief in the Fantasy Frame', *Mythlore* 35, 95–113.

Christensen, B. (2003), 'Gollum's Character Transformation in *The Hobbit*', in Lobdell 2003, 9–28.

Cianci G., and Harding, J. (2007), *T. S. Eliot and the Concept of Tradition*. Cambridge: Cambridge University Press.

Cilli, O. (2014), *Tolkien e l'Italia*. Rimini: Il Cerchio.

Cilli, O. (2023), *Tolkien's Library: An Annotated Checklist*. 2nd ed. Edinburgh: Luna Press [1st edition 2019].

Cilli, O., Smith, A. R. and Wynne, P. H. (2017), *J.R.R. Tolkien the Esperantist: Before the Arrival of Bilbo Baggins*. Barletta: Cafagna.

Collier, I. (ed.) (2015), *Journeys & Destinations: Proceedings of the 22nd Tolkien Society Seminar, Sir John Soane's Museum, Lincoln's Inn Fields, London, June 27th 2009*. Wolverhampton: The Tolkien Society.

Collins, R. (2000), '"Ainulindalë": Tolkien's Commitment to an Aesthetic Ontology' *Journal of the Fantastic in the Arts* 11, 257–65.

Conrad-O'Briain, H. and Hynes, G. (eds.) (2013), *Tolkien: The Forest and the City*. Dublin: Four Courts Press.

Cook, S. J. (2016), 'How to Do Things with Words: Tolkien's Theory of Fantasy in Practice', *Journal of Tolkien Research* 3.

Cristofari, C. (2012), 'The Chronicle without an Author: History, Myth and Narration in Tolkien's Legendarium', in Klinger 2012a, 173–90.

Coutras, L. (2016), *Tolkien's Theology of Beauty*. London: Palgrave Macmillan.

Croft, J. B. (2004), *War and the Works of J.R.R. Tolkien*. Westport, CT: Praeger.

Croft, J. B. (ed.) (2015), *Baptism of Fire: The Birth of the Modern British Fantastic in World War I*. Altadena, CA: The Mythopoeic Press.

Croft, J. B. (2017), 'The Name of the Ring; Or, There and Back Again', *Mythlore* 35, 81–94.

Croft, J. B. (2018), 'Doors into Elf-mounds: J.R.R. Tolkien's Introductions, Prefaces, and Forewords', *Tolkien Studies* 15, 177–95.

Croft, J. B. and Donovan, L. A. (eds.) (2015), *Perilous and Fair: Women in the Works and Life of J.R.R. Tolkien*. Altadena, CA: The Mythopoeic Press.

Croft, J. B. and Röttinger, A. (2019), *"Something Has Gone Crack": New Perspectives on J.R.R. Tolkien in the Great War*. Zurich and Jena: Walking Tree.

Currie, E. and Lewis, A. (2016), *On the Perilous Road: An Unauthorised Biography of J.R.R. Tolkien*. Scotts Valley, CA: Create Space.

Curry, P. (2004), *Defending Middle-earth: Tolkien, Myth and Modernity*. 2nd ed. Boston, MA: Houghton Mifflin.

Daniélou, J. (2018), *From Shadows to Reality: Studies in the Biblical Typology of the Fathers*. Transl. by M. Heintz. Jackson, MA: Ex Fontibus Company [1st ed. Paris 1950].

Davidsen, M. A. (2016), 'The Religious Affordance of Fiction: A Semiotic Approach', *Religion* 46, 521–49.

Davidsen, M. A. (ed.) (2018), *Narrative and Belief: The Religious Affordance of Supernatural Fiction*. London and New York: Routledge.

Del Rincón Yohn, M. (2021), 'J.R.R. Tolkien's Sub-creation Theory: Literary Creativity as Participation in the Divine Creation', *Church, Communication and Culture* 6, 17–33.

Denisoff, D. (2007), 'Decadence and Aestheticism', in Marshall, G. (ed.), *The Cambridge Companion to the Fin de Siècle* (Cambridge: Cambridge University Press), 31–52.

Devaux, M. (ed.) (2003a), *Tolkien: Les racines du légendaire. La Feuille de la Compagnie 2*. Geneva: Ad Solem.

Devaux, M. (2003b), 'Les anges de l'Ombre chez Tolkien: chair, corps et corruption', in Devaux 2003a, 191–245.

Devaux, M. (2007), 'The Origins of the Ainulindalë: The Present State of Research', in Turner 2007a, 81–110.

Devaux, M. (ed.) (2014), *J.R.R. Tolkien, l'effigie des Elfes. La Feuille de Compagnie 3*. Paris: Bragelonne.

Devaux, M. (2023), 'Hope and Its Meanings in the *Athrabeth* and Tolkien's Theological Dialogue', in Pezzini and O'Brien 2023, 127–42.

Devaux, M., Ferré, V., and Ridoux, C. (eds.) (2011), *Tolkien aujourd'hui: Colloque de Rambures 13–15 juin 2008*. Valenciennes: Pu De Valenciennes.

Devine, C. (2016), 'Fertility and Grace in *The Lord of the Rings*', *Mallorn* 57, 10–11.

Dickerson, M. T. (2003), *Following Gandalf: Epic Battles and Moral Victory in The Lord of the Rings*. Grand Rapids, MI: Revell, Baker.

Dickerson, M. T. (2007), 'Theological and Moral Approaches in Tolkien's Works', in Drout 2007a, 643–5.

Dickerson, M. T. (2011), 'Water, Ecology, and Spirituality in Tolkien's Middle-earth', in Kerry and Miesel 2011, 15–32.

Dickerson, M. T. (2012), *A Hobbit Journey: Discovering the Enchantment of J.R.R. Tolkien's Middle-earth*. Grand Rapids, MI: Brazos Press.

Dobie, R. J. (2024), *The Fantasy of J.R.R. Tolkien: Mythopoeia and the Recovery of Creation*. Washington, DC: The Catholic University of America Press.

Donovan, L. A. (ed.) (2015), *Approaches to Teaching Tolkien's The Lord of the Rings and Other Works*. New York: International Association for the Fantastic in the Arts.

Donovan, L. A. (2022), 'Middle-earth Mythology: An Overview', in Lee 2022a, 79–92.

Doyle, M. (2020), *Utopian and Dystopian Themes in Tolkien's Legendarium*. Lanham, MD: Lexington Books.

Driggers, T. (2023), *Queering Faith in Fantasy Literature: Fantastic Incarnations and the Deconstruction of Theology*. London: Bloomsbury.

Drout, M. D. C. (2004), 'Tolkien's Prose Style and its Literary and Rhetorical Effects', *Tolkien Studies* 1, 137–63.

Drout, M. D. C. (2005), 'Towards a better Tolkien criticism', in Eaglestone, R. (ed.), *Reading The Lord of the Rings: New Writings on Tolkien's Classics* (London and New York: Continuum), 15–28.

Drout, M. D. C. (ed.) (2007a), *J.R.R. Tolkien Encyclopedia*. New York: Routledge.

Drout, M. D. C. (2007b), 'J.R.R. Tolkien's Medieval Scholarship and its Significance', *Tolkien Studies* 4, 113–76.

Drout, M. D. C. (2013), 'The Tower and the Ruin: The Past in J.R.R. Tolkien's Works', in Conrad-O'Briain, and Hynes 2013, 175–90.

Drout, M. D. C., Hitotsubashi, N. and Scavera, R. (2014), 'Tolkien's Creation of the Impression of Depth', *Tolkien Studies* 11, 167–211.

Dubs, K. and Kaščáková, J. (eds.) (2010), *Middle-earth and Beyond: Essays on the World of J. R. R. Tolkien*. Newcastle: Cambridge Scholars.

duPlessis, N. M. (2018), '"Changed, Changed Utterly": The Implications of Tolkien's Rejected Epilogue to The Lord of the Rings', *Tolkien Studies* 15, 9–32.

duPlessis, N. M. (2019), 'On the Shoulders of Humphrey Carpenter: Reconsidering Biographical Representation and Scholarly Perception of Edith Tolkien', *Mythlore* 37, 39–74.

Duriez, C. (2012), 'What Made J.R.R. Tolkien Tick and Why Was He Called "Reuel?": The Importance of Tolkien Biography?', *Mallorn* 53, 22–25.

Duriez, C. (2015), *The Oxford Inklings: Lewis, Tolkien and Their Circle*. Oxford: Lion.

Eden, B. L. (2003), 'The "Music of the Spheres": Relationships between Tolkien's *The Silmarillion* and Medieval Cosmological and Religious Theory', in Chance 2003, 183–93.

Eden, B. L. (ed.) (2014), *The Hobbit and Tolkien's Mythology: Essays on Revisions and Influences*. Jefferson, NC: McFarland.

Edwards, R. (2012), *J.R.R. Tolkien: His Life, Work and Faith*. London: Catholic Truth Society.

Edwards, R. (2014), *Tolkien*. London: Robert Hale.

Eilmann, J. (2011), 'I Am the Song: Music, Poetry, and the Transcendent in J.R.R. Tolkien's Middle-earth', in Kerry and Miesel, 99–117.

Eilmann, J. and Turner, A. (eds.) (2013), *Tolkien's Poetry*. Zurich and Jena: Walking Tree.

Eilmann, J. (2017), *J.R.R. Tolkien, Romanticist and Poet*. Zurich and Jena: Walking Tree.

Eilmann, J. and Schneidewind, F. (eds.) (2019), *Music in Tolkien's Work and Beyond*. Zurich and Jena: Walking Tree.

Ellison, J. A. (1991), 'The 'Why', and the 'How': Reflections on "Leaf by Niggle"', in Reynolds, T. (ed.), *Leaves from the Tree: J.R.R. Tolkien's Shorter Fiction* (London: The Tolkien Society), 23–32.

Emerson, D. (2008), 'Tolkien and Moorcock: Achieving Literary Depth through Vertical and Horizontal Explorations of Time', in Wells 2008, 1.233–7.

Estes, D. (ed.) (2023), *Theology and Tolkien: Practical Theology*. Minneapolis, MN: Lexington Books and Fortress Academic.

Estes, D. (ed.) (2024), *Theology and Tolkien: Constructive Theology*. Minneapolis, MN: Lexington Books and Fortress Academic.

Ferrández Bru, J. M. (2018), *"Uncle Curro": J.R.R. Tolkien's Spanish Connection*. Edinburgh: Luna Press.

Ferré, V. (2022), 'The Son behind the Father: Christopher Tolkien as a Writer', in Ovenden and McIlwaine 2022, 53–69.

Filmer-Davies, (2007), 'Theology in *The Lord of the Rings*', in Drout 2007a: 645–6.

Fimi, D. (2008), *Tolkien, Race and Cultural History: From Fairies to Hobbits*. Basingstoke: Palgrave Macmillan.

Fimi, D. (2018), 'Language as Communication vs. Language as Art: J.R.R. Tolkien and Early 20th-Century Radical Linguistic Experimentation', *Journal of Tolkien Research* 5.

Fimi, D. and Higgins, A. (2020), *A Secret Vice: Tolkien on Invented Languages, Introduction and Notes*. London: HarperCollins. [1st edition 2016].

Fimi, D. and Honegger, T. M. (2019), *Sub-Creating Arda: World-Building in J.R.R. Tolkien's Work, Its Precursors and Its Legacies*. Zurich and Jena: Walking Tree.

Fisher, J. (ed.) (2011), *Tolkien and the Study of His Sources: Critical Essays*. Jefferson, NC: McFarland.

Flieger, V. (1997), *A Question of Time: J.R.R. Tolkien's Road to Faërie*. Kent, OH: The Kent State University Press.

Flieger, V. (2000), 'The Footsteps of Ælfwine', in Flieger and Hostetter 2000, 183–97.

Flieger, V. (2002), *Splintered Light: Logos and Language in Tolkien's World*, 2nd ed. Kent, OH: The Kent State University Press [1st edition 1983].

Flieger, V. (2004), 'A Mythology for Finland: Tolkien and Lönnrot as Mythmakers', in Chance 2004, 277–83.

Flieger, V. (2005), *Interrupted Music: The Making of Tolkien's Mythology*. Kent, OH: The Kent State University Press.

Flieger, V. (2006), 'Tolkien and the Idea of the Book', in Hammond and Scull 2006a, 283–99.

Flieger, V. (2007a), 'Frame Narrative', in Drout 2007a, 216–18.

Flieger, V. (2007b), 'The Curious Incident of the Dream at the Barrow: Memory and Reincarnation in Middle-earth', *Tolkien Studies* 4, 99–112.

Flieger, V. (2007c), 'When Is a Fairy Story a Faërie Story?: *Smith of Wootton Major*', in Segura and Honegger 2007, 57–70.

Flieger, V. (2009), 'The Music and the Task: Fate and Free Will in Middle-earth', *Tolkien Studies* 6, 151–81.

Flieger, V. (2012), *Green Suns and Faërie: Essays on Tolkien*. Kent, OH: The Kent State University Press.

Flieger, V. (2014a), 'Tolkien's French Connection', in Eden 2014, 70–77.

Flieger, V. (2014b), 'The Jewels, the Stone, the Ring, and the Making of Meaning', in Houghton et al. 2014, 65–77.

Flieger, V. (2014c), 'But What Did He Really Mean?', *Tolkien Studies* 11, 149–66.

Flieger, V. (2014d), 'Tolkien and the Philosophy of Language', in Arduini and Testi 2014, 73–84.

Flieger, V. (2020), 'The Arch and the Keystone', *Mythlore* 38, 7–19.

Flieger, V. (2022), '"The Lost Road" and "The Notion Club Papers": Myth, History, and Time-travel', in Lee 2022a, 140–51.

Flieger, V. and Hostetter, C. F. (ed.) (2000), *Tolkien's Legendarium: Essays on The History of Middle-earth*. Westport, CT and London: Greenwood.

Flieger, V. and Shippey, T. (2001), 'Allegory versus Bounce: Tolkien's Smith of Wootton Major', *Journal of the Fantastic in the Arts* 12, 188–200.

Fontenot, M. N. (2019), 'The Art of Eternal Disaster: Tolkien's Apocalypse and the Road to Healing', *Tolkien Studies* 16, 91–109.

Forest-Hill, L. (2013), 'Poetic Form and Spiritual Function: Praise, Invocation and Prayer in *The Lord of the Rings*', in Eilmann and Turner 2013, 91–116.

Forest-Hill, L. (2015), '"Hey Dol, Merry Dol": Tom Bombadil's Nonsense, or Tolkien's Creative Uncertainty? A Response to Thomas Kullmann', *Connotations* 25, 91–107.

Forest-Hill, L. (ed.) (2016), *The Return of The Ring: Proceedings of the Tolkien Society Conference 2012*, 2 vols. Edinburgh: Luna Press.

Fornet-Ponse, T. (2010), '"Strange and Free": On Some Aspects of the Nature of Elves and Men', *Tolkien Studies* 7, 67–89.

Fornet-Ponse, T. (2011), 'Intertextuality in Tolkien and (un)informed Reader: *The Lord [of] the Rings* and the *Silmarillion*', in Devaux, Ferré, and Ridoux 2011, 253–68.

Fornet-Ponse, T., Aubron-Bülles, M., and Eilmann, J. (eds.) (2014), *Natur und Landschaft in Tolkiens Werk*. Düsseldorf: Scriptorium Oxoniae.

Fornet-Ponse, T., Honegger, T., and Eilmann, J. (eds.) (2015), *Tolkien's On Fairy-Stories*. Düsseldorf: Scriptorium Oxoniae.

Fornet-Ponse, T., Honegger, T., and Eilmann, J. (eds.) (2016), *Tolkien's Philosophy of Language*. Düsseldorf: Scriptorium Oxoniae.

Forster, L. W. (1961), 'Tolkien', in *Lexikon der Weltliteratur im 20. Jahrhundert. Zweiter Band K–Z* (Freiburg: Herder), 1080–81.

Foster, R. (2022), *The Complete Guide to Middle-earth*. 3rd ed. London: HarperCollins [1st ed. 1971].

Freeh, H. L. (2015), 'On Fate, Providence, and Free Will in *The Silmarillion*', in Wood 2015, 51–77.

Freeman, A. M. (2022), *Tolkien Dogmatics: Theology Through Mythology with the Maker of Middle-earth*. Bellingham, WA: Lexham.

Gallant, R. Z. (2020a), 'The "Wyrdwríteras" of Elvish History: Northern Courage, Historical Bias, and Literary Artifact as Illustrative Narrative', *Mythlore* 38, 25–44.

Gallant, R. Z. (2020b), 'Elessar Telcontar Magnus, Rex Pater Gondor, Restitutor Imperii' *Journal of Tolkien Research* 9.

Gallant, R. Z. (2024), *Germanic Heroes, Courage, and Fate: Northern Narratives of J.R.R. Tolkien's Legendarium*. Zurich and Jena: Walking Tree.

Garbowski, C. (2004), *Recovery and Transcendence for the Contemporary Mythmaker: The Spiritual Dimension in the Works of J. R. R. Tolkien*, 2nd ed. Zurich and Berne: Walking Tree.

Garbowski, C. (2007), 'Eucatastrophe', in Drout 2007a, 176–77.

Gardini, N. (2014), *Lacuna: Saggio sul non detto*. Turin: Einaudi.

Garnier, P. (2003), 'Les traditions textuelles des Jours anciens', in Devaux 2003a, 283–311.

Garth, J. (2003), *Tolkien and the Great War: The Threshold of Middle-earth*. London: HarperCollins.

Garth, J. (2014), '"The Road from Adaptation to Invention": How Tolkien Came to the Brink of Middle-earth in 1914', *Tolkien Studies* 11, 1–44.

Garth, J. (2020), *The Worlds of J.R.R. Tolkien: The Places that Inspired Middle-earth*. London: Frances Lincoln.

Garth, J. (2022), 'The Chronology of Creation: How J.R.R. Tolkien Misremembered the Beginnings of his Mythology', in Ovenden and McIlwaine 2022, 88–105.

Gavaler, G. and Goldberg, N. (2020), 'There and Back Again: A Philosophy of Revision for Fictional Narrative', *Narrative* 28, 304–26.

Geier, F. (2008), 'Leaf by Tolkien? Allegory and Biography in Tolkien's Literary Theory and Practice', in Hiley and Weinreich 2008, 209–32.

Gilliver:, Marshall, J. and Weiner, E. (2006), *The Ring of Words: Tolkien and the Oxford English Dictionary*. Oxford: Oxford University Press.

Gilson, C. (ed.) (2010), *Quenya Phonology: Comparative Tables, Outline of Phonetic Development, Outline of Phonology*. Mountain View, CA: Parma Elderlamberon.

Gilson, C. (2020), 'He Constructed a Language L and Another LL': Diachronic Aspects of Tolkien's Early Philology', *Tolkien Studies* 17, 75–116.

Glover, W. (2020), '"Where Many Paths and Errands Meet": Travel Writing in The Lord of the Rings', *Journal of Tolkien Research* 9.

González de la Llana, N. (2020), 'The Writer as a Scribe: Sub-creation in J.R.R. Tolkien and J.L. Borges', *Hither Shore* 14, 80–94.

Grein, C., and Wülker, R. (1883–1898), *Bibliothek der angelsächsischen Poesie*, 3 vols. Kassel: G. H. Wigand.

Groom, N. (2022), *Twenty-First Century Tolkien: What Middle-earth Means to Us Today*. London: Atlantic Books.

Grybauskas, P. (2012), 'Untold Tales: Solving a Literary Dilemma', *Tolkien Studies* 9, 1–19.

Grybauskas, P. (2021), *A Sense of Tales Untold: Exploring the Edges of Tolkien's Literary Canvas*. Kent, OH: The Kent State University Press.

Gymnich, M. (2005), 'Reconsidering the Linguistics of Middle-earth: Invented Languages and Other Linguistic Features in J.R.R. Tolkien's The Lord of the Rings', in Honegger 2005, 7–30.

Hall, A. and Kaislaniemi, S. (2013), '"You Tempt me Grievously to a Mythological Essay": J. R. R. Tolkien's Correspondence with Arthur Ransome', in Tyrkkö, J., Timofeeva, O. and Salenius, M. (eds.) *Ex Philologia Lux: Essays in Honour of Leena Kahlas-Tarkka* (Helsinki: Société Néophilologique), 261–80.

Halliwell, S. (2011), *Between Ecstasy and Truth: Interpretations of Greek Poetics from Homer to Longinus*. Oxford: Oxford University Press.

Halsall, M. J. (2020), *Creation and Beauty in Tolkien's Catholic Vision*. Eugene, OR: Pickwick Publications.

Hammond, W. and Scull, C. (1995), *J.R.R. Tolkien: Artist and Illustrator*. London: HarperCollins.

Hammond, W. and Scull, C. (2005), *The Lord of the Rings: A Reader's Companion*. London: HarperCollins.

Hammond, W. and Scull, C. (eds.) (2006a), *The Lord of the Rings 1954–2004: Scholarship in Honour of Richard E. Blackwelder*. Milwaukee, WI: Marquette University Press.

Hammond, W. and Scull, C. (2006b), '"And All the Days of Her Life Are Forgotten": *The Lord of the Rings* as Mythic Prehistory', in Hammond and Scull 2006a, 67–100.

Hammond, W. and Scull, C. (2011), *The Art of The Hobbit by J.R.R. Tolkien*. London: HarperCollins.

Hammond, W. and Scull, C. (2015), *The Art of The Lord of the Rings by J.R.R. Tolkien*. London: HarperCollins.

Hammond, W. and Scull, C. (2017). *The J.R.R. Tolkien Companion and Guide: Chronology and Reader's Guide.* 2nd edition, revised and expanded, 3 vols. London: HarperCollins.

Hanks, D. T. J. (2012), 'Tolkien's "Leaf by Niggle": A Blossom on the Tree of Tales', *Journal of Inklings Studies* 2, 23–48.

Hart, T. (2007), 'Tolkien, Creation, and Creativity', in Hart and Khovacs 2007, 39–53.

Hart, T. (2013), *Between the Image and the Word: Theological Engagements with Imagination, Language and Literature.* Burlington: Ashgate.

Hart, T. and Khovacs, I. (eds.) (2007), *Tree of Tales: Tolkien, Literature and Theology.* Baylor, TX: Baylor University Press.

Hausmann, M. (2015), 'Parallel Paths and Distorting Mirrors: Strategic Duality as a Narrative Principle in Tolkien's Works', *Mallorn* 56, 31–35.

Hausmann, M. (2019), 'Lyrics on Lost Lands: Constructing Lost Places through Poetry in J.R.R. Tolkien's *The Lord of the Rings*', in Fimi and Honegger 2019, 261–84.

Hazel, D. (2006), *The Plants of Middle-earth: Botany and Subcreation.* Kent, OH: The Kent State University Press.

Hefferan-Hays, C. (2008), 'Unlocking Supplementary Events in the Dreams, Visions, and Prophecies of J.R.R. Tolkien's Work', in Wells 2008, 1.122–6.

Helen, D. (ed.) (2017), *Death and Immortality in Middle-earth.* Edinburgh: Luna Press.

Hemmi, Y. (2010), 'Tolkien's *The Lord of the Rings* and His Concept of *Native Language*: Sindarin and British-Welsh', *Tolkien Studies* 7, 147–74.

Henige, D. (2009), 'Authorship Renounced: The "Found" Source in the Historical Record', *Journal of Scholarly Publishing* 41, 31–55.

Hieatt, C. B. (1981), 'The Text of The Hobbit: Putting Tolkien's Notes in Order', *English Studies in Canada* 7, 212–24.

Hilder, M. B., Pearson, S. L., and Van Dyke, L. N. (2020), *The Inklings and Culture: A Harvest of Scholarship from the Inklings*. Newcastle: Cambridge Scholars.

Hiley, M. (2004), 'Stolen Language, Cosmic Models: Myth and Mythology in Tolkien', *Modern Fiction Studies* 50, 838–60.

Hiley, M. (2011), *The Loss and the Silence: Aspects of Modernism in the Works of C.S. Lewis, J.R.R. Tolkien & Charles Williams*. Zurich and Jena: Walking Tree.

Hiley, M. (2015), '"Bizarre or dream like": J.R.R. Tolkien on *Finnegans Wake*', in Carpentier, M. C. (ed.), *Joycean Legacies* (Basingstoke: Palgrave Macmillan), 112–26.

Hiley, M. and Weinreich, F. (eds.) (2008), *Tolkien's Shorter Works*. Zurich and Jena: Walking Tree.

Hillman, T. P. (2023a), *Pity, Power, and Tolkien's Ring*. Kent, OH: The Kent State University Press.

Hillman, T. P. (2023b), 'The Great Tales, Tragedy, and Fairy-Story in "The Choices of Master Samwise"', *Tolkien Studies* 20, 47–58.

Hoffman, C. (2014), 'Wings over Númenor: Lucid Dreaming in the Writings of J.R.R. Tolkien', in Hurd, R. and Bulkeley, K. (eds.), *Lucid Dreaming: New Perspectives on Consciousness in Sleep* (Santa Barbara, CA: Praeger), 2.127–42.

Holland, M. and Hart-Davis, R. (2000), *The Complete Letters of Oscar Wilde*. New York: Henry Holt.

Holloway, C. L. (2011), 'Redeeming Sub-Creation', in Kerry 2011, 177–92.

Holmes, J. R. (2011), '"Like Heathen Kings": Religion as Palimpsest in Tolkien's Fiction', in Kerry 2011, 119–44.

Holtz-Wodzak, V. (2014), 'Travel, Redemption and Peacemaking: Hobbits, Dwarves and Elves and the Transformative Power of Pilgrimage', in Eden 2014, 181–94.

Honegger, T. (2003a), 'A Theoretical Model for Tolkien Translation Criticism', in Honegger 2003b, 1–30.

Honegger, T. (ed.) (2003b), *Tolkien in Translation*. Zurich and Berne: Walking Tree.

Honegger, T. (ed.) (2005), *Reconsidering Tolkien*. Zurich and Berne: Walking Tree.

Honegger, T. (2011), 'Time and Tide: Medieval Patterns of Interpreting the Passing of Time in Tolkien's Work', *Hither Shore* 8, 86–99.

Honegger, T. (2013), 'My Most Precious Riddle: Eggs and Rings Revisited', *Tolkien Studies* 10, 89–103.

Honegger, T. (2018), 'Splintered Heroes – Heroic Variety and Its Function in The Lord of the Rings', in Rateliff 2018, 157–75.

Honegger, T. (2020), '"Uncle Me No Uncle!" Or Why Bilbo Is and Isn't Frodo's Uncle', *Journal of Tolkien Research* 9.

Honegger, T. (2023), *Tweaking Things a Little. Essays on the Epic Fantasy of J.R.R. Tolkien and George R.R. Martin*. Zurich and Jena: Walking Tree.

Honegger, T. and Mann, M. F. (eds.) (2016), *Laughter in Middle-earth: Humour in and around the Works of J.R.R. Tolkien*. Zurich and Jena: Walking Tree.

Hooker, M. T. (2020), *Tolkienian Glôssology: Or a Study of the Primitive Elvish Vocabulary of Tolkien's Qenya Lexicon and Gnomish Lexicon from the Late 1910s, the Precursors of Quenya and Sindarin*. North Haven, CT: Llyfrawr.

Hooker, M. T. (2023), *Translating The Hobbit*. North Haven, CT: Llyfrawr.

Hooper, W. (2015), *C.S. Lewis and His Literary Circle*. Oxford: Oxford University Press.

Hostetter, C. F. (1991), 'Over Middle-earth Sent unto Men: On the Philological Origins of Tolkien's Eärendel Myth', *Mythlore* 17, 5–10.

Hostetter, C. F. (2006), '"Elvish as She Is Spoke"', in Hammond and Scull 2006a, 231–55.

Hostetter, C. F. (2007), 'Languages Invented by Tolkien', in Drout 2007a, 331–44.

Houghton, J. W. (2003), 'Augustine in the Cottage of Lost Play: The Ainulindalë as Asterisk Cosmogony', in Chance 2003, 171–82.

Houghton, J. W. et al. (eds.) (2014), *Tolkien in the New Century: Essays in Honor of Tom Shippey*. Jefferson, NC: McFarland.

Hunt, P. (ed.) (2013), *J.R.R. Tolkien: The Hobbit and the Lord of the Rings*. London: Bloomsbury.

Hutton, R. (2008), 'Tolkien's Magic', in Wells 2008, 175–86.

Hutton, R. (2011), 'The Pagan Tolkien', in Kerry 2011, 57–70.

Hynes, G. (2016), 'Theorists of Sub-creation before Tolkien's *On Fairy-Stories*', in Fornet-Ponse, Honegger and Eilmann 2016, 36–51.

Imbert, Y. (2022), *From Imagination to Faërie: Tolkien's Thomist Fantasy*. Eugene, OR: Pickwick Publications.

Isaacs, N. D. and Zimbardo, R. A. (eds.) (1968), *Tolkien and the Critics: Essays on J. R. R. Tolkien's The Lord of the Rings*. Notre Dame, IN: University of Notre Dame Press.

Izzo, M. (2019), 'Worldbuilding and Mythopoeia in Tolkien and Post-Tolkienian Fantasy Literature', in Fimi and Honegger 2019, 31–55.

Jarman, C. (2016) 'The Black Speech: The Lord of the Rings as Modern Linguistic Critique', *Mythlore* 34, 153–66.

Jeffers, S. (2014), *Arda Inhabited: Environmental Relationships in The Lord of the Rings*. Kent, OH: The Kent State University Press.

Joosten, M. (2013), 'Poetry in the Transmission Conceit of The Silmarillion', in Eilmann and Turner 2013, 153–62.

Joy, L. (2013), 'Tolkien's Language', in Hunt 2013, 74–87.

Judd, W. S., and Judd, G. A. (2017), *Flora of Middle-earth: Plants of J. R. R. Tolkien's Legendarium*. Oxford: Oxford University Press.

Kahlas-Tarkka, L. (2022), 'Finnish: The Land and Language of Heroes', in Lee 2022a, 260–70.

Kane, D. C. (2009), *Arda Reconstructed: The Creation of the Published Silmarillion*. Bethlehem, PA: Lehigh University Press.

Kascakova J., Levente Palatinus. D. (eds.) (2023), *J.R.R. Tolkien in Central Europe: Context, Directions, and the Legacy*. London: Routledge.

Kechan, A. (ed.) (2022), *Reimagining the Works of J.R.R. Tolkien*. Skopje: International Balkan University.

Kerry, P. E. (2005), 'Thoughts on J.R.R. Tolkien's *The Lord of the Rings* and History', in Honegger 2005, 67–85.

Kerry, P. E. (ed.) (2011), *The Ring and the Cross: Christianity and The Lord of the Rings*. Madison and Teaneck: Fairleigh Dickinson University Press.

Kerry, P. E. and Miesel, S. (eds.) (2011), *Light beyond All Shadow: Religious Experience in Tolkien's Work*. Madison, NJ: Fairleigh Dickinson University Press.

Kilby, C. S. (1976), *Tolkien & the Silmarillion*. Wheaton, IL: Harold Shaw.

Kilby, C. S. (2016), *A Well of Wonder: Essays on C.S. Lewis, J.R.R. Tolkien, and the Inklings*. Orleans: Paraclete Press.

Kirk, E. D. (1977), '"I Would Rather Have Written in Elvish": Language, Fiction, and *The Lord of the Rings*', in Spilka, M. (ed.), *Towards a Poetics of Fiction* (Bloomington: Indiana University Press), 289–302.

Klarner, W. C. (2014), 'A Victorian in Valhalla: Bilbo Baggins as the Link between England and Middle-earth', in Eden 2014, 152–60.

Klinger, J. (2006), '"More Poetical, Less Prosaic": The Convergence of Myth and History in Tolkien's Work', *Hither Shore* 3, 180–95.

Klinger, J. (2009a), 'Changing Perspectives: Secret Doors and Narrative Thresholds in *The Hobbit*', *Hither Shore* 5, 30–45.

Klinger, J. (2009b), 'The Legacy of Swords: Animate Weapons and the Ambivalence of Heroic Violence', *Hither Shore*, 132–52.

Klinger, J. (2012a), *Sub-creating Middle-earth: Constructions of Authorship and the Works of J.R.R. Tolkien*. Zurich and Jena: Walking Tree.

Klinger, J. (2012b), 'Tolkien's "Strange Powers of the Mind": Dreams, Visionary History and Authorship', in Klinger 2012a, 43–106.

Kokot, J. (2013), 'O What a Tangled Web We Weave': The Lord of the Rings and the Interlacement Technique', in Kowalik 2013b, 9–27.

Korpua, J. (2015), 'Constructive Mythopoetics in J.R.R. Tolkien's Legendarium', *Fafnir* 2, 54–58.

Korpua, J. (2016), 'J.R.R. Tolkien's Mythopoeia and Familiarisation of Myth: Hobbits as Mediators of Myth in *The Hobbit* and *The Lord of the Rings*', in Forest-Hill 2016, 1.241–49.

Kowalik, B. (2013a), 'Elbereth the Star-Queen Seen in the Light of Medieval Marian Devotion', in Kowalik 2013b, 93–113.

Kowalik, B. (ed.) (2013b), *O What a Tangled Web: Tolkien and Medieval Literature, A View from Poland*. Zurich and Jena: Walking Tree.

Kreeft, P. (2005), *The Philosophy of Tolkien*. San Francisco, CA: Ignatius Press.

Kullman, T. (2009), 'Intertextual Patterns in J.R.R. Tolkien's *The Hobbit* and *The Lord of the Rings*', *Nordic Journal of English Studies* 8, 37–56.

Kullman, T. (2013), 'Poetic Insertions in Tolkien's *The Lord of the Rings*', *Connotations* 23, 283–309.

Kullman, T. and Siepmann D. (2021), *Tolkien as a Literary Artist: Exploring Rhetoric, Language and Style in The Lord of the Rings*. Basingstoke: Palgrave Macmillan.

Lee, S. D. (ed.) (2017), *J.R.R. Tolkien (Routledge Critical Assessments)*, 4 vols. Abingdon and New York: Routledge.

Lee, S. D. (2018), '"Tolkien in Oxford" (BBC, 1968): A Reconstruction', *Tolkien Studies* 15, 115–76

Lee, S. D. (ed.) (2022a), *A Companion to J. R. R. Tolkien*. 2nd ed. Hoboken, NJ and Chichester: John Wiley & Sons [1st edition 2014].

Lee, S. D. (2022b), 'Manuscripts: Use, and Using', in Lee (2022a), 48–64.

Lee, S. D. (2022c), 'A Milestone in BBC History: The 1955–56 Radio Dramatization of *The Lord of the Rings*, in Ovenden and McIlwaine 2022, 144–65.

Lee, S. D., and Solopova, E. (2016), *The Keys of Middle-earth: Discovering Medieval Literature through the Fiction of J.R.R. Tolkien*. 2nd ed. Basingstoke: Palgrave Macmillan.

Lewis, P. W. (2007), 'Beorn and Tom Bombadil: A Tale of Two Heroes', *Mythlore* 25, 145–60.

Lewis, A. (1996), 'Historical Bias in the Making of The Silmarillion', *Mythlore* 21, 158–66.

Lewis, A. and Currie, E. (2009), *The Epic Realm of Tolkien, Part One: Beren and Lúthien*. Moreton-in-Marsh: ADC.

Lobdell, J. (ed.) (2003), *A Tolkien Compass*. 2nd ed. Chicago and LaSalle, IL: Open Court [1st edition 1975].

Lobdell, J. (2004), *Language, Religion, and Adventure in Tolkien*. Chicago and LaSalle, IL: Open Court.

Long, J. B. (2014), 'Pillaging Middle-earth: Self-plagiarism in *Smith of Wootton Major*', *Mythlore* 32, 117–35.

MacLachlan, C. (2012), *Tolkien and Wagner: The Ring and Der Ring*. Zurich and Jena: Walking Tree.

McIlwaine, C. (ed.) (2018), *Tolkien: Maker of Middle-earth*. Oxford: Bodleian Library.

Madsen, C. (2003), '"Light from an Invisible Lamp": Natural Religion in *The Lord of the Rings*', in Chance 2003, 35–47.

Madsen, C. (2011), 'Eru Erased: The Minimalist Cosmology of *The Lord of the Rings*', in Kerry 2011, 152–69.

Maillet, G. (2020), '"Meeting Somewhere in Truth": Allegory, Story, and the Significance of the Tale of *Beren and Luthien*', in Hilder, Pearson, and Van Dyke 2020, 189–91.

Manganiello, D. (1992), 'The Neverending Story: Textual Happiness in The Lord of the Rings', *Mythlore* 18, 5–14.

Martsch, N. (2011), 'Consider the Context', *Mallorn* 52, 4–6.

McBride, S. (2020), *Tolkien's Cosmology: Divine Beings and Middle-earth*. Kent, OH: The Kent State University Press.

McIntosh, J. S. (2017), *The Flame Imperishable: Tolkien, St. Thomas, and the Metaphysics of Faërie*. New York: Angelico Press.

Medcalf, S. (1999), 'The Learned Language of Elves: Owen Barfield, The Hobbit and The Lord of the Rings', *Seven* 16, 31–53.

Milbank, A. (2009), *Chesterton and Tolkien as Theologians: The Fantasy of the Real*. London and New York: T & T Clark.

Miller, L. (ed.) (2016), *Literary Wonderlands: A Journey through the Greatest Fictional Worlds Ever Created*. London: Modern Books.

Milon, A. (ed.) (2018), *Poetry and Song in the Works of J.R.R. Tolkien*. Edinburgh: Luna Press.

Monda, A. (2019), 'Tolkien and Manzoni', in Arduini, R., Canzonieri, G., and Testi, C.A. (eds.) *Tolkien and the Classics* (Zurich and Jena: Walking Tree), 167–73.

Morrison, R. D. (2005), '"I Much Prefer History, True or Feigned": Tolkien and Literary History', *Kentucky Philological Review* 19, 36–42.

Morton, A.H. and Hayes, J. (2008), *Tolkien's Gedling*. Studley: Brewin.

Moseley, C. (1995), *J.R.R. Tolkien*. Liverpool: Liverpool University Press.

Mosley, D. R. (2016), *Being Deified: Poetry and Fantasy on the Path to God*. Minneapolis, MN: Fortress Press.

Moulin, J. (2008), 'J.R.R. Tolkien's "Eucatastrophe," or Fantasy as a Modern Recovery of Faith', in Bray, Gavin, and Merchant 2008, 77–86.

Muir, B. J. (2000), *The Exeter Anthology of Old English Poetry*, 2nd ed., 2 vols. Exeter: University of Exeter Press.

Murray, R. (1999), 'J.R.R. Tolkien and the Art of the Parable', in Pearce 1999, 40–52.

Nagel, R. (2012), *Hobbit Place-names: A Linguistic Excursion through the Shire*. Zurich and Jena: Walking Tree.

Nagy, G. (2003), 'The Great Chain of Reading: (Inter-)textual Relations and the Technique of Mythopoesis in the Túrin Story', in Chance 2003, 239–58.

Nagy, G. (2004), 'The Adapted Text: The Lost Poetry of Beleriand', *Tolkien Studies* 1, 21–41.

Nagy, G. (2005), 'The Medievalist('s) Fiction: Textuality and Historicity as Aspects of Tolkien's Medievalist Cultural Theory in a Postmodernist Context', in Chance and Siewers 2005, 29–41.

Nagy, G. (2007), 'Authorship', in Drout 2007a, 44–45.

Nagy, G. (2012), *"Ye Olde Authour": Tolkien's Anatomy of Tradition in the Silmarillion*. Diss. Szeged.

Nagy, G. (2019), 'On No Magic in Tolkien: Resisting the Representational Criteria of Realism', in Fimi and Honegger 2019, 153–75.

Nagy, G. (2022), '*The Silmarillion*: Tolkien's Theory of Myth, Text, and Culture', in Lee 2022a, 93–103.

Nencioni, G. (1998), *Ascanio Condivi: Vita di Michelagnolo Buonarroti*. Florence: Studio per edizioni scelte.

Neubauer, L. (2016), '"The Eagles are coming!": Tolkien's Eucatastrophic Reinterpretation of the "Beasts of Battle" Motive in The Hobbit and The Lord of the Rings', in Fornet-Ponse, Honegger and Eilmann 2016, 236–46.

Neubauer, L. (2020), 'The "Polish Inkling": Professor Przemysław Mroczkowski as J.R.R. Tolkien's Friend and Scholar', *Mythlore* 39, 149–76.

Neubauer, L. and Spirito, G. (2024), *The Songs of the Spheres: Lewis, Tolkien and the Overlapping Realms of their Imaginations*. Zurich and Jena: Walking Tree.

Neuhaus, V. (1990), 'Illusion and Narrative Technique: The Nineteenth-Century Historical Novel between Truth and Fiction', in Burwick F. and Pape, W. (eds.), *Aesthetic Illusion: Theoretical and Historical Approaches* (Berlin: De Gruyter), 275–83.

Nicholas, A. P. (2012), *Aragorn: J.R.R. Tolkien's Undervalued Hero*. Edinburgh: Luna Press.

Nicholas, A. P. (2015), 'Female Descent in J.R.R. Tolkien's Middle-earth Mythology', *Amon Hen* 252, 11–18.

Noad, C. (2000), "On the Construction of *The Silmarillion*" In Flieger and Hostetter 2000, 31–68.

Noel, R. S. (1980), *The Languages of Tolkien's Middle-earth*. Boston: Houghton Mifflin.

Oberhelman, D. (2008), 'A Brief History of Libraries in Middle-earth: Manuscript and Book Repositories in Tolkien's *Legendarium*', in Himes, J. B. (ed.), *Truths Breathed Through Silver: The Inklings' Moral and Mythopoeic Legacy* (Newcastle: Cambridge Scholars), 81–92.

O'Neill, T. R. (1979), *The Individuated Hobbit: Jung, Tolkien and the Archetypes of Middle-earth*. Boston: Houghton Mifflin.

Ordway, H. (2021), *Tolkien's Modern Reading: Middle-earth Beyond the Middle-Ages*. Elk Grove Village, IL: Word on Fire.

Ordway, H. (2023a), *Tolkien's Faith: A Spiritual Biography*. Elk Grove Village, IL: Word on Fire.

Ordway, H. (2023b), 'The Mystical Face of Fairy-Stories: Tolkien and the Use of Allegory in Fantasy', in Pezzini and O'Brien 2023, 87–106.

Ovenden R. and McIlwaine C. (eds) (2022), *The Great Tales Never End: Essays in Memory of Christopher Tolkien*. Oxford: Bodleian Library.

Padley, J. and Padley, K. (2009), '"From Mirrored Truth the Likeness of the True": J.R.R. Tolkien and Reflections of Jesus Christ in Middle-earth', *English* 59, 70–92.

Painter, J. (2016), '"A Honeycomb Gathered from Different Flowers": Tolkien-the-Compiler's Middle-earth "Sources" in The Lord of the Rings', *Tolkien Studies* 13, 125–46.

Paprocki, M. and Matz, A. (eds.) (2022), *There and Back Again: Tolkien and the Graeco-Roman World*. *Thersites* 15. Potsdam: Universität Potsdam.

Pavlac Glyer, D. (ed.) (2007), *The Company They Keep: C. S. Lewis and J. R. R. Tolkien as Writers in Community*. Kent, OH: The Kent State University Press.

Pearce, J. (1998), *Tolkien: Man and Myth*. London: HarperCollins.

Pearce, J. (ed.) (1999), *Tolkien: A Celebration*. London: Fount.

Pearce, J. (2014), *Catholic Literary Giants: a Field Guide to the Catholic Literary Landscape*. San Francisco, CA: Ignatius Press [1st ed. 2005].

Pepe de Suárez, L. (2013), *Homero y Tolkien*. La Plata: Synthesis.

Petty, A.C. (2007), 'Allegory', in Drout 2007a, 6–8.

Pezzini, G. (2018), 'The Authors of Middle-earth: Tolkien and the Mystery of Literary Creation', *The Journal of Inklings Studies* 8, 31–64.

Pezzini, G. (2019), 'The Lords of the West: Cloaking, Freedom and the Divine Narrative in Tolkien's Poetics' *The Journal of Inklings Studies* 9,115–53.

Pezzini, G. (2020), 'Terence and the *speculum uitae*: "Realism" and (Roman) Comedy', *Harvard Studies in Classical Philology* 111, 101–61.

Pezzini, G. (2021), 'The Gods in (Tolkien's) Epic', in Williams 2021, 73–103.

Pezzini, G. (2022), '"Classical" Narratives of Decline in Tolkien: Renewal, Accommodation, Focalization', in Paprocki and Matz 2022, 25–51.

Pezzini, G. and Taylor, B. (eds.) (2019), *Language and Nature in the Classical Roman World*. Cambridge: Cambridge University Press.

Pezzini, G. and Spirito, G. (2023), 'The Maiar in Middle-earth: Sub-creative Collaboration and the Secret Fire', in Pezzini and O'Brien 2023, 161–77

Pezzini, G. and O'Brien, E. (eds.) (2023), *Tolkien and the Relation between Sub-creation and Reality. Journal of Inklings Studies Special Issue III*. Edinburgh: Edinburgh University Press.

Phelpstead, C. (2011), *Tolkien and Wales: Language, Literature, and Identity*. Cardiff: University of Wales Press.

Phelpstead, C. (2022), 'Myth-making and Sub-creation', in Lee 2022a, 67–78.

Pickstock, C. (2013), *Repetition and Identity: The Literary Agenda*. Oxford: Oxford University Press.

Pinsent, P. (2022), 'Religion: An Implicit Catholicism' in Lee 2022a, 424–36.

Poe, H. L. (2021), *The Making of C.S. Lewis*. Wheaton, IL: Crossway.

Potts, S. W. (ed.) (2016), *Critical Insights: The Hobbit*. Ipswich, MA: Grey House & Salem.

Prozesky, M. (2006), 'The Text Tale of Frodo the Nine-fingered: Residual Oral Patterning in The Lord of the Rings', *Tolkien Studies* 3, 21–43.

Purtill, R. L. (2003), *J.R.R. Tolkien: Myth, Morality, and Religion*. San Francisco, CA: Ignatius Press.

Purtill, R. L. (2006), *Lord of the Elves and Eldils: Fantasy and Philosophy in C. S. Lewis and J.R.R. Tolkien*, 2nd ed. San Francisco, CA: Ignatius Press.

Qadri, J.–P. (2014), 'Tom Bombadil ou le chant de la forêt' in Devaux 2014, 369–450.

Rateliff, J. D. (2006), '"And All the Days of Her Life Are Forgotten": *The Lord of the Rings* as Mythic Prehistory', in Hammond and Scull 2006a, 67–100.

Rateliff, J. D. (2011), *The History of the Hobbit*, 2nd ed. London: HarperCollins.

Rateliff, J. D. (2014a), 'Anchoring the Myth: The Impact of The Hobbit on Tolkien's Legendarium', in Eden 2014, 6–19.

Rateliff, J. D. (2014b), 'Inside Literature: Tolkien's Explorations of Medieval Genres', in Houghton et al. 2014, 133–52.

Rateliff, J. D. (ed.) (2018), *A Wilderness of Dragons: Essays in Honor of Verlyn Flieger*. Wayzata, MN: The Gabbro Head Press.

Rateliff, J. D. (2020), 'The Flat Earth Made Round and Tolkien's Failure to Finish the Silmarillion', *Journal of Tolkien Research* 9.

Rateliff, J. D. (2022), '*The Hobbit*: A Turning Point', in Lee 2022a, 104–15.

Rearick, A. (2012), 'Father Knows Best: The Narrator's Oral Performance as Paternal Protector in *The Hobbit*', *Inklings Forever* 8.

Reid, R. A. (2009), 'Mythology and History: A Stylistic Analysis of The Lord of the Rings', *Style* 43, 517–38.

Reid, R. A. and Elam, M. D. (2016), 'Authorizing Tolkien: Control, Adaptation, and Dissemination of J.R.R. Tolkien's Works', *Journal of Tolkien Research* 3.

Reinders, E. (2024), *Reading Tolkien in Chinese: Religion, Fantasy and Translation*. London: Bloomsbury.

Robbins, S. (2013), 'Beauty in Language: Tolkien's Phonology and Phonaesthetics as a Source of Creativity and Inspiration for *The Lord of the Rings*', *Zmogus ir Zodis* 15, 185–91.

Robbins, S. (2015), 'Old English, Old Norse, Gothic: Sources of Inspiration and Creativity for J.R.R. Tolkien's The Hobbit and The Lord of the Rings', *Zmogus ir Zodis* 17, 66–76.

Roberts, A. (2013), *The Riddles of The Hobbit*. Basingstoke: Palgrave Macmillan.

Robertson, R. (2016), *Jung and Frodo: 7 Paths of Individuation in Lord of the Rings*. Alhambra, CA: Manyhats.

Robinson, C. L. (2013), 'What Makes the Names of Middle-earth So Fitting? Elements of Style in the Namecraft of J. R. R. Tolkien', *Names A Journal of Onomastics* 61, 65–74.

Rosebury, B. (2003), *Tolkien: A Cultural Phenomenon*. Basingstoke: Palgrave Macmillan.

Rosegrant, J. (2019), 'Mother Music', *Tolkien Studies* 16, 111–31.

Rosegrant, J. (2021), *Tolkien, Enchantment, and Loss: Steps on the Developmental Journey*. Kent, OH: The Kent State University Press.

Rosenquist, R. (2008), 'Myth, Fact and "Literary Belief": Imagination and Post-Empiricism in C. S. Lewis and J.R.R. Tolkien', in Bray, Gavin, and Merchant 2008, 115–26.

Rutledge, F. (2004), *The Battle for Middle-earth: Tolkien's Divine Design in The Lord of the Rings*. Grand Rapids, MI: William B. Eerdmans.

Ruud, J. (2011), *The Critical Companion to J.R.R. Tolkien: A Literary Reference to His Life and Work*. New York: InfoBase Publishing.

Ryan, J. S. (2009), *Tolkien's View: Windows into his World*. Zurich and Jena: Walking Tree.

Ryan, J. S. (2013), *In the Nameless Wood: Explorations in the Philological Hinterland of Tolkien's Literary Creations*. Zurich and Jena: Walking Tree.

Saxton, B. (2013a), 'Tolkien and Bakhtin on Authorship, Literary Freedom, and Alterity', *Tolkien Studies* 10, 167–83.

Saxton, B. (2013b), 'J.R.R. Tolkien, Sub-creation, and Theories of Authorship', *Mythlore* 31, 47–59.

Scarf, C. (2013), *The Ideal of Kingship in the Writings of Charles Williams, C. S. Lewis and J.R.R. Tolkien: Divine Kingship Is Reflected in Middle-earth*. Cambridge: James Clarke.

Scull, C. (2006), 'What Did He Know and When Did He Know It? Planning, Inspiration, and *The Lord of the Rings*', in Hammond and Scull 2006a, 101–12.

Seeman, C. (1995), 'Tolkien's Revision of the Romantic Tradition', in Reynolds, P. and Goodnight, G. H. (eds.), *Proceedings of the J. R. R. Tolkien Centenary Conference 1992* (Milton Keynes and Altadena, CA: The Mythopoeic Press), 73–83.

Segura, E. and Peris, G. (2005), 'Tolkien as Philo-Logist', in Honegger 2005, 31–43.

Segura, E. (2007), '"Leaf by Niggle" and the Aesthetics of Gift: Towards a Definition of J.R.R. Tolkien's Notion of Art', in Segura and Honegger 2007, 315–37.

Segura, E. (2010), '"Secondary Belief": Tolkien and the Revision of Romantic Notion of Poetic Faith', *Hither Shore* 7, 138–50.

Segura, E. and Honegger, T. (eds.) (2007), *Myth and Magic: Art according to the Inklings*. Zurich and Berne: Walking Tree.

Sepe, K. (2008), '"Tell Them Stories": The Consciousness of Myth in Tolkien and Pullman', in Wells 2008, 1.266–73.

Shaeffer, A. B. (2017), *Spiritual Formation in Tolkien's Legendarium*. PhD. Durham.

Shank, D. (2013), '"The Web of Story": Structuralism in Tolkien's 'On Fairy-Stories', *Tolkien Studies* 10, 147–65.

Sherwood, W. (2020), 'Tolkien and the Age of Forgery: Improving Antiquarian Practices in Arda', *Journal of Tolkien Research* 11.1.

Sherwood, W. (ed.) (2022), *Twenty-First Century Receptions of Tolkien*. Edinburgh: Luna Press.

Sherwood. W. (ed.) (2023a), *Tolkien and Diversity*. Edinburgh: Luna Press.

Sherwood, W. (ed.) (2023b), *Translating and Illustrating Tolkien*. Edinburgh: Luna Press.

Sherwood. W. (ed.) (2024), *Tolkien and the Gothic*. Edinburgh: Luna Press.

Sherwood, W. and Eilmann, E. (eds.) (2024), *The Romantic Spirit in the Works of J.R.R. Tolkien*. Zurich and Jena: Walking Tree.

Shippey, T. (2000), *J. R. R. Tolkien: Author of the Century*. London: HarperCollins.

Shippey, T. (2005), *The Road to Middle-earth*, 2nd ed. Boston and New York: Houghton Mifflin [1st edition 1982].

Shippey, T. (2007), *Roots and Branches: Selected Papers on Tolkien*. Zurich and Berne: Walking Tree.

Shippey, T. (2008), 'Introduction', in *TPR*, ix–xxviii.

Shippey, T. (2011a), 'The Ancestors of the Hobbits: Strange Creatures in English Folklore', *Lembas Extra*, 97–106.

Shippey, T. (2011b), 'Introduction: Why Source Criticism?', in Fisher 2011, 7–16.

Shippey, T. (2013a), 'Goths and Romans in Tolkien's Imagination', in Conrad-O'Briain, and Hynes 2013, 19–32.

Shippey, T. (2013b), 'Tolkien's Development as a Writer of Alliterative Poetry in Modern English', in Eilmann and Turner 2013, 64–75.

Shippey, T. (2016), 'The Curious Case of Denethor and the Palantír, Once More', *Mallorn* 57, 6–9.

Shippey, T. (2018), 'Tolkien and "That Noble Northern Spirit"', in McIlwaine 2018, 58–69.

Shippey, T. (2022), 'Tolkien as Editor', in Lee 2022a, 34–47.

Shoopman, J. G. (2010), 'Tolkien's Composite Christ', *Silver Leaves* 3, 33–43.

Sibley B. and Howe J. (2024), *The Maps of Middle-earth: The Essential Maps of J.R.R. Tolkien's Fantasy Realm from Númenor and Beleriand to Wilderland and Middle-earth*. London: HarperCollins.

Siburt, J. E. (2023), *Myth, Magic, and Power in Tolkien's Middle-earth: Developing a Model for Understanding Power and Leadership*. Lanham, MD: Lexington Books.

Simonson M. (2008a), *The Lord of the Rings and the Western Narrative Tradition*. Zurich and Jena: Walking Tree.

Simonson, M. (2008b), 'Redefining the Romantic Hero: A Reading of *Smith of Wootton Major* in the Light of Ludwig Tieck's *Der Runenberg*', in Hiley and Weinreich 2008, 233–50.

Simonson, M. (ed.) (2015), *Representations of Nature in Middle-earth*. Zurich and Jena: Walking Tree.

Slack, A. E. (2010), 'Stars Above a Dark Tor: Tolkien and Romanticism', *Hither Shore* 7, 8–17.

Smith, R. (2006), 'Fitting Sense to Sound: Linguistic Aesthetics and Phonosemantics in the Work of J.R.R. Tolkien', *Tolkien Studies* 3, 1–20.

Smith, R. (2011), *Inside Language: Linguistic and Aesthetic Theory in Tolkien*, 2nd ed. Zurich and Jena: Walking Tree.

Smith, R. (2016), 'A Natural Product of our Humanity': Tolkien's Philosophy of Language', *Hither Shore* 13, 8–21.

Smith, A. R. (2017), 'A Secret Vice: Tolkien on Invented Languages by J.R.R. Tolkien', *Tolkien Studies* 14, 169–84.

Smith, A. R. (2022), 'Invented Languages and Writing Systems', in Lee 2022a, 202–14.

Solopova, E. (2009), *Languages, Myths and History: An Introduction to the Linguistic and Literary Background of J. R. R. Tolkien's Fiction*. New York: North Landing Books.

Stefani, M. (2020), 'Il Libro Rosso della Marca Occidentale: l'uso narrativo della critica testuale in J.R.R. Tolkien', *Classico contemporaneo* 6, 45–73.

Steimel, H., and Schneidewind, F. (eds.). (2010), *Music in Middle-earth*. Zurich and Jena: Walking Tree.

Stephen, E. M. (2012), *Hobbit to Hero: The Making of Tolkien's King*. Moreton-in-Marsh: ADC.

Stuart, R. (2022), *Tolkien, Race, and Racism in Middle-earth*. Basingstoke: Palgrave Macmillan.

Swank, K. (2013), '*The Hobbit* and *The Father Christmas Letters*', *Mythlore* 32, 127–44.

Tarr, C. C. (2017), *Gothic Stories Within Stories: Frame Narratives and Realism in the Genre, 1790–1900*. Jefferson, NC: McFarland.

Testi, C. A. (2016), 'Analogy, Sub-creation and Surrealism', in Fornet-Ponse, Honegger and Eilmann 2016, 178–93.

Testi, C. A. (2018), *Pagan Saints in Middle-earth*. Zurich and Jena: Walking Tree.

Thayer, A. (2016a), 'Stars Above a Dark Tor: Tolkien and Romanticism', in Potts 2016, 89–99.

Thayer, A. (2016b), *On Eagles' Wings: An Exploration of Eucatastrophe in Tolkien's Fantasy*. Edinburgh: Luna Press.

Thiessen, D. (2014), 'A Baggins Back Yard: Environmentalism, Authorship and the Elves in Tolkien's Legendarium', in Eden 2014, 195–207.

Thrasher, A. D. and Freeman, A. (eds.) (2023), *Theology, Fantasy, and the Imagination*. Lanham, MD: Lexington Books.

Tindall, R. and Bustos, S. (2012), *The Shamanic Odyssey: Homer, Tolkien, and the Visionary Experience*. Rochester, VT: Park Street.

Tolley, C. (1993), 'Tolkien and the Unfinished', in Battarbee 1993, 151–64.

Townend, M. (2024), *J.R.R. Tolkien: A Very Short Introduction*. Oxford: Oxford University Press.

Triebel, D. (2008), '"Sing We Now Softly, and Dreams Let Us Weave Him!": Dreams and Dream Visions in J.R.R. Tolkien's The Hobbit', *Hither Shore* 5, 67–81.

Turner, A. (2003a), 'Fronting in Tolkien's Archaising Style and Its Translation', in Tschichold, C. (ed.), *English Core Linguistics: Essays in Honour of D.J. Allerton* (Bern and Oxford: Peter Lang), 301–21.

Turner, A. (2003b), 'A Theoretical Model for Tolkien Translation Criticism', in Honegger 2003b, 1–30.

Turner, A. (ed.) (2007a), *The Silmarillion: Thirty Years On*. Zurich and Berne: Walking Tree.

Turner, A. (2007b), 'Language, Theories of', in Drout 2007a, 328–31.

Turner, A. (2008), 'Putting the Paratext in Context', in Wells 2008, 1.284–89.

Turner, A. (2019), 'One Pair of Eyes: Focalisation and Worldbuilding', in Fimi and Honegger 2019, 17–29.

Turner, A. (2022), 'Style and Intertextual Echoes', in Lee 2022a, 374–85.

Urang, G. (1971), *Shadows of Heaven: Religion and Fantasy in the Writing of C. S. Lewis, Charles Williams, and J.R.R. Tolkien.* London: SCM Press.

Vaccaro, C. (ed.) (2013), *The Body in Tolkien's Legendarium: Essays on Middle-earth Corporeality.* Jefferson, NC: McFarland.

Vaccaro, C. and Kisor, Y. L. (eds.) (2017), *Tolkien and Alterity.* Basingstoke: Palgrave Macmillan.

Vanderbeke, D. and Turner, A. (2012), 'The One or the Many?: Authorship, Voice and Corpus', in Klinger 2012a, 1–20.

Vaninskaya, A. (2020), 'J.R.R. Tolkien: More Than Memory', in *Fantasies of Time and Death: Dunsany, Eddison, Tolkien* (Basingstoke: Palgrave Macmillan), 153–228.

Vassányi, M. (2015), '"At Journey's End, in Darkness": A Reticent Redemption in *The Lord of the Rings*', *International Journal of Philosophy and Theology* 76, 232–40.

Vink, R. (ed.). (2012), *Wagner and Tolkien: Mythmakers.* Zurich and Jena: Walking Tree.

Vink, R. (2020a), 'J.R.R. Tolkien, Translator of The Red Book: A Look at His Views, His Methods and His Work, in Vink 2020c, 47–62.

Vink, R. (2020b), 'Glorfindel's Body: The History of a Self–sacrificing Elf, in Vink 2020c, 113–23.

Vink, R. (ed.) (2020c), *Gleanings from Tolkien's Garden.* Beverwijk: Ahvô Braiths.

Walczuk, A. and Witalisz, W. (eds.) (2014), *Old Challenges and New Horizons in English and American Studies.* Frankfurt: Lang-Ed.

Weidner, B. N. (2002), 'Middle-earth: The Real World of J. R. R. Tolkien', *Mythlore* 90, 75–84.

Weiner, E. S. C. and Marshall, J. (2011), 'Tolkien's Invented Languages', in Adams 2011b, 75–109.

Weinreich, F. and Honegger, T. (eds.) (2006), *Tolkien and Modernity*, 2 vols. Zurich and Berne: Walking Tree.

Walker, S. C. (2009), *The Power of Tolkien's Prose: Middle-earth's Magical Style*. London: Palgrave Macmillan.

Wells, S. (ed.) (2008), *The Ring Goes Ever On: Proceedings of the Tolkien 2005 Conference celebrating 50 Years of The Lord of the Rings*, 2 vols. Coventry: The Tolkien Society.

West, R. C. (1975), 'The Interlace Structure of The Lord of the Rings' in Lobdell, J. (ed.) *A Tolkien Compass* (La Salle, IL: Open Court), 77–94.

West, R. C. (1981), *Tolkien Criticism: An Annotated Checklist*, revised edition. Kent, OH: The Kent State University Press [1st edition 1970].

West, R. C. (2003), 'Real-World Myth in a Secondary World: Mythological Aspects in the Story of Beren and Lúthien', in Chance 2003, 259–67.

West, R. C. (2004), 'A Tolkien Checklist: Selected Criticism 1981–2004', *Modern Fiction Studies* 50, 1015–28.

West, R. C. (2006), '"Her Choice Was Made and Her Doom Appointed": Tragedy and Divine Comedy in the Tale of Aragorn and Arwen', in Hammond and Scull 2006a, 317–29.

West, R. C. (2011), 'Neither the Shadow nor the Twilight: The Love Story of Aragorn and Arwen in Literature and Film', in Bogstad and Kaveny 2011, 227–37.

West, R. C. (2019), 'A Letter from Father Murray', *Tolkien Studies* 16, 133–39.

Whitmire, J. F. Jr. (2023), 'An Archaeology of Hope and Despair in the Tale of Aragorn and Arwen', *Tolkien Studies* 20, 59–76.

Whittingham, E. A. (2007), *The Evolution of Tolkien's Mythology: A Study of the History of Middle-earth*. Jefferson, NC: McFarland.

Widdicombe, T. (2020), *J.R.R. Tolkien: A Guide for the Perplexed*. London: Bloomsbury.

Wilcox, M. (2003), 'Exilic Imagining in *The Seafarer* and *The Lord of the Rings*', in Chance 2003, 133–54.

Williams, H. (ed.), (2021), *Tolkien and the Classical World*. Zurich and Jena: Walking Tree.

Williams, H. (2023), *J.R.R. Tolkien's Utopianism and the Classics*. London: Bloomsbury.

Williamson, J. (2015), *The Evolution of Modern Fantasy: From Antiquarianism to the Ballantine Adult Fantasy Series*. Basingstoke: Palgrave Macmillan.

Wise, D. W. (2016), 'Book of the Lost Narrator: Rereading the 1977 Silmarillion as a Unified Text', *Tolkien Studies* 13, 101–24.

Wood, R. C. (2003), *The Gospel According to Tolkien*. Louisville, KY and London: Westminster John Knox Press.

Wood, R. C. (ed.) (2015), *Tolkien among the Moderns*. Notre Dame, IN: University of Notre Dame Press.

Zaleski, P. and Zaleski, C. (2015), *The Fellowship: The Literary Lives of the Inklings: J.R.R. Tolkien, C.S. Lewis, Owen Barfield, Charles Williams*. New York: Farrar, Straus and Giroux.

Zimmerman, P. (2013), '"The Glimmer of Limitless Extensions in Time and Space": The Function of Poems in Tolkien's *The Lord of the Rings*', in Eilmann and Turner 2013, 59–89.

INDEX